Clinical Psychology in Action

A collection of case studies

To David, John, Hannah, Rachel, Emily and Matthew
who gave us time and support

Clinical Psychology in Action

A collection of case studies

Edited by

Jenny West

Penny Spinks

Wright
London Boston Singapore Sydney Toronto Wellington

Wright
is an imprint of Butterworth Scientific

First published 1988

© **Butterworth & Co. (Publishers) Ltd, 1988**

British Library Cataloguing in Publication Data

Clinical psychology in action: a collection of case studies.
  1. Clinical psychology
I. West, Jenny II. Spinks, Penny
157'.9

  ISBN 0-7236-0729-X

Library of Congress Cataloging in Publication Data

Clinical psychology in action.

  Bibliography: p.
  Includes index.
  1. Clinical psychology–Case studies. I. West, Jenny, 1947–
II. Spinks, Penny. [DNLM: 1. Psychology, Clinical–case studies.
2. Psychotherapy–case studies. WM 40 C641]
RC467.C5862 1988   616.89'09   88-10735
ISBN 0-7236-0729-X

Photoset by Butterworths Litho Preparation Department
Printed and bound in England by Hartnolls Ltd, Bodmin, Cornwall

Preface

The aims of this book are threefold. First, it sets out to illustrate the range and diversity of modern clinical psychology practice for all those who, for personal or professional reasons, have an interest in finding out what clinical psychologists actually do. Second, it aims to provide discussion material for all students and practitioners of psychological therapy. Finally, it provides a substantial body of case material for students of abnormal psychology or similar courses, and will, we hope, act as a companion volume to textbooks.

Clinical psychologists have established and developed their roles as scientist-practitioners over the past 40 years or so. Most see their task as using their scientific knowledge and expertise in the application of their professional and clinical skills, in order to develop and provide services for people in a wide range of health and social service settings. The findings and theories of the discipline of psychology can be applied and made accessible to services at three different levels (Bender, 1979): to the individual client with psychological problems; to other professionals such as nurses, medical practitioners, social workers, care staff, counsellors, managers and others whose work can be enhanced by the knowledge and application of psychological principles; and to organizations themselves, where issues of policy and planning can benefit from the psychological perspective. As well as providing the means by which psychology can be applied to human services, clinical psychologists also have the role of engaging in applicable research, where their scientific skills can be used to investigate the problems of the clients or organizations for whom they work or to evaluate the services which are being provided (Cooke and Watts, 1987). These two integral parts of the clinical psychologist's day-to-day work are illustrated through the cases presented here.

All the cases in the book are real-life examples selected from the work of practising clinical psychologists. Because all the cases are about real people (clients, their families and other professionals) and places (hospitals, community homes, health districts) we have considered it essential to take every possible step to preserve confidentiality. Besides changing all the names and omitting some relevant details, we have not attributed individual case studies to their respective authors. In some instances the name and location of the author could be sufficient to identify the individuals involved.

In selecting the cases, we have attempted to use a sampling procedure which reflects the major settings in which clinical psychologists work, the range of clients with whom they deal and the kinds of activities they carry out. Each section of the book contains cases of a particular client group or work in a particular setting. Part 1 is written by clinical psychologists working in the broad field of adult mental health, including work with elderly people and in both hospital and community settings. Part 2 contains cases of children and adolescents and their families. Part 3 describes work with people with mental handicaps and their families and carers. Part 4 is written by clinical psychologists who work in what we have described broadly as medical settings; this includes neurological, orthopaedic, rehabilitation, surgical, medical and primary care settings. These four sections describe direct therapeutic work with individual clients, couples, families or groups of clients; assessment and diagnostic work; applied research projects and staff training programmes.

The cases in Part 5 describe some of the more recent developments in clinical psychology practice in the area of service development and organizational planning. This work may be carried out in any setting and with any client group. There are examples from a psychiatric hospital, social services and NHS facilities for the elderly, a mental handicap service and community projects. In these cases the problems are those of organizational structure, or the most effective use of scarce resources or the development, maintenance and evaluation of improved quality of care.

The division of cases into these five sections and the allocation of cases to specific sections does not imply that clinical psychology practice is exclusively organized in this way. On the contrary, there is a considerable degree of arbitrariness in such a division. Although clinical psychologists, like other professions, do specialize in particular areas of work, the boundaries are by no means inflexible.

A brief explanation of the way in which these particular case studies were selected may be useful. We decided that there should be cases from all the major specialties (adult mental health, mental handicap, work with the elderly, with children, in neuropsychology, in primary care and in medical settings) and that different kinds of work (therapy, assessment, research, training) and different settings for the work (NHS or social services; hospital or community) should be illustrated within the specialties. In the scope of a single book it was not possible to illustrate each kind of work in each setting for each specialty. Then our authors were selected on the basis of their known reputations within a specialty and invited to select a case from their own practice to illustrate a certain kind of work: for example, a research study in the child field, or a staff training project in mental handicap, or working with the elderly in a community setting. Within this broad description authors were free to select their own particular case. As expected, the resulting collection of cases comprises a mixture of the typical and the rare, of the bread-and-butter work of clinical practice and the complex, multi-faceted problem that defies the textbook approach. Like any snap-shot approach to describing activities, what is presented here is not an idealized view of clinical psychology practice but one that reflects a slice, at least, of contemporary reality.

We would like to point out what the book does *not* aim to do. There has been no attempt to illustrate all the theoretical models which clinical psychologists use. The fact that the majority of authors have taken a cognitive-behavioural approach to therapy, for example, reflects the trend of current practice. There is no description of the profession of clinical psychology, its organization or training. Such information is well documented elsewhere (e.g. Liddell, 1983; Marzillier and Hall, 1987). Many of our authors have pointed out that frequently they work as part of a multi-disciplinary team. Here we have limited ourselves to looking at the clinical psychologists' input to such teams and at their perspective of the case. In doing so, we recognize that there is the potential for another fascinating book which focuses on team-work case studies. Finally, it is not intended that these cases should be seen as an attempt to evaluate the contribution of clinical psychology to health care. The concept of illustration is central to what we are trying to do, with the minimum of contextual information to ensure understanding. The brief scene-setting introductions to each section and the glossary of terms will, we hope, facilitate understanding for non-psychologist readers.

We would like to record our very sincere thanks to all the authors. Probably ours is not the longest list of contributors to a single volume (although we feel that 42 is quite an impressive total), but the extent of the cooperation and unfailing courtesy we have received in the face of our many demands must be unequalled. We are extremely grateful to Dr Anthony T. Carr, not only for his valuable comments and advice, but for the most constructive way in which he gave them. Our thanks also to Karen Flockhart for giving us a consumer's view of the book. Finally, a very special thank you to David Mulhall. He was responsible for the meeting on Reading Station early in 1981 which began a most rewarding professional partnership between us, and which has culminated in our producing this book.

Acknowledgements

Thanks are due to the many colleagues, both within and outside the profession of clinical psychology, who have inspired, worked with or assisted authors in these cases, including: Martin Churchill-Coleman, Rosemary Dennett, Mary Donald, Anne Dyckhoff, Valerie Elliott, Alison Farrar, Anne Fletcher, Clive Glover, Isky Gordon, Ros Harrison, P. Kendrick Thomas, Richard Lansdown, Barbara Laws, the Lowe-Costello Fund, Jacky McGuire, Derek Milne, Glynis Murphy, Penny Murphy, Gail Peterson, Judith Phillips, Sandra Powell, Maggie Randall, Dave Rhodes, Neil Sabin and Sheila Sharkey.

We are grateful to Baillière Tindall for permission to draw material from the article: Larner, S. (1984) The work of a clinical psychologist in the care of the elderly. *Age and Ageing,* **13**, 29–33.

The views expressed in these cases are those of the authors and not necessarily those of their employing authorities.

Contributors

Richard Ball Principal Clinical Psychologist, Kidderminster and District Health Authority (Social Services)

Nick Barlow Top Grade Clinical Psychologist and Senior Educational Psychologist; District Clinical Psychologist, Rugby Health Authority

Annabel Broome District Clinical Psychologist, Dudley Health Authority; Change Management Consultant, NHS Training Authority

Mary Brownescombe Heller Principal Clinical Psychologist (Adult Mental Health), Acting District Clinical Psychologist, South Tees Health Authority

Nicholas Canever Principal Clinical Psychologist, Plymouth Health Authority

David Findlay Clark Director, Area Clinical Psychology Services, Grampian Health Board

Marcia Davis District Clinical Psychologist, Coventry Health Authority; Senior Lecturer in Psychology, Warwick University

Hilary Davison Senior Clinical Psychologist, Oxfordshire Health Authority

Mary Dicks Senior Clinical Psychologist, Winchester Health Authority

Keren Fisher Head of Health Psychology Section, Bloomsbury Health Authority

Susan Gardner District Clinical Psychologist, East Berkshire Health Authority

Ann Green Top Grade Clinical Psychologist (Mental Handicap Services), Lothian Health Board; Honorary Fellow, University of Edinburgh

John Hall District Clinical Psychologist, Oxfordshire Health Authority; Clinical Lecturer, University of Oxford

Heather Hunt Principal Clinical Psychologist (Primary Care and Early Intervention), Redbridge Health Authority

Marie Johnston Chairperson, Department of Psychology, Royal Free Hospital and Hampstead Community, Hampstead Health Authority; Senior Lecturer, Royal Free Hospital School of Medicine, London University

Bernard Kat District Clinical Psychologist, Durham Health Authority

John Kincey District Clinical Psychologist, Central Manchester Health Authority

Richard Lansdown   Chief Psychologist, The Hospitals for Sick Children, London

Stuart Larner   Principal Clinical Psychologist (Services to the Elderly), Central Manchester Health Authority

Steven Lovett   Principal Clinical Psychologist (Mental Handicap Service), Hull Health Authority

Dougal Mackay   District Clinical Psychologist, Bristol and Weston Health Authority; Lecturer in Mental Health, University of Bristol

Edgar Miller   District Clinical Psychologist, Cambridge Health Authority

David Mulhall   District Clinical Psychologist, Plymouth Health Authority

Jim Orford   Reader in Clinical and Community Psychology, University of Exeter; Top Grade Clinical Psychologist, Exeter Health Authority

Roger Paxton   District Clinical Psychologist, Northumberland Health Authority

Derek Perkins   Chief Psychologist, Broadmoor Hospital

Stephen Pilling   Principal Clinical Psychologist, Islington Health Authority

Trevor Powell   Senior Clinical Psychologist, West Berkshire Health Authority

S. Jane Santo   Clinical Psychologist, Tower Hamlets Health Authority

Penny Spinks   Senior Clinical Psychologist, West Berkshire Health Authority

Timothy Stockwell   Principal Clinical Psychologist (Alcohol and Drug Services), Exeter Health Authority

Eddy Street   Principal Clinical Psychologist, South Glamorgan Health Authority

Charles Twining   Top Grade Clinical Psychologist, South Glamorgan Health Authority

Louise Wallace   Principal Clinical Psychologist (Physical Health), South Birmingham Health Authority

Jane Wardle   Senior Lecturer in Psychology, Institute of Psychiatry, University of London; Principal Clinical Psychologist, Bethlem Royal and Maudsley Hospital Special Health Authority

Geraldine White   Senior Clinical Psychologist, Sheffield Health Authority

Peter Wilcock   District Clinical Psychologist, Winchester Health Authority

Tim Williams   Principal Clinical Psychologist (Children's Services), West Berkshire Health Authority

Barbara Wilson   Senior Lecturer in Rehabilitation, University of Southampton

William Yule   Professor of Applied Child Psychology, University of London, Institute of Psychiatry; Head of Clinical Psychology Services, Bethlem Royal and Maudsley Hospital Special Health Authority

Contributions to individual cases from:

Christine Bundy   Research Psychologist, South Birmingham Health Authority

Verity Hobbis   Lecturer, Cheshire College of Further Education

Contents

Part 1
Work in adult mental health settings

Introduction

John Hall

Most clinical psychologists in Britain work with adults with mental health problems, and it is this area of work which has seen the greatest growth numerically, and probably the greatest development conceptually, over the past 25 years. In 1960 most clinical psychologists working with adults would have been acting primarily as assessors, usually using one-to-one psychological tests. In the late 1980s such psychologists are primarily therapists and therapeutic advisers, using a wide range of techniques and guiding and supporting other staff in using them. This section illustrates only some of the wide array of problems seen by clinical psychologists today, but conveys something of the therapeutic challenge and commitment required to try to solve them.

The World Health Organization (1951) has defined mental health so as to emphasize the fluctuating nature of this condition for most people, and the essentially individual way in which relationships with others, effects of environment, and internal factors are resolved to achieve a satisfactory synthesis. When the mental health of most people is disturbed, they often experience transient changes of mood or behaviour which improve spontaneously, or with commonly and domestically available methods of help and support. One product of clinical psychologists' work over the past few years has been the publication of books which can safely be bought by lay people to help them cope with such changes (such as Dorothy Rowe's 1983 book on depression). Other more enduring or more serious changes may not improve spontaneously or easily, and it is those more incapacitating problems which are the focus of these first 12 cases.

The range of problems displayed in this section can be viewed from several perspectives. One is the way in which a problem is conceptualized. Both of the first two cases illustrate the use of cognitive models of treatment, which examine the illogical thinking and inappropriate beliefs often apparent in the development of depression. These models, closely identified with the work of Aaron Beck and his colleagues (1979), lead to treatment procedures which help people to become aware of, and articulate, their own strongly held beliefs. Other treatment approaches stress the exposure of previously concealed anxieties and emotions. In the third case Mrs Ahmed is asked to keep a diary to identify the actual nature of her emotional upsets, as a prelude to eclectic psychotherapy. The fifth case, Phil, illustrates how an unexpressed crippling fear of cancer was related to a series of otherwise inexplicable shoplifting offences.

The work of Dorothy Rowe and Aaron Beck on depression illustrates how essentially psychological models of personal dysfunction have been developed to generate widely applicable and effective treatment methods. Traditionally, psychological treatment methods have been classified as behavioural, or psychoanalytic, or educational. The total range of psychological treatment approaches and techniques is enormous (as illustrated in Kendall and Norton-Ford's text, 1982); no one psychologist can expect to be proficient in more than a few. Most of these case studies show an appreciation of the value of several approaches, and the successful fusing of them into a therapeutic regime tailored to meet the needs of the individual.

Another perspective is the number of people involved in treatment. The second case involves essentially only the psychologist and Susan, two people, while many of the other cases involve whole families. In the sixth case the clinical psychologist is working with a psychiatrist and social worker to help Norman, the identified client, and both his parents, and in the twelfth case, on Lilac Ward, the psychologist is working with 16 staff and 27 clients. A psychologist thus has to be able to work with people in a wide range of social relationships and networks.

Several cases demonstrate the importance of providing clear information to clients in order to engage them in a therapeutic alliance, and of laying out a clear step-by-step treatment programme. The seventh case, concerned with stopping smoking, shows the range of information which may be required: the weight of each individual in the group; individualized information to help each person clarify their own motives for stopping smoking; and a standard handout. Some of this information may be gathered by using standardized measures designed for highly specific problem areas. The case of Albert illustrates the continuing use of psychometric cognitive testing, while the social skills group case shows the application of self-rating scales which can be used repeatedly to monitor progress. It is not enough simply to show that a client is 'better' at the end of a course of treatment, since some may relapse after a few weeks or months. The seventh case shows the steps that can be taken to help non-smokers continue to be non-smokers.

Although some clinical psychological techniques are very rapid, most of these cases show the sustained commitment by psychologists and clients — and others — that is required to produce long-term change. The case of Mrs Edwards involved a series of home visits that had to be arranged flexibly to cater for the demands of the client and the availability of family members. The persistent shoplifter was seen on 15 occasions over a year. It took 23 weeks to carry out the staff training course on Lilac Ward.

Some people with mental health problems present single problems, and they can be helped easily. Clinical psychologists are often asked to help people with multiple problems. The progress of Carol in trying to stop smoking is bound up with her social difficulties. Norman, identified as suffering from Asperger's syndrome, and Albert, the incontinent stroke victim, illustrate the highly complex interaction between genetic or acquired medical conditions and the presenting psychological problem. Psychologists need to be sensitive to both social and medical factors in their clients' problems, and need to work closely with the social worker and medical practitioner when the needs of the client require that cooperation.

By contrast with children and people with more serious mental handicaps, most adult clients can act as their own advocates, and can say what they want from the professional care that is offered them. Nonetheless, some adults place such heavy demands upon others (such as the burden upon Norman's father, who had had two coronary heart attacks) or are so unable to articulate their own wishes, that the views of carers or professional staff need to be taken into account in formulating therapeutic goals. It may be easy to reconcile such differing views; sometimes it is extremely difficult to agree on objectives of care or treatment when such issues arise as expression of sexuality, substance dependency, risk of self-harm or violent behaviour, or quality of life.

One major area, covered only in one case, that of Brian, is psychotic disorders. Although long-stay patients in psychiatric hospitals are steadily declining in number, new long-stay or long-term patients, many of whom have schizophrenic disorders, continue to present themselves for care and treatment. Most of the problems they present are amenable to treatment by the procedures described in this section and in the section concerned with mental handicap. While schizophrenic symptoms, including the experience of auditory hallucinations, can be modified by behavioural means (Gomes-Schwartz, 1979) the degree of modification is extremely variable.

The likelihood is that clinical psychologists will be asked over the next few years to take on an even wider range of mental health issues. This is because of the greater public and medical willingness to concede a specifically psychological perspective on some problems previously not referred to psychologists, and because of an increasing reluctance among some people to entertain a pharmacological solution, such as a minor tranquillizer, to problems of living. Some of these issues may be tackled preventatively by, for example, encouraging more active lifestyles that reduce the risk of some cardiological conditions. Some of the issues may be related to the growing number of older people, and of people with a chronic disability for whom medicine and surgery have done their best, but who still have difficulties of adjustment to changed roles and restricted lives. Whatever the issue, the evidence of these cases is that clinical psychologists possess a range of assessment, therapeutic, organizational and evaluative skills that enable them to make a continuing contribution to mental health.

1 Barbara and Simon: conjoint cognitive therapy in the treatment of depression

Introduction

According to the cognitive model (Beck *et al.*, 1979), maladaptive assumptions, inappropriate beliefs and illogical thinking errors play a primary role in the genesis of depression. By contrast, family therapists (Lederer and Jackson, 1968; Treacher, 1985) regard the depressed client as part of a complex and interlocking system of cognitions, emotions and behaviour in which the whole is more than the sum of the parts. From their standpoint, psychological interventions with a depressed person are unlikely to produce lasting change unless all members of the family unit are involved in therapy.

An attempt to resolve the cognitive/systems theory controversy is provided by Feldman (1976). Working with couples whose marriages are characterized by depression, he describes a model that enables the therapist to explore the dysfunctional beliefs of both partners which, he argues, collectively contribute to the maintenance of depression in the designated client. This model suggests a therapeutic approach involving the simultaneous modification of dysfunctional beliefs in both partners.

The case that follows illustrates how Beck's cognitive therapy can be adapted for work with couples to eliminate depression in the person presenting with the symptoms.

The clients

Barbara, a 40-year-old mother of two, had been treated for depression with medication for eight years before being seen in the psychology department. A small overdose precipitated the referral. At the onset of therapy, her main problems could be summarized as follows:

chronic low self-esteem;
lack of self-confidence in social situations outside the home;
obsessional regard for her appearance;
a perfectionist approach to housework, cooking and entertaining;
considerable apprehension about coping with life after the children leave home;
a pessimistic view of the future.

She spoke positively about her family but felt that she was a burden on her husband and an inadequate mother. She stated that she took great pride in her role as hostess and derived considerable pleasure from giving dinner parties.

Simon, a 42-year-old owner of a small business concern, described himself as relaxed and happy with life. While acknowledging Barbara's difficulties, he was quick to emphasize her positive qualities as a wife and mother. He expressed surprise at being invited to become involved in therapy but readily agreed, claiming that he was prepared to do anything to resolve his wife's problems.

Phase 1: Engagement, collaboration and early interventions

When working with depressed clients, it is advisable to intervene quickly and effectively in order to raise their morale, establish therapeutic credibility and thereby to increase their motivation to change. This means that the initial therapeutic techniques employed will be derived from an incomplete assessment and formulation of the problems. An added complication in relation to conjoint work is that the therapist must be satisfied that both partners accept their share of responsibility for helping to maintain depression before introducing techniques.

Assessment

In an endeavour to identify the triggers of emotional responses in the marriage, and the intervening cognitive events, both clients were asked to complete independently a simplified version of the Daily Record of Dysfunctional Thoughts (Beck *et al.*, 1979). Sample items from their mood diaries are presented in Table 1.1.

Table 1.1 Extracts from mood diaries for Barbara and Simon

DAY, TIME	SITUATION What were you doing or thinking about?	EMOTIONS What did you feel? How bad was it? (0–100)		AUTOMATIC THOUGHTS What exactly were your thoughts?
BARBARA				
Friday, 8 p.m.	The new neighbours are having a party. We're not invited.	Despair Anger	(70) (40)	They don't like me. I'm not good enough. After all I've done for them.
Saturday, 3.15 p.m.	Simon got cross because I got behind.	Despair Hurt	(80) (50)	I'm a hopeless wife. He's better off without me. He doesn't understand.
Saturday, 4.30 p.m.	Simon did the washing up, dusting and vacuuming.	Despair Anger	(60) (80)	He's taking over because I'm so inadequate. He's destroying the little bit of confidence I've got.
Saturday, 5.30 p.m.	Simon and the girls went out, leaving me behind.	Despair Anger	(70) (40)	They don't like me. After all I've done for them.
SIMON				
Saturday, 3 p.m.	Lunch was two hours late.	Hurt Sadness	(45) (65)	She ruined my weekend for me. She doesn't care about me.
Saturday, 4 p.m.	Barbara burst into tears.	Sadness Guilt	(70) (30)	She's depressed again. I should have realized. It's my fault.
Saturday, 5 p.m.	She's sulking because I helped with the housework.	Anger	(80)	I can't do anything right. She's impossible.

Formulation

An examination of Barbara's records indicated that her mood changes were invariably accompanied by negative thoughts concerning her worth as a person. Typically the initial trigger would be a perceived put-down from a social acquaintance which she interpreted as evidence of her inadequacy as a person. The consequent feelings of despair would lead, in turn, to emotional withdrawal and to a marked reduction in her effectiveness within the family system. When Simon attempted to help out, she tended to see this as undermining behaviour and responded through passive aggression.

Simon's mood diaries contained far fewer entries. From an examination of his records, it was immediately apparent that his emotional responses were invariably precipitated by variations in Barbara's behaviour. He tended to attribute her bouts of withdrawal and passivity to the fact that she did not care deeply for him. An additional factor to emerge was that, on the occasions when he recognized that she was low in spirits, he experienced guilt which he attempted to reduce by taking over the household duties. When his efforts were rebuffed, the consequent feelings of frustration would lead to a retaliatory response.

An attempt to synthesize the two sets of data sheets indicated a complex interactional sequence, with both partners' erroneous interpretations contributing to a rapidly accelerating downward spiral. Using Feldman's (1976) model, this process can be presented schematically as in Figure 1.1.

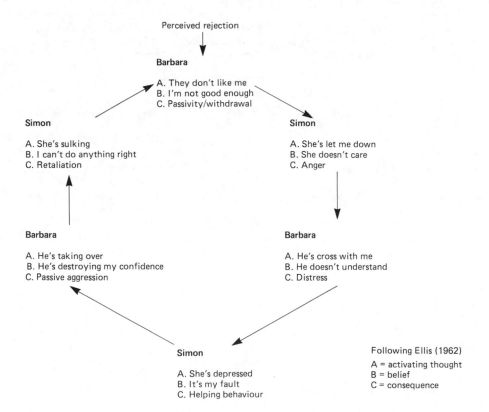

Figure 1.1 A cognitive/systemic representation of factors maintaining depression

Intervention

An advantage of conducting cognitive therapy conjointly, rather than with the depressed person alone, is that it enables clients to check immediately the validity of their beliefs and percepts. Thus the transition from the assessment to the treatment phase proceeds particularly smoothly.

On being shown the above diagram, both partners expressed surprise at the ways in which they had misinterpreted each other's behaviour. Similarly they were astonished that their own reactions could be so easily misread by a partner of some 20 years' standing. However their emotional reactions to these insights were sharply contrasted. Simon became quite excited that the puzzle had been unravelled so easily and felt optimistic that change would now be possible. Barbara, on the other hand, expressed considerable concern that Simon had apparently been so preoccupied with his own needs throughout the marriage that he had never fully understood the nature of her depression.

As so often happens in cognitive therapy, the sudden awareness that one's views of a situation are not supported by the evidence can produce a catastrophic reaction, accompanied by a significant lowering of affect. In this case, it appeared that Barbara had been holding on to one of the five most common irrational beliefs isolated by Eidelson and Epstein (1982) in their work with troubled marriages: 'mindreading is expected.' The psychologist's immediate task at this point was to help Barbara to consider how realistic it was to expect a partner, regardless of how loving, to understand intuitively his spouse's precise feelings, at a particular time, if these were never articulated. This intervention enabled Barbara to acknowledge her share of the responsibility for communication failures within the marriage and thereby prevented her from continuing to react inappropriately to Simon's disclosures.

Having induced a collaborative set for therapy proper, the psychologist then encouraged both clients to evolve rational responses to counter the maladaptive automatic thoughts which had emerged from their mood diaries.

Simon quickly proposed the following rejoinders to his negative inferences as recorded in Table 1.1:

She's feeling down about something. I wonder what's upset her.

She's clearly upset about something. Before jumping in, I'd better find out what's wrong.

She feels I'm taking over. Let her get on with it but be on hand to offer support and help.

Barbara, with noticeably less conviction, suggested more positive self-statements to counter her despairing thoughts, as listed:

Just because some people aren't very friendly towards me, that doesn't mean I'm a bad person.

How can I expect him to understand if I don't open up? No wonder he's fed up.

He's only trying to help. If I told him when I was wrong, he'd give me the support I need.

He's only cross because I rejected his offer of help. He still cares for me.

The final part of this phase of treatment was to request the couple to continue to monitor their mood changes and thoughts, but to include an additional column to record their rational responses to any negative reactions.

Outcome

Both partners complied with the homework assignment and discovered that mood monitoring, coupled with the systematic countering of negative thoughts, led to a period of emotional stability within the marriage. Barbara, however, carried out the task with little conviction. As she put it, 'Although I can see I'm being irrational, I don't *feel* any different.'

Phase 2: Facilitating cognitive change

The procedures described above are not radically different from those of the cognitive behaviour therapy approach described by Meichenbaum (1977). In cognitive therapy proper, however, such interventions serve merely as the groundwork for fundamental change. Beck *et al.* (1979) are particularly critical of programmes aimed solely at modifying superficial cognitions:

> By relying exclusively on the immediate raw data of the automatic thoughts, the therapist misses the crucial — but unexpressed — meaning: namely, the patient's anticipated consequences in terms of the rest of his life. (p.30)

In the second phase of this treatment programme, the psychologist attempted to uncover both clients' underlying cognitive structures in an endeavour to loosen their conceptual systems, thereby leaving them free to change.

Given that the exploration of hidden meanings and primary assumptions for living is a complex and intensive process, it is necessary, at this stage in conjoint therapy, to work with each partner in turn. There are, however, a number of advantages in having, say, the husband present when the wife's conceptual system is the focus of therapy:

(1) He will achieve a deeper understanding of the way she sees the world.
(2) With his knowledge of her past history, he can assist the therapist when she encounters blocks.
(3) Being involved in one's partner's change process can be a special experience for both parties.
(4) His wife serves as a model for self-exploratory work with the result that he will find it easier to enter this stage himself.

Barbara

Assessment

Using the mood diaries, the psychologist quickly focused on the dominant themes of 'feeling uncared for' and 'inadequacy'. Barbara revealed that she found any hint of rejection, from virtually anyone, quite intolerable. She volunteered the information that she dressed immaculately, kept the home spotless, brought up the children to be excessively polite and well mannered, and held exotic dinner parties so that no one could fault her. By becoming 'the perfect wife, mother and hostess' she hoped to avoid criticism from any quarter.

In an attempt to understand the factors which led to the establishment of such a narrow strategy for living, the psychologist explored the rejection theme in its historical context. It slowly emerged that, when her father died suddenly when she was 8, her mother removed all his effects from the house, destroyed all family photographs, and never referred to him again. She then began to victimize

Barbara, while the younger sister established herself in the goody-goody role. It seemed that everything Barbara did was wrong and she gradually formed the impression that she was 'stupid' and 'bad'.

Formulation

It seemed that Barbara had devoted her adult life to playing the part of the ideal woman in order that no one, not even Simon, might suspect how bad and useless a person she really was underneath. Any perceived rejection or criticism from others served to validate her fundamental negative beliefs about herself, which had arisen through her interpretations of her mother's behaviour towards her. Thus, when Simon took over the housework or went out with the children, he was inadvertently confirming her worst fears. Moreover, no amount of affectionate displays from Simon or compliments from guests had served to modify her core assumptions about herself. A simplified version of her belief system is depicted in Figure 1.2.

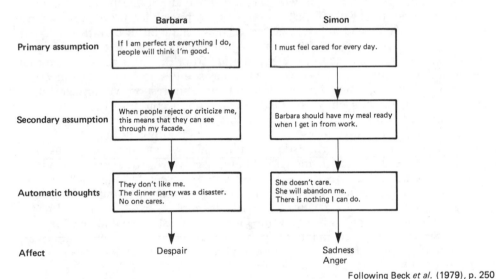

Following Beck *et al.* (1979), p. 250

Figure 1.2 Extracts from the clients' cognitive systems

Intervention

The psychologist began to question the advantages of pursuing a strategy for living which, despite her countless successes, had done nothing to dispel her low regard for herself. At this stage she became very tearful and expressed the view that life was futile and that she would be better off dead.

At the next session, Simon reported that she had been expressing considerable anger towards him throughout the week and that she had, in effect, gone on strike around the house. He himself felt extremely upset about these developments and proposed that therapy should be terminated immediately. As Barbara insisted on continuing, the focus of therapy then shifted to Simon and the work described later was instigated at this point.

When treatment with Barbara was resumed, the psychologist encouraged her to examine her interpretation of her mother's behaviour towards her. Did it follow that the perceived put-downs were a reflection of her worth as a person? Simon offered his opinion that, from his observations, Barbara appeared to be the favoured child but that her mother found it impossible to show affection to her.

Eventually a homework assignment was set up to check the various hypotheses. Despite being 'terrified' of her mother, Barbara agreed to set up a private meeting with the aim of discussing her never-mentioned father. It emerged from this that her mother had never come to terms with her husband's death and that Barbara, who was apparently similar to him in looks and personality, had served as a constant reminder of her loss. This was an extremely emotional meeting and one which left Barbara feeling confused initially but later relieved.

Simon

Assessment

The two main themes to emerge from Simon's mood diaries involved 'being cared for' and 'being appreciated'. He was happiest when the domestic arrangements were running smoothly, with all parties taking full responsibility for their respective duties. He quickly denied any suggestions of male chauvinism or inflexibility by pointing out that he was perfectly happy to help Barbara out if she was feeling down. However, in response to close questioning from Barbara, he conceded that he expected her to have his meal ready for him as soon as he returned from work. He admitted that he became disproportionately upset in response to any deviation from this part of the household routine but could not account for it.

A preliminary exploration of his childhood experiences yielded little of any significance. He was the youngest of six children and, although he described the household as rather chaotic from time to time, his overall impression was of a general atmosphere of warmth and good humour. However, on being pressed, he suddenly remembered a series of upsetting incidents between the ages of 12 and 14. As his elder siblings began to lead independent lives, his parents would spend many evenings in the local pub, having 'forgotten' to cook a meal for him. Images returned to him of the misery he felt waiting for them to return so that he could eat. On occasions, he even sneaked into the pub to try to entice them home. Moreover, an attempted strategy of helping his mother with the housework failed to produce any changes in her behaviour towards him.

Formulation

An analysis of these events revealed a long-standing association between delayed meal-times and the negative thought that 'nobody cares about me.'

Moreover, the fact that Barbara failed to respond positively to his unsolicited contributions to housework seemed to revive echoes from the past concerning his mother's lack of responsiveness to practical help. The automatic thought, 'I can't do anything right,' reflected the hopelessness he felt in his early adolescence. The interrelationships between his beliefs are illustrated in Figure 1.2.

Intervention

The main thrust of therapy involved systematic questioning with regard to the rationality of the above beliefs. As with Barbara, this took the form of generating alternative hypotheses to account for his mother's behaviour. The one that seemed to have some validity for him was Barbara's suggestion that his mother had devoted so many years of her life to looking after six children that she felt she had earned the right to some time for herself. Given that there was considerable evidence that she had cared for him in many other ways, he was able to accept this in due course. However, since she had died five years earlier, it was not possible to test this hypothesis.

Outcome

After ten weekly sessions of intensive therapy, a number of monthly follow-ups were arranged. At termination, the gains Barbara had achieved through therapy can be summarized as follows:

(1) She had become far less perfectionistic with regard to her appearance and performance of household duties in order to spend more time on leisure pursuits.
(2) She organized dinner parties only very occasionally and now viewed them as a source of enjoyment rather than as a vehicle for demonstrating her prowess.
(3) She formed much closer relationships with her mother and younger sister, culminating in the first family visit ever to her father's grave.
(4) She went off alone to a health farm for a week — her first holiday from the family.
(5) She encouraged her daughters to apply for courses which would entail them leaving home.
(6) She came off all her anti-depressants.

The changes in Simon were less dramatic. At first he was suspicious of Barbara's demands for freedom, fearing that she might leave him. Her trip to the health farm was an important test for him. However, when these fears of abandonment were shown to be ill-founded, he quickly adapted to the changes. He became much less concerned about the regularity of meals and allowed Barbara to pull his leg about his former quirk.

Of particular interest is the fact that the children found it more difficult to adjust to the systemic changes which had occurred. As they had not been involved in therapy, they tended, at first, to dismiss Barbara's change of attitude by referring to it as 'Mum's Women's Lib phase'. However, as the benefits of the new arrangements became apparent, their expectations and behaviour altered also, with the result that homeostasis was re-established within the system.

Discussion

This case illustrates many of the advantages and difficulties which can arise when conducting cognitive therapy on a conjoint basis. It is argued here that only by working on Simon's irrational beliefs did it prove possible to enable Barbara to change to such a degree. Moreover, by establishing the meaning of the maladaptive cognitions in both partners, the psychologist was able to achieve more than the containment of a potentially explosive situation. Finally, the experience of working collaboratively on each other's difficulties led to a joint determination to make their marriage a platform for personal growth rather than a cage within which to trap each other.

The major problems when practising this form of therapy arise around the mid-point when the partial facilitation of insight in the designated client can lead to both partners catastrophizing simultaneously. In this example, the psychologist had to abandon work with Barbara at a critical stage in her therapy to focus on Simon's difficulties. There is always the risk that such a tactic may backfire.

A possible criticism of conjoint cognitive therapy is that it involves a subsystem of the family unit rather than the totality. As illustrated in this case, the children proved to be relatively resistant to change and their exclusion from therapy undoubtedly impeded the progress made by their parents. Moreover they were deprived of a potentially valuable learning experience concerning family relationships. As techniques become more sophisticated it may prove possible to develop a cognitive/systemic approach in the full sense of the term.

2 Susan: cognitive-behavioural treatment for bulimia

The past decade has witnessed the identification of a disorder characterized by episodes of binge eating, followed by vomiting, purging and strict dieting. Russell (1979) coined the name 'bulimia nervosa' for this condition, which he described as 'an ominous variant of anorexia nervosa'.

In its brief history, bulimia appears to have overtaken anorexia nervosa in prevalence, and has captured the interest of the public and clinicians alike. Stangler and Printz (1980) found it to be the fifth most frequent diagnosis in women attending a university clinic, and community surveys estimate the prevalence of the full syndrome at about 2–4% (Halmi *et al.,* 1981; Cooper and Fairburn, 1983).

In earlier reports, the prognosis for bulimia was thought to be very poor indeed (Russell, 1979), but with the development of a spectrum of behavioural and cognitive treatment approaches there are grounds for more optimism. The present case study is from a cognitive-behavioural treatment programme which was based on a psychobiological perspective of the aetiology of bulimia (Wardle and Beinart, 1981).

Background

Susan was a 24-year-old editorial assistant, who had completed a university education. She was in regular contact with her family, including a younger sister and brother, with whom she got on well. She lived in a flat shared with two other women, and had a boyfriend whom she had known for just over a year. None of her family or friends had been told about her present difficulties.

Her presenting problem consisted of regular bouts of binge eating followed by self-induced vomiting. She also suffered from almost continuous preoccupation with food and weight, and from depressed mood. Binges occurred several times most days, with the highest frequencies in the evenings and on Sundays. Her referral had been prompted by her dentist who had noticed erosion of the tooth enamel and suggested that she should seek help.

The clinical history revealed that Susan had no problems with eating or weight in childhood, and reached menarche at 12 years. There was no family history of psychiatric illness, but her mother had always been overweight. Between ages 12 and 14 Susan's weight went up to 9 stones, and she began to feel sensitive about being fat. Despite dieting she remained slightly overweight (between 9 and 9½ stones) and very self-conscious, until, after her first holiday with friends of her own age, she decided to lose weight seriously. Over the next six months she lost 2 stones in weight, and at this point (under 8 stones) she received considerable positive reinforcement from friends and family. However, she was still sometimes troubled by feeling fat, and in her first year at college she lost another stone and ceased menstruating. At this point she came to the attention of the college staff and was admitted to the student health centre with a diagnosis of anorexia nervosa. She agreed to gain weight and gradually increased to 8½ stones, but over the holidays at home with her parents she had her first experience of binge eating. The days were marked by increasing depression about her appearance, weight gain, renewed resolution to diet and secret binges. Later that year she read an article about bulimia nervosa which described self-induced vomiting, and although it had stressed the harmful aspects of vomiting, she decided to try it. It took some practice but she persisted, and eventually could vomit with only slight pressure on her abdomen. At first, vomiting appeared to be the ideal solution, and her weight went down. However, with time, both the size and frequency of the binges increased and, correspondingly, the frequency of vomiting. She became increasingly preoccupied with food, and felt progressively less in control of her eating. Her social life was reduced, and her contact with her boyfriend was limited by her avoidance of public eating and her fear that he would find out about her problem.

Assessment

In the first few sessions several standardized assessments were completed, and Susan was asked to keep a diary covering what she ate, the circumstances of eating, and how she felt before and afterwards. Intake was recorded on a form divided into two parts, one for non-binge eating and one for binge eating, which Susan found an easy distinction. She also recorded all episodes of vomiting. Eating style was assessed with the Dutch Eating Behaviour Questionnaire (DEBQ) (van Strien *et al.*, 1986) to measure restraint, externally cued eating and emotionally cued eating. Attitudes to food and eating were assessed with the Eating Disorders Inventory (EDI) (Garner *et al.*, 1983). A baseline measure of intake control problems was based on a list, made by Susan, of six foods ranging from a highly preferred to a less highly preferred food. Each food was rated for how anxious she would feel eating it, and how difficult she would find it to stop after a small amount. Her height, weight and girth were also measured, and percentage of desirable weight was calculated with reference to the published norms (Metropolitan Life Insurance Company, 1983). Body image was assessed in two ways, first by asking Susan to rate how satisfied she felt with each of ten body parts, and then by asking her to estimate her body width (using the Slade and Russell (1973) moving lights techniques) at shoulders, bust, waist and hips. Body width estimates were compared with actual width (measured with calipers) to get a value for percentage overestimation. To complete the general assessment, a self-esteem scale (Rosenberg, 1965) and the Beck Depression Inventory (Beck, 1976) were given.

The results showed that Susan was fairly depressed (BDI score 35) and low in self-esteem. She had an EDI profile characteristic of patients with bulimia, with high scores on drive for thinness, bulimia, and body dissatisfaction. She also had high scores for ineffectiveness and interpersonal distrust. Her eating style was marked by exceptionally high scores for restraint, external eating and emotional eating, and her weight was 89% of the Metropolitan desirable weight. Her body satisfaction was low, and she showed marked overestimation of her waist, hips and bust (averaging 20%). The food intake records showed that her non-binge food intake was very low. Coffee with skimmed milk at breakfast time, an apple and an orange at midday, two slices of Ryvita with low-fat spread and ¼lb grapes would not be atypical. The binge section was in stark contrast. Beginning at around 6 p.m. but sometimes earlier, she would consume cakes, biscuits, sweets, tins of rice pudding and custard, sandwiches and ice cream along with large quantities of sweet drinks. She would then induce vomiting. This could happen up to five times in an evening. At the weekend, particularly on Sunday, binging could go on all day. Once or twice a week she had what she called 'good days' in which she didn't binge, and her caloric intake was below 700 kcals. This would usually occur if she spent the evening in company.

Formulation

Susan's problem was formulated in three ways: (1) overvalued ideas about thinness, (2) conditioned overeating, and (3) the psychobiological effects of starvation. In adolescence she had experienced worries about weight and dieting which were not unusual for girls of her age, and were exacerbated by the media. She then found a successful weight loss regime, and the positive reinforcement she experienced added to her sense that well-being and success were dependent upon thinness. However, her weight loss inevitably induced an increased drive to eat and preoccupation with food, just as in starving people (Keys et al., 1950). When her resolve failed and she ate, she had a greatly increased appetite due to low body fat stores. Food was therefore strongly rewarding, and hence eating was powerfully reinforced. Furthermore her malnourishment effected a readily learned preference for calorie-rich food. Finally, her satiety mechanisms could well have been attenuated due to long-term starvation. Even after weight was restored, other psychological processes could have maintained binge eating, including the constant intention to abstain which might enhance appetite in the short term. Vomiting would also have enhanced appetite by preventing the longer-term nutritional consequences of eating, and so recalibrating the appetite to demand ever-increasing quantities of food.

Susan's depression and low self-esteem were seen as essentially secondary to her food intake problem, principally because they varied with the success of her dieting. However, the possibility that they might require independent treatment was not rejected.

Treatment plan

Susan was offered a 12-session out-patient treatment programme, organized along cognitive-behavioural lines. The initial stages of the treatment were essentially educational, and a simplified version of the formulation (above) was presented to Susan. Nutritional education was also given to provide information about what a balanced diet might include and to reduce some of Susan's prejudices against high calorie foods. As Susan was interested she was given several papers and books to read including 'Bulimia: A psychoeducational perspective' (Garner et al., 1985). Emphasis was also placed on identifying the general sources of cultural pressures for slenderness, and their specific impact in her own life. This was particularly crucial when some of Susan's friends, who were themselves dieters, reinforced her negative views about 'fattening' food.

Binge eating and vomiting

In order to monitor her eating behaviour Susan was asked to keep dietary records continuously for the treatment period. The emphasis in the treatment was upon reducing dietary restraint, resuming an adequate and regular food intake without vomiting, and maintaining a healthy body weight. These goals were acknowledged to be difficult and anxiety-producing, but their importance was underlined regularly over the course of treatment. Modelling, graded exposure, goal setting and cognitive techniques were all used to help to achieve a healthy eating pattern. For example, over the treatment sessions Susan brought progressively more 'difficult' foods with her to eat with the therapist. Vomiting was prevented in the sessions. She was encouraged to eat part of the food, and then to keep the remainder for progressively longer times. Susan then used that food as 'practice food' over the next week, to be eaten, in moderate quantities, in successively more difficult situations without binging or vomiting. Susan was advised that when her non-binge food intake adequately met her nutritional needs, then she would experience a reduced urge to binge. A meal pattern comprising three main meals and two snacks was recommended, initially utilizing the less threatening 'diet' foods, but gradually incorporating the foods she felt less confident about. She was encouraged to include foods that she enjoyed in her meals, although this proved difficult at first in view of her negative attitude to most foods. She tended to say, for example, that she preferred All-Bran with water and no sugar for breakfast, low-fat spreads instead of butter, etc. While these could be genuine preferences, the coincidence with calorie avoidance, and the contrast with the food choices she made during binges, belied this statement. Susan had been binge eating consistently in certain environmental conditions (e.g. being alone in her parent's home with a well-stocked larder), and in particular emotional states (e.g. depressed mood) and so the likelihood of some conditioned overeating was also emphasized. She was encouraged to avoid exposure to difficult situations at first, and to use various self-control strategies to avert binges (self-talk, distraction etc.). A graduated exposure hierarchy of progressively more difficult trigger situations was then constructed, which was worked through over the weeks.

The therapeutic approach to vomiting began by simple advice to refrain from vomiting where possible. This advice was reinforced with information on the harmful effects of vomiting and on the mechanisms whereby persistent vomiting can increase appetite and maintain binge eating. This was put in the context of a general restoration of normal experiences of hunger and satiety. It was explained to Susan that this would depend on several factors including: (1) a nutritionally adequate diet, (2) meals of familiar foods eaten at regular times, and (3) ensuring that every caloric intake was followed by its natural nutritional consequence, uncontaminated by vomiting or purging. Advice on coping with the urge to vomit was given, including coping self-talk (e.g. 'If I'm sick now it will only make me want a bigger binge tomorrow.' 'I managed to resist yesterday and felt better after an hour, I'm sure I can do it again.'), and active distraction. Physical exercise (within normal limits) also proved a useful alternative activity, with the additional benefits of increased fitness, increased psychological well-being and a sense of taking positive steps towards weight control.

Fear of fatness

Like many bulimic patients, Susan's fear of fatness and her over-valuing of thinness had motivated her to keep her body weight down. Early in treatment therefore it was necessary to negotiate a target weight which she could accept. Guided both by the standard healthy weight, and by her own weight history and her family background, a target weight of 9–9½ stones was agreed. Susan was reassured that the therapist would help her not to lose control of her weight, and a variety of behavioural and cognitive manoeuvres were used to help her become less distressed about weight.

The general background of the sessions was a discussion of Susan's beliefs and anxieties about weight. Using the techniques of cognitive therapy she was helped to develop more adaptive alternatives: for example, the thought: 'Everyone will notice if I put on 3 lb' was replaced with 'It's unlikely that anyone will notice a weight change of that amount'. 'People will only think I'm attractive if I am thin', was replaced with 'Thinness can be attractive, but many women who are much fatter than me are thought to be very attractive.'

A behavioural approach was also used, encouraging and targeting previously avoided behaviour. This included wearing more revealing clothes, using public fitting rooms in shops, and letting her boyfriend see her with fewer clothes on. Susan herself gradually became confident enough to reveal the numerous subtle avoidance behaviours she practised, and helped to set goals for change. She also began physical exercise, which integrated exposure (e.g. wearing track suits, leotards etc.) with increased physical self-confidence. She aimed for three exercise sessions a week, to be increased in intensity as her level of cardiovascular fitness increased. Careful records of exercise levels were kept so that she could see an improvement in her physical capacity.

Results of treatment

Susan was enthusiastic about the programme, and readily grasped the essential points. However she was doubtful about the possibility of tolerating weight gain. After the third session the treatment programme was implemented. Her non-binge caloric intake increased steadily over the weeks of treatment, until she was eating a full and well-balanced diet (see Figure 2.1). In the later weeks she needed help in

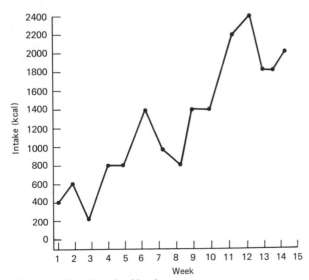

Figure 2.1 Non-binge food intake

coping with the reactions of her flatmates and colleagues, many of whom also had very restrictive eating patterns.

The binge and vomit frequency also showed a fairly steady decline until week seven, when an episode of weight gain caused her to panic and reinstate some dieting and vomiting behaviour (see Figure 2.2). She needed a lot of support at this time and made several telephone calls between sessions. The basic principles of the programme were re-emphasized and Susan was helped to develop some more positive cognitions about her weight change. The importance of continuing an adequate food intake was stressed again, and she was given help preparing meal plans. The re-emergence of a strong urge to binge was dealt with in two stages: when the urge appeared she was encouraged to attempt to control it for the first hour by strategies of distraction and arranging to include in her next planned meal any foods she craved. If the urge had not diminished after an hour, she was 'given permission' to eat.

Susan agreed to tell her boyfriend about her problem, and he came with her to one of the sessions. He proved very supportive about the programme, and they were also able to resolve some of the other difficulties between them.

The binge and vomit frequency dropped close to zero, and Susan's weight, which increased to 8st 12lb over the first seven weeks, reached a stable level. In parallel with the improvement in her eating problems, Susan's preoccupation with food was reduced and her general mood was dramatically improved. She became more socially active, more assertive and her relationship with her family and her boyfriend improved. After the planned 12 sessions of treatment the assessment battery was repeated, revealing an improvement in self-esteem and depression, improved body satisfaction, positive changes in the EDI scales, reduced restraint, and reduced overeating. Her anxiety about eating was much reduced, and control over eating was improved. Susan was seen again at a four-month follow-up. During that time she had maintained her gains, although she had one recurrence after Christmas. She succeeded in getting over this during a holiday with her boyfried and otherwise remained well. She then moved away from the area, but wrote a year later to say that she was married and expecting a baby, and that all was going well.

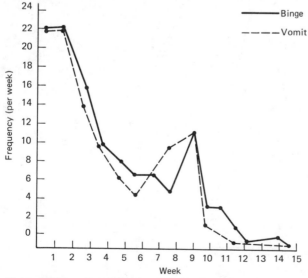

Figure 2.2 Binge/vomit frequency during assessment and treatment

20

Discussion

This case study shows that bulimia, and the associated emotional difficulties, can be modified with a relatively brief, straightforward treatment programme. The clinical impression was that the educational background to the treatment programme was important in setting the conditions in which Susan was able to comply with the difficult behavioural advice. The role of the cognitive component also appeared to be a facilitative one, helping Susan to tolerate a radical change in her lifestyle, and to reassess her attitudes to weight and eating. Finally, the relationship with the therapist was warm and easygoing, with an emphasis on the exploration of social ideals of slenderness which can be biologically and psychologically unattainable.

3 Mrs Ahmed: an eclectic approach to psychotherapy

This case demonstrates the use of an eclectic approach to psychotherapy in which the psychologist draws upon a wide range of psychological models and techniques (Garfield, 1980). Therapy is guided not by one single theoretical model but by the needs of the client as identified by the psychologist and the client working together in a therapeutic alliance.

Presenting problem

An attractive and articulate 25-year-old woman of Indian parentage, Mrs Ahmed was referred for help with feelings of depression, moodiness and aggressive outbursts. At times she felt suicidal. These feelings were reportedly worse pre-menstrually and were associated with a sense of being overwhelmed and unable to cope with her roles as wife, mother and homemaker. She had two daughters aged 6 and 1 year.

Background

Mrs Ahmed grew up in Africa in comfortable circumstances as part of an extended family. The second oldest of four children, her closest friends were two maternal aunts of her own age. Her mother was a businesswoman and the driving force in the family, while her father was more understanding and passive. Although Mrs Ahmed described her childhood as a very happy time she said that her mother had been very strict and violent towards her during her childhood and early adolescence. Her mother would beat her with 'whatever came to hand' and then lock her in her bedroom for hours, refusing to let her out no matter how much she pleaded. Mrs Ahmed said this had occurred over small infringements and she had felt very resentful at being so unjustly treated. She used to feel hatred for her mother and would act rebelliously to hurt her back. Mrs Ahmed had felt jealous of the attention her mother gave to others, especially her sister and her aunts. However, their relationship improved considerably once Mrs Ahmed became engaged, and she missed her mother greatly since coming to England.

Mrs Ahmed met her husband when she was 15, in her last year at school. They secretly courted briefly before becoming engaged by 'arrangement'. After obtaining good O level results she followed her fiancé to England to do A levels at a college some distance away. This period was marked by Mrs Ahmed's moodiness and ambivalence towards her fiancé. A perfectionist, she also felt under severe pressure about her studies. Prior to her exams she made a suicide attempt by slashing her wrists, and returned to her parents' home for a year. At first, Mrs Ahmed was set on breaking her engagement but decided to return to England at 19 to marry and make a new start.

Mrs Ahmed felt that her problems had been worse since marriage. At first she attributed this to living with her in-laws where she felt 'like a servant'. She took an overdose at this time. Her problems persisted when the couple moved to their own home and their first child was born.

Mrs Ahmed had looked to various solutions to her problems. She started a college course and did well but withdrew because she felt she was not working up to her standard. There were also two extended visits to her parents, where she felt 'looked after', but the benefits were short-lived. She had a second child about one year prior to therapy, hoping this would keep her busy and not give her time to brood.

Mrs Ahmed described her husband as extremely good, considerate and helpful. She said she had nothing to be angry with him about and could not understand her moods. He was a very stable and logical person who did not himself express much emotion. One of a large family of brothers, Mr Ahmed seemed to be the one his family turned to for support and help and Mrs Ahmed resented this. She disliked herself for being possessive of him and envious of others. She felt very dependent on her husband and wished to be less so.

Assessment

When Mrs Ahmed was first seen there were several questions to be asked. First, her style of presentation was as interesting as the content of her difficulties. For example, did her affect match the content of what she was saying? Did she seem to have an understanding or insight into her feelings and behaviours or did they seem to her to happen out of the blue, beyond her awareness?

Second was the question of why she was seeking help now. What was her motivation for change? Was she seeking help for herself or was it because someone else — a relative or a professional — thought she should? Did she feel it was her problem or someone else's?

Third, it was important to pay close attention to what Mrs Ahmed presented as *her* major worries or problems. While the psychologist had several hypotheses about the underlying dynamics giving rise to her complaints, the development of a good working relationship or therapeutic alliance (Bordin, 1979) with her would depend on addressing, at least initially, the issues most salient for her.

Fourth, her level of distress: how anxious or depressed did she seem? If her anxiety level was very high, for example, then a first task of therapy would be to help her reduce it so she could be comfortable enough to examine important but possibly painful issues.

Last, there was a need to be very aware of the relationship with Mrs Ahmed. How did she relate to the psychologist? Did she seem to be looking to her for directives and answers or could she take some responsibility for raising areas of concern and elaborating on them? Did she keep herself at an emotional distance or was she open and warm? How did she make the psychologist feel: like mothering her? threatened by her? In considering these relationship aspects, it is always important for the psychologist to separate the feelings which belong to herself because of tiredness or some personal problem from the feelings engendered by the client. The feelings the client brings to the therapeutic relationship can give important clues both to central issues for her in her relationships with others and to emotional conflicts within herself.

As this brief description illustrates, the psychologist can use herself as a clinical instrument rather than rely on formal assessment measures and this was how the assessment of Mrs Ahmed proceeded.

Formulation

The psychologist's view of Mrs Ahmed was that she was a sensitive person who had inner emotional conflicts stemming from her childhood which pulled her in opposing directions. The core or central conflict was between wanting to be very close to another person and her sense of rejection, hurt and anger at the slightest hint that she was not the most preferred person in their lives. Mrs Ahmed would retaliate by rejecting the other, and feel very hurt, abandoned and despairing. Thus her present problems in her marriage, her terrible moods with her husband, could be seen as a re-enactment of the pattern she experienced with her mother as a child and adolescent when she repeatedly felt abandoned, resentful and jealous.

A related inner struggle was between her desire for perfection and her sense of inadequacy and failure. She felt she was either 'all good' or bad, and was not tolerant or accepting of herself. This also seemed to relate to her earlier experiences. The hypothesis was that she had struggled to be the good child who would please her mother. Receiving unwarranted punishments when failing in small ways had made her feel worthless, bad and guilty.

Some of Mrs Ahmed's attitudes and behaviours were probably also learned within her family. For example, her mother's family were described as wilful, quick-tempered and a little arrogant, which was also how she saw herself. Her mother had had a bad relationship with her own mother, having also been harshly disciplined as a child.

Although these were the central formulations there were additional hypotheses to be tested as therapy progressed. It was tempting to understand Mrs Ahmed's problems purely as current relationship difficulties in an arranged marriage and to consider marital therapy as the approach of choice. However, as Mrs Ahmed presented it, she and her husband did genuinely care for each other and got on reasonably well except when she had her 'attacks'. The information available indicated that the problem was worse after marriage but had always been there. Also she was concerned to sort herself out and did not consider that it was her husband's fault or problem. Therefore, the possibility of marital work was kept in mind for a later date.

Although the formulation of Mrs Ahmed's problems was essentially dynamic, it was not felt that an exploratory approach on its own would be the best way to begin therapy with her. She was in very considerable distress about her emotional outbursts. She felt very out of control, particularly with her 6-year-old daughter with whom she was too strict and critical. Mrs Ahmed felt very guilty for 'terrorizing' the child, though she did not hit her. A most immediate issue therefore was to give some concrete help towards improving her sense of control, especially with her children.

Mrs Ahmed was personally highly motivated for therapy at this time, both by her own distress and her recognition that previous attempts to solve her problems by external measures such as bursts of activity, return to her family of origin and crisis contacts with the mental health services had failed. She had had antidepressant medication for postnatal depression and courses of hormonal therapy for pre-menstrual tension, all with little effect.

However, she tended not to look inside herself; she kept a certain distance from her feelings especially when describing what must have been a very painful childhood. It was felt that an approach which put pressure on her to explore feelings in an unstructured way from the beginning would feel so uncomfortable and anxiety-provoking that she might well reject therapy by dropping out.

With these considerations in mind, it was decided to begin with a more structured cognitive/behavioural approach aimed at helping Mrs Ahmed identify the triggers for her emotional upsets and the feelings and thoughts which went with them. The hope was that once her emotional reactions became understandable to her there would be a base from which to explore their meanings, possibly in the context of what was happening in the therapeutic relationship.

The therapy

The therapy can be divided into phases, though, as with love, its course was not smooth. From the beginning Mrs Ahmed was asked to keep a diary where she wrote about her emotional upsets as well as noting her menstrual cycle. First the focus was on her irritability with her children, which led on to the perfectionistic demands she made of herself. Giving her permission to value her ability to enjoy herself as well as to work hard helped reduce the conflict she felt between gratifying her needs and her over-strict conscience. Her view of spending time playing with the children (something she enjoyed doing) rather than doing housework was positively reframed as 'good mothering' and not laziness. It also emerged that Mrs Ahmed did not show the children much affection. Once she was able to link this with the lack of affection shown in her family of origin, she made conscious efforts to change. Her relationship with the children improved early on in the therapy, giving her encouragement and hope.

Increasingly, Mrs Ahmed shifted to recounting the angry outbursts or sullen withdrawals she had in relation to her husband. Most awful for her were her feelings of being out of control and often unaware of why she behaved as she did. Glimpses began to emerge; she felt she was unreasonably jealous of help he gave to his family, she got angry if he did not give her his complete attention, yet she often pushed him away when he did. In this phase, she fluctuated between coping quite well and emotional upset followed by despair.

As she had done previously, Mrs Ahmed also took flight to advanced studies for a career as a hoped-for solution to her personal unhappiness. When this quickly failed she decided she must return home to her parents to be looked after and sort herself out. This was a time of uncertainty for the psychologist, who temporarily lost sight of initial formulations as she fluctuated between hope and feeling that she was failing Mrs Ahmed. Reviewing the therapy from the beginning made it possible to step back and see that she was getting caught up in Mrs Ahmed's feelings and patterns of avoidance rather than helping her gently but steadfastly to look within and face possibly painful aspects of herself.

Having grasped this, it was possible to hold up a mirror to Mrs Ahmed to see this pattern for herself. This was aided by her parents' lack of enthusiasm about her return home. Deep feelings of abandonment were stirred within her which she recognized as similar to her feelings in childhood when she had cried herself to sleep after beatings.

It was perhaps a turning point in the therapy when Mrs Ahmed wept in the therapy session, as she actually re-experienced those very hurtful memories. She became aware that she had not wished to remember that aspect of her life. She realized she had been unwilling, perhaps unable, to be a wife and mother as she 'yearned to be a child still and get the love I feel I lacked as a child'. By the use of the 'empty chair technique' (Page, 1984) (that is, imagining that a relevant person is sitting in an empty chair in the room) Mrs Ahmed was encouraged to express her feelings to her mother — her puzzlement, her resentment, her desire for love now. The psychologist also comforted her as she cried. It is not something that is usually done, but it felt natural and spontaneous, perhaps a way of offering her the 'good-enough' mothering (Winnicott, 1965) she had not had.

As the therapeutic relationship became close, Mrs Ahmed seemed more able to risk her feelings in therapy. As she recalled more and more from her childhood she made increasing links between her current emotions and reactions and the past. It was very clear by this time that her moods were not related to her menstrual cycle. She became aware that she often overreacted in her current relationships, especially with her husband, as if she were still being rejected, when in fact this was not actually the case.

Mrs Ahmed began to see that she wished to be very close to her husband, but became increasingly insecure as she drew closer. Hence she tested him a good deal; when he failed her secret tests she became angry and withdrew in a mixture of rage, hurt and abandonment to her bedroom, as she had done in childhood. Now, though, she was putting herself in prison and denying herself the comfort he offered to her.

Therapy progressed a stage further when she began sharing these insights with her husband. Small but significant changes occurred. She cried with him and allowed him to comfort her for the first time. She began to say 'sorry' — something she had never done even as a child when her mother had demanded it of her. Mrs Ahmed herself picked up a suggestion made early on in therapy that her husband be included in some of the sessions. This seemed to signify her readiness to share the psychologist with her husband as well as a clear commitment to sharing herself more with him.

In the conjoint meetings Mrs Ahmed initially needed some encouragement to take responsibility for sharing her feelings with her husband, rather than hope the psychologist would do this hard work for her. To complement work on improving understanding and communication at the feelings level, tasks were agreed on as homework experiments which would put some of the insights into action. The aim was to encourage change at the emotional, cognitive and behavioural levels. For example, Mrs Ahmed practised accepting comfort and giving comfort to her husband, something she had no real experience of previously. As she felt able to recognize her needs more, she was also better able to appreciate the needs of others and to meet them better.

Outcome

Mrs Ahmed has made great leaps forward in understanding herself and in relying less on denial as a way of coping with her needs. She is no longer stuck unknowingly in her past. Now much more in touch with her emotions, she can express these more appropriately by asking directly for what she wants. She will continue to struggle with her great sensitiveness, a basic insecurity, and a low frustration tolerance. However, she now has an ally in her husband who can help in the reparative process. She has become more of a whole person who can empathize with the needs of others and can now better extend herself to them. Her relationships with her husband and her children are much more satisfying for all. Mrs Ahmed has also managed to sustain a course of study, doing well without pressurizing herself unduly. She and the family are more relaxed and contented.

Discussion

This case illustrates the use of an eclectic approach to psychotherapy. Within an overarching framework of the therapeutic alliance, the flexibility an eclectic view affords has many advantages.

It does not close off any possible problem areas, whether these are the role of intrapsychic conflicts, the influence of significant others, or faulty learning patterns. The case also shows the usefulness of drawing on a variety of techniques to facilitate change in the cognitive, emotional and behavioural domains rather than relying on one sphere as the prime focus of therapy. Why work with one hand tied behind one's back by theory if two are needed to do the job effectively?

Meeting the client on her ground initially felt very important, to give her some encouragement and to develop mutual trust. The major disadvantage of not working more strictly within one therapeutic framework is that it can be hard to know when to stick and when to change. The point in therapy where the psychologist felt she lost sight of the core issues illustrates the difficulty of changing gear, from a more directive to a more explorative mode.

This leads to the last lesson, the regular need to take time to review a case alone and in consultation or supervision with a colleague. In using the self as the instrument of change, there is a continuing need to step back and review the process of which one is a part.

4   Mrs James: treating agoraphobia

Presenting problem

Mrs James was referred by her GP to the district psychology department for treatment of 'her nerves and agoraphobia'. The referral was precipitated by the recommendation of a consultant gynaecologist after Mrs James had prematurely discharged herself from the general hospital in a state of panic before having a hysterectomy.

After discharging herself from hospital she said that she had lost all her confidence, was avoiding friends, taking extended time off work and feeling generally desperate and miserable. In her words, 'I cannot go out of the house on my own because I'm scared I'll flake out.' She described feeling generally tense and having panic attacks characterized by breathlessness, dizziness, pains in the chest and feeling unsteady on her feet. The thoughts that accompanied these sensations included 'I'm going to pass out or go completely out of control,' 'There must be something seriously wrong with me — maybe I'm cracking up?' She avoided going anywhere on her own; her husband drove her to work, her father-in-law picked her up, and her friends and children accompanied her on shopping trips. Situations she particularly avoided included crowded shops, long queues, coaches, trains, cinemas and travelling a long way from home.

She vividly described her first, and worst, panic attack which had occurred, out of the blue, 14 years ago while shopping in a crowded supermarket. At the time she was three months pregnant and experiencing serious marital difficulties. Her first thought was that she was having a heart attack, but her GP assured her she was just under stress and prescribed a course of tranquillizers.

Her more recent panic in hospital was different, as she was aware of her anxiety gradually building up, and of being 'tipped over the edge' by a number of factors, such as her husband being asked to leave before the operation, the telephone being removed from her room, and an unfamiliar nurse arriving to take her down for her operation.

Mrs James said that she was initially reluctant about being referred, but recognized the time had come when she needed professional help. She wanted to work primarily on her agoraphobia and secondly on attempting to return to hospital.

Background

Mrs James was 38, married, with two daughters aged 8 and 13. She worked as a secretary for a firm of solicitors. Her 13-year-old daughter accompanied her to the out-patient clinic. Mrs James described her father, a retired electrician, as 'a rather calm, passive man'; her mother was described as 'a hard bitter woman' who at the age of 20 lost the sight of one eye and was badly scarred by the explosion of a bomb in the Second World War. After the accident the mother did not like leaving the house and was prone to anxiety and depression. Mrs James was the second of three children, but had little contact with her elder sister who lived in Australia and her younger brother who was described as 'Mum's favourite'. She did not feel close to her parents, only visiting them once a year.

Mrs James married her first husband, Michael, at the age of 17. Her parents disapproved of the relationship and refused to attend the ceremony. The marriage survived eight volatile years although her husband was described as uncaring and physically violent. At the age of 25, nine months after her first panic, she left her first husband and, together with her 3-month-old daughter, moved into a friend's house. Two years later she married a GPO engineer called Tony whom she described as 'a gentle, kind man'. She described their marriage as marvellous, although she acknowledged that she was completely dependent on him.

Assessment

The assessment involved an interview and the completion by Mrs James of a number of self-report questionnaires. The small battery of questionnaires completed before the first consultation included:

(1) the short version of the Leeds Scale for the Self-Assessment of Anxiety and Depression (Snaith et al., 1976);
(2) the short 15-item Fear Questionnaire (Marks and Matthews, 1979);
(3) the Spielberger State-Trait Anxiety Inventory (STAI) (Spielberger et al., 1970);
(4) the Cognitive Anxiety Questionnaire (Lindsay and Hood, 1982);
(5) the Effects on Life Inventory (Matthews, 1983).

Alongside these recognized inventories there were sections devised by the psychologist on the client's experience of physical symptoms, panic attacks and rating of severity of her problem.

These inventories were used to help establish a clinical profile of Mrs James's anxiety across a number of areas. They also acted as a useful baseline from which progress could be measured, and were quick to administer.

The assessment interview followed a standard multi-modal assessment, where the client's problems were assessed for behaviour, affect, sensation, ideation, cognitions, interpersonal aspects and drug influences (Lazarus, 1976). Questions concerning the what, where, when and how of the problem were asked, as were questions to elicit relevant antecedent and consequent events. Examples of episodes of anxiety and panic were examined using the three-systems model of anxiety (Lang, 1971) — physical sensation, thoughts and behaviour. Information concerning family background, personal history and present situation was also elicited. Finally Mrs James was asked about her expectations for treatment and what specific changes she would like to make.

Formulation of the problem and treatment

Mrs James could be described as suffering from agoraphobia with panic attacks. She had an exaggerated fear of being alone or in public places from which escape might be difficult. This fear and subsequent avoidance behaviour restricted her normal activity and dominated her life.

A number of authors, (for example, Chambless and Goldstein, 1982; Hallam, 1978) have argued that in many cases agoraphobia is best viewed as a fear of panic rather than a fear of specific situations. The experience of panic, often occurring during periods of stress, predates the onset of situational avoidance (Matthews *et al.*, 1981). Given the extreme nature of these attacks, which may be qualitatively different from the experience of anxiety because of the effect of hyperventilation (Garssen *et al.*, 1983; Ley, 1985), it is easy to understand the development of intense and enduring avoidance behaviour.

Clark (1987) suggests that panic attacks such as those experienced by Mrs James result from the misinterpretation of certain bodily sensations (for example, palpitations, breathlessness, dizziness) where the client perceives these sensations as more dangerous than they really are (for example, perceiving palpitations as evidence of an impending heart attack). A number of recognized catastrophic thoughts have been associated with the experience of panic; these include thoughts about loss of control, illness and death, injury, failure to cope and social embarrassment (Hibbert, 1984). They are all themes which appear to form the basis of a vicious circle involving physical symptoms, cognitions and avoidance behaviour (Matthews, 1984). Mrs James's avoidance of surgery appeared to be typical of this pattern.

The treatment of choice for agoraphobia has been shown to be graded *in vivo* exposure to feared external situations (Matthews *et al.*, 1981). In practice this is normally augmented by teaching the client a variety of coping skills or anxiety management techniques to help control anxiety and break the vicious circle. Inevitably there is a large educational component in this treatment approach, as new information is given to the client concerning such areas as the mechanics of physical symptoms and the role of hyperventilation in panic. Clark *et al.* (1985) suggest that this informational aspect is important in altering the catastrophic thoughts in clients who experience severe anxiety and panic attacks.

Alongside this cognitive/behavioural approach it also seemed important to work with Mrs James's family who appeared to collude with her avoidance behaviour. Hafner (1982) concluded that agoraphobic symptoms emerge or are exacerbated as part of a couple's attempt to adjust to one another and the constraints, demands and conflicts of marriage. In some cases it is argued that agoraphobia stabilizes the relationship and the spouse may become depressed if the agoraphobic person starts to function normally again.

On another front it was considered useful to look specifically at Mrs James's psychological preparation for surgery (Ridgeway and Matthews, 1982), and also to examine possible changes that could be made to the hospital environment.

What happened

At the end of the assessment interview Mrs James was given:

(1) a self-help treatment manual (Matthews *et al.*, 1981) which she was asked to study with her husband;

(2) a relaxation tape, accompanied by an explanation of the rationale for relaxation training (relaxation as an incompatible physiological response to anxiety); and

(3) a number of diary sheets to monitor incidents of increased anxiety.

Mr James was invited to attend the second session but was unable to take time off work. A number of further excuses precluded his attendance until the fifth session. The first four treatment sessions with Mrs James followed the same format: diary sheets and homework tasks were reviewed in the light of antecedent events, physical symptoms, catastrophic thoughts and subsequent coping strategies. Coping skills were taught for controlling physical and cognitive manifestations of anxiety (relaxation, respiratory control, positive self-talk and distraction). In the second session a hierarchy of fear-provoking situations rated on a ten-point scale was constructed and worked upon as homework tasks. At the bottom of the hierarchy was, 'Go around the corner to the local shop at lunch-time;' half-way up was, 'Go to work on the bus unaccompanied, followed by husband in the car;' and at the very top was, 'Go back to hospital for my operation.'

Mrs James was well motivated and always conscientiously completed her self-monitoring sheets and homework tasks. Considerable progress was made although new fears and phobias were unearthed. For example, she had the habit of avoiding eating any food that she felt someone could have poisoned. Because this avoidance behaviour was a way of coping with anxiety, homework tasks involving food were added to the hierarchy. Examples of these tasks included eating an apple without first deliberately sharing it with somebody else, and sitting down and eating a meal with her family rather than eating her food five minutes after they had all started.

A joint session was then arranged with Mr James after an incident when his wife became more aware of his resistance to her changing. She had set herself the task of going to work on the bus unaccompanied, but that morning, because it was raining, her husband insisted on giving her a lift. After initially refusing she accepted his offer but was angry and disappointed with herself. In the subsequent joint session Mr James came across as a rather passive man with little to say. The importance of his role in Mrs James's programme was emphasized and the sensitive issue of his needs in their relationship was gently explored without much headway. No further joint sessions were held.

After considerable progress had been made regarding her general mobility, attention was turned to Mrs James's return to hospital. Because she was so well motivated, a self-desensitization programme was implemented which she carried out outside the sessions. Progressively more anxiety-provoking scenes were described on cue cards, and in imagination were paired with relaxation, for example, 'ringing up the hospital to arrange my admission' or 'packing my suitcase in preparation to go to the hospital'. Nearer the date of her operation Mrs James revisited the ward and discussed with the nursing staff some of her anxieties. They arranged for her to have a shared dormitory, for her husband to be on hand until the last minute, and for her operation to be carried out as soon as possible after her admission.

Outcome

Mrs James successfully underwent her hysterectomy operation, the task at the top of her hierarchy, eight months and ten sessions after the beginning of treatment. Although she acknowledged that she still felt very anxious at times, she reported that she had not had a major panic attack since the start of therapy. Her mobility was greatly increased; she travelled to work unaccompanied, daily, on the bus. She reported that she still felt a little uneasy travelling long distances from home and in very crowded supermarkets. The nature of her catastrophic thoughts appeared to have shifted as she no longer feared that she was 'seriously ill, or going mad', but often worried that she might 'look a fool' and wondered, 'why do others cope better'.

Self-report data from questionnaires completed before and after treatment suggested substantial changes in all areas of her anxiety. These changes were maintained at three-month follow up (see Table 4.1).

Table 4.1 Outcome measures: pre-treatment, post-treatment, and three-month follow-up scores

	Pre	Post	Follow-up
*Severity of Problem	13	4	4
Leeds Scale – Self-Assessment Anxiety	16	7	6
Leeds Scale – Self-Assessment Depression	11	2	2
*Physical Symptoms Inventory	16	7	8
Cognitive Anxiety Questionnaire	20	8	9
Fear Questionnaire	57	21	18
Spielberger STAI	56	42	41
Effects on Life Inventory	33	16	14

* Scales created by psychologist

Discussion

Mrs James was in many ways classically agoraphobic, demonstrating the complex multi-faceted nature of the condition. When under stress she experienced severe somatic symptoms (panics), which tended to be misinterpreted and catastrophized, leading to avoidance of situations with an element of entrapment. Alongside this process, important relationships colluded with that avoidance.

It is interesting that Mrs James did not develop a more fully blown agoraphobia earlier on, when, in her mid 20s, she had her first major panic attack. With hindsight she could recognize why, saying, 'I wasn't allowed to. Mike [her first husband] would laugh at me saying, "Well pass out on the floor then." He was really very cruel to me, but in some ways it was good for me.' Mrs James's second husband allowed her to avoid situations and become dependent on him, eroding her confidence in her ability to function independently.

A number of treatment options could have been taken. A psychodynamic approach might have focused primarily on exploring conflicts arising from early relationships and separation anxiety, but this would not have dealt directly with the problems she was concerned with. A systemic approach might have focused on the family as a system which allowed her to be agoraphobic, but that system was able to cope with her more assertive behaviour without major readjustment. The cognitive/behavioural approach adopted, acknowledged and discussed these areas, but did not choose either of them as the main focus of therapy.

In clinical practice it is always difficult to assess what the most important components of the intervention are. At the end of treatment when the client was asked what she had found most helpful she replied, 'Finding somebody who understood and could explain to me what was going on — and then could offer me a way out.' The therapeutic relationship also seemed important and she reported often being able to hear the psychologist's voice encouraging her and telling her what to do when feeling anxious. In the exposure tasks Mrs James ultimately helped herself but stressed that she felt that she 'needed pushing'. She also invented a number of personalized anxiety management strategies along the way. For example, after her operation she took to carrying her temperature chart from the hospital in her handbag and, whenever she felt anxious, she took it out and looked at it. This acted as both a source of positive self-statements and a distraction technique and reduced her anxiety levels.

Mrs James still gets anxious and still does not like large crowds, situations of entrapment, or being far from home, but this anxiety does not unduly interfere with her life or restrict her mobility and she now feels much more able to cope on her own.

5   Phil: a shoplifter with compulsive problems

Introduction

For clinical psychologists working in prison or forensic out-patient centres, the focus of most cases referred for treatment is the modification of offence behaviour. These are mainly sex, violence and arson offences, but some lesser offences, including shoplifting, are also involved. The following case is somewhat unusual by virtue of both the client himself and the approach to treatment. Psychologists who normally work within a cognitive/behavioural framework sometimes need to adapt their approach to focus on the emotional needs of the client when these are the dominant aspects of the problem.

The referral

Most shoplifters seen for treatment are middle-aged to elderly women. One interesting exception was Phil, a young, good-looking, quietly spoken married man in his early 30s with a young daughter. Phil had ten convictions dating back to his early 20s for stealing items from stores. These included clothes, electrical goods, food and luxury items. According to previous social enquiry reports, Phil had offered no explanation or excuses for his offending and had apparently accepted without question whatever punishments were meted out by the court. At first, he had been fined but, as his offending continued, courts had finally begun to impose short periods of imprisonment.

For some time, Phil's case had presented something of a dilemma for the courts and probation service. His offending, while clearly carried out in a deliberate fashion, was sometimes so blatant as to almost guarantee apprehension. He appeared to gain nothing from his offending, about which he seemed genuinely ashamed and distressed.

The letter of referral about Phil's case noted his hesitant manner and apparently high level of anxiety, particularly around the time of his offences. The referral letter raised the possibility that his offending might be stress-related and amenable to anxiety management techniques.

Background

Referral to the psychology department from the probation service noted that Phil was the elder of two brothers. Their father died from a stroke when Phil was 23, and his mother from cancer when he was 26. The relationship with his mother had apparently always been difficult, and her death left him with many unresolved feelings about their relationship.

Phil's schooling was disrupted when the family moved and, unlike his younger brother, he was left feeling rather isolated at his new school. Nevertheless, he obtained a number of GCE O levels and went on to work first as an assistant in a menswear shop and later as the manager of a bicycle shop.

Apart from his stealing, Phil's behaviour was seemingly unremarkable. He and his wife appeared to have a good marriage and, with their daughter, were a happy and financially well-organized family. Phil's offending was their only major concern.

Assessment

The usual assessment procedure for offenders referred for psychological treatment begins with a broad-based, multi-modal behavioural analysis (Crawford, 1979; Lazarus, 1976). Within this framework, interview and other data are assembled so as to ascertain as many antecedents and consequences for the offender's behaviour as possible at various levels of functioning — behaviour, emotions, cognitions, attitudes, relationships and opportunities for offending.

Both Phil and his wife were interviewed and details of their past and present circumstances elicited. Phil's wife gave a clear account of his offending which was in line with the probation officer's report. Phil found it much more difficult to talk about his offending and, in so doing, periodically 'blanked off', as he called it. On these occasions he would cease talking and his attention would become fixated on some minor aspect of his immediate environment such as a door handle or carpet pattern.

When Phil blanked off, further questioning had no effect in restimulating the conversation. Only a change of topic brought his concentration and conversation back to normal. He was able to report that, when blanked off, all thoughts of the conversation became lost to him.

Psychometric testing

In an attempt to derive additional clues about Phil's cognitive and emotional functioning, he was asked to complete a number of personality and symptom questionnaires. This was not carried out with any narrow diagnostic intention, but rather as a kind of broad sweep for psychological clues, as in Cronbach and Gleser's (1965) 'high bandwidth-low fidelity' dilemma in which evidence can usefully be sampled over a wide area of interest (high bandwidth) but at the cost of reduced efficiency or validity for any one aspect under consideration (low fidelity). Of particular interest were the results from the Fear Survey Schedule (Geer, 1965) which yielded minimum scores on all items except 'prospects of a surgical operation' and 'failure', on which he scored 'a little fear', and 'loss of loved ones', on which he scored 'maximum anxiety'. Also of interest was Phil's very high score on the Middlesex Hospital Questionnaire's 'free-floating anxiety' (three standard deviations above the mean for men in Phil's age group seen in a general practice setting) and a moderately high score on 'obsessionality' (one standard deviation above the mean) (Crown and Crisp, 1966).

Intervention

The aim of intervention with Phil was to explore with him, and help him control, his shoplifting. Fifteen sessions were held over a period of a year. Early on, discussions with him about the results from the questionnaires led to the psychologist describing how some people with high obsessionality scores engage in checking rituals which are carried out to protect them from some imagined problem. Phil expressed great surprise that this hitherto secret aspect of his life had somehow been uncovered, and he went on to describe how he had indeed engaged in checking rituals since his early teens. He was, however, totally unable to explain the function of these rituals, and again 'blanked off'.

In talking further about his shoplifting, Phil falteringly explained that this usually occurred while he was engaged in some other task, such as collecting stock for his shop, and usually when he felt under some kind of pressure, but again he was unable to elaborate on this. He was prepared to concede that anxiety or stress might play a part in his offending but how, he asked, could this be the total explanation? Why was it that he responded to stress by shoplifting? Why was it that he had had periods of up to five years following his mother's death when he had engaged in no shoplifting?

Asked about the consequences of his offending for him and his family, Phil reported that he felt numb at the time of his offences — he was 'in a state of limbo' — and that he generally wished to get the legal consequences of his offending over with as quickly as possible, and with as little involvement as possible from other people, including his family.

Unlike interviews with many offenders who either appear to give information freely or to deliberately withhold it, the impression gained from interviewing Phil was that, on one level, he wished to cooperate but, on another, simply could not follow this through into revealing and discussing his thoughts and feelings.

Dreams

Subsequent to the session in which the questionnaire results were discussed, Phil reported having experienced a series of distressing nightmares. He felt that these were somehow important, and said that he wished to describe them. Having agreed to do this, however, he found difficulty beginning his account. A few hesitant words would be followed by long silences. It was suggested to Phil that he just begin talking about anything in the sequence of the dreams which he could remember and to proceed from there. This he did, and gradually the content of the dreams unfolded. In the most distressing of the dreams, Phil was standing in a dark, futuristic landscape sweeping down from the hospital at the brow of the hill. He was dressed in old thin clothes and carried an old-fashioned flame thrower. At the top of the hill, the psychologist appeared, dressed in strong, durable clothes carrying a laser gun. He was accompanied by three darkly clothed assistants standing in a triangular formation.

With the psychologist in this dream was Susan, a colleague who had sat in with him during a previous interview with Phil. In the dream, the psychologist discharged the laser gun at Phil, his only escape being an ability to jump great distances. In the course of this, Susan was severed in half by the laser beam and Phil could see the cross section of an abnormally large spinal cord running through her body. He aimed his flame thrower at the psychologist and his assistants and imagined that he had destroyed them. As he continued his escape, however, he turned round to see the psychologist moving ominously over the brow of the hill, still alive and in pursuit.

Interpretation

Having given his account of these and other dreams, Phil was asked to comment upon them and, in so doing, made what turned out to be a number of clinically significant comments. He fairly quickly drew the analogy between the psychologist's probing questions during sessions and the laser beam in the dream. His escape from the laser beam (that is, the questions) was accomplished by jumping great distances (that is, avoiding questions by blanking off).

Phil was later able to relate that the bone in the cross-section of Susan's body was very much as he had imagined cancer to be, although he acknowledged an ignorance of the precise nature of the disease. He was also able to acknowledge that the triangular formation of the three assistants in the dream was significant in that his compulsive rituals were all carried out in threes, a point he had been unable to make previously.

Formulation

Although Phil's fear of illness had been partially revealed during previous discussions, he commented that he had never really discussed its precise, cancer-related nature before. Neither, he said, had he ever revealed to anyone the precise details of his obsessional rituals, partly through shame and partly because he felt such revelations might somehow bring about the illnesses from which he felt he was protecting himself and his family.

Subsequent discussions with Phil indicated that he had engaged in various rituals as a teenager while his mother was ill, 'to protect her', but each time he noticed her condition worsen, he had assumed that it was his fault because he had not carried out the rituals satisfactorily. His expectations about illness and death became distorted by the deaths of his father and then his mother. He began to feel that death by the mysterious disease of cancer, to which he had developed phobic reactions, was a quite likely event. Having uncovered and been able to discuss these hitherto secret fears and rituals, Phil and his wife noted a progressive loosening in his manner both at work and at home.

It also emerged that Phil was extremely careful, almost over-cautious in his management of the family finances, and was keen for everything to be neat and tidy at home. His hobbies of collecting and meticulously sorting toy cars and soldiers reflected similar characteristics. Phil said that his collections gave him satisfaction both in the collecting process — obtaining the items and creating sets — and in obtaining items he had wished for but never been able to obtain in his early childhood. Many of the items stolen by Phil possessed a similar quality for him in that they were ones he would have liked to have possessed but which his obsessional concern for financial stringency would not allow him to purchase.

Further intervention

Further sessions involved piecing together with Phil the jigsaw of factors from his past and present. This led to him achieving, only for fleeting moments to begin with, an understanding of possible connections between the unfairness and missed opportunities (as he saw it) of his childhood and his later desire for similar gratifications in adult life.

The anxiety which surrounded his family relationships as a child, focused upon fears about his parents' health, resulted in his taking responsibility for this by performing rituals to protect them. This contributed to the development of an over-cautious personal style, but one in which a delayed streak of adolescent rebellion periodically emerged.

Phil's thinking was characterized by rigidity (in that, having once picked up an item in a shop to admire it, he believed that he was on the inexorable path to stealing) and fragmentation (in that his daily rituals and stealing were aspects of his life which did not enter his thinking at other times).

As to why Phil's stealing had occurred only occasionally, sometimes with substantial periods between incidents, it emerged that his fears of illness could generally be contained by his pattern of rituals. When these became insufficient, however — for example when his daughter went to the doctor — shoplifting occurred and served the function of replacing his major anxiety (cancer) with a lesser anxiety (legal prosecution).

In summary, stealing not only fulfilled historical needs to obtain luxury items upon which he could not bring himself to spend hard-earned money, but also served the function of deadening the crippling anxiety Phil felt about the risks of cancer.

At a meeting in the later stages of contact with Phil, he reported having handled an item in a store and having thought about stealing it. For the first time, however, his thinking had not been so channelled as to exclude the possible consequences of such stealing for his wife and family. He was able to think through possible courses of action, including replacing the item rather than automatically proceeding with the theft as in the past, and the item was in fact replaced.

Outcome

Retesting on the Fear Survey Schedule showed Phil to have the same fears as before — 'prospects of a surgical operation' and 'failure'. On the Middlesex Hospital Questionnaire, while 'obsessionality' remained high (two standard deviations above the mean), 'free-floating anxiety' had reduced from its previously very high, to an average level.

The concept of multi-modal behavioural analysis (Lazarus, 1976) draws attention to the fact that clients' problems can have representations in a number of modalities or levels of functioning, such as cognitive processes, attitudes, emotions, behaviours and relationships. Some clients' problems are concentrated in some modalities, or combinations of modalities, more than in others. Some clients, for example, are primarily cognitive responders, others emotional responders and so on. However, there are typically interconnections between these levels of functioning about which the client may well be aware, for example thinking of being cheated leading to being angry leading in turn to physical aggression.

In Phil's case it was evident that his knowledge about the links betwen many of the aspects of his functioning were unknown to him and that treatment, on one level, involved helping him become aware of these connections. With these connections understood, changes in the key aspects of his problem behaviour (shoplifting), emotions (anxiety) and thinking (obsessional) began to occur.

At six-month follow-up both Phil and his wife reported being happier, more communicative and less anxious about the future than when first seen (perhaps related to the reduced score on free-floating anxiety). Even though his illness fears and rituals (reflected in the questionnaire results) persisted to a degree, he appeared to have gained insight into, and control over, his presenting problem of shoplifting. When last seen he had been free from offending for over two years.

6 Norman: convergence of physical, social and psychological problems

The referral

Norman, aged 30, was having infrequent consultations with a consultant in medical genetics when he was referred for a psychological opinion. He was suffering from a rare type of muscular dystrophy known as Landouzy-Dejerine or facio-scapulo-humeral muscular dystrophy. Sufferers from this condition have no movement in the musculature of the face. They have a fixed and unvarying facial expression. They are unable to smile or frown or to give any facial indication of their feelings. In Norman's case this already unprepossessing appearance was compounded by an acneform rash.

None of this need in itself have led to a referral to a psychologist. However, Norman was notably uncommunicative and was thought to be depressed or mentally handicapped or both. It was known that he had been a source of much concern to his parents, although the full extent of this had not been discussed until the department of medical genetics recruited a specialist social worker. She soon realized that the family were having grave problems and suggested that a psychologist should be involved.

Background

Norman was the first of four children born to Tilly and Eric. There had been a difficult labour lasting two days and ending with a high forceps delivery. He was of relatively low birth weight (6lb.3oz.) and was separated from his mother for 48 hours because of cerebral twitching. His early progress was slow although Tilly only recognized this retrospectively when she had had other children. There was some suggestion that his motor development was delayed, but his general progress was such that at age 5 he started at a normal infants school. It was not long, however, before his teacher reported that he tended to isolate himself from other children. Perhaps because of this he was vulnerable to being bullied, but he put up no resistance. In addition, he was said to be preoccupied by whatever activity he was pursuing.

By age 11 his scholastic progress was limited and it was thought unlikely that he would pass the eleven-plus. Eric, his father, took the view that he would be unhappy at a secondary modern school and first considered private secondary education, perhaps in a Rudolph Steiner School, but then, on the advice of a school medical officer and an educational psychologist, turned his attention to a school for emotionally disturbed children. Norman settled well in this school and for the first and, to date, only time, developed a friendship with one of his peers.

Eric was in government service and had tours of duty in a variety of places. This meant that the family had to move several times. Sometimes there were delays between his taking up post and the family selling the house and moving into a new one. This involved separations which on one occasion lasted a year. Such a pattern is disruptive and it became clear that Norman was particularly resistant to change. For this reason it was decided that he would have a more stable existence if he became a boarder at the school. This decision turned out to be prudent as he seems soon to have made the necessary adjustment. By now he was about 12 years old and, while undergoing treatment for a minor condition, the possibility of muscular dystrophy was first raised. This was confirmed about 12 years later.

There were continuing reports of Norman's diffidence and when he was 15½ the head teacher indicated that he would be unlikely to gain anything more by staying at school. He therefore left, and a round of assessments and unsuccessful placements began. From the time he left school until the present referral, Norman had not undertaken any permanent employment. Despite several assessment courses the only placements he attended for any length of time were sheltered workshops for physically or mentally handicapped people. During this period Norman lived at home, and any residential placements were rejected either by Norman or his parents.

Two other aspects of the history must be mentioned, not because they are relevant but because they have been culs-de-sac where various of those who have attempted to help Norman have become lost. The first is that Norman's youngest sister, some ten years his junior, tragically drowned when she was 4 years old. The second surrounds allegations that the parents' marriage had been difficult. This belief arose because Eric, being a man of high standards, tended to be harsh on his then adolescent daughters. Tilly's advocacy for the girls was mistakenly perceived by some outsiders as marital disharmony.

Assessment

When Norman was first seen he was, for the reasons given earlier, unexpressive. He weighed some 13 stones and had a lumbering gait. These features in combination with his limited speech gave him a rather menacing presentation. At best he would give single word answers to questions and it became clear that it would be an uphill task to administer any tests. His father made it known that he had been found, at age 25, to be of average intelligence. Thus testing was confined to sentence reading. This was given as much as anything to sample his speech so that the presence of a speech or language disorder could be excluded. He read fluently up to the 14-year level. This was the most he was heard to speak during the assessment and it revealed that his near-mutism was elective.

Records of the former psychometric assessment were obtained and a detailed history was taken from Norman's parents. This revealed that he was only marginally more responsive to them than he had been to the psychologist. He was said to go for walks alone, especially to a nearby stream. This had some stones in it over which the water flowed rapidly. Norman would sit and watch this waterfall for hours at a time.

He seemed to take a special interest in his money. He was alive to how to invest it so as to get the best return and kept an impressive portfolio. Because this was one of his few identifiable interests, his parents had encouraged him. The difficulty was that his interest was in accumulating money and not in spending it. For example, he contributed nothing to his keep and even refused to pay for holidays.

There was clear evidence that his physical condition was slowly deteriorating. From time to time he would fall and be unable to retrieve himself. On a recent occasion, his sister and her husband had visited for the day. Unbeknown to anyone Norman had gone out for a walk. This was discovered well after dark, and it was only after extensive searches that he was found sitting on a railway track, not far from the house, unable to get up. The temperature was below zero and the track was in use but, because it was a Sunday, no train had run. There was no evidence that he had called for help nor that he welcomed it when it arrived. It is difficult to know whether or not he recognized the realistic possibility of developing hypothermia or of being injured by a train.

Diagnosis

There were features of Norman's history and presentation that were suggestive of brain damage which was most likely to have been congenital. Against a measurably average intellectual level and no discernable speech or language disorder, his reclusiveness and his management of money amounted to gross social ineptitude. These features, together with the suggestion that his early development was slow, especially in the area of motor function, his failure to form friendships and his passive acceptance of being bullied, his resistance to change, and his apparent fascination with rapidly flowing water in the stream, pointed to an autistic condition. Yet he did have speech, he could read fluently and he had an area of real expertise, albeit unproductive, in his financial investment strategies. The only diagnosis that seemed to fit was the Asperger syndrome. This was described by Wing (1981) and it was she who confirmed the diagnosis when Norman was referred to her by the psychologist.

Management

So far, much emphasis has been placed on Norman, but clearly the problem has affected all members of the family, especially his parents. They had consulted many experts over the years and had received contradictory opinions and advice. Some had talked of psychosis, others about doubtful parenting, and yet others about unresolved conflicts arising from the bereavement following the death of the last child, but nobody had been able to put their minds at rest. Eric and Tilly had feelings of failure and had remained unclear as to how best to help Norman. They were past their first youth and, following two coronaries that had forced Eric into early retirement, they were having great difficulty managing Norman when he fell. They viewed the future with utmost concern, fearing that Norman would eventually end up in a mental handicap institution.

In view of these considerations there was much to be gained from clarifying the diagnosis. Although clinical psychologists are reluctant to apply diagnostic labels, especially when there are no clear treatment implications, there are times when doing so is of value. Wing (personal communication) has suggested the following justifications in cases of the Asperger syndrome:

(1) The diagnosis makes it clear that the strange behaviour is the result of a developmental abnormality due to brain dysfunction, and is not an 'illness' occurring in a hitherto normal person.

(2) The parents are relieved of the burden of guilt, and stop wasting time trying to work out where they went wrong in bringing up their affected child. They are mostly glad to know the truth even though the abnormalities in Asperger's syndrome are life long.

(3) The parents and professionals can work out appropriate ways of managing the behaviour problems and encouraging the development of constructive activities, based on an understanding of the nature of the handicap.

(4) Practical plans can be made for the future of the person concerned, including finding sheltered accommodation and/or occupation and leisure, depending on how much support is necessary.

(5) People with Asperger's syndrome can be given emotional support and counselling pitched at a simple level, appropriate to their degree of insight and understanding. The abstract concepts involved in psychoanalysis can be avoided, since these inevitably confuse and distress people with Asperger's syndrome.

(6) The parents have access to a reference group, so they no longer feel as if they are the only people in the world to have such a strange child. They can join the National Autistic Society. This covers Asperger's syndrome and other conditions related to autism as well as the classic autistic syndrome. The Society has set up special schools and adult sheltered communities.

(7) The change of attitudes following diagnosis and a full explanation of the nature of the condition often lead to some lessening of the severity of the behaviour problems, some of which are due to too high expectations on the part of parents and professionals.

Assessment of relationships within the family

In order to understand more clearly the mutual influence between Norman and his parents, a technique known as the Personal Relations Index (PRI) was used (Mulhall, 1977). This helps the participants of dyadic relationships to construct a personal model of their interactions in a way that portrays some of the relevant dynamics. These models are made up of attributes provided by either or both of the two people. In this case Tilly described Norman and herself and Eric described Norman and himself. Both parents independently constructed a model of their own relationship with their son. The process began with a free discussion during which the attributes emerged. In each case both people are described in seven ways. These data are fed into a computer which generates a unique questionnaire. The questionnaire gives equal weight to both people and to each of the attributes. Taking Tilly's questionnaire, some questions asked how she reacted to Norman, and others asked how, in her view, he reacted to her. 'Shutting himself away in his room' is an example of one of Norman's attributes. It was something to which she reacted and one of his reactions to her. In other words this attribute is sometimes a stimulus and sometimes a response, context dictating which of these two roles it plays at any given moment.

The questionnaire enables respondents to impose a structure on the attributes. The means of achieving this need not be considered in detail here but its purpose is to demonstrate in an unbiased way the most likely outcome or outcomes of each attribute. On the assumption that the respondent has an overall perception of the relationship, in the form of an implicit model, often not articulated, it is possible to construct an easily understood diagramatic representation by connecting each attribute with its outcome(s).

Figure 6.1 portrays the models produced by Tilly and Eric. By following the arrows it is possible to see the perceived flow of events.

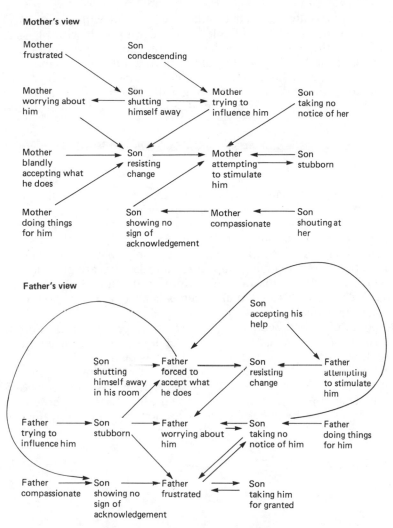

Mother's view

Mother frustrated

Son condescending

Mother worrying about him ← Son shutting himself away → Mother trying to influence him

Son taking no notice of her

Mother blandly accepting what he does → Son resisting change → Mother attempting to stimulate him ← Son stubborn

Mother doing things for him

Son showing no sign of acknowledgement ← Mother compassionate ← Son shouting at her

Father's view

Son accepting his help

Son shutting himself away in his room → Father forced to accept what he does → Son resisting change ← Father attempting to stimulate him

Father trying to influence him → Son stubborn → Father worrying about him ← Son taking no notice of him ← Father doing things for him

Father compassionate → Son showing no sign of acknowledgement → Father frustrated → Son taking him for granted

Figure 6.1 Model of parents' views of their relationships with their son

Intervention

Time was spent discussing these models with Tilly and Eric. The models were recognizable to them, giving a clear indication of how difficult it was for each of them to cope with Norman. These discussions helped them to crystallize and articulate their hitherto unformulated concerns and allowed them to talk about the conflict between the difficulties of living with Norman and the emotional ties that had made it impossible to accept living without him. What also emerged was that Eric, whose apparent *raison d'être* had been finding some appropriate placement for Norman, became slightly more accepting of a hidden reality: that it was he rather than Norman who had sabotaged the few offers of places they had received. It had generally been presented as though Norman was unhappy or dissatisfied.

The specialist social worker from the department of medical genetics and the psychologist did a nationwide trawl for suitable placements for Norman. For the most part he was too physically disabled for those who dealt with behavioural difficulties and his behaviour was too difficult for those who dealt with physical disability. Unfortunately the situation remains the same to the present.

However, the diagnosis of Asperger's syndrome confirmed the improbability of Norman's behaviour being amenable to substantial change and this, together with the acknowledgement of the difficulties of living with Norman, increased the chances of the family accepting an offer of a residential place for Norman should one be made.

Conclusion

This case highlights three points: lack of service provision, the value of clarifying the nature of the problem and the importance of considering family dynamics. On the first of these, it seems to be an endemic feature of the so-called 'young chronic sick' (that is, people between the ages of 16 and 55 with intractable physical disabilities) that service provision is either non-existent or patchy. This group of clients is small in relation to other client groups for whom services are provided on a planned basis, which in itself presents an administrative difficulty. More than this, they are a group with diverse needs so that arrangements have to be, or should be, tailor-made for each individual.

On the second point, disturbed behaviour is more often seen as a reflection of perversity, or even malice, than as a case for detailed scrutiny. When it is unexplained, parents in particular tend to account for it as their own failure. This can be largely prevented by analysing the behaviour and by offering a diagnosis.

The third point is that problems are as much between people as they are within the ostensible client. Therefore, it is of value to determine how those concerned are influencing each other with a view to helping them develop appropriate strategies.

7   Carol: stopping smoking in a group

Introduction

Treatment groups for smokers have been called a failure and compared unflatteringly with the possible benefits of brief but widespread advice by GPs. As will be seen, it is true that treatment groups are costly in time, and most participants do not succeed in becoming non-smokers. Nevertheless, treatment groups have probably been the activity most commonly undertaken by psychologists who have tackled smoking. The contradiction is only apparent. During the 1970s effective group treatment procedures were demonstrated (Lichtenstein, 1982). It is a pity that they are not more effective, but different approaches to the smoking problem — Britain's single largest preventable cause of death — are not only possible but easily compatible and even necessary. Psychologists have important work to do in supporting primary care staff and promoting health authority policies against smoking, to name but two other tasks. Treatment groups help some smokers, they indicate a constructive rather than restrictive approach, and they can teach the people who run the groups much about the severity and psychology of dependence.

The group described here was one of a series using the same core treatment package, based on operant psychology, with a focus away from reliance on will power and towards helping smokers to be specific in identifying the feelings, thoughts and actions they need to influence. It is the antecedents and consequences of these behaviours which are believed to maintain them. Therefore it is these rather than the feelings, thoughts and actions themselves which become the focus for change. There was an emphasis on making use of the social environment. Participants were asked to involve other people in reducing temptations to lapse and encouraging progress. Ideas from the relapse prevention approach (Marlatt and George, 1984) were incorporated. As the name implies, relapse prevention concentrates not on intiating but rather on maintaining change — undoubtedly the main difficulty with smoking and other dependence problems. It uses social learning methods to develop skills for preventing and managing lapses. The results of several variants of the programme have been evaluated and described elsewhere (Paxton, 1983).

The group

Information about the service for smokers was sent periodically to GPs and some hospital physicians. Participants were referred by these people or other health care staff. Every person referred was offered a place in a group. The programme consisted of 12 group meetings over 17 weeks.

45

The group described here totalled 24 members: 14 women and 10 men. Their mean age was 41, they had smoked for an average of 22 years, and they consumed an average of 29 cigarettes a day.

This group was larger than the average of 8 or 10, and it is for this reason that it is described here. To anticipate a conclusion, large groups can use psychological methods, and in an effective and cost-effective way.

To give a different slant on the processes and continuing puzzles about stopping smoking, particular attention is given to one member of the group: Carol, who was then 27 years old, a clerical worker, smoking 30 cigarettes a day. She had smoked for ten years. She had attended a group the previous year and stopped smoking for three weeks, but then lapsed and stopped attending.

The group meetings

Introductory meeting: session 1

This meeting was to prepare participants to stop smoking a week later, following Flaxman's (1978) finding that a preparatory meeting improved overall results. The activities of the meeting were described and each person was weighed. Weight gain after stopping smoking is common (Shiffman, 1979), and one function of the group is to help control this. Carol's weight was 7 stones 10 pounds, which she thought about right.

Group members were then asked why they smoked. Enjoyment, dependence, and habit were raised. Carol thought she smoked because she could not stop. It was acknowledged that cigarettes could be enjoyable and helpful in the short term and that this was partly why stopping smoking is difficult.

Reasons for becoming a non-smoker were discussed. Carol said that she felt weak and tied as a result of her dependence on cigarettes. The main reasons discussed were: reducing the risk of premature death and more common respiratory infections; improving fitness; being nicer to be with; saving money; and bringing freedom from dependence.

The help to be offered was outlined:

(1) information and discussion to help each person clarify her or his own reasons for and against smoking;
(2) practical advice on preparing to stop smoking, stopping, and remaining a non-smoker;
(3) using rapid smoking to help with stopping smoking abruptly rather than gradually. This is generally more effective and produces less discomfort (Flaxman, 1978; Shiffman and Jarvik, 1976);
(4) using group meetings so that each person can benefit from the experience of others and develop a commitment to them;
(5) meeting frequently in the early days and less frequently as difficulties ease;
(6) continuing group meetings for four months to help maintain non-smoking;
(7) noticing the benefits of stopping smoking;
(8) helping with weight reduction.

Members were then advised to make the preparations for stopping smoking a week later. First they should tell other people about the attempt to stop smoking. Smokers are understandably reluctant to do this, fearing loss of face if they later fail, but the anticipated loss of face is itself a help in maintaining abstinence. Second, they should ask friends and relatives to help. The most important help is to make cigarettes unavailable. Third, they were asked to notice smoking situations —

the occasions when smoking seems most necessary or enjoyable. Fourth, they should begin to plan ways of avoiding or dealing with smoking situations.

A handout summarizing the information given during the meeting was distributed. The meeting ended.

The stop-smoking meeting: session 2

A week later all 24 people returned. Most had told others of their intention to stop smoking, and all had been able to notice smoking situations. Carol said that she was shy, and smoked more when talking to men, especially those she found attractive. Her work was also a source of difficulty. She had many opportunities to smoke, and there were many smokers around.

The rapid smoking procedure and its purposes were described. The procedure, modified from Lichtenstein et al. (1973), consisted of three separate four-minute trials of puffing every six seconds. It was explained that this should help to provide a firm break from the habit. Because rapid smoking can cause breathlessness and raised heart rate, there are possible risks for people with actual or suspected heart disease and so they were not allowed to take part. One person in this group, suffering from angina, was not permitted to participate. The remaining 23 did so. Three sessions were interspersed with the other activities outlined below during the one-and-a-half hours of the meeting. Carol's report after the first was typical. She felt hot, uncomfortable, dizzy and nauseous.

The changes that might be experienced after stopping smoking were discussed. Those in the group who had previously stopped described their experiences. The main points follow. The difficulties are variable, unpredictable and usually not all avoidable. The duration of difficulties varies, but most people report them diminishing after ten days of not smoking (Shiffman, 1979). The difficulties include craving, tension, irritability, sleep problems, stomach upsets, depression, concentration problems and weight gain.

Practical advice on staying off cigarettes was then given and discussed. This included ways of avoiding cigarettes, taking care with alcohol, using distraction and relaxation, noticing improvements in fitness, and planning detailed coping a day at a time.

The next discussion point was coping with lapses. The relapse prevention approach concentrates both on preventing lapses and on avoiding continued smoking if a lapse should occur. Attention was drawn to the 'abstinence violation effect': the tendency for one cigarette to lead to others. The group would try to help people who had smoked to identify the causes of lapses, to see that lapses can be independent events rather than linked series, and to learn from them to prevent similar difficulties in the future. It was pointed out that people who have smoked may be reluctant to attend the next group meeting, but it is they who need it most.

After the final rapid smoking session, a summary handout was distributed.

The first non-smoking meeting: session 3

This was two days later. Each person was asked whether they had smoked. Lapses were discussed. Other group members were encouraged to offer advice on what might have been done, and on preventing continued smoking.

Each was asked to report on the time when they had felt worst or closest to smoking again. Reports of successful coping were encouraged and useful lessons summarized. Carol said that she missed the pleasures of smoking at work and after meals, but overall felt almost elated. She and several other people reported little or no craving and no other side effects.

Finally, each person was asked to anticipate problems they would face before the next meeting, three days later. It was then Friday. Several people reported social events where they would be drinking alcohol. They were advised to avoid alcohol for the first week, and ways of reducing consumption for those who did drink were suggested. Active coping methods were again encouraged with an emphasis on maximizing the support available from other people. Carol expected what she described as a boring weekend with no social activities.

The second non-smoking meeting: session 4

The meeting took the same form as the previous one. Most people were experiencing craving, tension, other physical complaints, and rationalizations about smoking. Carol reported few problems. The notions of 'apparently irrelevant decisions' and 'relapse road maps' (Marlatt and George, 1984) were used to illuminate discussion of the causes and prevention of lapses. An example of an apparently irrelevant decision is the choice of a route which took a member of the group out walking past a tobacconist's shop. He was experiencing strong craving, and then bought and smoked cigarettes from the shop. Was the decision to take that route irrelevant or had he, having made that choice, already decided to smoke? A relapse road map is simply a way of drawing the chain of decisions and events leading up to a lapse. Carol anticipated no difficulties except boredom at work before the next meeting, two days later.

One week after stopping smoking: session 5

The meeting took the usual form. Carol had not smoked and again described few difficulties. Her most worrying times had been in periods of inactivity, remembering the enjoyment of smoking. Weights were recorded in this and each subsequent meeting, and are summarized later.

The group discussed problems which might occur before the next meeting. Carol said that she was going out with a new boyfriend at the weekend and he was a smoker. Ways of explaining her commitment, refusing cigarettes and controlling her alcohol intake were discussed.

Two weeks after stopping smoking: session 6

Carol's date had been enjoyable. In anticipating future problems she was again concerned about socializing and periods of inactivity, but said that she felt more confident.

The first month: sessions 7 and 8

The next meetings were one and two weeks later. The most common problems reported were irritability and sleep difficulties. Carol's relationship had ended. Her main difficulty was missing the pleasures of smoking.

The second month: sessions 9 and 10

There were two meetings at fortnightly intervals. The second of these was two months after the stop-smoking date. The most prominent concerns expressed by the people who attended were irritability and weight gain. Carol said that she was getting used to being a non-smoker. Her life was uneventful. She still missed the pleasures of smoking.

The third month: session 11

The next meeting was four weeks later. A letter from Carol arrived that day in which she said that she had smoked two weeks previously while out on a date and drinking alcohol. In the letter she said that she had not smoked since, nor seen the man again. She was unable to attend the meeting that evening. The main concerns of the other people were weight reduction and missing the pleasures of smoking.

The fourth month: session 12

The next and last meeting was 16 weeks after stopping smoking. Carol did not attend, but wrote and was contacted by telephone. She had smoked again while socializing and drinking alcohol and had continued to smoke daily. She expressed disappointment and frustration, having stopped smoking for almost three months without much difficulty, but then found herself unable to face the future without 'the comfort of a cigarette'.

Outcome

When the group meetings ended four months after the stop-smoking date, Carol was one of 11 who were smoking. The numbers of people in the group not smoking each week are shown in Figure 7.1.

One month after the stop-smoking date, 15 people (63%) were not smoking; at two months 14 (58%); at three and four months 13 (54%) and at one year 9 (38%). The results show the familiar negatively accelerated survival curve. The longer a person has been abstinent the greater the chance of remaining so.

Attendances at meetings declined in a similar way. Most people who were succeeding in not smoking attended meetings. Most who were failing (reporting smoking in several consecutive meetings) stopped attending.

The average weight gain reached its maximum of three pounds at two months. At the final meeting it was two pounds. Carol never gained more than one pound. This is less than the weight gained in most groups. Reduction to the original weight is usually achieved only after around eight to 12 months.

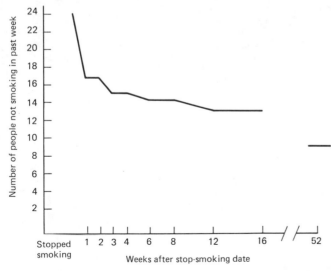

Figure 7.1 Number of people not smoking each week

49

Discussion

The results presented here were not validated by biochemical checks on self-reports of not smoking and so might be criticized as artificially high. However, they are very similar to the results of groups that were so validated (Paxton, 1983). The success rate is about the same as that of recent package treatment programmes, including those that have incorporated nicotine chewing gum (Lichtenstein, 1982). Most treatment methods still fail with most smokers. Perhaps treatment group attenders are a self-selected population for whom stopping smoking is exceptionally difficult or even impossible without help. If so, a success rate of 38% is worthwhile.

The results of the group and the experience of Carol in particular highlight continuing puzzles and difficulties. Carol's feelings and achievements were very different in the two groups she attended — illustrating the unpredictability of stopping smoking. Moreover, her difficulties did not diminish over time as the statistics of relapse lead us to expect (Hunt *et al.*, 1971). Deciding when group meetings should decline in frequency and end is difficult. If the group had been meeting weekly when Carol's lapses occurred her smoking might not have continued. It is clear that the subjective benefits of smoking are powerful and still missed a month after stopping smoking and later. Few methods exist for replacing them.

To end on a positive note, the group described here was the largest of nearly 40 run by the writer. The results were no worse than those of smaller groups. Psychological advice, and not just support, can be given effectively to groups of more than 20 people in meetings lasting one-and-a-half hours.

8   A social skills group: five years of follow-up

Introduction

The socially inadequate or unskilled individual is likely to find social situations frustrating, distressing or unrewarding. This results in social avoidance, increasing social isolation and further reductions in skilled and effective social behaviour. A self-perpetuating downward spiral is created which intensifies the felt lack of interpersonal effectiveness and decreases opportunities for some rewarding social interactions. While individual therapy can be appropriate in reversing these difficulties, the group setting provides unique opportunities to try out a new, more effective range of social behaviours, to receive supportive, constructive feedback on these and to view oneself not as an isolated social misfit but as a member of a group of people who all (including the leader) experience and share social anxieties which are both uniquely different and common to the group.

Recent work in the social skills remediation field (Trower, 1984) suggests that those social skills training (SST) packages that are more effective concentrate less on remediating skills deficits (the 'organism' or 'micro' approach) and more on the ability of the individual not only to generate her or his socially skilled behaviours, but also to generalize, maintain and modify these developing skills (the 'agency' or 'macro' approach). The latter approach includes a range of cognitive techniques in addition to the traditional behavioural components of the SST programme. This approach allows each individual to explore, test, expand and have validated, in the relative safety of the group situation, the kinds of social behaviours that feel uniquely right for that particular individual. The emphasis is on individual learning and the client as a social being rather than the adoption of a set of superficial social techniques which may feel personally invalid and alienating.

Selection of group members

The group described in this case comprised individuals who had been referred to the psychological service by their general practitioner and/or psychiatrist for help with anxieties of a broadly social and interpersonal nature. Initial pre-group interviews were offered to assess individual social dysfunction and to ensure that the group membership would include people from both sexes, from a range of backgrounds and of varying ages. In this way it was hoped that the group would provide a representational social microcosm in which members could try out and rehearse new behaviour in as realistic a social setting as possible.

Six people attended the group. They were:

Walter Aged 52, married, unemployed. Walter had suffered a 'depressive breakdown' five years previously and had spent several periods in hospital, each of a few months duration. He had retired from his job three years previously and was currently awaiting with considerable anxiety the results of a bankruptcy order. Walter was attending a social services day centre and had been referred because his psychiatrist felt that he seemed withdrawn from people and unable to converse with them. This was having the effect of alienating him from the day centre clients, and to some extent from the staff.

Pamela Aged 23, employed, married. Over the last year or so Pamela had experienced increasing difficulties with the supervisor of the office where she worked as a clerk and where she felt 'picked on' and humiliated. Pamela had reacted by suffering headaches and nausea. She had also 'fainted' two or three times at work. After various investigations her GP felt that the problem was psychological rather than physical. Pamela talked of uncomfortable feelings, particularly in relationships with older people, and said that she was beginning to avoid social occasions more and more. She had recently been married and described the ceremony as 'a nightmare'.

The other members were: *Alan*, aged 20 and unmarried, who had never worked and was described as a 'virtual recluse'. *Neville*, aged 32, unmarried and unemployed, was very anxious with people and conscious of his bald patch. *Donald*, aged 34 and unmarried, had a severe social stammer and consequent difficulties with women. *Debbie*, aged 28 and married with two school-age children, was unable to cope with situations such as job interviews which involved assessment and possible criticism.

Assessment

Before the training programme began, each group member was assessed on a self-rating Social Assertion and Satisfaction Scale (SASS). This was a 28-item, five-point scale based on a questionnaire from Trower, Bryant and Argyle (1978). Each item was rated from 'no anxiety' to 'extreme anxiety', such that the higher the obtained score, the more severe the level of assessed social anxiety. The SASS includes such items as: 'walking into a room full of people', 'being able to tell someone you disagree with them', and 'apologizing to someone'. Scores from a group of unqualified helpers at a local social services day centre were obtained for comparison purposes; the level of assessed social anxiety attained by this group was in the range 'little-moderate'. This was taken as a 'normal' rating. A comparison of pre-group SASS scores and those of this comparison group indicated a highly significant difference between the two groups on assessed anxiety, (Mann-Whitney U test; $U = 1$, $N = 5,6$, $p = 0.008$ two-tailed). The scores are shown in Figure 8.1.

The social skills programme

The training programme took place in the spring of 1980 and involved one session a week, each lasting one-and-a-half to two hours, over a period of eight weeks. Meetings took place in the psychology department, based in a large house in a residential area. It was felt that for a group such as this the type of setting had distinct advantages both in comparison with the clinical anonymity of the general hospital, and more importantly, with the local psychiatric hospital and its stigmatization effects.

The structured course included: identification of problem areas and problem solving skills; basic conversational/non-verbal skills; relaxation exercises; confidence-boosting and assertion exercises; role play; exploration and expression of feelings; exploration and monitoring of self-sabotage patterns of thinking; generation of individually appropriate, more realistic self-statements; development of anxiety control techniques — both behavioural and cognitive; and the use of constructive group feedback to individual members. Ideas for the structured exercises were gleaned from Brandes and Phillips (1977), Hoper *et al.* (1975), Priestly *et al.* (1978), Smith (1975) and Spence (1980).

Each session began with a round in which the members were asked to comment briefly on progress made during the week. A short teaching input followed, based on the theme of the week. Following this the group participated in structured exercises relating to the theme and geared to their individual needs. Group discussion followed and this usually included further individual behaviour rehearsal and/or exploration of cognitive put-downers which interfered with effective social functioning. A relaxation exercise followed which incorporated the use of anxiety control and skills enhancement imagery. Group members then shared their experiences of the relaxation exercise. Working in pairs or using the whole group, members decided what they would do for their individual homework assignments. Each session concluded with a round, using variations of 'something I enjoyed/learned in the group today'. The final session took the theme of relapse-prevention, and explored in detail the ways in which group members would maintain and develop their learning. In this session each person, including the leader, was given a 'goodbye present'. This involved a written comment from everyone regarding something positive that they had really appreciated about each other person — for example, 'nice sense of humour', 'a good listener', 'you were very helpful'. This 'goodbye present' exercise is useful since individuals report that it can provide an effective antidote to put-downers once the group has ended.

All members attended each session except one who was absent for three weeks due to influenza.

Outcome

The SASS was repeated at the end of the group. Follow-up assessments were carried out one, three and five years later. The small group of day centre staff was assessed on the SASS to provide a baseline and to discover whether SASS scores remained relatively stable over a three-year period. No significant changes in SASS scores occurred for the day centre staff over this period.

The protocols of all six group members showed a reduction in pre- and post-group SASS scores (mean reduction 23.2, range of reductions 3–45). Using the Wilcoxon matched-pairs signed-ranks test, this reduction was significant at $p = 0.05$ (two-tailed). Reductions were generally maintained at one-, three- and five-year follow-up and included some further individual improvements. The differences at one year between SASS scores of the social skills group and day centre staff, while clearly apparent on the graph, did not reach statistical significance (see Figure 8.1).

Follow-up details of individuals

All six members of the group reported positive changes in their lives in the five years following the group. For example, during the course of the group, Pamela

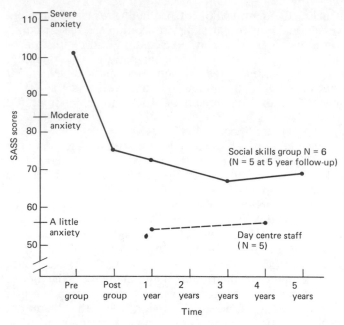

Figure 8.1 Mean group SASS scores for social skills group and day centre staff

managed to be appropriately assertive with her supervisor and consequently felt more relaxed and confident in her job. At the five-year follow-up she reported that she now had a small child and no longer worked. She wrote, 'It helped me to realize that there were other people so much worse than me!'. Walter has continued to see the psychologist for support at fairly regular intervals since the group ended. The bankruptcy proceedings were eventually dropped. He said, at the three-year follow-up, 'I still use the relaxation exercises we practised.' Walter has gone into craft work in a dedicated way and produces wood carving and metal jewellery which he sells to local craft shops. He has not been back into hospital, feels that he is 'better' with people and is less anxious about travelling, though he recognizes that it would be unrealistic to seek full-time employment.

Discussion

This small group is not untypical of the range of socially anxious individuals seen as outpatients by clinical psychologists working in the adult mental health area of the National Health Service. Before their group attendance, individuals produced high levels of anxiety as measured on the SASS instrument. For this group, assessed anxiety levels reduced significantly over the period of the group and continued to reduce to a plateau, mostly within normal limits (little-moderate social anxiety). It can be inferred from this observed reduction in SASS scores, and from the subjective comments and news follow-ups, that the members of this SST group were able to retain the effects of their social skills learning and to continue to use it, to a greater or lesser extent, in an active, goal-directed way, in order to obtain increased life satisfaction.

While it would be unwise to generalize from such a small sample, these results can be seen to add weight to the evidence that this type of social skills training programme — which utilizes a broad range of behavioural and cognitive interventions and strategies, and encourages individuals to adapt these creatively to their own needs and goals — is more likely to have longer-term, positive and generalized benefits for social effectiveness in comparison to the somewhat mechanistic, social skills deficit model that was developed originally in the early 1970s.

In this particular group, attendance for some brought fairly immediate benefits, for others the benefits derived were less obvious and objectively measurable. Each individual appeared to have derived different long-term benefits from the group experience. For example, for Walter it was the relaxation that was important; for Pamela it was the recognition that there were other people with more severe problems than hers; Neville developed sufficient confidence to tackle the problems involved in a hair transplant, while Debbie learned to present herself in a less overtly anxious manner and was thus able to secure employment shortly after the group ended. Alan overcame his social anxiety sufficiently to attend evening classes. At the five-year follow-up he wrote to say he had recently been accepted for a degree course. Donald largely overcame his stammer and is now happily married.

The individual comments at the three- and five-year follow-ups indicated that attendance at this social skills training group was at the least meaningful and at best an experience that had profound and positive impact. For the psychologist it has been rewarding to follow this group of six people over a period of several years and to be given access to the ways in which they have developed their lives since the initial period of the group.

9 Albert: treatment of fear of faecal incontinence

Presenting problem

Albert, a 74-year-old man, was referred to the clinical psychologist because the hospital staff were unable to control his demanding behaviour, principally his vociferous calls to be toiletted in excess of his need.

Albert had been a waiter in a hotel and had a history of heavy drinking. He had two daughters and six sons, many of whom visited him regularly. His daughters described him as selfish, lazy and very demanding of people. After his wife's death, when he was 65, he became more dependent on his daughters as they stepped in and did all his cooking, cleaning and laundry.

His medical history included an operation to remove a carcinoma of the rectum at the age of 70. He also had a history of suicide attempts by overdose, but had always refused the follow-up offered by psychiatrists. In fact it was never felt that he was suffering from a depressive illness.

At the age of 74 Albert sustained a severe stroke. This involved a left hemiparesis (paralysis of the left side of the body) with a left visual field deficit. He had extreme difficulty with self-care and needed two people to toilet him.

He was discharged after one year in hospital to an aged persons' home for a trial period. However, this did not last long because of his demanding behaviour. The staff were unwilling to attempt a behavioural programme for his toiletting because they felt that he was inappropriately placed there in view of his high dependence. He was then readmitted to hospital, and it was decided to try to discharge him to live at home with maximum support, since by this time he needed only one strong person to toilet him.

Assessment

On the ward the nurses took him to the toilet whenever he asked and noted whether he had passed anything on each visit. By this means they established that he asked to be toiletted at least three times more often than he actually used the toilet. Over one fortnight period he asked to go to the toilet 76 times, but actually defaecated only twice a day on most days.

A cognitive assessment using the Wechsler Adult Intelligence Scale (Wechsler, 1955) gave the following results: Comprehension 10, Similarities 4, Digit Span 9, Vocabulary 14, Block Design 4, Object Assembly 0 (all age-scaled). The performance subtests were obviously contaminated by his impaired sight, but there was a strong suggestion from the verbal scale that there was some intellectual deterioration (Nelson and McKenna, 1975). On a test of new learning there was no evidence of a learning impairment (Inglis, 1959).

In interview he said that he was afraid of being incontinent, and that he had to keep on going to the toilet. He admitted that he did not always pass anything, but was unable to reason that he was therefore calling excessively. As far as he was concerned, he felt that he really had the urge on each occasion.

Formulation and intervention plan

It was hypothesized that Albert was calling out excessively because he was afraid of being incontinent. He might also have the additional problem of not being able to correctly interpret signals from his bowel, since these may have been distorted by the operation and/or the stroke.

His potential for discharge depended on the extent to which he could care for himself. He had grown dependent on the staff and it would be hard to adjust to living by himself. From this point of view it might seem better to have left him in hospital. However, hospital could not be considered a suitable place for him because he was not physically ill and would block a bed and debar the treatment of other patients. In addition, acute geriatric wards are not geared up to provide a permanent home and people in them do not make adequate psychological adjustment. His home was considered a suitable goal because it was planned that he would be fitter on discharge than he had been when previously discharged into the social services' home. It would also have the advantage for him of signifying a quasi-independent existence.

A discharge plan was envisaged with the district nurse going in twice a day to get him up and put him to bed. His daughter would visit in the morning, his sister in the afternoon, and another daughter again in the evening. At each of these times, the visitor could toilet him. The longest gap would be in the afternoon when he would have to tolerate signals from his bowels for up to two to three hours. A training programme was thus required which would allow him to overcome his fear of incontinence, and to sit for this length of time without calling out.

Prior to training, a baseline phase was necessary during which behaviour was recorded in its untreated state. This allowed the extent of the problem to be seen so that the effectiveness of future treatments could be assessed. The nurses kept a chart of his bowel activity and this formed the nursing baseline (22 days). The date and time of his asking, and whether he defaecated or not was recorded.

This was followed by phase 1 (28 days) of the intervention period which involved monitoring by staff, and Albert was encouraged to keep a record as well. The purpose of his self-monitoring was to give Albert immediate feedback of his bowel function and also to engage him actively in the programme. Phase 2 (the next 22 days) was the learning part of the programme wherein he was asked to tolerate gradually increasing periods before going to the toilet. Albert was initially encouraged to wait for a quarter of an hour, then half an hour, then for gradually extended periods of time.

What happened

During the programme it was found that Albert also began calling out to pass water, so he was given a refresher training course in using a urine bottle. This additional training involved prompting and reminding by the nurses. There was also a problem with self-monitoring because of his partial sight. This was overcome by giving him a large record sheet and two crayons. He would colour a large square in blue if he asked to go to the toilet and another in red if he opened his bowels on that visit. He had to have training in the use of this recording method. His resistance to it may have been due partly to his personality, and partly to his brain damage. It is possible that the latter would make it more difficult to comply with treatment because the resulting impairments would make life harder, and being disinhibited he would be liable to take the easy way out and not comply with treatment. His personality was such that he would tend to give up easily anyway. He might also find it rewarding to stay in hospital because it was a safe environment and he could get attention from the staff.

Results

Considering only the number of toilet calls would not be meaningful because it would give no idea about incontinence although it may be related to his demanding behaviour. Similarly considering only incontinence would also have its problems because it may be affected daily by diet, bowel habit etc. A measure was needed which would incorporate these two indices, and would also show how Albert's learning during the programme had affected his behaviour and his approach to the problem.

Signal detection theory was chosen as the framework for this analysis because it allows study of the efficiency of people's decisions in uncertain situations. Table 9.1 represents an outcome matrix describing Albert's decision-making. If he calls out and defaecates, it is called a 'hit' since it was a correct decision to call out. If he calls out and does not defaecate, it is called a 'false alarm'. If he defaecates and does not call out — i.e. he is incontinent — then this is termed a 'miss'. 'Correct rejections' represents the number of times that Albert experiences a signal from his bowel, but then rejects it as a possible defaecation urge without calling out. Such data is not experimentally available and has to be estimated during the analysis, bearing in mind the assumptions of signal detection theory (Parks, 1966).

Table 9.1 Outcome matrix of patient's decisions

| | | Patient defaecates | |
		Yes	No
Patient calls out	Yes	Hit	False alarm
	No	Miss	Correct rejection

Table 9.2 shows the results of each of the three phases of the programme, each phase being presented in its own tabular format according to the layout in Table 9.1. For example, during the nursing baseline there were 24 occasions (hits) on which Albert had called out to go to the toilet and had actually used the toilet. There were also 82 other occasions (false alarms) on which Albert had called out to go to the toilet but had not passed anything. There were no occasions on which he had not called and been incontinent (misses). Additional calculations suggested that there were no times when Albert experienced a feeling in his bowel but

Table 9.2 Programme results

Baseline (22 days)		Phase 1 (28 days)		Phase 2 (22 days)	
24 hits	82 false alarms	36 hits	48 false alarms	23 hits	9 false alarms
0 misses	(0) correct rejections	9 misses	(0) correct rejections	5 misses	(19) correct rejections

rejected it as an urge to defaecate and thus refrained from calling (correct rejections). He seemed to be calling at every urge he experienced.

The theory of signal detection analyses Albert's behaviour into two independent components: his accuracy at detecting whether he needs to defaecate or not (called discriminability), and his willingness (called criterion) to call out regardless of whether or not he needs to defaecate. In learning theory, these variables may be thought to reflect competence and avoidance respectively. 'Competence' refers to his ability to discriminate successfully between different bowel symptoms (e.g. between faeces, flatulence, soreness etc.) and 'avoidance' refers to a tendency to call out for the toilet to try to relieve himself of discomfort. The values of discriminability and criterion are obtained from the raw data by substituting into formulae given by Parks (1966). For the purposes of the present analysis, both discriminability and criterion have a range of +4 to −4. A value of +4 on the discriminability variable would indicate perfect performance in detecting genuine urges to defaecate from normal background variation in bodily sensations. A value of 0 would indicate a performance no better than chance and −4 would indicate that the patient saw everything as background and missed a lot of genuine urges. On the criterion variable, a value of +4 would indicate extreme caution in reporting urges as genuine, and a value of −4 would indicate extreme liberalness whereby all urges are reported irrespective of how competent the patient was at telling the genuineness of urges.

During the nursing baseline the results showed that there was no incontinence, but this was at the expense of a large number of false alarms. During the nursing baseline his discriminability was negligible (0.00), and his criterion was extremely liberal (−4.00), (Parks, 1966).

During Phase 1 of the intervention (wherein he was asked to begin self-monitoring) his number of false alarms decreased, though this was at the expense of being incontinent. However, though his criterion improved (−0.84), his discriminability actually worsened (−3.16) possibly because the self-monitoring made him focus on his behaviour and pay extra attention to his symptoms.

During the learning phase, when the staff asked him to tolerate his bowel symptoms for increasingly longer periods, his false alarms and incontinence were reduced. Both his discriminability (1.38) and his criterion (−0.92) were found to have improved. By asking him to tolerate his symptoms for slightly longer periods of time, the staff demonstrated to him that he need not be afraid of all his symptoms and that tolerating them did not result in incontinence. This led to a reduction in his fear and less avoidance. With his fear reduced he could then analyse the feelings in his bowel and grow in competence in discriminating between faecal and non-faecal sensations.

A reduction in calling out for toiletting from ten times a day to twice a day had been achieved at the end of the programme and the tolerance periods extended from one hour to well over two-and-a-half hours. Thus he was now at a level for discharge home.

Outcome

Just before the day arrived there were problems about discharge. First, Albert began to feel unwell and so the day was put back a week. Second, his relatives began to have cold feet about whether they would be able to sustain for long the high level of input required of them, and really wondered whether discharge was such a good idea. Albert had become dependent on the hospital staff and preferred to be in hospital rather than at home where his quality of life might be poorer. Because he would not be able to go out of his flat readily, he would see only his family and nurse compared to the many people that he would interact with during the course of a hospital day. There is little doubt that such thoughts went through his mind during that final week before the discharge date, for he still remained ambivalent about discharge.

The new discharge date had been set and the time came round to virtually the eve of discharge. Albert had overcome his fear of incontinence and his dependence on others for long enough periods to make living outside in the community a real possibility. Though there had been many difficulties and moral questions in this case, overcome by frank discussion and forward planning by all involved, no one could really have been expected to predict what was to happen next.

On a routine visit to the ward during the week before discharge, the psychologist began as usual by reading the nursing notes from the previous day. It was a great shock to see the previous evening's entry: 'Albert was talking and behaving normally, but at 9.55 p.m. he suddenly threw up his right arm . . . which then started to jerk spasmodically and he became deeply cyanosed [turned blue]. The doctor was present within five minutes but death had been almost instantaneous . . .' The diagnosis was 'fit due to extension of stroke'.

Discussion

There are five points to be noted. First, the treatment was successful but the patient died. This is a recurring issue when working with elderly people. The elderly sick are a very dependent group who are expensive to maintain and are not easily helped. Success with this group brings tremendous rewards for the therapists as well as savings for the health service and benefits to patients. In this case one could argue that the extra stress of the treatment and impending discharge might have given Albert the further stroke, though the evidence is highly circumstantial and conjectural.

Second, it had been possible to provide a treatment for a very distressing and demanding problem. Eighteen months hospitalization had already occurred and without this intervention it is likely that the person would not have been considered fit for discharge and would have remained in hospital for the rest of his life.

Third, the problem illustrates a novel application in the analysis of the results. Though certain statistical assumptions were made, the use of signal detection theory was found to be illuminating and helpful in this case. It could be used in other cases of under-functioning where both real and ideal performances are measurable.

Fourth, with some patients who have spent a long time in a passive role and see only hopelessness in their futures it is important to show them that they are not beyond help.

Fifth, the patient, though physically handicapped, partially blind, and intellectually deteriorated, had no learning impairment and this last feature may have been an important outcome factor in this case.

10 Mrs Edwards: the interaction of physical illness and family pathology

Introduction

The relevance of clinical psychology to persons suffering from primary physical illness has been given increasing emphasis in recent years. In the care of elderly people one of the fundamental rules is that of multiple pathology: those elderly people needing help often have more than one problem. This makes it more essential than ever to work as a member of a multidisciplinary team. Within such teams the specific roles of individual members from different professions, who share mutual skills (such as interviewing, counselling, supportive psychotherapy) may sometimes become blurred. There are some interventions which may be successfully carried out by more than one member of the team.

The referral

Mrs Edwards was referred to the clinical psychology department by a specialist consultant physician in geriatric medicine. She was aged 82 and lived with her son and daughter. Mrs Edwards did not think there was any major problem but her son and daughter disagreed with her about this. Her daughter reported that the main problem was that Mrs Edwards was afraid to be left alone and appeared to resent the fact that her daughter had to leave her to go to work.

Physical examination had confirmed the presence of considerable obstructive airways disease. Mrs Edwards reported that she smoked ten cigarettes a day. Her appetite was poor and she had probably lost a considerable amount of weight.

Referral of this case to the clinical psychologist was based on the presence of evident anxiety and family tension in the absence of acute physical disease. The presentation of such problems in medical out-patients is well recognized. In particular it has been shown that disproportionate breathlessness associated with anxiety or other mood disorder can regularly be found in patients attending out-patient chest clinics (Burns and Howell, 1969).

Assessment

The clinical psychologist called to see Mrs Edwards at home four weeks after her out-patient visit. She said that she had lived in the house for the last 51 years. Her husband had died when the children were quite young and she had since then brought them up on her own. Her daughter was unmarried and worked as a nurse in a local hospital while her son, now aged 48, was in business. He was not at home on this occasion, but a second visit was arranged when he would be in as the major current life event for the family was his forthcoming marriage. Not only was he about to forsake bachelorhood, but the family had been joined in the last three weeks by his fiancée, a divorcee, and her 10-year-old daughter.

Mrs Edwards reported that she found it difficult to accept that her son was getting married after all these years and hinted that she felt that he should have done so earlier in order to spare her the upheaval at this time! She was able to discuss how the marriage would affect relationships in the household.

Her son was obviously acutely aware of the tensions currently affecting the family. He felt that his mother had both been a strong assertive figure and had leaned on him as the only male in the house. Mrs Edwards' daughter reported that there had been some problems of anxiety for up to 12 months and this seems to have started when the daughter suffered an accident and had to spend six or seven weeks at home. Difficulties really began when she had to return to work. There appear to be two sorts of disturbance. First, there were repeated episodes when Mrs Edwards felt ill in the morning, which seemed to be related to her chronic obstructive airways disease. She would become very distressed upon waking and would call for immediate help from her children, notably in helping her with her inhaler.

The second type of episode happened when she was left alone. She would become very distressed and telephone her son, daughter or GP, so that someone had to come to the house. When the GP had been called he had arrived at the house to find Mrs Edwards rapidly recovering from whatever it was that had happened. Mrs Edwards appeared to have some trouble recalling either of these types of episode but on questioning did admit to the second type. She seemed to have much more difficulty recalling the morning episodes.

Mrs Edwards herself described fears of being left alone and how these were heightened by thoughts that her son might be about to leave home altogether. This in fact was not the case as the house was large and the son was sure that it could easily accommodate all those at present living there. Mrs Edwards repeatedly asked for reassurance that it was quite normal for someone of her advanced years to wish not to be left alone. She said that she felt her daughter was not very sympathetic to her plight and did not fully appreciate just how old she really was.

Mrs Edwards admitted that loneliness was a real problem and she now had very few social contacts other than her immediate family. She used to be visited by an elderly lady who unfortunately had moved away some three years earlier. Many of her contemporaries had died.

Formulation

It was possible to identify a number of problems:

(1) probable panic attacks when left alone. Due to chronic airways disease, breathlessness was the most prominent symptom;
(2) early morning distress, probably due to her lung disease and associated with acute toxic confusion and consequent memory impairment;
(3) anxiety associated with the anticipated 'loss' of her son;
(4) conflict relating to the changing authority structure in the family;
(5) loneliness and isolation.

Actions aimed at relieving these might include:

(1) advice and training in anxiety management;
(2) advice to the family as to how some of the apparent inability to recall episodes might be due to acute confusion rather than denial;
(3) counselling regarding the actual likely outcome in terms of continued contact with her son;
(4) work with the family to encourage resolution of the new structure;
(5) arranging for a volunteer to visit Mrs Edwards regularly.

Interventions

Since there was some considerable reluctance on the part of Mrs Edwards to recognize that the episodes might be based on anxiety, direct attention to this was deferred. The psychologist undertook to look for a volunteer with interests similar to those of Mrs Edwards.

It was explained to the family that at least some of Mrs Edwards' 'forgetfulness' could be organic in origin and agreed with all of them that further contact would be made when a volunteer had been found. They could contact the psychologist in the meantime if they so wished. In the event, no suitable volunteer was forthcoming.

The following Monday morning Mrs Edwards' daughter telephoned in some distress as things had gone badly over the weekend. A visit was made to the house that afternoon. On this occasion the daughter evidently wished to talk. She revealed that she had for some years suffered from a drink problem and had in the past received in-patient psychiatric treatment. The present stresses, in particular the rows over the weekend, were once more causing her to seek solace in alcohol. Her previous treatment had not included work with the family.

On this visit it was also possible to talk with Mrs Edwards' prospective daughter-in-law. She was a determined and articulate woman who was insisting that her future husband should stand up to his mother and resist unreasonable demands. It was this which had brought things to a head over the weekend. Mrs Edwards herself would admit to very little being wrong and insisted that at the age of 82 she should be treated with more respect. In the course of quite a lengthy visit, it was possible to talk to these several people both individually and together.

The main focus of intervention was advice to the family on understanding and responding appropriately to the various types of problem behaviour. Appropriate limits for responding to requests for help were agreed and the importance of consistency was stressed.

In view of her particular problems in dealing with stress, it was arranged for the daughter to have an individual session with the psychologist. A further visit to the home was planned to monitor the agreed programme.

Mrs Edwards' daughter reviewed a number of the problems which confronted her. She was unsure whether she felt able to continue with her job but also knew that she could not cope with being at home with her mother full-time. Unfortunately Mrs Edwards steadfastly refused to concede that the stresses in the family might in any way contribute to her daughter's drink problem. Similarly she found it much easier to ascribe all of her symptoms to chronic obstructive airways disease than see a role for anxiety as a precipitant factor.

There was nonetheless general agreement in the family that things were beginning to resolve. It was stated that Mrs Edwards had become less demanding, suffered fewer panic attacks and seemed to have begun to accept that she would not be 'losing' her son. Her prospective daughter-in-law was much happier that relationships had improved although it was pointed out that some further problems might arise when the wedding actually took place. The family felt that if they were to continue the strategy of kind-but-firm towards Mrs Edwards things would continue to improve. It was therefore arranged that they should be left to contact the psychologist should the need arise.

Follow-up

There were no further requests to visit the family. However, hospital records indicated that about six months later Mrs Edwards was admitted with an acute exacerbation of her chest complaint. At this time it was noted that she was acutely confused, was restless and agitated. This improved with treatment for her physical condition. Her obstructive airways disease had, however, worsened and the family had been told that the outlook was poor.

Discussion

This somewhat complex and colourful case illustrates a number of points. There was a mixture of psychological problems and physical illness. It was not possible to treat either in isolation. Some possible interventions were ignored; for example, it might have been desirable to try to modify Mrs Edwards' smoking behaviour. However this was certainly not the client's wish and, however foolish such behaviour might be, such decisions must be left to the client.

The work was largely based in the home. Mrs Edwards was a somewhat frail if very determined woman and it would have been very difficult to transport the family to some special centre to work with them. It was important to let the various members of the family express their views in private, at least initially. In a busy hospital out-patient clinic, this is often difficult and can impede a proper understanding of the problems.

In this particular case, the clinical psychologist's role was primarily to assist the family in understanding the origin of the problems and in agreeing on a consistent strategy in coping with them. It is recognized that in senile dementia, even when relatives know that there is a permanent impairment of intellect, they still often interpret disturbed behaviour as being awkward or deliberate. Separating the organic from the functional in this case was especially difficult. Certainly the subsequent admission to hospital with accompanying acute confusion does suggest that the initial formulation was correct. In so far as the family appear to have coped without major crisis, the intervention would seem to have been successful.

At the time of referral, the consultant physician identified certain problems, such as anxiety and smoking, which suggested that psychological intervention using behavioural methods would have been appropriate. However, assessment of Mrs Edwards in the context of her family situation showed that such interventions would not have been acceptable to her and that family interactions should be the focus of attention. Clearly it was more appropriate for the psychologist, having made the initial contact, to maintain his involvement, albeit using skills that are not specific to a clinical psychologist, rather than to refer Mrs Edwards to another member of the team.

11   Brian: living with schizophrenia in the community

Introduction

Brian Wilson is a 64-year-old man resident in a six-person mixed group home which is managed and staffed by a voluntary mental health group. He has suffered from chronic schizophrenia for 30 years. This was first diagnosed in 1947 and he spent the following 28 years in a psychiatric hospital. The home is situated near the centre of a large city; he has lived there for five years since his transfer from another group home.

When the help of the clinical psychologist was requested, the present management body had been running the home for about one year, having taken over from an organization which had run into financial difficulties. The advent of new management had seen a number of changes. Three of the long-standing residents, who had lived together both in this home and the previous group home with Brian, had moved on to other residences. They had been replaced by younger people who were not as handicapped as Brian and who were using the home as a stepping stone to more independent living.

The major consequence of this was that the staff became concerned about the comparative lack of progress of Brian as he was the most disabled of the older group of residents. The home's managers were concerned that his mental state and self-care were deteriorating and began to question whether Brian might be better cared for in the long term in hospital. However, the direct care staff felt that Brian had considerable potential and that although his current demands for care were very high and probably higher than they would be able to meet in the long term, they were anxious to explore ways of developing and improving his personal and social skills.

The problems for Brian present in a number of interesting ways. First, there is Brian's individual health and behaviour, e.g. his mental state and self-care. Second, there is a question about the ability and skills of the staff to help him with his problems. Third, there is a question about the willingness of the organization to continue to care for him.

Assessment

Assessment in rehabilitation must be wide-ranging and cover a number of areas that may traditionally not be seen as part of psychologists' role or within their area of expertise. A full assessment should include details of an individual's physical and mental state, self-care, domestic skills, occupation/leisure skills, community living community living skills and work skills (Shepherd, 1983). It must concentrate on individuals' strengths as well as their weaknesses and provide a clear framework for any future interventions (Anthony and Farkas, 1982). This requires the contribution of a range of mental health professionals.

A brief interview with Brian (he communicated little and was obviously very distressed by the presence of strangers) revealed something of the nature of his psychiatric problems but it became clear that much of the assessment would have to be conducted through the care staff.

An initial interview with the care staff revealed the following areas of difficulty:

(1) social withdrawal. Brian spent much of his time in his room and communicated little with his room-mate or anyone else. His verbal communication was usually restricted to monosyllabic responses to direct questions. He avoided all communal areas of the house and would not eat meals with anyone else present.

(2) physical well-being. His diet was very poor. He refused much of the food that was offered by the home, preferring to buy his own bread and milk which he supplemented with chocolate bars and the occasional cereal and soup that the home staff could persuade him to eat in his own room. His teeth were in very poor condition, he needed spectacles for reading, his weight was low and he had a persistent chesty cough.

(3) self-care. With considerable prompting his basic self-care was adequate but particular problems remained with bathing and changing of clothes, both of which he would only do weekly after considerable efforts by the staff.

(4) mental state. There was some question as to whether some of his behaviour could be explained by the fact that Brian was influenced by either hallucinations or delusions. For example, he believed that other residents of the home and also the staff of the day centre were 'putting things in his head' and these were causing him so much pain that he had to avoid them if at all possible. He also had very limited concentration and was at times so thought-disordered that it was impossible to have any kind of conversation with him.

(5) daytime activity. Brian had no regular daytime activity and would spend his day 'travelling'; this meant leaving the house at 10 a.m. and returning at 2 or 3 p.m. It was suspected that much of his time was spent rather aimlessly travelling around on buses.

With long-term mentally ill people it is tempting to see their problems solely as the product of a long and debilitating illness or of a long period of hospitalization. However, a danger in seeing things in these rather narrow ways is that much of the meaning of the problems and hence potential ways of understanding and helping an individual can be lost. It is important to have as full a personal history as possible to provide a context in which the problems can be understood. As the hospital records were very inadequate in this respect it was decided to seek further information from Brian's family.

After some difficulty the psychologist arranged an interview with Brian's brother. It proved very fruitful, in that for the first time the group home had a clear picture of Brian's early life. He was born the second of four children. His father was a heavy drinker and an occasional street brawler. His father's drinking, along with the chronic physical illness of his mother, coloured the whole of Brian's childhood. His mother's illness was of particular importance because Brian was closest to his mother but her illness meant that she had repeated hospital admissions throughout his childhood.

Brian was described by his brother as a shy, withdrawn child who was often bullied at school. On leaving school at the age of 14 he worked as a bricklayer's labourer. He did this until the early part of the Second World War when he was conscripted into the Pioneer Corps. It was at this stage that his psychological problems first became apparent and, although no clear records are available, they eventually led to his discharge from the Army on medical grounds. For a period of about two years he continued to live at home with his mother, but became increasingly withdrawn and disturbed. He was unable to hold down a job and his eccentric behaviour made it difficult for him to stay at home. Therefore, in the late 1940s he was admitted to a large mental hospital where he was to stay for almost 30 years.

He had little contact with his family during this time. Both of his parents died and a decision had been taken by the family not to invite Brian to their funerals. In the mid 1970s he was discharged to a privately run group home. He lived in a series of group homes before the present one. His brother felt that the frequent moves over the past ten years had contributed to his difficulties.

Formulation

The above five problem areas are typical of those presented by people with long-term mental illness (Shepherd, 1984). They require different methods of assessment and treatment. Social withdrawal, one of the cluster of symptoms of schizophrenia generally referred to as the clinical poverty syndrome (in addition it includes emotional apathy, underactivity, slowness of thought and movement and poverty of speech (Wing, 1978)) can be very disabling and is not very responsive to medication but more to changes in an individual's social environment (Wing and Brown, 1970). Physical health problems and neglect of self-care and general well-being are frequent problems. Hallucinations, delusions and thought disorder are also common but their relationship to future community adjustment is not strong (Wing, 1978), although they are more responsive to medication than the symptoms of the clinical poverty syndrome. Appropriate day-care can have a valuable protective function in preventing further relapse and re-admission to hospital (Linn *et al.*, 1977), as well as developing the social role and community living skills that many long-term mentally ill people lack.

The various problem areas described above also demand different types of intervention at varying levels within the system. Bender (1979) has set out the three levels of intervention for a psychologist in such a setting as the group home. They are (1) working directly with clients at the individual or group level, (2) working with staff who will carry out the appropriate interventions and (3) working with managers in the development and monitoring of care policy and practice. Any intervention in a service system will require that some consideration is given to all three levels. The level of the major focus of intervention is determined by a number of factors including the resources available (in both personnel and facilities) and the varying capacities of all the individuals in the system to make a commitment to and allow, conduct or sustain an intervention (Lavender, 1985).

Prior to the request for help with Brian the psychologist had visited the group home regularly (once every three weeks) and had provided primarily a consultation and advisory service to the two staff members and also acted as a communication channel between the health services and the staff who might otherwise have become isolated from other developments in the mental health services. The psychologist was, therefore, familiar with the resources of the home and also with the capacity within it for change and development. The limited availability of the psychologist's time and the requirement for detailed individual behavioural work with Brian determined that much of the work would be conducted indirectly through the care staff. There was also a requirement for some work at the organizational level, both in reassuring the home managers of the appropriateness of the home for Brian and in initiating the contacts with a series of mental health workers including the consultant psychiatrist, general practitioner, community psychiatric nurse and day centre worker.

Intervention

The interview with the brother provided a very useful context in which to set the intervention. It provided some knowledge with which to begin to understand Brian's personal isolation and his inability to trust in the services offered by the home.

The intervention through the direct care staff focused on four areas of difficulty. It was decided to work on his self-care skills (particularly his bathing and changing of clothes), his eating habits, his social withdrawal and day centre attendance. This aspect of the programme was developed around a goal attainment scale (GAS) (Kirusek and Sherman, 1968) and is described in Table 11.1. The GAS was developed in close collaboration with the staff. It has the advantage of being tailored to individual needs and the clearly specified behavioural targets serve not only as evaluative tools but also as guides to the intervention. The instruction of the staff in behavioural techniques was also built around the development of the GAS. The importance of clearly objectified goals, consistency of approach, the contingency of any reward or feedback and the importance of durability and generalization were stressed. The importance of setting appropriate and achievable goals was emphasized particularly as it was probable that any change with Brian would be a slow and gradual process. This teaching of behavioural techniques was

Table 11.1 Brian's goal attainment scale (GAS)

	Social withdrawal	Eating	Self-care	Day centre
1 Least desirable outcome	Spends all time alone	Breakfast only downstairs	Constant prompts about bathing and clothing	No sessions
2 Poor outcome	Most time alone – will talk very rarely	Breakfast and occasional (10%) other meals downstairs	Prompts 75% of time	1 session per month
3 Moderate outcome	Sustain one 5-minute conversation per day	50% other meals downstairs	Prompts 50% of time	2 sessions per month
4 Good outcome	Sustain one 10-minute conversation per day	75% other meals downstairs	Prompts less than 10% of time	1 session per week – occasional lapses
5 Best possible outcome	Sustain two 10-minute conversations per day	100% other meals downstairs	No prompts required	1 session per week – no lapses

combined with more general teaching on mental health including the nature of disability in long-term mental illness, psychiatric symptomatology and the importance of social factors in affecting the course of a schizophrenic illness. In the initial stages of the intervention the frequency of the visits from the psychologist was increased to one per week for two weeks and then fortnightly for a further two months. The purpose of this was to advise and support staff while they learnt new skills and began to adapt to the slow and painful process of change.

At the same time as the behavioural interventions began, a series of appointments for Brian were made. Appointments with the consultant psychiatrist and general practitioner were arranged to review his mental state and physical state respectively. The staff also began a long, hard struggle to persuade Brian of the value of a visit to both the optician and the dentist. The GP passed Brian as fit and well and the psychiatrist adjusted his medication which resulted in some improvement in his mental state, in particular his thought disorder. This made communication with Brian about the behavioural interventions a little easier.

The necessity to try to rebuild something of the last 30 years of Brian's life was also recognized. The first step here was renewing the relationship with his family. Considerable tact was needed as the family were suspicious that the home might be trying to shift the burden of care to them. They were reassured on this point and then asked to provide further information including photographs from his past life. One staff member took on the responsibility for helping Brian to rediscover something of his lost past. They visited old work places, residences and his parents' graves. This had the dual purpose of providing a much fuller and richer picture of Brian's life and of developing his relationship with the staff. The same staff member also took on the role of key worker and was responsible for the daily monitoring of the behavioural work and the arrangement of all interviews.

Outcome

The primary method of evaluation was through the GAS which was reviewed monthly. The outcome of the evaluation at initiation of the programme, at three months and at one year are presented in Figure 11.1.

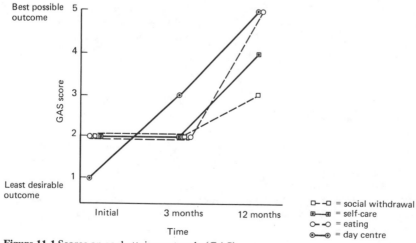

Figure 11.1 Scores on goal attainment scale (GAS)

Two months into the programme a problem arose when the consultant who usually saw Brian was on leave and as a result he saw a locum who admitted him to hospital in the belief (mistaken as it transpired) that he was suicidal. This was a very distressing period for both Brian, who was terrified at being returned to hospital, and for the staff who felt that much of the work of the past two months had been wasted. Fortunately the staff maintained contact with Brian and there seemed to be few consequences of his admission save an even greater reluctance on his part to go anywhere near any health service premises. The psychologist at this stage was required to support and reassure the care staff and spend further time with the managers in reassuring them of the appropriateness of Brian's placement.

Six months into the programme a further difficulty was encountered when the key worker left. Fortunately, this was known about well in advance and the difficulties that it might create were explored in detail with both staff members. A particular concern was how Brian might respond to the loss of what had become an important and trusting relationship for him. There were problems, but none were serious and it proved useful in focusing attention on the maintenance of Brian's improvement independently of the contribution of individual workers.

Evaluation

As can be seen from Figure 11.1 Brian has continued to make progress albeit in a limited way in some areas. Indeed, throughout the assessment and intervention period one of the major roles for the psychologist has been to stress to staff the slow nature of change for someone like Brian and to ensure they felt rewarded and recognized for their work.

Over one year after the work began Brian continues to live at the group home, and although he remains somewhat isolated, his attendance, for example, at meal times, has given him a place in the home which is respected by both residents and staff. This is reflected in the managers' pleasure in the progress he has made and their acceptance that he has a permanent place in the home. His attendance at the day centre has also provided him with a structure to his day and a range of social contacts which will continue to be of positive benefit.

12 Lilac Ward: staff training in a rehabilitation setting

The problem

Lilac Ward is home to 27 people — 15 men and 12 women — all of whom suffer from major psychiatric disabilities. A survey of all the longer-stay patients in this 350-bed hospital had led to regrouping the patients, to deliberately create more mixed-sex wards, while trying to preserve as many long-standing friendships as possible. In this regrouping Lilac Ward had been identified as the ward for older hospital residents who might be able to leave hospital, to go to some form of sheltered accommodation. As a result new staff groupings emerged, since each ward had to have staff of both sexes. These ward staff were consequently faced with new patients, and were apprehensive about the new expectation that some of the patients perhaps should leave hospital. The nursing officer for the ward was anxious that the staff be given some systematic training relevant to their work, but was not able to permanently allocate any extra staff to the ward to compensate for the time taken in training.

When the training course was being planned, the 27 residents were aged between 31 and 73, although half were aged over 59. Most were not thought likely to do well in unsupported accommodation, and it was accepted that some might need to return to hospital from time to time, and if so they would be re-admitted to Lilac Ward. Sixteen day staff were assigned to the ward: two charge nurses, three staff nurses, four enrolled nurses, and seven nursing aides. The number of staff actually on duty at any one time varied from three to five.

Assessment

The basic situation on Lilac Ward was that a newly formed team of staff did not possess a coherent treatment philosophy or relevant skills or knowledge to help a very mixed group of disabled patients. It was accordingly necessary to clarify what the staff already knew and could carry out, what care needs of the patients to address, and how best to organize a training course within the very real restraints of staff time that could be devoted to training.

Carrying out some standardized test of knowledge, such as the 229-item Behaviour Modification Test designed by Gardner (1972) right at the beginning of training ran the risk that it might alienate the ward staff. Initially, individual interviews with ward staff gave useful information on the level of existing knowledge and skills, and also revealed that most of the aides (except for one qualified teacher and one arts graduate) and the enrolled nurses were not used to reading nursing or technical literature. It was possible, by careful juggling of the staff rota, to take 11 of the staff for a day to a similar but longer-established unit at another hospital. This created an awareness that change in the patients *was* possible, and by judicious stops at pubs on the way there and back helped to draw staff together.

After this day, and at the beginning of the training course proper, a specially constructed 37-item training scale was administered. The scale consisted of:

(1) 14 attitude questions (derived from Caine and Smail, 1968), for example, 'Nurses should work alongside patients when they are working on the ward.' Respondents indicate whether they strongly agree, agree, are uncertain, disagree or strongly disagree with the statement.
(2) 14 multiple-choice questions, for example, 'Which of the following is the most important cause of institutionalization:
    (a) the way nurses and patients communicate with each other
    (b) lack of facilities on the ward
    (c) not having a homely physical appearance to the ward.'
(3) 9 open-ended questions, for example: "Please list three different things you could do to try to stop a patient lying down suddenly on the floor or pavement."

The core needs of the patients were assessed using a change-sensitive rating scale (Baker and Hall, 1983), supplemented by information about other patient characteristics, such as presence of major physical illness, and whether any family or friends were still in regular contact. By examining these measures, three clusters of patients were identified according to levels of ability. The most able group, interestingly enough, included a number of the older patients. It was agreed with the staff and the nursing officer that the therapeutic goal for the ward, to be reflected in the training course, would be primarily to improve independent social and activities-of-daily-living functioning by means of a behaviourally based regime which included attention to group functioning and a range of recreational activities. (Paul and Lentz (1977) outline many of the characteristics of such regimes.)

The training course had to be acceptable to and comprehensible by all ward staff, especially the enrolled nurses and aides with the greatest amount of direct staff-patient contact. It had to be attractive to the staff, since their motivation to carry through with such a course was essentially unproven. It also had to be attainable with the current ward staffing levels, which effectively precluded teaching sessions of more than two hours on any one day. An adult education model of training was adopted (Rogers, 1973) which was familiar to some of the staff already, and emphasized the need for their positive commitment to the course.

This model of training has been developed from experience in Workers' Educational Association and local authority evening classes, where students often arrive with negative experiences of education — frequently associated with bad memories of school — and continue to be anxious about criticism and difficulties of being an older learner. These issues suggest a model of training with a number of special characteristics, such as positive encouragement of innovation, and an emphasis on simulation and project work.

The training course

In the preliminary interviews it became apparent that the untrained staff were embarrassed that they might be shown up in front of their trained and ostensibly more knowledgeable colleagues. A reciprocal embarrassment was felt by some of the trained staff about some of the aides. Training groups were thus selected to be either trained staff, or untrained staff, taking groups of at least three on each occasion. Groups were on average five, very occasionally reaching seven. A room immediately adjacent to the ward, previously used as a small dormitory, was available because of the slow run-down in total patient numbers in the hospital. This room was not used for any other purpose, and it was initially agreed that at least two two-hour sessions a week would be run, and occasionally it was possible to run three sessions in a week. Even though ward staff were willing to adjust their days off to fit in with this schedule, on two weeks in February and March it was impossible to run more than one session because nurses were using up all their leave allocation before the leave year ended on 31 March.

The course consisted of ten two-hour units:

(1) people with chronic psychiatric handicaps: their main problems
(2) people with chronic psychiatric handicaps: the environment they live in
(3) observing and recording behaviour
(4) changing behaviour: staff-patient communication
(5) changing behaviour: laws of behaviour
(6) changing behaviour: setting goals and targets
(7) changing behaviour: discovering new opportunities and rewards
(8) changing behaviour: focusing on individuals (design of individual prog-rammes)
(9) maintaining behaviour
(10) social behaviour

The content of each unit was prepared with care. Although over half of the staff group had some formal training, it was apparent that relatively little training had focused on the specific disabilities of chronic patients, or on the environmental factors modifying the frequency with which bizarre or inappropriate behaviour was displayed. None had received any formal training in behavioural treatment methods, apart from the ex-teacher who was familiar with general learning theory. In the limited time available it was important to stress a relatively few key points, rather than attempt too much detail or qualification. These key points included, for example, the response latency of sufferers from chronic schizophrenia — leading to the practical point that prompting should not follow too quickly after an initial question; and the basic notion of schedules of reinforcement (for which fruit machines always act as an appropriate example) — leading to the practicalities of preparing a patient to do without immediate praise from nursing staff.

These key points were transmitted by an integrated set of handouts (the longest being four sides of A4), overhead projector transparencies, and practical assignments, with a set of questions for group discussion. The vocabulary level used in the handouts and OHP transparencies was deliberately kept simple, and psychological jargon avoided as much as possible. The assignments for each unit were reviewed at the beginning of the subsequent session, and typically involved observing an identified patient, collecting information about a patient, or carrying out a mini-programme with the patient. The main benefit of the assignments was the marked improvement in the nurses' ability to describe precisely what a given patient was doing over a particular period of time.

After the first two or three sessions, most staff became adept at role-playing, often with considerable sensitivity. At the end of each unit, a short quiz was held, at a very easy level for the first three or four units. This idea was introduced with caution, but in practice staff entered into the spirit of things, and it was well received, and enabled key points to be repeated at the end of each session.

The educational model used thus covered skills, knowledge and attitudes. The most important attitudinal shift was the realization by staff that there was a degree of variability of speech and behaviour in even the most handicapped patients, and that this variability was influenced by what staff did. The importance attached to the assignments stressed skill acquisition more than knowledge attainment; there was a degree of overlearning of key points, and also staff became accustomed to other people commenting directly on how they related to other patients. This emphasis on written and spoken material, observation of others, and personal performance matches the 'symbolic', 'iconic', and 'enactive' phases of learning noted by Milne (1986a) after this course was run.

To illustrate one of the units, unit seven was concerned not only to establish any event which the patient might enjoy, but also to exploit any residual interests in which the patient might still be able to engage. For example, one patient said he enjoyed reading, but he did not have any spectacles and could not read small print. The continuing involvement of one nurse in assessing the patient's interest in reading material, obtaining new spectacles, and selecting large-print books from the hospital library was of real value for the patient, and for the nurses' group in seeing how to follow through an individual problem. Reliance on material reinforcers was not over-stressed — just as well, since another patient expressed his fondness for tinned peaches, but, on being given a can as reinforcer priming, chose never to open it, despite repeated proffering of the tin-opener.

Outcome

It took 23 weeks to run the 47 unit sessions necessary to train all 16 staff, and by the end of this period two of the nursing aides had already changed. The 37-item scale was repeated after the course, and showed improvement in knowledge as assessed by the multiple-choice and open-ended questions. There was no change on the attitude questions, probably because the initial individual interviews and other preparatory discussions generated attitude change *before* the pre-test use of the scale. The most important outcome of the course was the ability of staff to feel confident in taking on-the-spot decisions about patients in the course of running the ward programme, and the maintenance of programmes for individual patients.

These programme records were maintained over many months, and were inspected for omissions of data. There was no evidence of increased 'missed days' in the records, and they were maintained during the holidays of both the psychologist and the charge nurses. The weekly review of the programme afforded an opportunity for staff both to report any variations in the programme they had to devise, and to suggest any new variations. Woods and Cullen (1983) have described the difficulties in maintaining this type of regime over many months.

Two years after the initial training course, the course is still offered to new staff likely to stay for more than six months, and the handouts have been modified in some respects. Of the original 27 patients, 10 have left hospital at some time or another, and three patients have needed to come back to hospital for some time. The new patients who have come into the ward are in general more disabled than those who have left, so the probability of discharge for the remaining patients is low, with implications for the design of the ward programme and hence of the training course.

Discussion

It was not difficult to obtain content-related material for the course, but British material written by nurses (e.g. Barker, 1982; Butler and Rosenthall, 1985) was more acceptable to staff than American material written by psychologists. It was more difficult to obtain guidance on how to structure the course, although Milne's (1986a) book, published since the course was run, is helpful in that respect.

The material available on methods for teaching skills to nurses tends to follow either an educational or an explicitly behavioural approach. Both of these approaches are useful, but tend to neglect the formal and informal interpersonal skills involved in nursing, especially in the type of psychiatric nursing required in a ward like Lilac. Kagan (1985) suggests that the teaching of interpersonal skills to nurses should be given greater prominence, and to the extent that it would also teach patient advocacy skills, the suggestion has particular appeal for this type of setting.

The three main lessons derived from this course were, first, the attention to timetabling and scheduling of the course that was necessary, in close collaboration with the nursing officer and charge nurses. Second, the ward staff were a very cohesive team. The group dynamics of the team were important, and it was valuable to spend time with staff before the course began, to understand their concerns. The awareness of the need for training was sustained day-to-day by the charge nurses, and cooperation with them was essential (Orton, 1984). Most important of all was the need to continually relate the emphasis of the course to the needs of the patients and ward regime, and to be prepared to change the course as patients' needs gradually changed.

Part 2

Working with children and adolescents

Introduction

William Yule

Clinical psychologists working with children, adolescents and their families are sometimes regarded as specializing in the age group 0 to 18. However, they are faced with a wide range of problems from early feeding and sleeping disorders, through the management of behavioural difficulties to depression, delinquency and identity problems. Far from specializing, they have to bring a developmental perspective to bear on the whole range of intra- and interpersonal difficulties that occur before legal majority is achieved.

Inevitably, the nine case studies presented here can only begin to illustrate the range of cases seen and approaches used to help. What comes across is the complexity of even the simplest problems, the need to undertake a broad-based functional analysis of the presenting problem, the importance of considering the problem within the surrounding social setting, and the range of settings within which clinical psychologists are working.

With pre-school children it is frequently the parents who act as the agents of change. Problems such as tantrums, disturbed sleep patterns, toiletting and eating behaviour are common causes for referral to a clinical psychologist. In young children passing rapidly through stages of development, such problems may be transient. However, as in Tom's case, these problems can be distressing and disruptive for families, and therefore intervention becomes valuable.

The idea of a child having a phobia of custard pies is initially amusing, until one realizes how much the problem dominates the boy's daily life. The case of Keith illustrates how treating children's phobias differs from treating adults' phobias, and how real-life problems are often more complex than simplified textbook examples. Interventions are adjusted to meet different needs of individual clients, making it difficult to identify which element of treatment is most important.

Health services and hospitals are usually seen to be in the business of curing people. Staff find it difficult to acknowledge problems surrounding dying and when the dying patient is a child, the process is particularly emotionally painful. The third case study, Christopher, draws attention to the need for more open communication among staff, parents and child, and for mutual support. There is a growing consensus that children's questions should be answered honestly. This study illustrates how psychologists can help determine how much the child understands about death in general and the illness in particular, and how this information can be used to make dying more bearable for all.

The first three cases focus on different sorts of presenting problems and involve parents in different ways. The fourth, the Adams family, uses a systems approach to family therapy both in assessment and intervention. The study illustrates how therapists can use their intervention to alter alliances within a family. The report is particularly interesting in showing how, at a crucial point, clinical psychologists can call on their generic training involving adult clients to offer some marital therapy.

The fifth case study illustrates yet another role of the clinical child psychologist — that of conducting action research to improve a particular area of service delivery. In this case, the focus of interest was on whether a painful radiological procedure used in a paediatric out-patient setting could be made less problematic by preparing the children. In the event, observational data and self-report data gave contradictory results, but overall client satisfaction increased.

Social services have often called for psychological assessments as part of their work in preparing reports for courts. The past few years have shown how the intervention and other skills of clinical psychologists can also be used to the advantage of child clients, whether in teaching social skills as part of intermediate treatment, advising on token economies in residential treatment of delinquency, or, as in this case, advising on alternative care. Often there is long-term work involved in treating children who have been rejected by their parents. The case of Steven shows how alternative care proved to be appropriate. The team were forced to reconsider their policy of opposing all care orders. It reminds us that the needs of individual clients have to take priority over global policies based on premature theorizing.

Adolescence is the time when substance abuse is first manifest. Sometimes it amounts to little more than transient experimentation as part of asserting independence. At other times, as in the case of Lulu, it is part of a more serious set of problems. The case study illustrates how a treatment programme within a closed institution broke down even when (or perhaps because) it was beginning to be successful. It also illustrates the well-known finding that factors that maintain a problem may be different from those that caused it.

The eighth case study shows the complex problems of an adolescent striving for independence at a time when her family had collapsed around her. Many adolescents are truculent and resentful at being offered therapy. Charlotte attended regularly but remained silent for nearly a year. The case illustrates the need for counselling to proceed at a level and pace acceptable to the adolescent. In this case, the use of a repertory grid to explore Charlotte's construct system was especially valuable.

The final case, again involving an adolescent girl, shows another apparently circumscribed problem set within a complex web of family problems and aspirations. It illustrates how focusing on the presenting problem helped to force out into the open additional factors maintaining the problem. Acknowledgement of these aspects helped to resolve Katie's distressing hair-pulling.

Overall, the cases presented here show that clinical child psychology is in a healthy state and has come a very long way from solely diagnostic testing. The writers of these case studies show a sensitivity to the children and their predicaments while remaining aware of the relevant literature and applying it in a flexible yet imaginative way. They are aware of the need to evaluate their interventions to protect them and their clients from following expensive, ineffective treatments.

Not only is the range of ages and types of problem impressive, but the range of techniques is also worthy of comment. Most psychologists made heavy use of interviews in assessing problems with little use of direct observation in natural settings with these particular cases. Traditional psychometric assessment was less relevant in most of these cases, but would have been more central in cases of language disorder, learning difficulties, developmental neuropsychological problems, school refusal and family placement issues. Self-report questionnaires were used appropriately. Treatment approaches encompass a spectrum from systematic desensitization through supportive and Kellyian counselling to systems family therapy. All of these have roots in scientific psychological studies. Other less empirical approaches were not represented and this reflects the practice of clinical child psychologists in Britain in the mid-1980s.

13   Tom: sex role and expectations

The problem

Tom was referred by a health visitor because of his parents' concern about his behaviour. He was spending much time wearing a black petticoat on top of his ordinary clothes. He wanted to be called by a girl's name. The problem was exacerbated at Christmas with nativity plays and other dressing-up activities, and Tom engaging in imaginary play as an angel or a fairy. The health visitor had suggested that his parents ignore the behaviour, but this had if anything increased its frequency.

Background

At the time of referral Tom was 4½ years old. His younger brother Ben was 8 months. Their father, Mr Mason, worked in an office locally and their mother Mrs Mason, stayed at home to look after the children. Both sets of grandparents lived close by and weekends were often spent with them.

Tom was born following an emergency caesarean section and was described by his mother as being 'not very easy' as a baby. He was upset by anything unusual, for example seeing his mother in a hat, or by sudden noises such as aeroplanes. As he grew up he became fussy about food, disliking anything with a strong smell or messy appearance. In themselves these behaviours are not uncommon in young children, but Tom's distaste for anything messy became more marked. The sight of spilt food or his brother's food-smudged face could induce vomiting. Tom tended to leave the room when Ben was being fed.

As a result of Tom's difficult behaviour, he and his mother had become very close. This was reinforced by his father working very long hours. Since starting play-group at the age of 3 Tom had accepted separation from his mother, although it had taken a term for him to settle down. At the time of Mrs Mason's hospital admission for the birth of Ben, Tom had been very upset, frequently vomiting and refusing to let his father comfort him. The family coped with this by Mr Mason looking after the baby, so that Mrs Mason could spend time with Tom.

Assessment

Mr and Mrs Mason were asked to monitor Tom's behaviour using a chart which divided each day into intervals of one hour. Intervals when Tom was not wearing the petticoat were marked 'NP'; when he was dressed up they were left blank and activities with his father were marked 'DA'.

At the start of monitoring Tom was wearing the petticoat for approximately one-third of his waking time. He removed the petticoat when going out or going to bed, and did not wear it in stressful situations nor when separated from his mother. There was therefore no evidence to suggest that Tom used his petticoat as an attachment object nor that it served to reduce anxiety in the way that some children have a favourite toy or blanket.

At the time of the referral Tom had been wearing the petticoat for about a year. Often it was part of a solitary imaginary game in which he would pretend to be a butterfly or an angel. However, he would also wear the petticoat when engaged in other activities such as reading, watching TV or eating. He often asked his mother to call him by a girl's name. At play-group he would make straight for the dressing-up box and spend the whole morning wearing a skirt or a dress.

Tom expressed a preference for toys usually given to girls, but would also play with Lego, a toy fort and cars. He generally preferred playing with girls, but would play with boys although he often complained that their games were too rough.

Tom shared very few activities with his father, despite Mr Mason now spending more time at home than when Tom was a baby. Mr Mason was disappointed about this. Although he had suggested games and other activities Tom had refused, preferring to be with his mother. Mr Mason was particularly concerned about Tom's dressing up and 'feminine' behaviour.

Tom's close attachment to his mother was apparent when the family was seen together. He would go to her whenever he wanted anything, and she was sensitive to his needs, anticipating when he needed help. She presented as a mother who was involved with her children and their activities, wishing to provide a stimulating environment for them both within and outside the home. She found Tom's dressing up and other 'feminine' behaviours somewhat embarrassing. Friends and play-group leaders had commented on it. She was also concerned that it had a negative effect on Tom's ability to relate to other children.

Formulation

The first decision for the psychologist was whether any intervention was appropriate. Had close links not existed between the psychologist and the primary care team it is possible that the referral would not have been made. It could be considered that Tom's behaviour was a problem only when considered in the light of sexist expectations of small boys. However, Tom's behaviour was setting him apart from his peer group in a way that could influence his adjustment, especially when he started school. Furthermore, Green (1985) states that there is a tendency for 'feminine' boys to be bisexually or homosexually oriented in early adulthood unless the behaviour is checked. It may also be that during puberty, a link is established between cross-dressing and sexual arousal, providing a necessary condition for the development of fetishistic cross-dressing.

From the psychologist's viewpoint, also of concern was Tom's poor relationship with his father. Bandura (1971) reported that modelling is more likely to occur when the model is relatively nurturant or rewarding. For Tom, his mother was clearly the more rewarding of the two parental models and it could be hypothesized that this was a factor underlying his desire to be a girl and adopt female clothing.

The objectives of intervention were therefore to improve Tom's relationship with his father, and to help him adopt appropriate sex-role behaviour. The decision as to what was appropriate was necessarily subjective and was decided in discussion between Mr and Mrs Mason and the psychologist. It was agreed that the goal of intervention should be for Tom to dress up only when engaged in fantasy play but not at other times. He should accept his own name and not express a desire to be a girl. Provided he played with a wide range of toys his parents and the psychologist agreed that it was not inappropriate for some of these toys to be those more commonly associated with girls.

The method of intervention needed to be home-based in view of the impact of Tom's relationships with his parents on his behaviour. In his studies of triadic work with children (the triad being therapist, parent(s), and child), Herbert (1987) has outlined ways in which parents can be taught techniques to bring about change in their children's behaviour.

In the case of an individual child, parents do not need in-depth understanding of operant conditioning. Instead, teaching can relate to specific instances and draw attention to the way in which certain antecedent and consequent events serve to change and maintain problem behaviour. As behaviour change is taking place within the child's natural environment, using the most available sources of reinforcement (the parents), problems of generalization do not arise, as would be the case if the psychologist was undertaking the intervention personally, one or two hours per week.

Intervention

Stage 1

Initially steps were taken to increase contact between Tom and his father and to involve Mr Mason in activities that Tom enjoyed. It was hoped that the positive reinforcement value of these activities, which included reading, swimming and going shopping, would then generalize to other contacts with his father. It was agreed that Mr Mason would read Tom's bedtime story each evening and spend time with him at weekends. Mr and Mrs Mason were content that activities for Tom (and Ben) should have high priority at weekends even if this interfered with visits to the grandparents.

If Tom objected to his father reading to him, Mrs Mason would stay in the room as well, but she would not read the story. Within a week Tom was looking forward to his father reading the story and no longer asked for his mother. At weekends Tom and Mr Mason would go swimming or shopping, play football or just spend time together at home. Green (1985) suggests that in enhancing the father-son relationship, shared activities need not be overly masculine. Hence if Tom preferred to go shopping or read with his father these were the appropriate activities to share. The time Tom spent with his father enabled Mrs Mason to go out and enjoy activities she had not had time for since before Tom's birth, so great had been her involvement with the children.

After three weeks of increased interaction with his father, there was a slight drop in the amount of time Tom was dressing up, from 33% to 23% of his waking time. This reduction was most noticeable at weekends when Tom spent very little time dressed up (and also saw more of his father). However, the behaviour then stabilized at this level for four weeks. There had been a slight change in that Tom wore not only the petticoat when dressing up, but also one of his mother's aprons.

Stage 2

At no time had the target behaviour (dressing up in female clothing) been addressed directly. In view of the improvement in Tom's relationship with his father and the plateau in incidence of dressing up, it was decided to tell Tom to take off the petticoat (or apron) at certain times. He would be asked not to dress up when involved in other play activities, watching TV, reading with his parents and so on, in the same way as when he was taken out. Mrs Mason would ask the play-group leaders to adopt the same approach. If Tom did not take off his dressing-up clothes, the activity would be refused. (In practice this never happened.)

This part of the intervention followed the techniques of a DRO programme (differential reinforcement of other behaviours) (Murphy, 1980). Thus, the 'other' behaviour (not dressing up) was reinforced by enjoyable activities (being read to, watching TV and so on). Concurrently, reinforcement for dressing up was withdrawn.

Outcome

There followed a rapid reduction in the amount of time Tom spent dressing up. After two weeks Tom was wearing the petticoat or apron only once or twice a day when playing imaginary games. Similarly at play-group he dressed up only at times when the other children were doing so. There was a generalization of this more appropriate behaviour to other areas and Tom no longer asked to be called by a girl's name. He asked for toys usually associated with boys of his age, but continued to play with 'girl's' toys as well.

Unfortunately, as Tom's behaviour changed his parents were less motivated to complete behavioural charts and a precise record of his behaviour is not available for this stage of the intervention. The only indicator of outcome is parental report. However, they have reported that the change in Tom's behaviour has been maintained at three- and 12-month follow up. Tom still enjoys dressing up to play imaginary games at home and plays with some 'girl's' toys, but he no longer stands out from his peer group and has maintained a good relationship with his father.

Discussion

Prior to the second stage of the intervention there had been a reluctance on the part of Tom's parents, play-group leaders, the health visitor and the psychologist to ask Tom to stop wearing the petticoat or apron. Goldiamond (1974) has suggested that reinforcement of alternative adaptive behaviour — in Tom's case contact with his father and not dressing up — is more effective than focusing on the maladaptive behaviour as with extinction or punishment techniques. Punishment or extinction techniques used in isolation could have had a side effect of increasing other inappropriate activities in place of dressing up and could have deprived Tom of sources of reinforcement such as contact with his parents or play activities. In the event the change in Tom's behaviour was brought about by an increase in reinforcement which came from both his parents instead of just his mother as previously.

The other point to consider is whether *any* intervention should have taken place. As sex-role stereotypes are increasingly challenged, and questions are raised about child rearing practices which impose these roles at an early age (Oakley, 1982, Sharpe, 1976) it may be argued that Tom was not behaving inappropriately. However, studies quoted by Green (1985) suggest that distinctive play patterns for girls and boys have emerged by the age of 3 or 4 years, and failure to adopt these can be a precursor of later homosexuality. Although homosexuals are increasingly accepted by and integrated into contemporary society, such orientation is likely to be a disadvantage in a predominantly heterosexual culture. In addition, Tom's behaviour was isolating him from other children and seemed to reflect an over-close relationship with his mother at the expense of contact with his father. The important contribution fathers can make to the upbringing of children has been described by Lewis (1986). Providing the opportunity for a close relationship between Tom and his father within which appropriate sex-role modelling could occur was an integral part of the intervention.

14 Keith: the custard pie phobic

Introduction

Childhood fears are very common, so common that it has been said that 'adults seem to minimize the importance of children's fears, viewing them as common and transitory and thus not particularly serious parts of normal development' (Graziano *et al.*, 1979). Judged by self-report on Fear Survey Schedules, Ollendick *et al.* (1985) found that boys aged 7 to 18 years reported an average of eight fears and girls an average of 16 fears.

Fears which intrude on the child's everyday life to a great extent are much rarer. Only 16 handicapping phobias were identified among 2199 children studied in the Isle of Wight epidemiological studies (Rutter *et al.*, 1970). Little is known about what determines whether a mildly inconvenient fear develops into a handicapping phobia. There are different views regarding how to treat such phobias. The case to be described here illustrates how an apparently simple, circumscribed phobia can affect a child's whole life, and how the problem was treated.

Presenting problem

Keith was 11 when referred by his general practitioner to the clinical psychology department. The GP reported that Keith had a fear of custard pies and circuses, and that this had generalized to avoiding looking at any faces with similar substances on them, to the extent that he got upset when his mother wore make-up. Otherwise, the GP saw him as a healthy, normal, well-adjusted boy.

At the first interview, the extent of Keith's distress was quickly apparent. He could not mention the word 'custard' and became tearful when gently pressed to pinpoint his fears. He said he felt sick and scared, as well as angry, wanting to hit somebody when confronted by the things he feared. At these times, he would cry and on occasions get hysterical. He tried to avoid situations by looking or running away, and it was several hours before he felt calm again.

While the primary fear was of custard pies and custard pie fights, he was also upset by make-up on faces, shaving cream, some masks, edible custard, trifles, crazy foam, silly-string and the words 'custard' and 'pie'. He spent much time worrying whether something might happen to upset him, and avoided any situations where he perceived himself to be at risk. Thus, he was unable to watch many children's television programmes which might include slap-stick sketches involving throwing foam around; he was very wary of going to friends' parties or pantomimes; he would not go to a children's holiday camp in case there was larking around involving crazy foam or going to a fun fair. Despite his elaborate precautions, he was frequently upset — for example, by seeing glue on boys' faces in a serious drama on glue-sniffing or by a newspaper photograph of Prince Charles indulging in Goonish antics.

Keith's mother reported that the problem had started when he was taken to a circus at the age of 3. He had become extremely distressed by the clown act which had involved the throwing of custard pies. Subsequently, he refused to go to circuses. From then until referral, his fears had gradually generalized. Keith himself did not think that things had got very much worse over the preceding two years, but having newly transferred to secondary school, he was increasingly anxious about what his friends would think. He was also scared they might taunt him.

Otherwise, the history given by Keith's mother confirmed the GP's impression. Keith was the middle of three children. His father was a successful businessman and his mother had a part-time clerical job in addition to running the home. His junior school described him as a high achiever, successful and popular with his peers. In secondary school, he participated actively in rugby, soccer, judo, swimming and scouts. Apart from his mother, no other family member was reported to have many fears.

Assessment

Although there seemed to be evidence of a clear, traumatic event — being frightened by the clowns — which gave rise to Keith's fears, a number of other aspects complicated the picture. It was not entirely clear whether it was the covering of the face or some other aspect which caused most distress. Keith was reported by his mother to be unduly fastidious and avoided getting dirty. He was the only boy who would play a hard game of rugby and still come off the playing field looking as pristine as a Persil advert. He reported being upset by violence — was it the clown's apparent violence rather than the custard pies that worried him? His mother was scared by many things. To what extent had he modelled his behaviour on her? The whole family were now controlled by his fears: their viewing habits were restricted, custard and trifles could only be prepared when Keith was out. To what extent did their reactions reinforce his maladaptive behaviour?

To help clarify these issues, Keith and his mother both completed lengthy fear survey schedules designed by the psychologists. Out of 45 almost identically worded items, mother and son gave concordant responses (i.e. both high or both low rated) on 33 (Chi = 12.6, df = 1, P < 0.001). The items on which both gave high ratings of fear included death, people with deformities, having an operation, airplanes, darkness, enclosed spaces, snakes, public speaking, failure, fighting, anger, arguing, teasing, separation.

Keith completed the Junior Eysenck Personality Questionnaire (Eysenck and Eysenck, 1975) which indicated that he was quite introverted and very conscious of what others thought about him.

Both to explore further the stimulus conditions giving rise to his fear and to provide a possible baseline against which to measure treatment outcome, Keith was asked to rate his personal discomfort from 1 (OK) to 10 (most upsetting) on seeing 12 pictures which depicted people of all ages varying in the degree to which their faces were covered by various substances. These included a woman whose face was half-shadowed by her hat, Robert Morley with very bushy eyebrows, and a clown wearing make-up. The before and after ratings can be seen in Table 14.1.

Table 14.1 Ratings of pictures

Picture	Before intervention	After intervention
Meter maid	1	1
Old woman with wrinkled skin	5	1
Topol (bearded)	4	1
Model with shadowed face	7	1
Black person with spectacles	1	1
Grandfather	1	1
Clown	9	5
Philipino woman	1	1
Robert Morley (eyebrows)	3	1
Model with face pack	10	5
Boy with eye patch	6	2
Black dancer	8	2

Key to rating scale: 1 = OK; 10 = most upsetting

The *ad hoc* picture rating scale provided evidence that Keith could make finer discriminations about face coverings than had been evident in interview. However, it remained clear that his greatest fears involved a combination of throwing things, messy material and covering of the face.

Selection of intervention

In view of the shared fears between son and mother, and of Windheuser's (1977) work on treating mothers' fears in front of children to act as coping models for the children, working in this way was considered. It was decided against because Keith exhibited such extreme anxiety during baseline assessment. It was feared that, if treatment for his mother's fears was started, he would refuse to come back for treatment himself.

A major issue is how to confront the feared object or situation. Although Graziano *et al.* (1979) argued that modelling was the most effective treatment, Morris and Kratochwill (1983) pointed out that most studies using modelling were of relatively minor fears and they recommend the use of systematic desensitization. Marks (1981) argues that exposure to the feared object is the critical feature in treating adult phobias and so recommends flooding, but this has rarely been used with children. The authors agree with Yule *et al.* (1974) in believing that flooding should only be used with children after systematic desensitization has failed.

In systematic desensitization the psychologist establishes one or more hierarchies, getting the client to rank situations from the least feared to the most feared. Separately, the child is taught to relax at will. This can be achieved in a number of ways. The preference in this case was to ask Keith what he did to relax and to build on that. Alternatively, children can be shown the difference between being tense and being relaxed by clenching a fist then letting go and noticing the difference. In practice, the psychologist pairs the command, 'Relax!' with the child's breathing out. Indeed, good breath control is an important aspect of relaxation training. Children are instructed to practise relaxation daily between sessions. Once they can relax at will they are introduced to the lowest ranked (least feared) item on the hierarchy. They are told that it is impossible to be both afraid and relaxed at the same time, hence the reason to teach them techniques of self-control to counter feelings of fear. The presentation of feared items can be done in real life (*in vivo*) or by getting the child to imagine the scene (imaginal desensitization). Which technique is chosen depends on what the child can tolerate, how well the child can imagine scenes and how easy it is to arrange for real life exposure. The child is assured that if he or she feels anxious, that part of the session is terminated for a few minutes until he or she is fully relaxed again.

Description of intervention

Sessions were approximately one hour long and each began with a discussion of whether Keith had managed to practise relaxation, and what had happened in the interval between sessions. He required constant reassurance that treatment would not move too quickly. Sessions were scheduled for one or two weeks apart. It was decided to combine methods of imaginal desensitization with *in vivo* work. The first part of each session concentrated on imaginal desensitization.

A hierarchy of feared situations was elicited from Keith using a forced choice ranking paradigm. This was necessary because, left to himself, he categorized items as either fear-free or totally unmanageable. The hierarchy is seen in Table 14.2

Table 14.2 Keith's hierarchy of fears (1 = most frightening)

1. Someone throwing custard pie at K's face and it hitting
2. Someone throwing crazy foam at K's face and it hitting
3. Someone throwing custard pie at K's shoulder and it hitting
4. Someone throwing crazy foam at K's shoulder and it hitting
5. Squirting crazy foam at the cat
6. Seeing a custard pie being thrown at someone else
7. Seeing crazy foam being squirted at someone else
8. Seeing a film of a custard pie being thrown at someone else
9. Watching 'Game for a Laugh'
10. Seeing a photograph of a custard pie being thrown at somebody
11. Squirting crazy foam on the table
12. Going to a circus where there are no clowns
13. Sitting in a circus tent where there will be no clowns
14. Watching a comedy programme on television
15. Someone throwing water at K
16. Throwing water at the cat under the car
17. K pouring water
18. Throwing water on the grass
19. Squirting a fly spray can
20. Squirting some Pledge on the table
21. Sitting at home and reading

Keith was introduced to the idea that it is impossible to be relaxed and afraid simultaneously, and he quickly learned to relax. He was asked to imagine a 'safe' scene at home while relaxing. The psychologist then described a scene from the hierarchy and Keith had to give further details, such as the expression on a participant's face, as a way of checking that he was visualizing the scene. As more difficult items were presented, so it became necessary to present scenes several times before Keith could imagine them. He was required to visualize each scene for several minutes until he reported feeling 'fine'.

Within six sessions, Keith was able to visualize items 21 to 8 on the hierarchy. He blocked at imagining seeing crazy foam being thrown at someone else. It was necessary to spend two sessions on this item alone, getting him to elaborate details.

He imagined a young boy throwing the foam at an older man. Both characters were smiling, but Keith was sure that the older man was angry underneath. He had to be repeatedly asked to 'see' that the foam really did touch the man's face, and he eventually imagined that the foam covered the ear and part of the side of the man's face.

The second part of each session involved some *in vivo* work. Keith was too scared initially to contemplate facing any of the feared situations and the hierarchy of activities was developed by the psychologists rather than elicited from Keith. In part, this aspect of the treatment grew out of the behavioural assessment and in part from the psychologists' feeling that Keith needed to confront his fears within a safe setting.

In the second session, Keith agreed to let the psychologist squirt a can of air freshener and then did it himself. This was seen as a first step on the hierarchy towards squirting crazy foam. Next, Keith was asked to squirt the air freshener at his own reflection in a mirror. This permitted him to see his reflection getting covered without it happening to his own face. He then squirted the can on a wooden doll. He placed detergent bubbles on his own hands, but became upset when the psychologist placed some bubbles on the psychologist's face.

No *in vivo* work was undertaken during sessions three and four. In session five, the psychologist produced a can of silly string and squirted some on the floor outside the treatment room. Keith held the can at arm's length and likewise squirted some outside the room without undue reaction. He was praised for his bravery. During session six, he repeated this action and also sprayed the string on to a plate. It quickly dries to a solid consistency, and Keith touched it. The psychologist discussed the consistency of the material with him, trying to get him to look at the substance more objectively. Then the psychologist produced an aerosol can of artificial snow which is not as thick as crazy foam and which dissolves quite quickly. Keith sprayed a mound of snow on a plate.

In session seven, Keith again squirted a mound of snow onto a paper plate. The psychologist casually touched the snow, rubbing it between his fingers and watching it dissolve. Keith copied this action without being asked. Another aerosol of yellow-coloured crazy foam was produced and, although visually nervous, Keith squirted a mound onto a plate.

In the final session, Keith again squirted foam onto the plate, piling it up to look like custard pies used in slap-stick comedy. Both Keith and the psychologist handled the foam freely.

Keith's mother was invited to sit in on the sessions from session five onwards. In the last two sessions, she spontaneously joined in the touching and talking about 'snow' and foam.

Outcome

Evaluation depended on two main sources — Keith's subjective reports and observations of him during the sessions. He reported that in real life when he had to face something which produced intense fear, his fear habituated more quickly. Initially, it took several hours to clear his mind of the image; by the end of treatment he said it took nearer to 20 minutes. Within the sessions, he was able to visualize increasingly difficult scenes, including the details of foam being thrown in a man's face. Initially, he simply blocked on this scene. He was able to confront a plate of custard foam during the session and tolerated the psychologist and his mother using the words custard and foam freely. His mother confirmed that things were better at home, but no other measures were taken of his behaviour outside the clinic setting.

Table 14.1 shows some indirect evidence for therapeutic improvement. After the eight sessions, Keith was again asked to rate the 12 pictures on the ten-point scale. The average fear rating fell from 4.66 at baseline to 1.83 after treatment, a significant drop (Wilcoxon's $T = 0$, $N = 8$, $P = 0.01$).

By mutual consent, it was agreed to stop the sessions after the eighth, even though Keith had not reached the final items on the hierarchy. He reported feeling much more confident in facing the perceived threats of exposure to crazy foam or custard pies at friends' houses, parties and elsewhere. It was clear that he was never going to be the sort of boy who would initiate or even willingly participate in actual pie throwing contests and so it was judged unnecessary to test him to the limit.

In all, treatment took about ten hours of direct contact time, with about half as much again in preparation time. At follow-up, four months after the last treatment session, progress had been maintained. Keith had coped well with his first year of secondary schooling and with a move of house. He was looking forward to trips abroad with the school. He still avoided some situations where slap-stick might occur, but such avoidance was not interfering with a very full life. His mother was able to wear make-up without comment from her son.

Discussion

There is scarcely an object or situation which someone, somewhere, does not fear. When the reaction is of phobic intensity, even fears as apparently ludicrous as the fear of custard pies, can have serious impact on a child's life. In Keith's case, his social life was greatly restricted, both at home and outside. He was so afraid that it was initially difficult to obtain clear evidence for the most important dimensions of the fears, or even to get him to grade his reactions to different situations. Thus, the broad-based evaluation continued into treatment, resulting in a somewhat messy combination of imaginal desensitization, *in vivo* desensitization, modelling and the involvement of the mother.

A number of issues are highlighted in this case. First, how can the psychologist be sure that there were real changes in the boy's behaviour? The speed with which the hierarchy was gone through, his behaviour in confronting plates of crazy foam, his ratings of the pictures and his subjective reports do point in the direction of improvement. Should physiological measures have been taken, and if so, which ones? In the end, the views of the patient and his family have to have primacy.

Second, the formulation raised the question of the interrelationships of Keith's concern about aggression and his fastidiousness. His mother commented increasingly on the latter during the last few sessions. Initially, his fear of mud was interpreted as a specific instance of fear of substances on the skin. The relationship between fastidiousness, aggression and phobia was not explored any further, partly because the data did not fully emerge until treatment was underway.

Third, it was not clear how best to involve his mother during treatment. Mother and son shared many more fears in common than expected by chance, in keeping with Windheuser's (1977) hypothesis. However, not only were Keith's fears so intense that it was feared he would cease cooperating if work began with his mother's fears, but also she denied that any of her own fears were handicapping. Even so, it was necessary to help her reinforce Keith's progress during treatment as otherwise she tended to ignore progress and report current problems.

Although systematic desensitization has a long history in the treatment of children's phobias (Miller *et al.*, 1974; Graziano *et al.*, 1979) there is a dearth of literature teasing out the crucial elements or suggesting better ways of monitoring progress. Until larger scale studies of the sort reported with adult patients are undertaken, therapists working with children will have to continue to adopt procedures showing as much ingenuity as possible.

15 Christopher: support for a dying child and his family

Background

Christopher (his real name is used at his parents' request) was 5 when he first came to hospital. The diagnosis was neuroblastoma stage IV, a particularly nasty form of cancer with a bleak outlook. Treatment consisted of chemotherapy and irradiation involving the well-known side effects of nausea, lassitude and hair loss.

One facet of supportive work is described in this case but much else went on. The philosophy of the haematology/oncology unit at Christopher's hospital is one of team work, with medical and nursing staff joining with social workers, play leaders, teachers, the hospital chaplain and a psychologist to offer psychosocial care alongside medical attention. An essential characteristic of the team is the aim to achieve easy communication between all the members, an aim which is greatly helped by a weekly psychosocial ward round, when staff have an opportunity to meet, to exchange information and to plan future work.

In the last few years the team has come to realize the importance not only of communicating with each other but also of communicating with the children. In order to do this the professionals involved need to have some notion of the children's level of understanding, in the case of Christopher an understanding of both death and illness.

Christopher's father asked if he could see a psychologist because he wanted to know how best to talk to his son. Accordingly the psychologist met both parents and Christopher, and after several sessions spent getting to know him, when all sorts of things were talked about, he was questioned one afternoon on the subject of his disease and of death.

The development of the concept of death in children is now well documented (Lansdown and Benjamin, 1985). It is clear that it is not a unitary all-or-nothing concept; you do not go to bed one night without it and wake up next morning with it: rather it is made up of a number of components which accrue gradually (Kane, 1979).

Most 3-year-olds have some idea of the difference between living and dead, but they are likely at that age to be hazy about many components. The 4-year-old George Sand, for example, displayed an ignorance of permanence when, the day after being told that her father had been killed in a riding accident, she asked 'Is daddy still dead today?' Children sometimes express anxiety that a person just buried will be bored with no books or toys in the coffin. They may assert that only old people die or that the dead can return. One child said to her parents that she wanted to go to God for just one day to find out what she had done that was so wicked that she was being punished.

Assessment

To find out more about Christopher's understanding of death he was given some puzzles, including a vocabulary test. Among the words was the word 'dead' which he defined as 'not living any more'. Various probe questions were then asked, the answers to which indicated that he had a good grasp of causality ('illness and battles') and of universality ('everyone dies at the end of their life'). Most interesting were his responses to questions on the afterlife (his family are practising Roman Catholics). When you die, he said, you go to heaven where there is more life. And yes, people who have died can come back, 'a little bit of heaven floats down to earth and the people can see us but we can't see them; they are invisible.'

So far so good. But equally important if one is to communicate with children about their own death through illness is some understanding of their concept of disease and its place in a developmental sequence. The sequential steps which can be helpful as a framework are:

(1) I am very sick.
(2) I have an illness that can kill.
(3) I have an illness that can kill children.
(4) I am dying.

When Christopher was asked when he was going to die he answered, in a voice that suggested he was surprised at such a silly question 'at the end of my life'. Readers who think it strange to ask a 5-year-old with cancer when he is going to die can be reassured: not only did Christopher know the psychologist quite well by this time, but also children are much more matter-of-fact than we sometimes think they will be.

Further questioning yielded the information that he thought he would probably be killed in a war since he was planning to join the RAF. He discussed his disease almost entirely in terms of the unpleasantness of what was done to him during treatment.

The conclusion to be drawn from this conversation was that Christopher had a pretty good idea of what death was all about but that he was not, at this stage, associating his disease with his death. Those concerned could take their cue from this; Christopher was prepared by staff and parents for the next steps in his treatment, he was able to talk easily about his condition but there was no direct focus on his death.

Outcome

Time passed and he had long spells as an out-patient but also some time on the ward again. He remained alert and aware and it was thought likely that he had moved to a further stage of concepts about the implications of his illness. Accordingly the psychologist saw him again for another semi-structured interview. This time there was ample evidence that he had moved on in his thinking about his illness. He had, he explained, developed another tumour behind his eye. With only a little prompting he went on to say that he thought that one tumour was enough, two tumours were too many. Fortunately he had had radiation and the second tumour had gone down. Had it not, 'I would have got so poorly I might have died.'

It was possible to put this realization of his understanding alongside another general finding, that young children's greatest anxiety around the time of death is related to separation. This point was well illustrated by another boy with neuroblastoma. A few days before his death, at the age of 5, he told his mother he did not want to be an angel. He also said that he did not like going to sleep because he had bad dreams. He explained that he dreamt that he was dead and this was upsetting: 'I shall miss you and daddy.'

Discussion

As Christopher's condition deteriorated his parents were able to consider the final months of his life and to plan for his death. The aim of help at this time is to achieve a good death, not only for the sake of the patient but also for those who survive. The memory of a person's last few days takes on a special significance; what happens at this period is unalterable. What is more, many parents feel de-skilled in hospitals since they are no longer primarily responsible for their children. Once the last stage has been reached parents are back in their old place, but with such a difference. They remain as parents but need massive support in this variation of their role.

Christopher's parents and the psychologist talked of the importance of separation for a 6-year-old and it was arranged that he would die at home. (All parents in the unit are given the choice of home or hospital.) Apart from other considerations there was a near certainty that at home there could always be a familiar person with him. Also discussed was the need to maintain communication at several different levels, with the power of the non-verbal exchange being emphasized. Because of the openness that had been established already, because Christopher knew that his parents knew that he was aware of the likely outcome of his condition, there could be an extra meaning in the everyday hug or squeeze of the hand. Because they had heard him speak of heaven as a place where there is more life, they could share something of his anticipations.

Not that his experience was trouble-free. His parents tuned into his drawings and the stories he told as well. Once he offered an illustrated story about a ship in rough seas that was being attacked by sharks. Two huge whales swam alongside and protected the little ship.

His death was good. He was last seen a few days before he died when he was in bed in the sitting room at home where visitors could come and go quite easily. He could not see or speak, but his hearing was intact and visitors and family held his hand while they spoke to him or read him a favourite story. When he had had enough he let go of the other person's hand. His parents were able to be with him constantly, reassuring him that he would not be left alone, receiving in return a squeeze of their hand from him. He died peacefully.

Increasingly attention is paid to the techniques of communicating to patients or, in paediatrics, to patients and parents. Christopher's story illustrates the need always to see this as a two-way process. Staff were able to help his parents to help him primarily by listening to what he had to say, and certainly Christopher had a great deal to tell.

16 David Adams: family therapy using a systems approach

Presenting problem and referral

Mrs Adams had been concerned about her 12-year-old son, David, for some time. She was worried by his tendency to have 'sulky tantrums' when she attempted to discipline him and also felt that he was becoming 'distant' from her. She took David to the family's general practitioner who made a referral to the clinical psychologist at a Child and Family Centre. In his referral letter the GP reported on the presenting difficulty and also mentioned that Mr Adams was a building worker. David was the only child of the marriage.

Assessment interview

As is customary at the Child and Family Centre, an appointment letter was sent requesting that all family members attend. Mr and Mrs Adams and David duly arrived for their appointment.

The initial interview followed the four phases of a family interview as outlined by Haley (1976). Following the social phase when the family were met and introduced to the therapy situation, the psychologist moved on to the problem phase, in which each family member was asked to give their view of the problem. Mrs Adams gave the fullest account, focusing on David's difficult sulkiness and his distance from her. This was described with smiles and many giggly glances at David. At various points during her report Mrs Adams indicated that she believed that her husband 'did not do enough' with David. Mr Adams was quite willing to let his wife outline the difficulties and, when questioned directly, referred to his wife's account of the problems with his son. He readily admitted his own failings in a very passive, resigned manner. David was unable to give any reasonable account of what happened except that he 'got angry and fed up sometimes'. He presented as a boy who was somewhat immature for his age and when asked a question David always looked initially at his mother.

During this phase, the psychologist also questioned the family about the sequence of events which characterized the problem. Mrs Adams admitted that often the problem began with her being concerned and irritable at David's being distant. She then told him off about some minor misdemeanour and David would become angry at this and sulkily withdraw to his bedroom. Mrs Adams then told her husband that 'something would have to be done' about David. Mr Adams did not know what to do: on some occasions he would try to jolly David out of his sulk, while on others he would talk to David about other things. He never told David off for anything that might have happened earlier in the day. Eventually David 'settled down' and Mrs Adams felt that the problem had passed until the next time.

Further information gained during this part of the interview focused on other aspects of the family's activity. Mr Adams spent a lot of time working and often had a drink on the way home. Mrs Adams often organized trips for herself and David and these never involved Mr Adams.

The third stage of the initial interview is the interaction stage during which the therapist invites the family to talk to each other about their difficulties so that the therapist can gain an appreciation of the family's principal interactive patterns. When the Adams family interacted it was evident that Mrs Adams was quite dominant; she did most of the talking and directed what should happen. Mr Adams did not make any original contributions to their discussion; he tended to agree with whatever his wife said. At one point it appeared that Mr Adams had a different view of some event from his wife's. However, she rapidly reiterated her point and her husband made no attempt to argue his point further. At various times during the interaction Mrs Adams involved David on her side in the discussion and he often made spontaneous interjections into his parents' conversation. Once it appeared as if mother and son were having an adult discussion with father just sitting and watching.

During this phase of the interview Mrs Adams made several attempts to include the psychologist in the family interaction. She did this in a way which sought approval and agreement for her view about David's difficult behaviour and her husband's lack of involvement. The attempt to involve the therapist in the family system is a variety of triangulation, which is a process of relating to a third person in such a way that the emotional intensity is reduced between any two individuals or group of individuals. Street (1985) has listed the common varieties of triangulation that are found with child-focused problems. The variety that the Adams family were offering was based on the psychologist dealing principally with the husband rather than with the problems of the family as a whole or the couple in particular.

It was clear that this family did not feel threatened if the psychologist took on a role of someone who was closely allied to mother and critical of father. This role, if readily accepted by the psychologist, would represent a position from which it would be very difficult to embark on a change process. Therefore, the psychologist had to avoid adopting this role.

Before the fourth stage of this initial interview is described, it is necessary to look at the picture presented by the family so far.

Formulation of the problem

As the family is a system that operates through interactive sequences, it was now possible to construct a simple diagram of the Adams family interactive pattern.

Figure 16.1 demonstrates the circular nature of causality in the family system. No one piece of behaviour is the direct cause of another, but all behaviours are causally linked by the self-regulating character of the system. Adopting a systems approach enables the therapist to avoid blaming individuals while at the same time acknowledging that every participant contributes to the process.

It was then possible to develop from this a view of the family's structure. Minuchin (1974) has defined family structure as 'an invisible set of functional demands that organise the ways in which family members interact'. He has provided a number of concepts for describing the outcome of these functional demands. The Adams family presented with a weak generational boundary in which David's role was elevated, on occasions, almost to that of an adult.

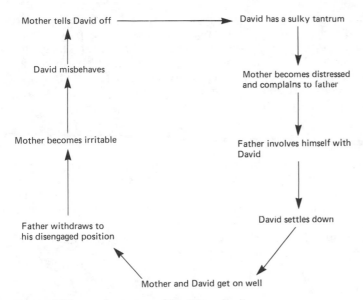

Figure 16.1 Interactive pattern of the Adams family

Consequently, the boundary around the spouse subsystem was not clear. Mr Adams's position was disengaged from the centre of the family's functioning, as demonstrated by his peripheral activity. Such a structure would indicate that the function of the symptom (David's difficult behaviour) was to involve the father in some aspect of the family's interaction. However, the complementary nature of the system's interaction also meant that the boy and the mother behaved in ways that kept the father peripheral. Obviously the developmental stage that David was entering would have a considerable bearing on the problem, for his emerging adolescence would result in his making some moves to be more independent from his parents. This developmentally appropriate behaviour might threaten both parents for it would disturb the balance of relationships that had developed over his younger years.

The implication of this formulation was that the boundary between the generations needed to be strengthened and the father needed to be brought more into the central area of the family's functioning. In attempting to deal with the second of these implications, the psychologist saw the danger that simply telling Mr Adams that he was not involved enough would place the responsibility for change on him. This would merely confirm the existing pattern of interaction in the family and was not an appropriate intervention.

The intervention strategy

After gaining the information and arriving at the initial formulation the psychologist was able to construct an intervention strategy.

Intervention within sessions

Throughout all sessions the psychologist encouraged those interactions in which Mr Adams was just as central as his wife. This was done by asking questions and opinions of the family and by the way the psychologist interacted, both verbally and non-verbally. For example, when Mrs Adams apparently wished the psychologist to criticize her husband, the psychologist would then turn to the husband to ask his opinion directly. Additionally, Mr Adams was given the responsibility for telling David off when he inappropriately interrupted the conversation. These interactive interventions naturally varied in style and strength, depending on the nature of the topic and the intensity of emotion involved.

Interventions outside sessions

During the fourth stage of the first session, the goal-setting stage, the psychologist set a homework task for the family. Mrs Adams was given the responsibility of keeping a daily diary of David's behaviour and of reporting this to her husband regardless of whether David had misbehaved. If David misbehaved the parents would jointly decide what action they should take with him. This task met the requirements of strengthening the parental subsystem by involving the father and sharing the responsibility.

Intervention

Session 2

Three weeks later the family returned, reporting that there had been no problems with David and therefore no diary had been kept and the parental discussions had not taken place. Even though the family were still interacting in the identical manner, they queried whether there was any need for further work as the problem had 'gone away'. Since many things in the family presented as similar to the first interview, the psychologist construed this change in David as merely 'first order' change: that is, there had been a change but the system itself remained unchanged. A 'second order' change (Watzlawick *et al.*, 1974) was required: that is, an alteration in behaviour, the occurrence of which changes the system itself. David's behavioural change could be conceived as a homeostatic mechanism designed to maintain the family system's usual way of functioning. The psychologist dealt with this by entering into an alliance with David against the parents, telling him that his parents needed to be 'tested' and the psychologist needed David's help to test them. He was told to be naughty so that his parents could have some practice in dealing with the matter as the psychologist wished. This intervention maintained the generational boundary even though the psychologist adopted a clear position within the family, a position which could only be transitional in respect of the overall aims of the therapy. David seemed quite pleased to be recruited in this way, particularly as the psychologist suggested some activities which were age-appropriate but which Mrs Adams had labelled as 'naughty' and 'distant', such as playing football on the way home from school.

Session 3

The family reported that David had indeed misbehaved and there had been some attempts to tackle the problem jointly by both parents. There had been some successes and some failures which were discussed openly. The psychologist reinforced the successes within the context of the same intervention strategy. The family were asked to continue with the same tasks.

Session 4

The family, through the mother, reported that the problem of David's 'distance' had increased. It was evident that the parents had argued about some aspect of David's management and that the issue had not been resolved. During the course of the session it became evident that this argument masked another conflict between husband and wife. The couple had in the past encountered financial difficulties and Mrs Adams now attempted to fully control the family's purse-strings. Mr Adams did not like this, but had not been able to confront his wife. He frequently asked his boss for 'subs' from his wages so that he did not receive a complete wage packet at the end of the week. When this occurred it was noticeable that father would be told off (just like David) and (again, just like the boy) he would withdraw. This marital interactive sequence now indicated that the original symptom served another function, for it was a means of reducing the tension between the parents as it diverted the conflict through their son. As the marital issue of unexpressed and unresolved conflict was now clearly to the fore, the psychologist suggested that a marital session was necessary and the couple agreed. They were asked to maintain the same parental tasks with David.

Sessions 5 and 6

In these sessions the psychologist worked from the premise that Mrs Adams, by dominating, acted like a parent to her husband, and Mr Adams, by his withdrawal and acquiescence, acted like a naughty boy. Some tasks were constructed so that they could take joint decisions about their financial arrangements. Additionally, issues relating to their respective relationships with their families of origin were discussed. At these sessions the parents reported on their success in bringing about a change in their way of handling David. These sessions, by their very nature, strengthened the marital subsystem and maintained the appropriate generational boundary.

Session 7

A follow-up appointment was held for all the family when it appeared from their report and their interaction that they were functioning adequately.

Discussion

This case highlights how all family members are involved in the problems that beset one of them. In particular, it can be seen that the marital subsystem provides the fulcrum on which the functioning of the family pivots. By adopting a family systems perspective the psychologist was able to move freely, adopting differing positions vis-à-vis family members. This was necessary in order to avoid the dangers of dealing with one person as the one at fault. Each intervention set a problem for the family to solve and its solution led to an elaboration of the psychologist's hypothesis of how the family functioned. By being an integral part of this active elaboration the psychologist was then able to direct and join the different ways of interacting between family members. The Adams family were faced with typical difficulties that can confront any family. Their usual ways of functioning prevented the construction of effective solutions and family therapy served to establish a different system of functioning which allowed them to tackle the problems of life more effectively.

17   Preparing children for painful hospital procedures: action research

Introduction

This research study looks at methods of reducing the stress on children induced by one aspect of 'high-tech' nuclear medicine — invasive radiological procedures. The setting is a Special Health Authority postgraduate teaching hospital for children. The features that contribute to the eminence of such a hospital can also affect the welfare of children: high technology, a hierarchical structure and high status given to diagnostic research. A clinical psychologist in this setting aims to engage with others to find ways to minimize children's and parents' distress; to facilitate more active participation of patients in medical procedures and decisions; and to use methods of monitoring and evaluation which enhance participation in these innovative procedures.

Invasive radiological diagnostic tests are common procedures for children with renal disorders. Children who were in-patients from the renal unit and who were going to have a specific radio-isotope kidney scan were selected for study. This examination involves the injection of radioactivity tagged isotope, usually into a vein in the arm, followed at two later periods in the day by the scans. Children lie in fixed positions for 20 minutes or so on a raised platform while pictures are taken with a gamma camera from underneath. There is an array of sophisticated equipment, lights, monitors and machinery in the imaging room.

The aims of this study were:

(1) to learn more about the children's reaction to and experience of stressful radiological procedures and to investigate individual differences;
(2) to explore how best to prepare children and their parents and to investigate any particular methods for certain groups of children;
(3) to help promote more child-centred practices in the X-ray department. It was hoped that, when staff from different disciplines learned together about children's reactions and discussed preparation methods, psychological sensitivity and sophistication would be enhanced, waiting time for children would be reduced and communication between X-ray and ward staff aided. Only a small part of the total study is described here.

Description of the study

An action research methodology for evaluation was decided on. Action research is usually undertaken in a clinical or natural setting, involves the introduction of a new procedure, is sensitive to current service needs and is intended to be clinically relevant and immediately applicable. It therefore does not usually utilize experimental methods like randomization of cases to treatments. In this case, the random allocation of children into preparation and control groups was seen as neither feasible nor desirable.

Prior preparation of children for hospital and medical procedures has been shown in other studies to be beneficial (Rodin, 1983; Eiser, 1984). The aims of preparation were to provide information to the child and parent, encourage emotional expression, aid the development of coping strategies and establish a trusting relationship with staff. The aim was not to assuage all anxiety as a moderate amount of anticipatory fear about realistic stress can aid mental rehearsal. Melamed (1977) describes this protective, adaptive process as 'the work of worrying'.

Preparation took the following form. The play leader discussed with the parents the issue of preparation and how best to help their child. With parent's consent, the play leader accompanied the child and parent to the X-ray department the afternoon before the day of the test. A radiographer showed the room where the test would be carried out, the equipment to be used, sometimes actively involving the child in a demonstration of how it moved or sounded and outlined what would happen including telling the child about the injection if the parent had agreed to this. The radiographer answered a child or parent's questions and suggested what they could do to help. On return to the ward the play leader allowed the child to worry and maybe to cry, but combined this with developing distraction techniques or coping strategies with the child and parent. A nurse was encouraged to support both the child and parent during the night if required. It was agreed that as many children as the staff could allow time for would be prepared in the general way described but methods would be individually tailored to adapt to the child's age and temperament based on discussions between parent, play leader and radiographer.

The child's behaviour was observed before and during the injection and subsequently during the imaging or scans by the radiographer and separately by the parent or nurse escorting the child. The parent and radiographer independently wrote down their free description of the same child's behaviour during these three discrete points in the procedure on separate forms provided. These participant observers then independently chose for each of their descriptions a rating of calm, anxious, distressed or very distressed. These were allocated 0,1,2,3, respectively to provide a quantitative distress measure. A measure of cooperation was also obtained. The observer noted whether the child was cooperative, needed physical restraint to gain cooperation or whether the procedure had to be abandoned through lack of cooperation. A score of 0,1 or 2 was allocated. This behaviour rating scale (BRS) was developed and piloted specifically for this purpose with the help of an undergraduate psychologist (Murphy, 1985).

A project meeting was held once a month. Those attending included radiographers and consultant radiologist from the X-ray department, play leader, staff nurse or sister and paediatrician from the renal unit, an undergraduate psychologist (who acted as independent observer) and the clinical psychologist. The clinical psychologist facilitated the meetings with the intention that they should be participatory, non-hierarchical forums. The direction and methods of evaluation of the project were decided here. These meetings also discussed individual children's reactions and needs, and ideas for improving preparation (often inspired by recordings of interviews with the children). Differing views were aired. In the early stages, radiographers had serious misgivings about the project, seeing it as implied criticism of their practice. There were clearly different views among the team and between disciplines about the benefit of preparation of children, particularly the wisdom of telling children in advance about the injection.

Results

Every child of 18 months or over on the renal unit having this particular radio isotope examination was observed by a parent, radiographer and ward staff over a 12-month period. There were 20 girls and 38 boys. Forty-one children had some preparation. Eighteen children were interviewed within 24 hours of their examination. Of all 51 children observed, 21 were rated as very distressed at some point during the procedure by either a parent or a radiographer. Eighteen children were observed to be calm throughout the procedure by both parent and radiographer. Ten children in both the very distressed and calm group had been prepared the day before for the test and the injection (50% and 55% respectively). Thus the preparation experience had a negligible effect on the extremes of children's manifest distress. The younger the child the more distress was observed; 78% of all children under 6 were seen as very distressed at some point. This compares with 36% of the total group. Pearson correlation co-efficients of -0.30 and -0.40, significant at more than the 1% level, were obtained for age correlated with total distress ratings made by parents and radiographers respectively.

The effect of preparation was examined by comparing the observations on the 18 children aged 6 and over who had been prepared for the procedure and the injection the day before with the observations on the ten children in this age range who had not been given the opportunity for preparation. Children under 6 were excluded from this comparison because of the age/distress effect which had been established, and the facts that young children were over-represented in the prepared group and the preparation experience of the young age group was quite varied. The parent and radiographer observations for children aged 6 and over are shown in Table 17.1. (There are more radiographer observations than parent observations as a few children were observed by radiographers only).

Table 17.1 Observations in X-ray of prepared and unprepared children aged 6 and over

	Before the injection		During the injection		During the scans	
	Prepared	Not prepared	Prepared	Not prepared	Prepared	Not prepared
Parents' ratings	n = 15 (%)	n = 9 (%)	n = 15 (%)	n = 9 (%)	n = 16 (%)	n = 9 (%)
Calm	7 46	3 33	7 46	3 33	15 94	7 78
Anxious	6 40	6 66	4 27	4 44	1 6	2 22
Distressed	0 0	0 0	0 0	2 22	0 0	0 0
Very distressed	2 13	0 0	4 27	0 0	0 0	0 0
Cooperative			13 86	9 100	16 100	9 100
Physical restraint required			2 13	0 0	0 0	0 0
Radiographers' ratings	n = 18 (%)	n = 10 (%)	n = 17 (%)	n = 10 (%)	n = 18 (%)	n = 10 (%)
Calm	7 39	6 60	9 53	3 30	17 94	8 80
Anxious	8 44	4 40	6 35	6 60	1 6	2 20
Distressed	1 6	0 0	0 0	1 10	0 0	0 0
Very distressed	2 11	0 0	2 12	0 0	0 0	0 0
			n = 18		n = 17	
Cooperative			17 94	9 90	17 100	10 0
Physical restraint required			1 6	1 10	0 0	0 0

Inspection shows no marked difference between the groups. Numbers are small. The tendency for more of the prepared children to be seen by both parents and radiographers to be very distressed just before and during the injection did not reach statistical significance. No child of 6 or over was observed to be distressed or very distressed during the scans, and all cooperated. The tendency for parents to see their children as more distressed than the radiographers saw them, particularly during the injection procedure, did not reach statistical significance. Overall there was a high degree of agreement between parent and radiographer observations (Pearson correlation coefficient = +0.72).

There was no significant difference between the groups on rated anxiety on the ward at any of the time intervals, including during the night before the test.

These results suggest that the particular experience of being prepared or not does not contribute to a child's manifest distress to a sufficient extent to outweigh all the other factors. The result suggests that preparation does not diminish a child's cooperation with the procedure, hence the chances of obtaining a good image are not affected. So although analysis of the observational data does not indicate whether preparation is advantageous to children, it does indicate that it is not prejudicial.

Interviews

Eighteen children from the sample were interviewed by the clinical psychologist within 24 hours of their examination. By chance 14 were boys and four were girls. Sixteen were aged 6 or over. Ten had been prepared in advance for the procedure and the injection. The aim of the structured interview was to elicit the children's thoughts and feelings about their experience in the X-ray department, the preparation, personnel involved, their rationale for the procedure and their understanding of their illness.

Fifteen children aged 6 and over responded to the question, 'If you were to have a similar investigation, when would you want to know all about it? Does that include being told about the injection bit?' Table 17.2 shows that there was a unanimous verdict from the seven children who had the experience of preparation that they would like to be prepared in advance again, including being told about the injection. Five of the eight children who were not prepared also said that they wanted to know ahead of time if they were to have a similar test again. Of the 88% who wanted preparation, 50% wanted it to 'give me time to get prepared' and 33% wanted information in advance.

Table 17.2 Children's attitude to preparation

	X-ray prep	No X-ray prep	Total
Want to know all about it at least a day ahead (including the injection)	7	5	12
Not want to know until just before	0	2	2
Don't know	0	1	1
Total	7	8	15

Some examples of children's comments follow:

Fred, aged 11, prepared:

Interviewer: If you had a similar test again, when would you want to learn all about it?
Fred: As soon as they know.
Interviewer: But you were a bit frightened.
Fred: I know, but I want to know everything that is going to happen to me so I can get familiarized.

Patrick, aged 7, not prepared:

Patrick: It would have been better if I had been told about the injection a day ahead.
Interviewer: Why is that?
Patrick: So that I can think about it and try not to be so worried when it happens. If I had been to X-ray the day before I would know about the rolling over too.

Of the 16 children over age 6 interviewed, two-thirds reported some anxiety about the injection; 70% of the children said the injection hurt a little, 15% said, 'quite a bit', 8% said 'a lot' and 7% said it did not hurt at all. Eighty per cent said it was better than they expected. Ali, aged 13, commented, 'The needle is very long. It looks so wicked. It would help if it were shorter or covered up a bit. And those syringes! Seeing them makes you think it will hurt.'

It was not unusual for children to show no distress even though they rated the injection as hurting a bit or hurting a lot. There is a lack of concurrence between the child's rating of pain and the observations of distress by both radiographers and parents. The inference is that children's experience of distress or pain cannot be inferred from observations of their behaviour. For children of 6 and over, there was a nearly significant trend for boys to be observed to be less distressed than girls. However, boys were prepared to tell an interviewer that the injection hurt or that they were anxious, but, unlike a lot of the girls, they had put on a brave face at the time.

Some of the children's comments stressed their need for accurate information at different levels. Patrick, aged 7, was not prepared, but worked out his own rationale. He thought he had the test 'because the blood is sort of poisoned and they had to pump water into it'. He was the only child interviewed who had such a misguided belief, but 21% said they did not know the reason for the test and 36% had only a general idea (e.g. 'something to do with the kidneys').

The interview data leaves little doubt that children aged 6 and over wanted preparation in advance, including information about the injection. Two-thirds of children interviewed said they worried when told, but they worried anyway, but had strong convictions that they wanted to know what was going to happen to them, where, when and why (and what bits would hurt) and in good time to feel prepared.

Discussion

The first aim of the study was to learn more about children's reactions to stressful radiological procedures. The combination of using observations, interviews and team discussions aided this process. It leaves no doubt that one cannot assume a child's emotions from observing behaviour only. Invasive radiological procedures are distressing for most children. Doctors who order such tests may benefit from this awareness so that such tests are ordered only when absolutely necessary.

The second aim was to explore how best to prepare children and their parents. Analysis of observational data did not indicate whether preparation was beneficial or otherwise. However, the interview data leaves little doubt that children aged 6 and over want preparation in advance including information about the injection.

The third aim was to effect a more child-centred approach in the X-ray department. Very noticeable changes took place in the department during and following the study. It is now an attractive place for children, with play materials and a part-time volunteer play helper. A greater degree of explanation is now offered to children and parents as part of the department's policy. Preparation has come to be seen as essential rather than an optional extra service. This change has resulted from positive consumer feedback regarding preparation visits as part of this study. It is of note that the radiographers became convinced about the benefit of preparation before the results from the analysis of the observational data were available.

It is interesting to consider the methods used to stimulate and evaluate change in this action research project in a clinical setting. This study raises the question of the value of observational data. Radiographers and parents reported benefits from the *process* of developing accurate observations of children and the subsequent discussions. However, the results from the *analysis* of the observational data had a negligible bearing on the development of the project. If time had been spent interviewing more children and furthering preparation work with parents instead of coding and analysing data, it is interesting to speculate whether the project would have been enriched or would have lost some credibility without the respectability generated through the statistical analysis.

In the climate of economic constraints and emphasis on efficiency in the Health Service, coupled with increasing high technology in medicine there is a need to raise the status of the caring processes and the caring professionals. Clinical psychologists' roles can be to stimulate and evaluate research into effective patient-orientated health care delivery systems and to develop appropriate research methodologies. It is significant that the changes that have ensued as a result of this study, and have continued after formal evaluation was completed, have taken place precisely because the evaluation method enabled children and parents to be participants rather than mere objects of study, and because ideas developed through sharing ideas and team-work rather than the more arid testing of a single hypothesis through a controlled trial.

18   Steven: psychological support to a long-term social services client

The referral

Steven was referred to the social services psychology team when he was 9. His parents asked a social services area office for help with Steven, because of problems with managing him. In addition to non-compliance with their instructions, they cited evidence of withdrawal, sleep problems, soiling problems, and petty theft within the house. Steven's father thought that he was beyond control of his parents and was investigating the possibility of a care order for the child (Children and Young Persons Act 1969).

Background

Steven and his family had always lived in a financially deprived, overcrowded part of the city. His father had been married before, and the son from that marriage, described by his father and stepmother as 'no problem', now lived with them and Steven. Steven's attendance at school had been 'reasonable', but since he was 8 he had occasionally left school on his own and wandered around the streets. The school also complained of Steven's lack of concentration and motivation. They described Steven as a loner and unable to play with other children. The headmaster spoke of one occasion when Steven had been suspected of deliberately starting a fire.

His father had attempted to control Steven by corporal punishment since Steven was five. Before this time, Steven had caused no great problems, and his physical development was described as 'normal'.

Assessment

Members of the psychology team read the files and the first investigations were made in the family home, with all members present after school with the television switched off.

Steven's father gave most of the information about the problems. A structured interview was difficult to conduct. Framing the questions so that the focus was on Steven's good points, as well as his bad, was also difficult. No one in the family acted as advocate for Steven, who remained silent.

When negotiating a programme for managing the major problems, neither parent was happy about the idea of reward, praise or affection. Steven's father was not prepared to negotiate with Steven as, he said, 'We want more control over him, not less.'

Perhaps it is of interest that the father had recently lost his job, but appeared to dress as though he were still a security guard. Father himself said that he was angry about not being admitted into either the police or the armed forces. He said that he had been on several SAS training missions and had held 'the most powerful rifle in Europe'. He had received a commendation for helping the local police. He had apparently had a violent and punitive background.

Steven's mother said she felt unable to discipline Steven and left it to her husband. She realized Steven was unhappy at home and felt that the psychologist could work with him if he were in care. Both parents felt that Steven would do better in care and both felt guilty that they had not been able to provide adequate parenting for him.

Steven's brother felt that his parents' attempts should have been adequate to 'control' any child and he was, therefore, beginning to think that Steven was, indeed, different from the rest of the family. After five minutes of the first assessment interview, Steven strode out into the garden because of his disagreement with the family's account.

When the psychologist eventually joined Steven outside for a more structured interview, he was unable to speak about most of his worries. However, he gave frequent 'don't know' and 'don't care' answers. The psychologist thought Steven may have over-learnt such responses through fear of punishment for the 'wrong' answer.

Steven did not seem far off tears at any time, although his parents had said that this was his present continual state. Steven was mildly hostile about his mother and his brother, but spoke in admiring terms of his father. He felt that his father should 'make him' go to school and should 'punish him' if he didn't do as he was told. At all times, Steven seemed tense and under great stress but did not want to leave his bedroom and his home.

Other interviews followed with both parents, and with Steven separately, but no formal psychometric assessments were used at this stage.

Intervention

It is psychology team policy to challenge all referred requests for care orders (Barlow, 1982a). In spite of the problems mentioned, it was not deemed beneficial to take Steven away from those comforts he did have, nor did there seem any chance of rehabilitation once Steven had left home.

It was therefore decided, with the help and agreement of social services department colleagues and the family, that with intensive befriending and discussion, a period of specific tutoring for a behavioural programme would be instigated which would be based on extrinsic rewards for compliant behaviour. Social praise and informal, non-threatening discussions were to be used to the maximum with Steven. Evidence from their interactions was quoted to both parents to show that punishment techniques had not worked with Steven. Both Steven and parents were to be responsible for records and feedback at the end of each week. The school was to be informed of the progress.

Father was involved in a tense one-to-one discussion about the problems of care orders with special regard to subsequent feelings of guilt and possible damage to

Steven (Millham, 1986; Cornish and Clarke, 1975). It was hoped that if the family could enjoy each other's company a bit more the parents would not wish to have Steven on a care order and would perhaps plan more appropriately for his future happiness and normal cognitive development.

Outcome

Steven's father came to the social services office, saying that he could not carry on with the programme. He felt that he could not change his attitude towards Steven; the two of them had just had a fierce argument and Steven had run away from home, saying that he would never return.

The father was in tears and felt that no programme would alter his views about Steven, which seemed a mixture of guilt at not being a good father and anger at his son's extreme dissatisfaction. He was, however, not prepared to put Steven on a voluntary care order. He said that Steven's presence in the household was breaking up the family and that his elder son's future was being jeopardized.

When Steven was found by the police, alone and very resentful of the family's apparent rejection, he was placed at the children's district centre (the short-term placement for emergency admission and decision-making) under a place of safety order (Children and Young Persons Act 1980).

With the psychologist as mediator, reintegration home was attempted, but met with no success, so that three months later the parental rights were assumed by the local authority and a full care order made (Children and Young Persons Act 1969).

It later transpired that while Steven had been missing from home he had gone into his school and set fire to some papers behind a wardrobe. Apologists for Steven said he had 'just been playing with matches'. The school, however, suspended Steven, saying that they could no longer ensure the safety of other children, and the headmaster asked the psychologist to look for 'more appropriate' schooling. This was seen as very unfortunate as Steven would have fewer community links, and placement in other school units would mean a more narrow curriculum. Steven would have to undergo important radical changes, both at home and school.

Reassessment of problem

Steven was now in care, and the local authority was reponsible for encouraging his normal development up to the age of 18. Because Steven's problems seemed so generalized to other areas of care and management, it was decided by the psychologist, with the encouragement of the social services department, that any plans for his future should encompass programmes at school and within the setting where he was to live, and he was to be fully involved in all decisions (Vernon and Fruin, 1986). Although the parents felt he had now gone, they were encouraged to remain in contact, but both parents refused. Steven was fortunately admitted to a new junior school and the senior staff were made aware of the circumstances. Although naturally hesitant, they realized that Steven's self-image should not be undermined and all staff should regard him as needing normal mainstream education rather than specialist education in a school with children with other problems. However, because of fears about the chances of Steven being suspended over behavioural problems in such schools, it was felt that preparation of a statement of his special educational needs, under the 1981 Education Act, might aid his retention in normal schools, or facilitate a quick removal to an appropriate placement should this fail. At the very least, it would allow continual monitoring of his educational progress and his social standing within schools (DES, 1983).

Interviews with Steven were now easy and he was most cooperative and constructive about his future plans, although he was not prepared to admit that his parents' demonstrable rejection indicated anything long-term.

While Steven was in the children's district centre (the hub of child care for that part of the city) he displayed few problems of management. Indeed, he was more compliant than others in the same situation, and was noted to be less competitive and assertive than many. As might have been expected, he hoped for an eventual return home, 'like other children', even though he realized that this was not possible.

Psychometric testing suggested that questions of intelligence, educational or neurological impairment were not relevant to his present problems. Steven was found a satisfactory place in a group one (i.e. structured, and with a large staff-to-client ratio) children's home close to his home by the psychologist and social services colleagues. The psychologist arranged for Steven to be placed in the first instance on a positive feedback system of reporting, which was rewarded each day with a half-hour's individual time from his key worker. Steven was responsible for the negotiation of his day-to-day programme.

Qualitatively, Steven was reported to be 'unhappy, but coping' at school and in the home. He was frequently tearful, wandered off for short periods, and often preferred the silence of his own company. However, he was not ostracized by other children, nor was he socially incompetent with his peers. It was questioned whether some help should be given with his attitudes towards his parents, but Steven categorically asked for no such counselling and, therefore, none was given at this point. In spite of frequent offers of guidance and facilitation, the parents wished for no further contact with Steven.

Rehabilitation

At the change to secondary school, Steven was not accepted by any of the local schools. For a short time he attended a special school on the other side of the city, but constant problems of attendance soon led to a re-referral to the psychologist. A place was negotiated at a local intermediate treatment centre with a plan to reintegrate Steven to the local mainstream school (2010 pupils). This plan never worked; incidents of petty pilfering and glue-sniffing frustrated plans of integration. Eventually Steven started in a school unit for children with special needs because of the lack of more suitable resources.

Happily, Steven settled in well here, and the psychologist was involved in the individual social and educational programme negotiated by the school and Steven. On one occasion, Steven had to appear in court, charged with taking and driving away a motorbike. The psychologist was asked to prepare a report. This recommended a conditional discharge so that Steven's rehabilitation should not be further jeopardized by removal from his present placements. The psychologist was only involved in statutory reviews every six months over the next two years, but a short investigatory interview was held with Steven before each review.

In the children's home, Steven struck up a close friendship with his link-worker who wished to become 'social uncle' to Steven. The psychologist was approached by the social services department to comment on problems of a conflict of interest on the link-worker's part in the children's home if he were to take on this role of a caring adult with a special interest in Steven. More controversially, the psychologist was asked to assess this social worker's suitability for being a social uncle with a view to possible fostering of Steven. The psychologist felt no psychometric or questionnaire methods had any prediction value, and that mutual motivation and ability to solve problems might be a better indicator of success.

The special school asked the psychologist to look at the possibilities of mainstream schooling, which was fairly quickly arranged. This allowed Steven to attend normal mainstream school while, at the same time, enjoying a home-on-trial arrangement with his social uncle, who had now been redesignated as foster parent. This foster parent and his girlfriend had firmly expressed a desire to eventually adopt Steven should the social services department agree. The psychologist was involved in the shaping of skills deemed by all concerned to be necessary for the adoption of Steven, in conjunction with discussion, programming and two role-play sessions with Steven. The psychologist's approval was requested for his 'freeing for adoption'.

Conclusion

Steven is now 15, living with his adoptive parents and coping well with the demands of mainstream schooling. It would seem that, in spite of the frequency of placement breakdowns, long-term plans for children in care need not always be as destructive as had been thought when the care order was challenged, providing monitoring, problem-solving and rehabilitation are prime concerns. Even though Steven's case lasted six years and no single long-term behavioural targets were planned, it would seem that the psychologist's role was important in assessment, intervention and in maintaining continuity of care.

19 Lulu: the treatment of chronic solvent abuse by an adolescent

Problem and background

Lulu was 15. She was detained as one of ten teenaged girls in a social services custodial treatment centre. The girls had been deprived of their liberties by care orders. Most of them had a criminal record and all had been assessed as a risk either to themselves or to others.

The stated intention of the unit was to rehabilitate the girls if possible to their original communities. However, the priority for most of the social services care staff was to ensure that the girls remained in security and adhered to a strict regime designed to prevent absconding, violence, stealing, damage and drug abuse — activities in which their charges had already become expert.

Lulu had already acquired a string of offences which included fraud, shoplifting and burglary. She had been living with her mother and co-habitee in a house dominated by a considerable number of attention-seeking cats. She had also maintained contact with her natural father, an alcoholic. Attempts over the past year to provide Lulu with a stable domestic setting in a council children's home had failed due to Lulu's persistent offending, absconding, and her blatant and chronic glue-sniffing.

The clinical psychologist working as a member of the unit's multi-disciplinary team was asked to treat Lulu for her addiction to glue.

Assessment

Lulu and the care staff who worked most closely with her were interviewed, as were her field social worker and the staff of the children's home who had had to reject her. Previous medical, social and school reports were consulted.

From these sources it emerged that Lulu had started to sniff glue about two years before and now sniffed alone. Her preference was for Evo-Stick, but she was prepared to sniff anything — even the disinfectant used in the sanitary disposal unit. It seemed that the effects of glue were initially pleasurable, but she now simply 'needed it'. Although her habit was chronic it appeared that a family row was a common antecedent event. While under the effects of glue she became atypically belligerent, abusive and physically violent. She would go to enormous lengths to procure solvent including subterfuge, stealing, smuggling and bodily concealment.

She had few interests or ambitions, appeared to have no close friends or lasting social relationships and had limited social skills. Although her formal educational attainments were poor, she was, like her fellow inmates, street-wise and was of average intelligence. She hated being 'banged up' and her only pleasure was in attempting to outwit the system, particularly with regard to smuggling glue.

Her addiction had never been formally treated although her social worker and the children's home staff had experimented with a mixture of threats, bribery and coercion. These had had no lasting effects.

Formulation of the problem

Lulu had resorted to solvent abuse to avoid tackling the developmental tasks for which she was ill-equipped due to the compounded effects of an eccentric domestic background, her relative social isolation, her poor social skills and her negative view of her own potential.

The theoretical rationale on which the programme was based was as follows. Glue-sniffing was originally established and reinforced by peergroup approval and curiosity and excitement. For the majority of more psychologically robust adolescents this form of reinforcement dissipates and they move on to fresh ventures. However, it was felt that in Lulu's case the effects of the glue were also found to reduce the distress she was suffering from the unsatisfactory aspects of her life. Although the effects of glue were no longer pleasurable, they were preferable to the discomfort experienced when sober. It seemed to be avoidance of this discomfort which maintained the habit, in much the same way that phobias are seen to be maintained.

This formulation led to the adoption of a programme similar to systematic desensitization. The aim was to systematically desensitize Lulu to exposure to abstinence from glue, that is, to introduce her to situations in which glue was more easily available, but she was able to resist abusing it.

A major difficulty with treating addictions is getting the addict sufficiently motivated to undergo the discomfort of abstinence. One way is to counteract this discomfort with conditions which are even more aversive. For Lulu, this had already been achieved by locking her up. The essence of the programme was to make reduction of imprisonment contingent upon reduced glue-sniffing.

Treatment

The treatment objectives were

(1) to stop Lulu using glue inappropriately;
(2) to develop appropriate uses of glue;
(3) to identify and reduce sources of conflict in the family network using family therapy;
(4) to develop Lulu's social skills, particularly with peers;
(5) to identify and develop other interests.

In this brief case study only the first two of the above objectives will be described although all were considered crucial and integral to Lulu's rehabilitation.

Treatment strategy

Following the initial assessment a 'glue team' was set up which consisted of Lulu, her social worker, her residential key worker and the psychologist. It was agreed that regular meetings would be held, and were to be conducted in a businesslike fashion with a chairperson (the psychologist), an agenda and a written record of any decisions made.

At the first meeting it was agreed that Lulu's motivation to stop using glue was non-existent. It was therefore agreed that the team would overtly exploit her very strong motivation to leave the unit. This would be done by making the length, extent and frequency of her trips out and her eventual discharge contingent upon her unequivocal demonstration that she would not sniff glue.

It was further agreed that the availability of glue would be gradually and systematically increased, and that, provided she did not abuse the glue, she would be allowed more and more time away from the unit. The precise details of glue availability and time away would be reviewed and negotiated by the glue team each week.

What happened

For several weeks progress was smooth and uneventful. Lulu worked through various stages of increasing exposure to glue, for example,

(1) sealed tube in the room accompanied by key worker (one hour);
(2) sealed tube in room with staff member outside (one hour);
(3) top removed

and so on until Lulu was allowed to use glue to repair some coffee mugs, using a large pot which remained in her room throughout the day. During these weeks, each successful step earned credit points which went towards her spending increasing amounts of time away from the unit. At this stage things started to go badly wrong.

Problems encountered

Each step had to be renegotiated with the unit management staff. They expressed increasing doubts about the programme and became more and more reluctant to relax 'the rules', such as 'No glue in living quarters'. They insisted on each step being repeated several times. The management staff invoked a 'policy rule' which stated that no resident could be discharged in under six months. (It had become apparent that Lulu could earn her discharge in less than this time.)

Trips out, earned via the glue programme, were summarily cancelled by staff for various misdemeanours extraneous to the glue programme, for example, swearing or being rude. Intensive family therapy work, also orientated towards Lulu's discharge, put Lulu under increasing emotional pressures. Other girls, resentful about the disproportionate attention Lulu was receiving and envious of her apparently rapid progress towards discharge, put Lulu under intense pressure to sniff the glue and to misbehave.

Outcome

After one month, Lulu's key worker resigned from the glue team (probably due to pressure from her line manager). Lulu expressed doubts about the psychologist's ability to secure management approval for her programme (entirely justified). Other care staff, drafted in to replace her key worker, acted inconsistently and unreliably.

Lulu became increasingly difficult to manage on the unit. She was suspected of smuggling things in from her trips. She absconded and the glue programme was abandoned.

After considerable debate a guarantee of clinical autonomy was given by the managers to the psychologist and team members for future treatment programmes.

Discussion

An attempt was made to wean a poorly motivated girl from substance abuse using a behavioural programme within a closed institution. A promising start was made but eventually progress was impeded largely due to factors within the institution. It proved impossible to achieve sufficient control over the security conditions demanded by the institution.

Despite the unhappy outcome, it is important to note that at no time did Lulu resort to sniffing the glue which had become readily accessible. It can be argued that it was just these sorts of pressures which in the past had led to substance abuse. To this extent, then, the programme was a success in that real life conditions had been created in a closed institution, which would make generalization of treatment effects more likely.

Even an apparently straightforward treatment intervention requires extensive planning when undertaken in closed institutions. It seems essential to either gain the enthusiastic support of the entire staff group or to be given clinical autonomy to work as a sub-team. Such a sub-team should be familiar with unit policy (even if unwritten) and be prepared to challenge it.

Innovative work in closed institutions places high demands on diplomacy, persuasiveness, political acumen and tenacity. The problems encountered in such institutions are intensified when working with untrained staff.

Notwithstanding the problems generated by the institution itself, young, poorly motivated teenagers can be productively involved in the treatment of their chronic solvent abuse. The magic ingredients seem to be to adopt a businesslike contractual style, and to grant teenagers a major say in expressing opinions and making decisions. It is important to stick to agreements and to be completely open and honest. In addition, conditions should be created which are as close to real life as possible.

20 Charlotte: therapy with an adolescent using a personal construct approach

Introduction

Charlotte Norris was almost 13 when she was referred to the Department of Psychological Medicine by her GP. She had had a series of physical ailments including abdominal pain, her school reported that she had been boasting of sexual exploits and she had made, or said she had made, at least two suicidal gestures.

Background

Her physical problems had begun two years before when her 20-year-old sister, Kathryn, left home. She had been her father's favourite and Charlotte had responded to her departure by 'shutting her father out'. Kathryn herself was not without her problems: she had a history of school refusal, drug-taking and an abortion. One other sister had married at the earliest possible opportunity and was in only sporadic contact with the family.

Mr Norris had left home three months before; just after that the presenting symptoms of sexual boasting and suicidal gestures began. At home Charlotte was reported to sit crying in her bedroom for hours, alternating with going into the garden to swing in the rain, also for hours at a time.

Charlotte's mother said that her husband was a man with high expectations of his daughters, with whom he had always had a closer relationship than he had with his wife. Her immediate fear was that Charlotte would turn out like Kathryn.

Charlotte was doing well academically in a grammar school. A picture of her behaviour in school was obtained from a rating scale completed by one of her teachers. This consisted of questions about her behaviour, for example whether she was a fidgety child. The pattern of reported behaviours indicates whether problems fall into two broad categories: neurotic or antisocial. Charlotte's total score suggested quite serious difficulties, with an emphasis on the neurotic.

Assessment

She and her mother were seen by a diagnostic team made up of a psychiatrist, social worker and psychologist. Mrs Norris was perceived as obsessionally neat, close to tears. Charlotte seemed confused much of the time, avoiding eye contact by hiding behind a thick curtain of hair, speaking only in response to a direct question.

At the end of this session there was no simple formulation. Mrs Norris agreed to come again; Charlotte remained impassive. They were seen together by the psychologist and the social worker on three more occasions; little fresh factual information emerged but a clearer picture of needs was obtained. Mrs Norris complained about everything: her family, her financial problems, her lack of friends, her boredom without a job. Charlotte maintained the impassive silence of the first meeting. It was not difficult to see that Charlotte and her mother were locked into a negative relationship; neither could give the other any support. Mrs Norris's depression was seen as a possible mainspring to Charlotte's problems, but her resolute silence suggested that there was more to it than that. It was agreed that Mrs Norris be seen fortnightly for casework with the social worker while Charlotte came for individual sessions with the psychologist.

Intervention

The theoretical approach taken was based on personal construct psychology (Kelly, 1955; Epting, 1984). This sees people as constantly erecting hypotheses about themselves and their world and testing these hypotheses with experience. The aim was to try to help Charlotte understand something of her own construct system, and possibly those of significant others, and to explore ways of behaving alternative to those adopted so far. In explanation of the approach, the metaphor of the jigsaw was used: she was a 'puzzle' and it would be necessary to work together to solve it since, although the psychologist had some experience of jigsaws, only she was an expert on Charlotte.

The immediate problem was not only that Charlotte would not speak, she refused to make eye contact. Every two weeks she came, for six months, and, apart from a very occasional 'yes' or 'no' towards the end of the fifth month, she said nothing. She sat, with her black curtain of hair completely covering her face. To remove some of the tension in this situation the psychologist explained that he knew that he could not force her to speak and that he respected her right to remain silent. This enabled him, at least, to relax and it seemed, judging by her body language, to help her.

Two techniques were used quite extensively. One was the psychologist thinking aloud, then giving Charlotte a task to think about. In this way it was possible to get across to her some of the hypotheses that were being considered. In one session, for example, feelings of aggression were raised; in another, relationships with siblings; in a third, the need to impress one's school friends. Once the task had been set there was silence for 10 to 15 minutes. Over the months there was a gradual relaxation in her guard. At first a nose appeared from behind the hair, then an eye and a cheek and, by the end of the fifteenth session, her whole face. Her expression changed from time to time in response to some of the psychologist's thoughts so there was a degree of communication.

The second technique was a repertory grid. This has been developed in several ways from Kelly's original and is described in Fransella and Bannister (1977). The aim is to explore a construct system by ranking what Kelly called elements (in this case people known to Charlotte) according to relevant constructs to find out how one construct relates to another. In this way one might discover, for example, that clever people are perceived as threatening. Normally constructs are elicited so that each person's grid is personal, but as Charlotte was still not speaking when this was first carried out, the psychologist provided them all, choosing those that seemed to be relevant. The results were cast in the form of a linkage analysis, in which those

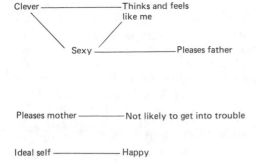

Figure 20.1 Repertory grid analysis

constructs that correlate together significantly are put together as shown in Figure 20.1.

This was shown to Charlotte and it was suggested that her sexual boasting was a way of pleasing her father, possibly even of trying to get him back to her. After this, the focus was on her father and the session ended with Charlotte in tears. From that moment she began to talk, at first hesitantly, later more freely. Two major parts of the jigsaw had been put together.

Throughout this time Mrs Norris had seen the social worker. One theme was envy, envy of her daughters and her husband; another was her inability to get out and about, to make friends or to work.

Intervention: phase two

Phase two began with the same format as phase one, the difference being that Charlotte was talking. During the next seven moths she was seen for ten more sessions in which she was able to reconstruct her perceptions of how her family had viewed her. The discussion began at the point when she was 5 and moved up to the present. She was able to elaborate her sense of loss not only of her father when he left, but of how she had stopped being the much-loved baby. There was discussion of construct systems and of how one develops an internal map or set of guidelines determining behaviour. She could, by this time, talk about her depression during the previous summer and how much better she and her mother were. She was able now to begin to explore, through her behaviour, different approaches to her mother and her school and there seemed to be a general relaxation and freedom of movement in both areas.

Following further discussions it was agreed to tail off treatment over a four-month period. During this time, however, she began a further symptom: nocturnal bleeding from the ear and then the mouth. Investigation by ear, throat and nose specialists could shed no light on the origin of the blood; no lesion was found despite investigation of her as an in-patient. Charlotte herself remained, perhaps predictably, indifferent; on being asked how she was, she invariably replied, with a grin, 'bleeding well'. It was agreed that too early an ending to treatment had been planned. Various interpretations of the psychological cause of the bleeding were tried. The psychologist speculated, for example, on the meaning of menstrual blood and tried to explore any points of contact between the two, but to no avail.

The psychologist next embarked on an analysis of her dreams, within a personal construct psychology framework. The hypothesis was that dreaming is an exercise in which one's mind is like a computer, needing to be cleared each night to allow a new programme to run next day. Regularly recurring themes might thus be detected from those immediate preoccupations which were powerful enough to require clearing. Together Charlotte and the psychologist searched for themes that might be relevant. The most dramatic to emerge were related to death and to being trapped. This theme was taken up in relation to her stage in the life cycle and her need to get away from her mother emotionally as well as physically. After three months of this approach the bleeding stopped gradually, and never returned.

No certain explanation of the beginning or ending of the bleeding emerged. It is possible that she had a physical vulnerability and that the need to remain in treatment expressed itself somatically. The working through of dream themes may have given her sufficient self-confidence, arising from self-awareness, to carry on alone. This seemed confirmed by the fact that at about this time she had a good school report and it was once again agreed that treatment should come to an end, which it did a month later.

Mrs Norris had continued in casework with a social worker and she was now able to go out to work again. Both she and Charlotte agreed that they had come a long way in the two-and-a-half years that had elapsed since their first interview.

Postscript one

Charlotte was kept on review and came back when she was having severe sore throats. Although Mrs Norris said firmly that there is no such thing as psychological tonsillitis, it was interesting that she wanted to discuss it here. Contact was maintained at a lower level than before between the social worker and Mrs Norris. The case was eventually closed.

Postscript two

It was reopened when the school phoned to say that Charlotte was refusing to take her mock A level exams, without which she could not go into the second-year sixth form. She was seen as an emergency and an easy communication was immediately resumed. It was clear that she still had some ambivalence about leaving her mother, which she would do both physically and psychologically if she passed her A levels and went on to higher education. This was talked through and she returned to school to take the exams.

Outcome

She was seen a year later. In the waiting room, she was wrapped round her boy friend and she told cheerily of her place in a Scottish university. Not only had she come back, she had brought with her evidence of social and academic success. All the symptoms for which she had been referred and which had come during treatment had disappeared.

Discussion

Charlotte was seen several years ago. With hindsight one might postulate the possibility that sexual abuse by her father was a major contributory cause of her problem. From the history the speculation arises that she was aware of her father having abused her sister Kathryn, hence the 'shutting out' behaviour when Kathryn left, since Charlotte did not want to replace her. The repertory grid provides some support for this theory and would have given an opportunity to take it up with Charlotte herself.

Whatever the validity of the sexual abuse hypothesis, the outcome for Charlotte seems to have been satisfactory. Mrs Norris had also been helped to some extent. Looking back over time it is likely that several factors combined to bring this outcome. One was that Charlotte had contact with a male therapist, old enough to be her father, who manifestly made no demands on her and who was able to live with her aggressive silence. On the other hand this male figure was also interested enough in her to explore her thoughts with her, the crucial emphasis here being on a collaborative exploration; there was constant reiteration of the need of her help to complete the jigsaw. Perhaps Charlotte felt relieved of the burden of carrying her mother since there was another to assist in this task. And when a second crisis came, the hospital team was still there, ready to offer support.

This was a case whose complexity became increasingly obvious as time wore on and it was by no means a one-therapist affair. It was, rather, one in which team-work played a major role: the case work carried out with Mrs Norris has not been given a great deal of space here, but that is not to minimize it. There were regular, supportive discussions between the therapists and the psychiatrist's input was of great value, especially at the time of the bleeding from the ear. The notion of team-work is passing rapidly in some quarters, disciplines going their own way. Historically and professionally this is probably inevitable, but Charlotte's case illustrates that the team is not without value.

21　Katie: trichotillomania in an adolescent girl

Introduction

Fiddling with hair is common in social primates and is quite a normal activity in many people (Horne, 1977). In some cases the fiddling goes on to pulling out so much hair as to cause bald patches, tissue irritation and varying degrees of hair follicle damage (Mehregan, 1970; Muller and Winkelmann, 1972). Hallopeau (1889) first used the term 'trichotillomania' to describe alopecia produced by somebody pulling out his or her own hair.

Trichotillomania is considered to be a rare condition (Anderson and Dean, 1956; Mannino and Delgado, 1969; Schacter, 1961) but its prevalence is likely to be underestimated for two reasons. First, cases are treated by both dermatologists and psychologists (McLaughlin and Nay, 1975) and, second, hair pullers often deny their habit, lessening the likelihood of identification (Greenberg and Sarner, 1965; Sanderson and Hall-Smith, 1970; Azrin and Nunn, 1978).

Psychoanalytically based psychotherapeutic approaches regard the problem as severe and chronic in nature, highly resistant to treatment (Cordle and Long, 1980) and as a manifestation of serious disturbance in individuals with pathological self-destructive tendencies (Friman et al., 1984). The aetiology was viewed as a function of disruptive psychosexual development attributable to disturbed family dynamics (Greenberg, 1969; Monroe and Abse, 1963).

Behavioural approaches to treatment have included thought stopping (Taylor, 1963), self-monitoring (Anthony, 1978), mild aversive control by saving the hairs pulled (Bayer, 1972), habit reversal (Azrin et al., 1980; Rosenbaum and Ayllon, 1981; Fleming, 1984), a mixture of positive reinforcement and punishment (Gray, 1979), contingency contracting (MacNeil and Thomas, 1976; Stabler and Warren, 1974), covert sensitization (Levine, 1976; Bornstein and Rychtarik, 1978), cognitive/behavioural coping procedures in conjunction with habit reversal (Ottens, 1981), facial screening (Barmann and Vitali, 1982) and a combination of aversive therapy, hypnosis, sexual and family therapy (Horne, 1977).

In general, behaviour therapists take a more optimistic view of the problem and have achieved greater success in treatment (Friman et al., 1984). However, behaviourally treated cases tend to have no other major symptoms whereas the psychoanalytically treated cases present a range of major problems of which hair pulling is but one.

A major methodological problem in all the reports concerns the validity of their assessment of the dependent variable — length, amount and quality of hair. Most studies rely on self-monitoring but apart from that of Rosenbaum and Ayllon

122

(1981) no reliability data are reported. The studies of small children and developmentally handicapped individuals rely more on therapists to manage the treatment, and outcome data are more reliably reported (Barmann and Vitali, 1982; Friman *et al.,* 1984).

The case to be described here concerns an adolescent girl whose hair pulling had not responded to over six months intervention by straightforward behavioural methods. It illustrates how a flexible application of behavioural techniques combined with an attempt at more rigorous monitoring helped to uncover family problems which were maintaining the hair pulling and so to effect a good therapeutic outcome.

Presenting problems

Katie, aged 13 years, had always been anxious, with nervous mannerisms such as facial tics and coughs being noted at her junior school. Her parents had been advised by her GP to ignore these. She was doing reasonably well at an independent secondary school, studying for examinations in cello and piano, in both of which she excelled. However, her immediate ambition was to attend the school at which her father taught, but this involved taking a competitive examination. Her parents thought she would have no difficulty doing so, but shortly after she had been entered for the exam she began hair pulling. Around this time too, the family learned of her paternal grandfather's terminal illness. To her parents, Katie appeared to take these stresses in her stride.

Her GP referred her to a clinical psychologist who treated her for seven months. At that time she was pulling out her hair, eyebrows and eyelashes. She was given training in relaxation and the therapy plan was to apply habit reversal techniques. However, Katie was unable to monitor her hair pulling despite considerable efforts by her mother and the psychologist. She did take part in swimming and long walks, suggested as stress reduction activities, but she was very embarrassed by her patchy hair and wore a beret to hide it. Her parents were dissatisfied with her progress so a referral was made to the present psychologists some distance from her home.

Assessment

At interview, Katie felt more able to confide in the female psychologist and no longer denied pulling out her hair. She did not know why she had denied it to her father, her GP or the previous male psychologist. It appeared that she pulled at her hair mainly when she was bored, especially when she first arrived home from school. She had resisted pulling (or at least had not done it) when abroad on holiday.

The whole family clearly had high academic aspirations and Katie was much more worried about taking the entrance exam than her parents appreciated. Formal psychometric assessment revealed that she obtained a Full Scale IQ of 109 on the WISC-R (Wechsler, 1974) and that her reading and spelling were in advance of her age. Thus, she was achieving well compared to all her peers, but there had to be doubts as to whether her performance would be good enough to get her into her father's school. Her headmistress had reservations about the course of action and linked the exam with the hair pulling. The contrast between her good average ability and the family's high expectations in part helped to explain her high anxiety and overwhelming fear of failure.

Katie's parents had been married for nearly 20 years. Her father was a headmaster in a public school and worked all hours during term time. About the onset of Katie's problems, he suffered from a stress-induced alopecia which slowly improved. He placed great emphasis on achievement. Her mother supported her husband in all his work and was very sympathetic to Katie. Her older brother was doing well at the father's school and was embarrassed by Katie's disorder and often fought with her. He coped with household tensions by working in a nearby shop whenever possible.

Formulation

Katie's hair pulling seemed to serve a stress-reducing function, but it was not clear what stresses were affecting her. The reassessment uncovered two new factors that better helped to understand the problem. The first was Katie's fear of failure in the entrance exam for her father's school. The second factor — more strongly suspected than openly discussed — was that there were problems in her relationship with her father. It was predicted that stress reduction techniques would make some impact on the hair pulling and that, in implementing the treatment, the underlying dynamics of the family would be clarified. Treatment goals might then be revised.

Intervention

Good records were seen as a key to monitoring progress, so Katie was asked to keep a daily record of the number of hairs pulled, along with an account of the surrounding circumstances. From Week 9 she also recorded the number of times she resisted hair pulling (Horne, 1977) in order to give more recognition to her efforts to overcome her problem. She kept the hairs and brought them to sessions (Bayer, 1972). To obtain more objective evidence of progress, her head was photographed each session in a standard pose that protected her anonymity (Santo and Yule, in preparation).

Because previous intervention was seen as unsuccessful, although along the right lines, by the present psychologists, therapy was initiated immediately without further lengthy baselines. It was acccptcd that Katie's reports might be unreliable, but it was important to give her the responsibility rather than continue her parents' involvement, which had been unhelpful previously. For the most part, Katie was seen by one psychologist alone, her parents being seen occasionally and briefly to review progress.

The first phase of treatment built on the earlier techniques, including practising relaxation exercises. On the assumptions that the hair pulling served a tension-releasing function and that relaxation was incompatible with the build-up of tension, Katie had been taught progressive relaxation. That is, she had learned to relax major and minor muscle groups in a pre-determined order so as to achieve an overall state of relaxation.

Some time was spent identifying an activity which was in itself relaxing, pleasant, a change from the usual and incompatible with hair pulling. It had to be unstructured, not involve her mother, but should involve her hands. It emerged that Katie wanted to throw paints on to large sheets of paper from big paint brushes. She enjoyed planning how and where to do this and scarcely believed it when her parents agreed to her doing it. She felt freed to express herself. Her mother saw the value of her activity; her father had reservations but agreed as he was desperate to try anything. Katie was to use the paints whenever she felt the urge to pull out her hair. Nobody was to comment on or to criticize her painting or her hair pulling. The family accommodated the painting rather well.

The next breakthrough occurred when Katie admitted to feeling embarrassed at the freedom of her painting. She needed an activity which was as satisfying but less conspicuous. At this stage she admitted that she pulled her hair when she felt angry. This usually occurred at home and was usually directed at her parents and brother. She felt it wrong to be angry with her parents and, although she felt it more natural to be furious with her brother, she blamed herself and went for long walks to escape the home. It was often during these long walks that she pulled her hair. This story rang true and provided a better understanding of the tension-releasing function of the hair pulling. It was decided that Katie would carry around a sketch pad and draw whenever she felt the urge to pull her hair or felt angry. During this phase, her hair pulling decreased considerably.

At half-term there was a relapse, under clearly provoking circumstances. Her mother and brother were away for a few days and Katie was at home with her father. By this time she had stopped keeping pulled hairs and needing to use the sketch book. She had a sudden increase in hair pulling, about 60–70 hairs over three days, but was too ashamed to report what happened. It was clear to the psychologists that her father had been critical of Katie as well as ignoring her during the period.

Despite the relapse, sessions were scheduled less frequently. With holidays identified as high-risk times, appointments were arranged for half-term and other longer breaks. Both parents were involved in the next few sessions and Katie was encouraged to spend more time with her father in pleasurable and appropriate activities. To Katie's surprise, this resulted in more relaxed holiday times.

Although her father had gone along with all the suggestions, the final breakthrough occurred when Katie produced a set of data sheets full of zeros, announcing that she was better. Her mother supported her. Her father became very angry with Katie, accusing her of lying and deceit. He had been suppressing his anger and had found it hard to say nothing about the hair pulling. Nevertheless, his fury had been apparent non-verbally. The whole issue was discussed openly and he realized how high his standards were for Katie. For the first time he began to realize the pressure she was under. In this session Katie admitted to her father for the first time that she did pull her hair out.

From this point onwards Katie's improvement was dramatic and the tension within the family dissipated. Relations improved among all family members even though her brother had never been seen in sessions. Her father was satisfied with Katie's progress and openly said so. Katie herself felt less self-conscious, began to go out more and started to grow her hair long.

Outcome

All this happened over a 38-week period during which there had been 11 clinic appointments. One month into treatment Katie was successful in obtaining a place at her father's school. Follow-up appointments were given until the end-of-term exam and subsequent summer holidays were over. Katie and her parents confirmed the continuing effectiveness of the treatment. These sessions concentrated on stress management and the continuing need to include relaxing activities in her routine.

The results of treatment are reflected in Katie's self-report data in Figure 21.1.

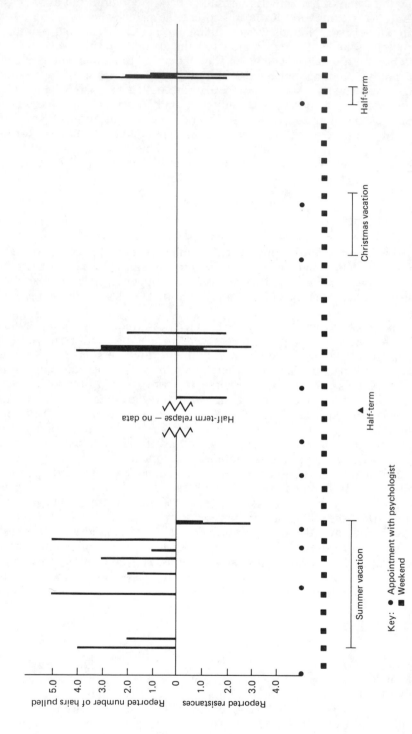

Figure 21.1 Self-report data showing the relations between number of hairs pulled and number of times hair-pulling was resisted with time periods

The records were notable for the low number of hairs she reported pulling out and the few times she reported resisting the habit. Clearly there were discrepancies between her reports and what the parents and psychologists could see with their own eyes (confirmed by the photographs). A more detailed analysis suggested that hair pulling was highest at weekends and school holidays when Katie's days were least structured.

Discussion

When a client arrives convinced that a prior treatment was unsuccessful and yet the therapist believes that the earlier treatment was basically sound, there can be difficulties in re-engaging the client in therapy. In the present case the psychologists agreed with the previous psychologist that Katie's hair pulling served a tension-reducing function, although they could not fully identify the sources of the tension. However, by acknowledging Katie's worries about the entrance exam and her distress over the grandfather, her problems were recast in a sufficiently different perspective to allow therapy to continue.

Even though Katie's self-monitoring was far from accurate, it was adequate enough to pinpoint situations that caused most distress. This brought her inability to cope with anger towards her parents into the open and eventually forced her father to be angry about her 'deceit'. Allowing them to express their anger without destroying the family was undoubtedly therapeutic.

This raises the problem of which elements in the therapeutic package were effective, if any. It is possible that the problem would have disappeared spontaneously. Given that it had not done so during the previous seven months of therapy and that the improvements followed particular breakthroughs, this explanation seems unlikely. Pursuing relaxation activities in part to counteract tension and in part to divert from difficult situations seemed to be helpful. Although similar to the previous strategy, it may have been more effective this time because Katie felt more able to confide in a female psychologist who showed a broader understanding of some of the sources of tension. Finally, forcing her parents to acknowledge her father's high expectations and the stress these placed on Katie was seen as an essential element.

The self-monitoring data are insufficiently reliable to allow detailed analysis and the photographic data largely confirm the general overall progress.

In general, the approach adopted used behavioural intervention and monitoring to begin treatment while clarifying the functional utility of the presenting problem. In some ways this is similar to Horne (1977). Given the earlier failure of a focused behavioural approach, it suggests that combined treatments may succeed better in treating trichotillomania (Friman *et al.*, 1984). The need for better measures, both objective and self-reported, is highlighted by the case.

Part 3
Working with people with mental handicaps

Introduction

Peter Wilcock

The case studies chosen for this section provide a fascinating historical insight into how the role of clinical psychologists working with people with mental handicaps has changed and broadened dramatically over the past 20 years. They illustrate how working from a theoretical base and applying research findings in practice, among other factors, has had a considerable impact on increasing the relevance of their work to the lives of their clients.

The explosion of research into the use of operant learning theory with people with a mental handicap that began in the early 1960s (e.g. Ellis, 1963) provided a framework for analysing their learning difficulties and planning interventions to overcome them. This, in turn, had an impact on people's attitudes, and workers in the field began to understand that they must actively accept the responsibility to teach new skills and behaviour to their clients.

The stereotyped behaviours described in the case study of John would at one time have been considered an inherent part of his mental handicap and something to cope with rather than change. However, knowledge of behavioural research findings in this case guided the preparation of an intervention plan and provided the framework for monitoring its success.

The second case study uses the same theoretical approach to address a very different set of problems relating to a person whose learning disability is compounded by his inability to control his body. An interesting feature of this case is the imaginative use of knowledge from the newly emerging field of micro-electronic technology within a behavioural framework to teach vital new skills to Martin who, like John, once would have been considered unteachable.

These first two case studies illustrate the impact of a new theoretical approach when applied intensively to individuals. The third, about Mary, takes this a step further. The initial assessment identified the influence of a number of different factors on her life which all needed to be tackled. Once again a behavioural approach was used and in addition to suggesting ways to work with Mary directly, it identified a broader range of organizational issues relating to the institutional setting in which she was living. It highlights the difficulties of helping people learn new skills when there are few natural opportunities to use them and when their living environments are themselves a major cause of much unacceptable behaviour (Tharp and Wetzel, 1969).

Part of the answer for Mary was to make opportunities for contact outside the institution increasingly available. Implicit in this is recognition that the best way to help people learn the skills to lead ordinary lives is to support them in living in ordinary houses among ordinary people. Mary's case is, therefore, an example of how the use of a powerful new theoretical approach indirectly challenged the currently accepted service model.

The work with Charles in the fourth case describes the clinical psychologists' attempt to help a young man with severely challenging behaviours live such an ordinary life. It is an important example of the use of a behavioural approach in an ordinary house as they attempt to test ways of changing this person's behaviours. Success was limited, and the work highlights the need to work at a number of different levels and tackle issues of staff skills, staff support and developing successful interdisciplinary team working. Perhaps most fundamentally, it emphasizes that if we are to develop services that really address individual needs, the greatest challenge lies in understanding what this means and developing more sensitive ways to explore this with our clients.

A further implication of the trend towards ordinary living is the need to avoid exposing people with a mental handicap to situations with which they do not have the skills to cope. One crucial area is the development of interpersonal relationship skills and especially their needs and rights for sexual relationships. The sixth case study tackles these specific issues, and describes how the psychologist's knowledge of learning theory is applied to staff teaching. More generally it reflects the need for clinical psychologists to work in ways which will create settings where staff can pro-actively work towards meeting identified client needs. This work takes place at a level removed from direct client contact, but is essential if the clinical psychologist is to avoid being used as a firefighter, to be called in when crises arise. This type of work (Wilcock, 1985) will become increasingly necessary if the newly developing services are to be of a high quality.

The case of Molly describes work with a woman who might well have been admitted to hospital for reasons that had little to do with her mental handicap. The psychologist needed to use a broad range of skills and also be sensitive to the needs of other members of the client's family. In order to be successful, it was necessary to approach the family as a vulnerable system with a set of very delicate balances maintaining its equilibrium. In this case the need was for the whole family to live as ordinary a life as possible and it emphasized the need for the psychologist to consider the whole family as the client, rather than just the person who was referred.

In summary, these case studies reflect how the advent of a new theoretical model and an increasing body of research findings have had a major impact on the work of clinical psychologists with people with a mental handicap. Further, they demonstrate how the application of new research knowledge has significantly influenced service design and how members of the profession are having to considerably broaden their roles as they pick up the challenges of the new services.

It is also worth noting that these theoretical and professional advances have taken place at the same time as there has been a growing campaign to defend the human rights of people with a mental handicap to live as ordinary members of the community. It is interesting that the goals which arise from the theoretical position coincide with those of the rights movement and, indeed, clinical psychologists have an important role to use the former to help achieve the latter (Independent Development Council for People with a Mental Handicap, 1982).

The focus of this movement has been the increasing emphasis on using the principles of normalization to guide thinking about services for people with a mental handicap. Normalization has been defined as 'the use of means which are valued in our society in order to develop and support personal behaviour, experiences and characteristics which are likewise valued' (O'Brien and Tyne, 1981).

These principles have been much misunderstood and clinical psychologists within the UK have made a major contribution to fostering a better understanding at a political level and clarifying their implications for service planning. They have been instrumental in the increasing acceptance of normalization as providing a statement against which to judge service quality in the provision of ordinary living experiences for people with a mental handicap by using it to make a common vocabulary available to those responsible for the services.

At a more individual level, the principles of normalization have provided a framework for making decisions about people's needs for intervention. They suggest criteria for goals related to ordinary needs rather than goals constrained by the fact of a person's mental handicap. Consistent reference to these within the individual programme planning approaches that are inherently part of the process has helped create a climate which has, in itself, produced pressure for change in the services being provided.

22   John: treating stereotyped behaviours

Stereotypies or stereotyped behaviours are generally defined as repetitive and invariant actions that appear to serve no obvious purpose, for example, foot-tapping or head-banging. Although they occur in most if not all people and animal species, they are particularly common in people who are handicapped or institutionalized. Stereotypies present a problem to teachers and others working with handicapped people, since they may prevent new learning and the expression of adaptive skills.

Most theories assume that the function of stereotypies is to enable a person to cope with a particular type of event, internal state or environment. For instance, one group of theorists (Baumeister and Forehand, 1973) have suggested that stereotypies are due to frustration. Certainly their experimental studies demonstrate that frustrating handicapped individuals induces them to show stereotypies. Other theories have proposed that stereotypies modulate arousal both by reducing it (e.g. Berkson and Mason, 1963) and by increasing it (Ellis, 1973). The evidence suggests that such theories can provide only partial explanations of stereotypies, and indeed that most of the occasions on which stereotypies are induced are not under such straightforward control (Romanczyk et al., 1982). Unfortunately, therefore, theories of stereotypies do not provide us with clear treatment methods.

The referral

John was 11 years and 10 months old when first seen. He suffered from a number of the effects of infection with German measles virus during pregnancy. He was profoundly deaf, and had had cataracts removed from his eyes in early childhood. He remained partially sighted, although he could see well enough to walk around without help.

His mother had died when he was only 5 years old, since which time he had been resident either in hospitals or in boarding schools for mentally handicapped people. At the beginning of the study he had just arrived at a specialist child treatment unit sited on the campus of a large mental handicap hospital.

John was referred for treatment of his apparent unresponsiveness and failure to learn. He would spend most of the time with one finger in his eye or flapping his hands in front of his face. This case study is intended to demonstrate how research methods enabled techniques for teaching him new skills to be formulated.

Assessment

John was assessed in two ways: first by observing his behaviour, and second on the Reynell-Zinkin scales of development (Reynell and Zinkin, 1975) which have norms for both blind and partially sighted children. Only the non-verbal scales were administered because John neither spoke nor appeared to hear speech.

John was observed during the assessment by recording every behaviour that occurred in any ten-second period during one block of ten minutes each day during an assessment period of one week. He showed some stereotyped behaviours in each ten-second period. The observations also demonstrated the wide range of stereotypies he indulged in. Six behaviours occurred particularly frequently: poking his eyes; hitting his face; flapping his hands; pulling his hair; pinching himself; shaking his head.

John's results on the Reynell-Zinkin scales revealed that on the social adaptation sub-scale he was functioning at about 3 years 6 months, on the sensorimotor understanding sub-scale he was at the 2 year 2 month level, and on the exploration of the environment sub-scale he was at about the 3 year 4 month level.

The results suggest that he had particular problems in early cognitive skills such as comparisons of size and shape. Comments in the notes at the time suggest that he was interested in the test materials but had only fleeting concentration. Treatment and teaching of methods would therefore need to be non-verbal and immediately contingent on his behaviour.

Problem formulation

The biggest problem for teachers working with John was his inability to concentrate on tasks. Observation suggested that he could not be attracted to a task because he was involved in eye-poking or flapping his hands, and that if he did perform a task, he would immediately return to these behaviours. Behaviours such as eye-poking and flapping occur frequently as stereotypies in partially sighted and blind children. Eye-poking is of particular concern in partially sighted children because it tends to damage their remaining vision. Therefore it was decided that the first goal of treatment with John would be to attempt to control his stereotypies. Before considering the methods used, literature on the treatment of stereotypies will be summarized.

Treatment of stereotypies

Operant behavioural theories have suggested a large number of techniques for the control of behaviour. The basic premise is that positive and negative reinforcers can be used to change the frequency of behaviours by making their occurrence contingent on the behaviour. In principle at least, stereotypies could be controlled using operant methods. In the case of stereotypies, recent reviews have identified at least 13 different methods of intervening (LaGrow and Repp, 1984). Three refer to the use of positive contingencies. None of the positive techniques used alone were found to be as effective as aversive techniques alone.

Seven of the treatment methods involved aversive techniques, in which a punishment is applied contingent on the occurrence of the stereotypy. However, some of the techniques described are dubious ethically (e.g. electric shock or aversive physical consequences such as a slap from staff), and so could not be used.

Other techniques such as aversive music or verbal punishment were inappropriate in John's case because of his deafness. Another technique that is sometimes used with stereotyped behaviours is time out from positive reinforcement. The usual method is to place the person where there is nothing interesting happening, such as the corner of a room. In John's case such a technique would have been ineffective because he would have been able to engage in stereotypies just as easily.

The most popular aversive technique reported in the literature is that of over-correction in which the client is required to practice alternative behaviours whenever he tries to start a stereotypy. The rationale is that it enables an alternative behaviour to be learned and that it is aversive to be compelled. LaGrow and Repp (1984) reviewed 23 studies of over-correction alone and concluded that it was as effective as most other forms of aversive treatment for stereotypies. However, when over-correction was attempted with John, he became more upset than was felt desirable or appropriate.

A few studies have investigated the effect of contingent restraint, but there is a danger of increasing the rate of other stereotypies (e.g. Bitgood *et al.*, 1980). It was felt that the most effective method would be to prevent the stereotypies occurring and at the same time indicate activities that would be more appropriate in a classroom setting. The simplest technique that could be devised required the teacher to push John's hands away from his face, around which many of his stereotypies occurred. In effect this was a form of brief restraint contingent on the stereotypy starting.

Design of study

The study of the effects of the treatment involved a multiple baseline design (Hersen and Barlow, 1976). This type of single case design requires that a baseline is taken for each behaviour of interest. Interventions are then planned to occur in a staggered fashion so that no two interventions take place at the same time. Multiple baseline designs, in which a single treatment is used for a number of behaviours, enable one to assert with some confidence that the effects observed are due to treatment rather than to effects such as attention or maturation.

In this study only three of the six most frequent behaviours were treated with the brief restraint technique. The remaining three behaviours were not treated in order to ascertain whether they would increase in frequency as a result of the treatment. The treatment consisted of five phases of ten sessions, each lasting 20 minutes. The phases were:

(1) baseline;
(2) treatment of eye-poking;
(3) treatment of face-hitting;
(4) treatment of hand-flapping;
(5) follow-up.

Each behaviour was treated separately.

Methods

All the sessions occurred during the normal school day. John was seated at a table with toys in one corner of a large classroom so that he could neither see nor hear other teachers or children. The teacher did not intervene in John's activities during the baseline and follow-up sessions. During treatment sessions, if John began a particular stereotypy, his hands were pushed firmly down onto the table, and he was encouraged to explore the toys.

All the sessions were recorded on videotape and a complete transcript of the occurrences of each of the six behaviours was made.

Results

The number of occurrences of each of the six behaviours during baseline, treatment and follow-up is shown in Figure 22.1. Inspection of the graphs suggests that the treatment had the effect of reducing the occurrence of treated stereotypies but without increasing or decreasing the frequency of untreated ones. It is also worth

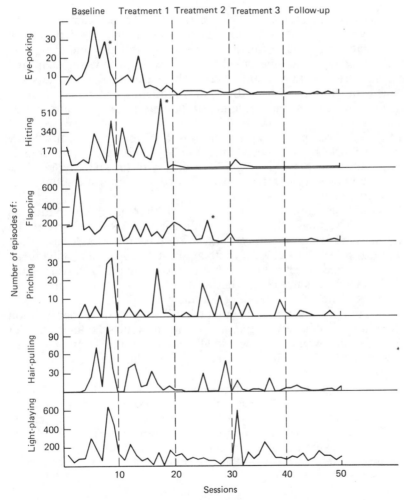

Figure 22.1 Changes in the number of episodes of stereotyped behaviours. During baseline and follow-up phases the stereotyped behaviours were not treated. During treatment 1 only eye-poking was treated. During treatment 2 only hitting was treated and during treatment 3 only flapping. The remaining three stereotyped behaviours (pinching, hair-pulling and light-playing) were not treated in this study. The asterisks indicate the point of maximum overall change on the graphs and suggest that treatment has the effect of reducing stereotyped behaviours

noting that in general there are only small increases in the rates of stereotyped behaviour in the follow-up phases. Indeed in one case, eye-poking, the rate continues to decrease after the treatment has stopped (see Treatment 2 phase in Figure 22.1). A statistical analysis of these results is possible using a technique described by Clements and Hand (1985) which assesses where the maximum changes in level of slope of a graph occur. The asterisks on the graphs indicate where the maximum change occurs, which is almost identical to the point at which treatment starts. The treatment therefore appears effective and durable, since it does not seem to promote an increase in the frequency of untreated behaviours. It also seems to be reasonably free of side-effects, unlike over-correction.

Discussion

The results from this study suggest that a brief restraint procedure can reduce the frequency of stereotypies without deleterious effects on other stereotypies. The follow-up suggests that the effects of treatment are reasonably durable at least in the short term. As a result it became possible to teach John new self-help and communication skills. Brief restraint could therefore be a useful aid to teachers and therapists working with children with multiple and frequent stereotypies. It is an eminently practical technique in that it requires relatively little time and energy from the teacher.

The treatment differs from previous interventions with John in its consistency and its structure. Previously John had been taught in larger groups and, therefore, less time was available to his previous teachers to deal with his stereotypies. It is likely that the stereotypies would have been prevented intermittently, thus prolonging the extinction period.

The study as reported has significant limitations. First, there is no information on generalization to other settings. Second, the follow-up is rather short so the stability of the changes in behaviour is uncertain. Third, it is only a single case study and therefore it is not possible to be sure of its applicability to other individuals. Finally, there must be some doubt about the use of the technique with very small stereotypies. For instance, it is not clear whether brief restraint would affect eye blinking, a stereotypy which John developed some years later.

On a more positive note one might predict that both follow-up and generalization to other settings could be achieved by the use of intermittent schedules of brief restraint. In practice this would involve slowly changing the contingency of treatment from being applied every time the stereotypy was initiated to every other time and then progressively less often.

In conclusion, the study reported here has demonstrated the utility of a brief restraint procedure in reducing the frequency of stereotypies in a multiply handicapped boy. It became possible to teach him self-help and communication skills such that he moved on to a staffed house in the community. Now, about six years later, he attends classes in a local special school, and enjoys a range of activities. He remains prone to stereotypies but it is much easier to prevent them by signing to him to stop.

23 Martin: using microelectronic technology with a profoundly and multiply handicapped child

Introduction

There is a steadily growing use of microelectronic and computer-based technology in intervention programmes with people who have a mental handicap. Because of this there have been increased demands placed upon clinicians to become familiar and proficient with such technology. It is likely that within the next five years many professionals working in the field of mental handicap will have some direct involvement in the development of such intervention strategies. The purpose of presenting this case study is to illustrate one way in which microelectronic technology can be used to increase the range of adaptive skills within even the most profoundly and multiply handicapped people. These highly dependent people represent the lowest level of adaptive functioning found, suffering from profound mental retardation, severe neuromuscular dysfunction and some degree of sensory deficit. A useful description of work with this group of people is given by Wehman (1979).

Although the group in question represents only a small percentage of the total population of people with mental handicaps, they pose a formidable challenge to those involved in environmental design and planning. At present there are no accurate prevalence figures for the group, who are typically found to function below the six-month level of development compared with normal children.

Background and assessment

Martin is an extremely multiply handicapped 5-year-old child with little opportunity to interact with his environment. His height and weight are typical of a child of 18 months. In addition to his profound mental retardation caused by lack of oxygen at birth, he also suffers from severe spastic quadriplegia, his lower limbs being totally paralysed. Martin is unable to move his body in any meaningful way but does have gross sweeping arm movements and can open and close his fingers. He has poor head control but is able to lift it for several seconds at a time. He responds well to auditory stimulation but his vision appears to be very impaired. Martin is also severely epileptic and receives medication for this. He suffers from constant ill health and is prone to chest infections. Although he is grossly multiply handicapped Martin appears to be happy, with some social responsiveness by smiling. He does not appear to be in any obvious pain. In assessing Martin using the Bayley Scales of Infant Development (Bayley, 1969) it was found that he was functioning below the two-month level on both mental and motor development. In fact Martin only passed the very earliest times but did well on auditory responsiveness and social responding.

Martin attends a special school where he is in a special care class. However, because of the magnitude of his problems, staff had great difficulty in developing an appropriate curriculum to meet his needs. A particularly difficult problem for staff was that Martin would not grasp or hold objects even though he had good movement in both hands. It was the staff's request for assistance that led to the development of a programme to initiate this skill through the use of some microelectronic equipment.

Formulation

From the brief description given, it can be seen that the constraints placed upon Martin by the combined effects of his multiple handicaps prevent him from having any meaningful interactions with his environment. So great are the effects of these constraints, the amount of active control over his surroundings is essentially zero. In order to plan any effective intervention with Martin therefore, the effects of these multiple handicaps had to be reduced and modified. It was hypothesized that if this could be done then Martin would be 'free' to interact with his environment in a limited way and that he would then have some degree of control over his surroundings. The particular behavioural response that the teachers were interested in developing lent itself very well to the use of existing microelectronic technology (Lovett, 1985). In general terms what was required was a reinforcer that was perceived by Martin and a device that required a grasp-type movement to initiate it.

Intervention

The equipment

The equipment used with Martin consisted of a microelectronic car and a specially designed grip switch which, when activated, operated the car.

The car consisted of a modified go-cart frame to which a child's safety seat had been attached. The car had two high-torque motors and gearboxes. The first of these was used to propel the vehicle at a speed of 0.35 m per second, a very slow walking pace. The second motor was fitted to drive the transmission to steer the front wheels. Although the car can be steered by the use of a microprocessor which follows a black line on the floor, it was set to travel in a fixed circular pattern when used with Martin. Two electronic counters were fitted to the car, one to record the total number of times the grip switch was operated by Martin. The second was a liquid crystal clock to measure the time the grip switch was operated.

The grip switch is an extremely simple mechanism, but requires skilled engineering in its construction. The switch is activated by making a grasp response which forces a contact, thereby completing an electrical circuit. The switch can thus act as a simple on/off switch for any battery or electrical device. It is possible to vary the strength of grasp required to make the contact and for Martin the sensitivity of the grip switch was set at its maximum value.

The procedure

Martin had 40 daily sessions of ten minutes each in the car. After Martin had been lifted into the car the grip switch was attached to his hand using velchrome tape. Then electronic counters were activated so that any degree of grasp response would produce an electrical contact and the car would begin to move. If the grip was released the car would stop.

Three separate conditions were used with Martin: a baseline period, a non-contingent reinforcement period and a contingent reinforcement period. All sessions were carried out in the school hall which was free from noise. Both baseline and non-contingent conditions were made up of ten ten-minute sessions, while the contingent reinforcement condition was made up of 20 ten-minute sessions.

During baseline (sessions 1–10) no consequences resulted from the grasp responses made by Martin, this being carried out to establish his operant rate of responding. During non-contingent reinforcement (sessions 11–20) reinforcement was given to Martin but this was not contingent upon his making a grasp response. During this condition Martin received movement in the car continuously through each session. During contingent reinforcement (sessions 21–40) Martin was able to control the onset and length of time the car moved by making a grasp response. As long as he exerted sufficient force on the grip switch the car would continue to move. If Martin released his grip the car would immediately stop.

In addition, throughout this study both the numbers of vocalizations made and smiling behaviour exhibited were recorded, measured in frequency only; no analysis of qualitative aspects was undertaken.

Results

Martin's results in total grasp responses made and length of time the grip switch was activated are shown in Figure 23.1. The results show that Martin was able to learn the association between response required and contingent reinforcement. There is a progressive increase in grasp responses made during the contingent reinforcement condition. His overall rate increased from four to 63 responses per ten-minute session. Martin also showed a slightly increased response rate during non-contingent reinforcement sessions, but this was not progressive in nature.

The total time the grip switch was activated showed a strong positive relation to grasp responses made in each of the three conditions. Martin's time for operating the grip switch increased from four to 44 seconds during the contingent reinforcement condition. In addition, there was clear evidence to show that the length of time Martin was grasping the grip switch was increasing, suggesting that within sessions learning was taking place.

The results relating the vocalizations made and smiling behaviour showed a similar pattern to that of overall response rate. There is an increase in both these measures during periods of contingent reinforcement.

Discussion

The results from this case study clearly demonstrate that even the most profoundly and multiply mentally handicapped people are able to learn adaptive skills once their environments are modified. It is the very existence of the constraints of multiple handicap that normally prevent such people from being able to interact with their surroundings and to control them. In Martin's case it was shown that once the response requirements for him to exert an effect upon his environment had been reduced to a sufficiently low level, not only did he become more active but he quickly learned that operating the grip switch would activate the car.

In this study three conditions were presented to Martin. The non-contingent reinforcement phase represented an investigation into the effects of increasing environmental stimulation *per se*. For instance, it might have been the case that by increasing Martin's daily stimulation, his own activity, including grasping, would increase. However, the results show that it is only when reinforcement is made contingent upon Martin operating the grip switch that his behaviour altered.

After this initial study the equipment remained at the school for a year. From time to time Martin was unable to have sessions in the car but he always showed a good response when given the opportunity to go in it again. One way that staff

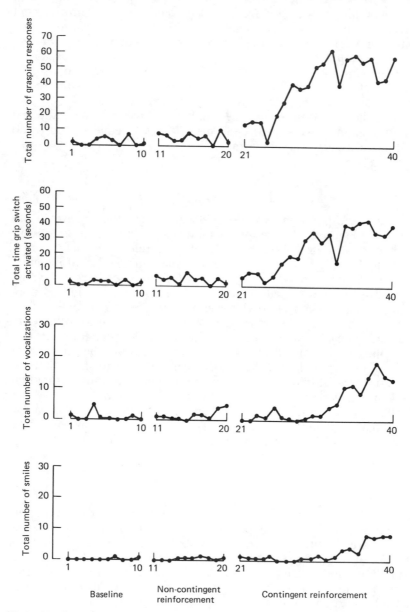

Figure 23.1 Results of intervention

began to use the equipment was to let Martin (and other multiply handicapped pupils) ride in the car during lessons in the school hall while ambulant children had physical education. In this way Martin was able to be much more part of the class and was no longer excluded from these sessions.

Over the period of the study Martin showed no signs of transferring his new skill to other settings, although teachers reported that he did seem more interested in objects and toys. This result is not surprising when one considers the extent of Martin's handicaps, the magnitude of which prevented him from interacting with his environment before the intervention took place. During his sessions in the car he showed clear enjoyment of the situation. Evidence of this came from the results of his vocalizations and smiling. So sensitive are these measures that in the absence of electronic counters it would seem quite realistic to use them to evaluate new techniques and equipment with the group in question.

In conclusion, the present case study represents a demonstration of one way in which microelectronic technology can be used effectively to develop skills within a multiply handicapped person. The cost of such equipment need not be great. However, it is necessary to have the expertise of a mechanical and electronic engineer. It may be that the services of such people can be found through local medical physics departments, colleges or universities or through REMAP, an organization of skilled people who provide their services free to build equipment to help handicapped people.

24   Mary: progress in socialization

Background

Mary was admitted to care as a baby and boarded with foster parents in a Scottish fishing village in October 1951. She had been there for nine years when she was taken to a reception centre where she stayed for four years before being placed in a children's home. She was then admitted to a hospital for people with mental handicaps. As a young child she had been described as a big girl, friendly, talkative and trusting. She was educated at a 'special' school up to the age of 18. Her mother was known to be mentally handicapped but her brother had a successful career in the RAF and her four sisters, although boarded out eventually, coped with normal schooling.

Because of a series of apparently unprovoked attacks on people round about her, Mary was admitted to a mental handicap hospital as a compulsory patient in 1967. The psychiatric and social work reports which were available at that time suggested that Mary had for some years presented significant behavioural problems which may have been accentuated by her large, heavy-boned stature and rather loud style. She had attacked a number of people both inside and outside the family, beating them up in what appeared to be very violent rages. There was a suggestion that she was suffering from epilepsy. She showed some difficulty with word-finding and apparent changes in level of responsiveness and even consciousness during interview. A skull X-ray proved normal but an EEG showed abnormality of parieto-occipital wave forms which were non-specific for epilepsy. Nevertheless, Mary was prescribed a small dose of anticonvulsant medication together with a minor tranquillizer.

Mary continued to be a compulsory patient. On the official form of certification the psychiatrist wrote that she was 'prone to outbursts of excessive violence and aggression whereby she is a danger to herself and others. She is emotionally unstable and has no insight into the deficiencies in her behaviour.'

Referral

In 1971 Mary was referred to the psychology department. She had had a particularly difficult period of both active and latent aggression, was neither working nor eating appropriately, and had been threatening to break windows and doors and to abscond. This phase lasted some weeks, during which time Mary was unable to develop any therapeutic relationships.

Assessment

A number of psychological tests were administered. The Eisenson Aphasia Test (Eisenson, 1954) showed some word-finding difficulty; the Gibson Spiral Maze (Gibson, 1965) score suggested poor motor control; the Bender Gestalt Test (Bender, 1938) performances showed significant perceptual motor disturbance, possibly indicating parieto-occipital dysfunction. On the Holborn Reading Scale (Watts, 1948), Mary's reading age of 7 years 9 months was perhaps a little low for her Wechsler Adult Intelligence Scale (Wechsler, 1955) score of 59. There was no excessive variation in WAIS sub-test scores and it was concluded that Mary could be seen as a moderately handicapped person whose perceptual motor defects and history of violent outbursts might fit with an epileptic disposition rather than indicating straightforward psychopathic behaviour in a way that had been suggested by some previous witnesses. At this time there was also noted a peculiarity of interactional style, which was characterized by very loud explosive speech, uncontrolled motor behaviour and, at times, lapses into long periods of hesitance, near silence and apparent blocking.

Formulation

At a clinical level, Mary's outbursts might have been seen sometimes to be environmentally provoked by people crossing her, but in general these seemed to occur out of the blue. Because of her considerable bulk and strength these outbursts were seen by most of the observers and recipients as being more drastic and damaging than they might have been had she been more slightly built and less loud. The psychologist considered that in the continuing absence of any positive signs of epilepsy and because of the significant threat that Mary posed to other residents and staff, an attempt should be made to reduce her aggressive behaviour and if possible, in parallel, to reduce her weight. In the course of arranging interviews with Mary and with other staff to clarify how to go about this, the psychologist also decided that one of the most significant features of Mary's behaviour was that she shouted, rather than spoke, and seemed incapable of carrying on a conversation at anything under about 80 decibels. This, in conjunction with her fairly thick glasses and obesity, made her a fairly unattractive social being and seriously reduced her rehabilitative potential. Programmes were therefore required (a) to reduce Mary's weight, (b) to reduce speech loudness, (c) to minimize her involvement in situations where overt aggression would fit, (d) to maximize and reinforce social cooperation and Mary's own self-esteem where appropriate and possible.

Intervention

In many ways the dietary problem was the easiest to tackle. Exact dietary details are not reported here but Mary was kept scrupulously to them. To support the dietary regime, Mary was weighed daily and the psychologist arranged for this to be charted on her locker door daily by one of the ward staff. Mary was rewarded with a yellow star each day her weight dropped and a gold star if it dropped for three days continuously. These stars were then associated with special privileges or activities in or out of the ward and later became associated with parole outside the hospital, interward visiting and increased pocket money as her general behaviour improved. Her weight had been generally around 12 stone 5 lbs. On the diet it settled for just over a year at around 11 stone until the social reinforcers operated more effectively as her other social skills developed. She then settled to just under 10 stone. Mary was still a bulky girl but at least her weight was now more in keeping with her height and bone structure.

One of the problems for Mary was the fact that she was largely confined to a ward where there were a number of disturbed residents of lower ability than her and where in fact many of them were physically smaller. It was also apparent that she had insufficient stimulation and because of her loud voice and tendency to speak peremptorily to others, she was seen as antisocial and unable to converse appropriately. High levels of frustration consequently occurred and culminated usually in a physical assault. In spite of the gloomy prognostications of ward staff, it was suggested that two general lines of activity should be initiated to minimize her boredom and restriction: first, she would go to work in the laundry with other of the more able residents and, second, she would attend a group therapy session with the clinical psychologist once a week. This group was one in which there was a good deal of free discussion but this was interspersed with sessions of didactic therapy and social skills training.

The underlying idea was to extend opportunity for diversity of social skills and at the same time to give Mary a range of environments in which she could test different kinds of social behaviour and be appropriately reinforced.

In her work at the laundry Mary was originally placed with another very large resident who could hold her own in any physical contretemps. She was also given fairly physically demanding work there which would enable her to burn up calories and keep her attention.

The most noticeable change in Mary occurred in the group therapy where she was initially one of eight or nine residents of both sexes, all of whom had a history of fairly violent, disturbed or unusual behaviour. In this setting, she became remarkably reticent and literally silent, often for 40 or 50 minutes at a time. However, it was noted that she was always a keen observer of how others behaved and what they said. At the conclusion of groups she would speak loudly and effusively on the way back to the ward as if releasing pent up energy which she had stored during the group.

The general thrust of the training and rehabilitation programme undertaken was the operant reinforcement of acceptable behaviours and the simultaneous changing of the general pattern of daily experiences and contingencies so as to extend her behaviour repertoire. As weekly sessions in therapy continued, the range of topics discussed, at least by other residents, gave Mary increasing opportunities to make brief contributions. This she did initially in her very loud voice until other members of the group asked her to quieten down when she spoke, often in no uncertain terms. At this point the therapist would encourage the other members of the group to pay a good deal of attention to what Mary said when she spoke more normally and in the same way the therapist would reinforce, with smiles, nods and general approbation, occasions when Mary presented a point in a normal voice. A number of variants of this occurred to draw Mary's attention to her habit since she was initially unconscious of it. For example, the therapist, when addressed by Mary in her very loud voice, would respond in a voice at an equal decibel level, to 'mark' or signal her behaviour. Initially this embarrassed her but within two or three sessions she began to speak at a more normal conversational level.

An adjuvant feature of these sessions was that Mary was given an opportunity to engage in a variety of role playing and conversational activities which both maintained her attention level and increased her sense of social status, since even being invited to these groups was seen as a significant privilege by the members of the group. Group members, for example, always had some say as to whether a new member could be admitted, and could, if there was consensus, also exclude a present member. As a consequence of this, Mary's social learning was much facilitated. After some months of this regime, Mary also began to take an interest in the opposite sex and established a fairly longstanding relationship with a boyfriend who was also a hospital resident.

Outcome

Mary was now working regularly in the hospital laundry without mishap. Her behaviour improved to such a degree that the psychiatrist who had always, as a safeguard, treated Mary with anticonvulsants, reduced and finally terminated these in February 1977 with no adverse effects.

Mary went with several boyfriends over the next year or two on a casual basis while her social skills progressively developed. Her weight had more or less stabilized on a normal diet by this time and eventually in 1980 she had had a sufficiently longstanding relationship with another resident to consider marriage. Her general behaviour was stable and she was given full parole for the first time to visit a nearby town with her boyfriend and again no mishaps resulted.

By the end of 1982 Mary was progressively weaned from the planned programme of behaviour modification. She was taking a low level of minor tranquillizer and had been put on a hostel waiting list. Mary had by this time given up the idea of marriage and had in fact changed to another boyfriend with whom she made a number of successful visits to a nearby city at weekends.

Early in 1983 Mary was given a place in a group home in a local town and after six months it was clear that she could cope well with a permanent placing there. Her compulsory detention was discharged in August 1983. Although the freedom of the group home did lead to some increase in weight because of more opportunities to buy casual snacks, Mary's general social behaviour was completely adequate. She visited banks, shops and other facilities in the town, continued with a number of boyfriends, dressed tidily and related well to people around her. Needless to say, there was a complete absence of aggressive verbal behaviour or physical attacks and to the time of writing Mary continues to be a reasonably well-adjusted citizen. On first greeting, she tends to be over-loud but most of her conversation is at a normal level.

Discussion

One of the most distressing features of this case was that the specific attention of a clinical psychologist was not drawn to it until 1971, some four years after Mary's admission to hospital. Perhaps this makes some kind of statement about the tolerance of ward staff for disturbed behaviour, or it may indicate that they harboured the notion that Mary might grow out of her disturbed behaviour because she was still developing through her adolescence. Even as a 16-year-old when she was admitted, she was really seen as a fat and clumsy child rather than as a young adult. It is perhaps significant that four years of physical growth had changed her into something of a physical threat to other residents and staff at the time her case was referred to the department of clinical psychology.

A second significant characteristic of the course of training and treatment arranged for Mary was that her home and relatives played no part in it. None was interested in making or sustaining any contact with her, and any goals for her developing socialization had to be couched in terms of hostel care or some even minimally supported environmental back-up apart from her family. One by-product of this was, however, that she became particularly responsive to social and other pressures from her peer group within the hospital and from members of the staff with whom she had some rapport.

There was good interdisciplinary cooperation throughout Mary's treatment. The psychiatrist, clinical psychologist, ward sisters, occupational therapists and several other staff who met Mary incidentally in her work and activities through the hospital each made their contribution to the success of the programme. Information about what was going on in the programme was made readily available to all participants by the psychologist and this is thought to have played a large part in the success of the programme.

The programme of treatment and training extended over a period of 11–12 years. The constraints of a hospital setting where, for example, a large number of residents require time from a very small number of specialist staff, such as psychologists, partly accounts for this. Despite the organizational difficulties, a programme of selective reinforcement, applied in a number of different contexts, all with the aim of minimizing destructive and aggressive behaviour, maximizing social skills and developing a positive self-image, was sustained consistently over a prolonged period.

During the period of this programme (1970s and early 1980s) there were considerable changes of attitude and approach to the care of people with mental handicaps. It is unlikely that compulsory hospitalization would now be considered appropriate for someone like Mary. However, in 1983 there were still 49 600 people with mental handicaps who remained in hospital in the UK (DHSS, 1986) and this case illustrates that constructive long-term goals can be worked for and achieved.

25 Charles: meeting extraordinary needs in an ordinary house

Introduction

Charles is in his late twenties. From about the age of 11 he has exhibited difficult behaviour in the form of aggressive attacks on other people and himself and has been treated with a variety of major tranquillizers.

He lived at home with his parents and sisters until the age of 16, attending special schools for children with severe learning difficulties. At 16 he went to live in a hospital for men with a mental handicap, where he stayed for the next 11 years. During this time he grew into a tall, strong, physically able man who continued to use sporadic aggressive behaviour towards other people.

Charles learned to wash, dress, eat and generally look after himself, but never learned to speak or use an alternative form of communication. If left alone, he would spend long periods of time lying down or sitting in a chair, rocking.

Reason for referral

National policies relating to mental handicap services direct that institutional care should be replaced by alternatives that afford people opportunities for community, integration, and for living an ordinary life (King's Fund, 1980). With local implementation of this policy, the hospital in which Charles lived was scheduled to close. All the residents were to be resettled in ordinary houses in groups of five to eight people with staff support.

An evaluation of the first such house to be opened had shown that people with difficult and disruptive behaviour could be successfully integrated. Additionally, with individualized programmes, people could be helped to develop new skills and to lose much of their disruptive behaviour (Felce *et al.*, 1986).

During Charles's stay in hospital, the main form of therapy he had received was medication. Attempts were made to analyse his behavioural problems, but due to the restrictive setting, the custodial philosophy and the low staffing levels, it was not possible to implement programmes which were devised to help Charles to develop appropriate and competent behaviour.

The initial request for assistance from the psychologist came from the staff in the house to which Charles moved from the hospital. The referral was to work with the staff to assess the nature of Charles's difficulties and needs (including his aggressive behaviour) and then to develop strategies for meeting those needs (including the need to be less aggressive).

The approach

The approach that was used and which determined the various assessment and intervention measures employed was that known as applied behavioural analysis. This approach, based on operant learning principles, centres on the belief that a person's behaviours are functionally related to other events in that person's environment (including other people's behaviour) and that these other events are critical for the maintenance and/or change of individual behaviour.

It is through the observation, interpretation and manipulation of these functional relationships between behaviours, their antecedents and consequences, that behavioural analysis is applied to individual problems. The process involves: observation and data collection; interpretation; intervention; evaluating the effects of intervention (Tennant *et al.*, 1981).

Intervention

First period

Charles was moved from hospital to a new staffed house in February 1985. There were four other residents who had recently moved from hospital, and the nine new care staff were inexperienced. All residents were required to participate in structured activities, both in and outside the home. The staff were committed to the principles of normalization. Data were collected on all incidents of aggressive behaviour, using the Specific Incident Sheet (Cameron *et al.*, 1984). From this came the formulation that Charles's aggressive behaviour was maintained by social reinforcement. A programme was instigated to differentially reinforce alternative behaviour, as follows:

(1) positive attention, interaction and access to preferred place and activities for appropriate behaviour, that is, compliance and engagement in prescribed tasks;
(2) withdrawal of these reinforcers following aggression;
(3) use of skilled key workers for Charles and to act as a model to other staff.

As a result of this programme, the number of aggressive incidents decreased from 29 in week one to an average of less than nine in weeks three to nine, until Charles's medication was changed (Figure 25.1).

Levels of appropriate behaviour were high. However, the inexperience of the care staff led to the programme placing unacceptably high demands on senior staff, and consequently Charles was admitted to another hospital, at the beginning of May 1985.

Charles remained in a locked villa in hospital until September 1985. Attempts were made to control his aggressive behaviour with medication, but no beneficial effects were observed. No systematic records were kept of Charles's behaviour during this time. He was considered suitable to return to a community unit and was discharged.

Second period

Charles was removed to a small bungalow, which was temporarily vacant, where he lived alone for two weeks with two staff to help with self-care, domestic and recreational activities. Observations made by a speech therapist at the hospital indicated that, in addition to being maintained by social reinforcement, Charles's aggressive behaviour was elicited by the use of verbal language during interaction.

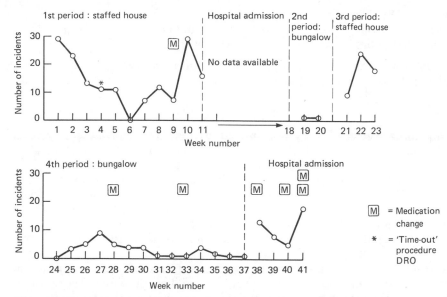

Figure 25.1 Frequency of physical aggression to others, objects and self

An additional formulation was made, that Charles's aggressive behaviour was an attempt to escape or avoid demands and that aggression was more probable with a more difficult task. While there was no danger to other residents, the opportunity was taken to set up experimental sessions which were designed to elicit the aggressive behaviour. These sessions consisted of Charles working with an experimenter and an observer, on table-top tasks of varied levels of difficulty and either verbal or verbal plus demonstration cues. Charles was required to continue tasks following aggressive behaviour and sessions alternated between interaction and non-interaction — that is, sessions in which Charles was requested to perform tasks were interspersed with sessions in which the experimenter was seated in the room but away from Charles and apparently engaged in another activity. 'Simple' tasks involving pointing to pictures were alternated with 'difficult' tasks involving the manipulation of objects according to instructions given by the experimenter. Gestural demonstration cues were given in some conditions and Charles's responses were observed and recorded.

For this period Charles was very compliant and relaxed. There were only two aggressive incidents (one during an experimental session), but the time was considered too short for firm conclusions to be drawn.

Third period

Charles was returned to the staffed house in October 1985, where there were seven other residents now living. A rota of skilled back-up staff was arranged and his room was made into a bed-sitter, enabling him to be alone if he wished. Staff had the same commitment to engagement in activities and participation in tasks on request.

The previous formulation was continued, that Charles's aggressive behaviour was elicited by verbal interaction and was an attempt to avoid demands. The following intervention was implemented:

(1) use of minimal verbal prompts and maximum use of gesture in interaction with Charles;

151

(2) strong verbal reprimand following aggression;

(3) no escape following aggression, that is Charles did not leave the room and was expected to continue with his previous activity.

The outcome was a rapid increase in the number of aggressive incidents, causing unacceptable stress to other people.

Fourth period

After only three weeks Charles was moved back to the bungalow where he remained until January 1986. For the first four weeks Charles shared the bungalow with two other people who then chose to leave because of his behaviour. He lived alone with staff for seven weeks, after which time it was possible to introduce another resident to share with Charles. Due to the failure to develop appropriate strategies to manage Charles's behaviour when it was elicited, the approach was changed to finding ways of reducing Charles's aggressive behaviour by changing the antecedents, rather than by manipulating the consequences after the aggressive incidents.

It was formulated that Charles's aggression was a means of communication that he was upset and that the events which upset him could be identified. Therefore, it was decided to minimize demands on him to engage in activities and staff were instructed to comply with his requests. At the same time he was given maximum possible control over his environment.

Consequently the frequency of physical aggression decreased and remained at a low level, especially when there were no other residents. However, the financial cost of maintaining this environment was deemed by the service managers to be too high and Charles was returned to a third hospital, where at the time of writing (October 1986) he remains.

Summary

Looking at the information obtained from this series of interventions, several conclusions can be drawn.

There are environmental events with which Charles has difficulty coping and which act as antecedents to physical aggression. These events are one or a combination of noise, numbers of other people and inability to control his own environment.

The consequence of physical aggression has usually been for such events to be removed from Charles's environment. Therefore physical aggression is functional for Charles.

The effects of medication are minimal compared with the above environmental influences on Charles.

Two options were identified for providing a service for Charles. First, place him in an environment which elicits the aggressive behaviour frequently, so that he can be taught coping strategies, for example, removing himself from the room before he becomes agitated. This approach was adopted in the small staffed house. It resulted in distress and physical harm to other residents and staff, low staff morale, a refusal to work with Charles and extreme pressure on the person in charge of the house.

Alternatively, place Charles in an environment which reduces his need to use physically aggressive behaviour and slowly build on his strengths. This approach was adopted during his final stay in the bungalow and resulted in special accommodation having to be identified for him, boredom in staff, some feelings of resentment in staff caused by Charles controlling his own environment (including them), low staff morale and a refusal to work with Charles.

Both options would require an experienced support team to be employed to work specifically with Charles.

Discussion

The small staffed house faced a number of difficulties in attempting to absorb disruptive behaviour. The needs of the seven other people in the house had to be considered, particularly their right to live peaceably in their own home. They also required some specialist intervention to maintain their quality of life. This was difficult to provide, when all existing resources were being allocated to Charles. Inexperienced staff in the house also had their own tolerance levels which were stretched to the limit with little or no possibility of replacement staff to provide relief cover.

The number of moves which Charles was required to make meant that during the year three different community teams became responsible for Charles as he moved to different neighbourhoods. Liaison between the three psychologists involved was sufficient to ensure consistent data collection to begin to understand Charles's behaviour using applied behavioural analysis but there was intense pressure on each psychologist to arrive at solutions before the tolerance level and coping ability of staff and residents became overstretched. Under such constraints it was not possible to spend much time simply observing Charles and his reactions to the manipulation of variables within a particular environment.

Throughout the intervention each psychologist adopted a variety of roles which included direct intervention, behaviour analysis, support to senior and direct care staff, acting as a model for the staff, acting as an advocate for Charles, reporting to service managers and planning alternative ways to meet Charles's accommodation needs. The work of the psychologist at a number of different levels at any one time was no different from the work which would be undertaken for any other client. However, the intensity of the work for this particular client, and the drain on community resources which were already stretched, must be an issue to be faced by service managers who may be planning to move people with special difficulties to live in the community. A particular issue in this case was the conflict between the needs of the individual and the needs of the service system.

26   Helping Molly and her family

Introduction

There is now greater understanding of the complex nature of stress and the importance of family interaction in adapting to significant events (Byrne and Cunningham, 1985). For example, in any family there are major adjustments for all members when a child reaches adulthood and leaves home. This event presents particular difficulties when the young adult has disabilities, as uncertainties arise about obtaining meaningful employment, the level of independence in which they can live, and prospects for the future, when parents can no longer cope or after their death. For such adults and their families, therefore, the usual stresses can be magnified and additional support is often necessary. These were some of the issues facing Molly and her family when they were referred to the Community Mental Handicap Team (CMHT).

CMHTs usually consist of a group of nurses, social workers, psychologists and others who work together as a multi-disciplinary team to help people with mental handicaps in the community. The referral was made by the family's general practitioner who was asked for sleeping tablets by Molly's mother. The GP thought that Molly might be placing too much strain on Mrs Smith.

Background

The family consisted of Mr and Mrs Smith and their two children, Molly, who was 20, and David, who was 17. There were no other relatives apart from a sister of Mrs Smith's who lived with her family in Canada. Mrs Smith was not close to her sister, and had not seen her for several years.

They lived in a three-bedroomed house which was very neat, and well looked after. Mr Smith was an invoice clerk in a large local department store, and was retiring in 12 months' time. He had been seriously injured in the Second World War, and was registered as disabled. He used a stick for walking short distances, and relied on his invalid car to get to and from work. Mrs Smith and Molly worked at home all day. Molly did not attend the local Adult Training Centre (ATC). It was learned from the team social worker who made sensitive inquiries at the ATC that the Smiths had withdrawn Molly after she told them she had a boyfriend. The Smiths had told the ATC that they were frightened that Molly would be 'interfered with'. David, Molly's brother, was in his final year at the local comprehensive school where he was studying for A levels.

Assessment

The first visit to Mrs Smith and Molly was made by the community mental handicap nurse. On this occasion Mrs Smith denied that there were any problems with Molly and gave the impression that no professional help was required. However, this provoked an angry response from Mr Smith who felt that Molly was 'a serious problem' and he rang the team to demand a further visit during one evening at which he could be present. A further visit was made by the community nurse with the clinical psychologist, to meet the whole family.

From this visit it emerged that Molly had a number of behaviour problems such as swearing in public and waking at night. However, her parents held different views on how to cope with her and, because of this, the problems had never been fully discussed in the family, and there was no consistency in the family's reactions to Molly's behaviour. It was agreed that a more detailed assessment of Molly would be carried out with a view to setting up a number of goals aimed at improving the family's life with Molly.

The psychological assessment was carried out over eight weeks. The information was gathered by interviewing Molly and her family, from diaries kept by Mrs Smith, by observation and by formal psychometric assessment. The following aspects of Molly's life were covered:

early development	cognitive skills
social background	daily activities
physical capabilities	leisure and recreation
self-help skills	significant relationships
communication skills	behaviour
social skills	strengths and needs

(This list of aspects to cover in an assessment was compiled by the psychologists in the team.)

Molly's strengths were her social, communication and self-help skills. On the Wechsler Adult Intelligence Scale (WAIS), (Wechsler, 1955) she had a Full Scale IQ of 58 (verbal IQ = 64, performance IQ = 56). Her needs seemed to be for more opportunities for daily activities and leisure, and for more appropriate ways of responding to stress. Mrs Smith had kept behavioural records, in which were noted any behaviours which would be considered unusual or inappropriate in a woman aged 20. Once this list had been obtained an ABC chart was kept, where A = antecedents, B = observable behaviours and C = consequences or subsequent events (see Table 26.1).

Table 26.1 An extract from the ABC chart

Name: Molly Smith   Date chart started: 7 June
                     Date chart finished: 28 June

Date and time	A What happened beforehand?	B What did you see and hear?	C What happened afterwards?
7.6	Molly was watching TV with us. (*Coronation Street*, Dad's favourite programme). Asked Dad to pass her a jigsaw (several times). Dad ignored her.	Asked Dad to pass her a jigsaw. Dad told her to shut up. Molly began to swear at him.	Dad shouted at Molly. Molly shouted back. Mum passed jigsaw and helped Molly to do it.

In addition to this, a 24-hour chart was kept of the main difficulties. On the basis of this information it transpired that they were:

(1) inappropriate behaviour when Molly was out of the house. She would swear, at first quietly then with increasing frequency and volume, on the rare occasions that she went out (five outings were recorded over four weeks);
(2) talking when the television was on. This was a major cause of irritation to Mr Smith as Molly was most disruptive during his favourite programmes;
(3) getting up at night. Mrs Smith had moved into Molly's bedroom so that she could tend to Molly in the night and so that David and Mr Smith would not be disturbed.

During subsequent visits, over a period of approximately six months, other significant concerns within the family were revealed. David obtained surprisingly disappointing results in his mock A level exams, possibly as a result of his ambivalent attitude to leaving home. The hypothesis was that David might be afraid to do well in case this meant that he would have to leave home to carry on with his studies or to get a job. When this was discussed with Mrs Smith, she agreed with this explanation. The community nurse had established a good rapport with Mrs Smith who then began to reveal some of her own problems. Mrs Smith was extremely unhappy with her marriage and was still distressed by having conceived Molly before marriage and the subsequent discovery of Molly's mental handicaps. Mrs Smith felt that she was being 'punished by God'. The connection between her own unhappiness and Molly's problems became clearer. Mrs Smith said that she herself was unhappy out of the house, that her fitful nights had 'caused' Molly's sleep disturbance and that, by sleeping in her daughter's room, she was 'free of her marriage duties'. She had always looked to her son for support and his quiet maturity had sustained her, but she 'could not be so selfish as to ruin his prospects for a career and an independent life'.

Formulation

The problems confronting each member of the Smith family were woven into the family interactions in a complex way. For Mr Smith, the 'problem' was Molly, and he had little insight into his own maladaptive ways of coping with his fears of retirement and illness. For Mrs Smith, her marital relationship was non-existent and her husband was dependent on her almost as a child. The bond with her son, David, took precedence, and she needed to understand that this was possibly preventing him from maturing and to learn to help him be more separate from her. For David, there was the need to look to a future away from his family in ways and at a pace with which both he and his mother could cope. For Molly, there was a need to be more independent, and to learn more acceptable ways of coping with stress.

Having formulated the problems, the task for the CMHT was to decide how best to help and how to establish priorities for any intervention plan. This was done by starting with the need to improve the family's management of Molly's behaviour and then to move towards providing practical support and strategies to reduce stresses on Molly and other members of the family. Regular objectives-setting exercises were held by the nurse and the psychologist with the whole family.

Intervention

Over the next three years, the community nurse and psychologist helped the Smiths in several ways, using a mainly behavioural approach together with therapeutic strategies evolving from other family therapy approaches, such as structural, strategic and family systems therapies (see Walsh, 1982 for an overview).

To begin with, the family were advised on behavioural strategies to help improve Molly's behaviour and the success achieved allowed family members to explore goals for themselves, both as individuals and in relation to each other.

A practical programme was devised to reduce Molly's inappropriate behaviours without increasing Mrs Smith's unhappiness. The following plan was drawn up with the family:

(1) Outings would be made once a day for a short length of time, determined in advance, during which Mrs Smith would talk to Molly about how good it was to be going out. Various ways of doing this were discussed and noted down. For example, Molly liked flowers and Mrs Smith said that she could point out any pretty gardens or ask Molly for her opinions of the attractiveness of plants and could also teach her the names of plants and trees.

(2) When the television was on, Mrs Smith would enlist Mr Smith's help in interesting Molly in the programmes that Molly liked or give her something else to do during programmes that she did not enjoy.

(3) When Molly got up at night, it was usually (according to the diary and other data collected) for a drink. She was also regularly having a nap in the afternoon. The naps were to be discouraged and Mrs Smith was to give her a drink to keep beside her bed. Mrs Smith suggested that she herself could sleep downstairs so that Molly would be less able to get her mother's attention at night.

The family helped to supplement these broad strategies with practical details and continued the recordings. The level of success was agreed to be a maximum of five disturbances a day where 'a disturbance' was defined as either:

(1) any inappropriate behaviour during the daily outing, or
(2) any disturbance during Mr Smith's favourite programmes (this covered about one viewing hour each night), or
(3) any action of Molly's that woke another family member.

Clear guidelines were also agreed about what was to be done if a disturbance did arise during an outing, television programme or at night so that the family gave Molly more attention and rewards for appropriate behaviours, but gave less attention for inappropriate behaviours. The occupational therapist and psychologist also gave Mrs Smith some ideas as to how to train Molly in using her existing skills and learning new skills. The results of the programme over the next six months for the total number of disturbances are given in Figure 26.1.

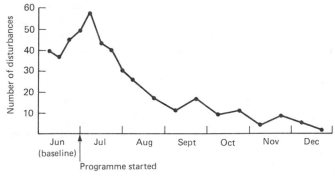

Figure 26.1 Number of disturbances recorded: weekly, then fortnightly averages

As Molly's disturbing behaviours decreased in frequency and duration, the family and therapists were able to pay some attention to the other difficulties within the family. For example, Mrs Smith helped David to join a local club and to get additional support from his sympathetic form teacher. Mr and Mrs Smith were encouraged to talk about and resolve difficulties between themselves in a more constructive way.

Outcome

After about two years the situation in the family had changed considerably. David had done well in his A levels and had started work in a bank. Molly displayed only occasional outbursts of inappropriate behaviour and, with the family's agreement, was attending an Adult Training Centre five days a week, which she enjoyed. Mrs Smith felt she had gained more control over her life; she saw that she was able to help Molly herself and she had also weaned herself off her sleeping tablets. Mr Smith had retired and settled down to his new life. Together Mr and Mrs Smith had worked out a pattern of life that was relatively peaceful.

At this stage it seemed appropriate to continue promoting Molly's independence by introducing her to the idea of short stays away from home at a local hostel for people with mental handicaps. Mr and Mrs Smith visited the hostel and the officer-in-charge invited the whole family to an evening meal there. This was very successful and Molly asked to go again. Some of her friends from the ATC lived there and she visited regularly and with increasing frequency over the next few months. It was agreed with the Smiths that this should be encouraged with a view to preparing Molly to leave home.

Unhappily this plan had to be speeded up when Mr Smith had a stroke from which he never fully recovered. Mrs Smith nursed him at home for the next four months until he became too ill. He died shortly afterwards in hospital. Mrs Smith was too busy and tired while nursing her husband to look after Molly at home, and Molly was persuaded to stay at the hostel. She settled in fairly well considering her distress at knowing that her father was ill. She occasionally became upset and her behaviour disturbances re-emerged. The ATC and hostel staff were helped to implement programmes along the same lines as had previously been used, and these were successful. The community nurse and psychologist continued to visit Molly and her parents and Molly was taken home each Sunday until her father died. The visits continued for a while after the funeral and the local MENCAP Society befriended Mrs Smith. She had not previously been a member, but the community nurse had encouraged her to make contact with them, and had taken her to a social evening.

At the final meeting with the family, Mrs Smith had plans to develop more interests outside the home. David was engaged to be married and Molly was full of stories about the ATC and hostel and showed a picture of her new boyfriend.

Discussion

The long-term needs of families with a mentally handicapped member include alternative residential care for the person with mental handicaps, training, further education or employment opportunities once school-leaving age is reached, and advice and support on a number of practical issues such as aids, financial help and ways for the family to best assist their own member. The interface between families with needs and statutory agencies, sometimes with inadequate resources to meet these needs, can often be made more flexible by a team who can understand both. The team therefore has a role in providing information to planners.

In the case discussed the team's contribution was the reduction of Molly's behaviour problems, assistance in increasing her freedom and independence and support to other family members while they accepted these changes. Some of this support need not have been the concern of a CMHT, it might be argued, but Molly's handicaps and their negative connotations prevented her family from realistically appraising their own problems. One family member's problem (the mental handicaps) came to be seen as the cause of all the family's problems. Once Molly had left home the team gradually reduced its involvement but recognized the need that Mrs Smith still had for some longer-term support which, fortunately, a voluntary agency was willing and able to provide.

27 Sex education for people with mental handicaps: a staff training package

The problem

Developments towards care in the community for people with mental handicaps over the past 10–15 years have led to a reduction of the number of such persons entering long-term institutional care, and a simultaneous increase in the number of former hospital residents returning to the less restricted, and often more demanding, patterns of life in a range of community settings.

Many such persons may have received little or no formal sex education in their childhood and adolescence. They may be ill-prepared to cope with interpersonal relationships and the complexities of appropriate and inappropriate social and sexual behaviours. More seriously, they may (often unwittingly) transgress the law (Craft and Craft, 1982), the accepted moral code, or the customary standards of the settings in which they live.

Staff working with mentally handicapped people in residential, day-care and support settings (mainly social services staff, but also staff of voluntary agencies) have been challenged by the clear need to provide sex education and counselling for their clients in order to enhance the process of integration.

In addition, two social trends have led to a greater concern with the issue of sexuality in the lives of people with mental handicaps. First, society's attitudes have become more liberal and open discussion of sexual matters is accepted and even encouraged (although the effects of the AIDS publicity on this are still to be gauged). Second, there has been a growth of interest in the rights of people with mental handicaps, including their rights to sexual expression and fulfilment, as embodied in the principles of normalization (Wolfensberger, 1972).

In practice, many staff have found that neither their qualification training nor any in-service training has equipped them to deal comfortably with this essentially complex and sensitive topic, which may be further compounded by legal, moral and religious overtones. It is common in such circumstances for a variety of outside expertise to be sought. In areas where clinical psychology services are well developed in the community, it is likely that both client problems in the area of sexuality, and associated staff training needs, may be referred to the service. It was from a series of such requests — for both staff and client education and counselling — that the staff training package described in this case study was evolved.

Formulation

The problem as presented comprised two sets of converging, but essentially competing needs for psychological time.

Clients, mainly with mild or moderate mental handicaps were being presented with clear needs for either sexual counselling (e.g. referrals as a result of demonstrations of inappropriate socio-sexual behaviour) or a structured programme of sex education (e.g. referrals of engaged couples; referrals of individuals whose gaps in sexual knowledge were cause for concern).

Staff generally had expectations that such client problems required so-called expert treatment, but they, or in some cases their managers, also requested basic training in the issues of sexuality and mental handicap, in order to prepare direct care staff to support and maintain the treatment/training offered to referred clients. In some cases, they also wished to extend this work themselves to other clients in the same facility.

From the point of view of the allocation of psychological time, and the appropriate use of psychological skills, much of the sex education or counselling required by the clients did not necessarily need the specific skills of a clinical psychologist. Some complex cases, requiring treatment rather than training, were of course appropriate psychological referrals, but these were in the minority. For those people with mental handicaps requiring sex education or counselling at a basic level, it was argued that direct care staff themselves were in the optimum position to provide either planned programmes, or occasional interventions, supported by their senior managers and, where appropriate, by clinical psychologists. Such staff already knew their clients well, had established rapport, and were well placed to monitor progress and maintain desired change.

This contrasts to the position in which many clinical psychologists find themselves. As a scarce resource, dealing with competing priorities on an episodic referral system, their interventions are often characterized by the hit-and-run formula. They commonly have little or no prior knowledge of, or relationship with, their client and are likely to maintain only time-limited management of a case.

This has led to two developments in the professional practice of clinical psychology which underpin the present work. First, the model of giving away psychological skills and techniques which has become widespread (and caused considerable debate); and, second, the practice of working with clients both directly and indirectly at a number of different levels of proximity, for example, working through care staff or working with service managers. Each of these developments has implications for the potential spread of psychological knowledge and techniques (Wilcock, 1985), and together provide opportunities for the individual psychologist to teach specific skills to defined groups of staff and then support and monitor their subsequent practice either directly, or through their managers.

The staff training package

The basic module of the package has been developed and refined over a period of some five years. It was first devised and carried out with the assistance of a junior colleague and was subsequently developed into its final form in close cooperation with a middle manager from social services, with whom the course is now jointly organized and taught.

The course is designed for direct care staff working with adults with mental handicaps in a range of support, residential and day-care settings. In practice participants have included social workers, residential care staff, staff of adult training centres, teachers, staff of voluntary agency establishments, community nurses, and, on occasion, senior managers of the above groups of staff, and parents.

The broad aims of the basic module are:

(1) to provide opportunities to examine and discuss attitudes to sexuality — both in general terms and in the context of work with people with mental handicaps;
(2) to increase knowledge of sex and sexuality and to consider the topics which might require to be included in a sex education programme for clients;
(3) to develop basic skills in teaching and counselling people with mental handicaps;
(4) to develop awareness of curriculum design and the planning of teaching or counselling sessions;
(5) to increase knowledge of the resources (both material and personnel) available to support work in this area;
(6) to consider by example the issues involved in casework in this area.

The basic module is not designed to equip staff with skills to mastery level. It is essentially an introduction to the subject which provides a basis for supported, rather than independent, practice.

The course is demand-led, and operates on average once or twice a year. The preferred number of participants is 20–24, permitting the formation of four smaller groups of 5–6 people for practical sessions and discussions.

Within the general framework of the aims of the basic module, each course is customized by the use of information from pre-course profiles and questionnaires. These are designed to elicit and identify the concerns, interests and objectives of each group of staff, and the associated difficulties or problems demonstrated by the clients with whom they work. The course then lasts for either three or four consecutive days, six to eight sessions, depending on the assessed needs of staff.

In passing it is worth noting that the entire staff training package is organized and operated with due regard to basic behavioural principles: taking baselines; starting where the 'customers' are; using shaping and guided discovery techniques; providing feedback; reinforcing target behaviours; monitoring performance and evaluating outcome; and incorporating maintenance and follow-up schedules.

The course has six developmental stages:

Stage one

Participants complete a series of four questionnaires on knowledge of sex; knowledge of the sexuality of people with mental handicaps; attitudes to sex; and attitudes towards the sexual behaviour of people with mental handicaps. The questionnaires are broadly those designed by Kempton (Kempton and Foreman, 1976) with some omission of items which pertain only to the USA (e.g. those on state law) and some minor anglicization of other items for a UK setting. They are filled in anonymously if desired; and discrete supervision of this procedure helps ensure that individual and not collaborative responses are produced.

Two separate purposes underlie this task. First, participants are provided with the opportunity to confront their own knowledge or lack of it and their personal attitudes in these areas, in a relatively unthreatening manner. This serves to focus their subsequent practical work and group discussions. Although the task undoubtedly raises the level of anxiety of some participants, the vast majority, on post-course feedback, cite this exercise as one of the most valuable for orientation and personal baseline. Second, the results of the questionnaires allow further tailoring of the course material to be offered in stage two.

The data from the questionnaires are subsequently fed back to participants at the end of the course in the form of either answers to the knowledge questions, or grouped scores for the attitude items. (No attempt is made to repeat these procedures in the form of post-course questionnaires since it is known that any changes from pre-testing could not be attributed solely to the course, but might also be accounted for by informal non-course discussions and information exchange, together with concurrent personal reading.)

Stage two

This stage incorporates a taught component, together with associated group tasks and case discussions. The background to work on sexuality and mental handicap is reviewed, including issues of institutionalization, normalization, community care, rights, advocacy and sexual myths. (The extent of background coverage accounts for the main difference between the three- and four-day versions of this basic module.) Following from this, and from the stage one questionnaires, information is provided and references recommended to extend and fill the most obvious gaps in participants' sexual knowledge, consistent with the level of work to be undertaken, and the need to be clear, frank, unambiguous and intelligible in their discussions with clients. Finally, extensive consideration is given to the broad area of attitudes to sex, sexuality and mental handicap. Work on attitude formation and change is reviewed; issues of values, tolerance, prejudice, norms and ethics are explored; and the attitudes of staff, of parents and relatives of people with mental handicaps, of clients themselves, and of society, are discussed. Once again, the attitude questionnaires from the first stage guide the level, direction and specific content of the attitude work undertaken.

A number of case studies provide the vehicle for stage two work. They are introduced cold at the start of this section and repeated at the end of the course as one (albeit fairly crude) component of the evaluation procedure.

Stage three

This stage considers the necessary prerequisites of planned programmes of sex education or counselling: namely, clear policy statements and associated staff guidelines (Chamberlain, 1984; Hounslow Social Services Department, 1983). These need to take cognizance of the prevailing interpretations of the law and the Mental Health Act and these latter topics are separately covered by a legally qualified invited speaker.

Stage four

Here, in the largest single section of the basic module, participants have the opportunity to work directly on the preparation, planning and implementation of sex education, together with the skills, methods and techniques which may be required to achieve success in this work in the specialist field of mental handicap.

Detailed consideration is given to the range of subject matter which may have to be covered in planned programmes of sex education. Both physical/biological and social/emotional aspects of topics are emphasized; and the importance of clarity and directness of language is stressed.

Curriculum planning and aspects of the design of teaching/counselling sessions form the basis for group exercises. Teaching methods and the skills and models of counselling are reviewed with special reference to the needs of people with limited intellectual abilities; practical tasks focus on both planned and crisis interventions; and the relative merits of group versus individual programme plans are considered.

Finally, a range of audio-visual aids and other resources (see for example Craft, 1982) are introduced; and selected examples of some of the most useful commercially available resource packs (e.g. Kempton, 1978) are demonstrated.

Stage five

This stage identifies some issues which relate to the wider context of sex education and counselling with this client group, and which may require a sensitive approach if programmes are to succeed. For example, appropriate liaison with the parents/families of clients is discussed; effective communication within or between agencies providing services to the same client is considered, as is the need for a balance between maintaining the confidentiality of client disclosures and keeping appropriate records of the progress of interventions; the requirements for staff support and development, access to specialist advice, and further relevant training is pursued; and public relations with a variety of community facilities and resources (e.g. Family Planning Association, Marriage Guidance Clinics, Sexually Transmitted Diseases Clinics) are debated.

Finally, the procedures involved in setting up, monitoring and evaluating programmes of sex education for clients are considered, together with a variety of experiential accounts of problems encountered and troubleshooting strategies.

Stage six

This is the feedback and evaluation section of the basic module. The results of the stage one questionnaires and the implications of these are discussed; the case studies from stage two are reconsidered with a view to noting changes in intervention strategy which might be adopted as a result of the course; participants are invited to give feedback on the course as part of a plenary group discussion; and finally individual comments are sought by use of a semi-structured evaluation questionnaire which may be completed anonymously.

Outcome

Evaluation of a staff training course, such as the basic module on sex education here described, is fraught with difficulty. At least three matters merit consideration: first, the extent to which the aims of the course, as matched to the objectives of participants, are met: does the course meet the need?; second, the specific ingredients of content, methods and skill of presentation: is it a good course?; and third, the resultant effects on staff behaviour, both post-course and subsequently in their work settings: does it produce change?

In general, the course has been rated as successfully meeting the needs of staff at the level of supported practice and has received very positive comment from participants. A number of staff who have also attended other similar courses have reported favourably on this course, particularly in the breadth of subject matter, the balance of topics and the style of presentation.

Since each basic course differs slightly from every other — because of the development of the course over time and degree of customization undertaken — it is difficult to report detailed cumulative data in any meaningful way. Such soft data as are consistently available suggest that staff are frequently ignorant of areas of sexual knowledge which they may be required to explain to clients; that staff attitudes in the area of sexuality incline towards the liberal-mainstream as measured by the questionnaires, but are not always consistent with behavioural correlates displayed during practical tasks; that strategies for intervention in relation to hypothetical cases become more personalized, less restrictive and, interestingly, to some extent more tentative; and that many staff express post-course interest in, and need for, further training in the area of sexuality in order to engage in more independent practice with clients.

Evaluation of the extent to which the training positively affects subsequent staff practice is by no means straightforward. There is some evidence to suggest that staff attitudes may become more accepting of certain aspects of sexuality (e.g. masturbation, homosexuality); that staff interactions with clients are simultaneously less restrictive, less over-protective, and more inclined towards inculcations of appropriate standards of public and private behaviour; and that more open discussion of, and individualized response to, client problems ensue.

In evaluating a staff training programme such as this, the original problem, and the goals of the related intervention strategy, have to be borne in mind. However, if staff training is effective (for example, in the subsequent provision of suitable basic sex education and counselling for clients, which in turn changes clients' behaviour in the direction of enhanced normalization and integration) the results paradoxically may be unobservable. The index of referrals to psychological services for client sexual problems cannot be used unequivocally to demonstrate training effects , since improved staff practice might tend to reduce the overall referral rate, or alternatively to increase the incidence of appropriate and timely referrals.

The strongest evidence of the success of the staff training may lie in the repeated demand for the basic module and the associated requests for further training at an advanced level to prepare staff for more independent practice with clients.

An advanced module which forms the second phase of the staff training package has been piloted and is now available. It is designed for 12–14 staff, all of whom have to have completed the basic module and to have a commitment to undertaking client work in sex education and counselling.

The advanced course aims to provide staff with the skills necessary to develop and operate sex education or counselling programmes for specific clients, with only minimum levels of support from line management or from specialist services. As such it is more comprehensive and represents an extension of the basic module, building upon the knowledge, attitudes and skills developed by participants, towards increased comfort with the general subject area and greater confidence in dealing with problems as semi-independent practitioners.

The demand for the basic module of training has been high. It is expected that the advanced module will also be well supported. This poses problems of the amount of clinical psychology time available for training direct care staff and for supporting their emergent practice. For this reason, a third component of the staff training package — a training-the-trainers module — may be a cost-effective development for selected graduates of the advanced course, who have demonstrated their skills at client-based work over a minimum period of time.

Discussion

In overall content, the basic module of the staff training package owes much to the pioneering work of Kempton in the USA (Kempton and Foreman, 1976; Kempton, 1978; Kempton, 1983) and of the Crafts in the UK (Craft and Craft, 1979, 1982, 1983, 1985). It also has commonalities with similar courses organized by a variety of non-aligned agencies (e.g. Family Planning Association, British Institute of Mental Handicap).

The particular distinguishing features of this training package lie in the basic behavioural methods of operation; the resultant individual tailoring or customization of the training which this permits; and the building-block approach of the modular design which extends the course upwards to an advanced practitioner level, and sideways to incorporate a trainers' programme.

In addition, one of the strengths of the package derives from its in-house design and operation. The course tutors have influence in the matter of which staff graduate from one level of training to another and subsequently engage in client-based work; they remain accessible to staff for continuing support and guidance; they can assist with the monitoring and evaluation of the training programmes which staff operate for clients; and can offer an associated crisis intervention service if required. This level of post-training support is rarely available to staff who attend non-local events, or those which are based on outside expertise.

A number of problems associated with both the training package and the sex education/counselling work of duly trained staff remain to be solved. First, the training modules may benefit from the complementary use of well-designed course manuals. Care staff are not always confident of their skills in working from first principles in intervention strategies: this is particularly noticeable in such a sensitive and difficult area as sex education. Although there can be no blueprint of interventions, some limited used of standard examples, which then could be individualized, might be appropriate as a teaching tool, at least at the advanced course level.

Second, the current training is mainly designed to enable staff to redress the lack of sex education received by their adult clients in earlier years. There is still a need to pursue opportunities to provide appropriate age- and stage-related sex education for children and young people with mental handicaps.

Third, some staff who do undertake sex education or counselling with clients remain vulnerable and anxious in the absence of an agreed policy statement by their employing agency. The risks to both staff and clients can only be reduced by the adoption of clear policy and detailed guidelines on the organization and implementation of this work. Some agencies seem reluctant to make overt policy statements in this area, being concerned about the sensitivity of the issue, possible adverse publicity and the attitudes of the public.

Fourth, there are unresolved difficulties in evaluating much of this work. Evaluation methods and measures need to be refined in order to quantify and qualify not only the effectiveness of teaching packages for staff and for clients, but also the quality-of-life aspects of outcome for clients in their personal relationships and social interactions.

Part 4
Work in medical settings

Introduction

Marie Johnston

Health psychology as a discipline has developed rapidly since the early 1970s. Increasing theoretical sophistication and the accumulation of empirical findings have contributed to a sound body of knowledge which has been applied by clinical psychologists in a wide variety of health care settings. These clinical applications, by their use of suitably scientific approaches, have in turn advanced the basic subject.

Health psychology has addressed all stages of health, illness and treatment. In healthy people attention has been given to health promoting behaviours, such as taking exercise and consuming a healthy diet, and to health risk behaviours such as smoking, excess alcohol consumption and Type A behaviour. These have been identified as risk factors for cancer, central nervous system (CNS) damage and coronary heart disease.

Healthy subjects do not normally come to the attention of the hospital-based health professions and are most likely to come to the attention of clinical psychologists working in primary care or community settings. An example from Part 1 is the case of Carol: stopping smoking in a group. There is a transitional stage, when the individual experiences bodily changes which may or may not be perceived and presented as symptoms. Modern theories of pain and recent research on the perception and evaluation of symptoms illustrate the complexity of this area (Feuerstein *et al.*, 1986). It is not surprising that it can prove problematic in clinical practice, as illustrated here in the case of Mrs Ellis. The patient's social environment can be an important influence at this stage, as in the case of Neil.

When the patient decides to consult a doctor, the potential for dysfunctional communication patterns and relationships between doctor and patient arises, an area which has been heavily explored by health psychologists but which is only addressed indirectly in these cases. Psychologists can contribute to diagnosis, as in the cases of Mr Watkins and Mrs Ellis, where symptoms might be interpreted either within a behavioural or physiological framework. They can also contribute when a physical diagnostic or therapeutic procedure is planned, most obviously in enabling patients to cope well with stressful medical procedures. While most patients can benefit from such preparation, there are patients who have particular difficulties with planned procedures and an example is that of Derek.

Many of the cases deal with psychological treatments of physical complaints, an essential contribution of psychologists working in this field. Similarly, many deal with enabling patients to cope with persistent impairments, some of which are the result of medical procedures. Coping can be directed at the emotional or at the handicapping aspects of the impairment. The examples given focus on the latter, minimizing the patients' behavioural and social limitations, but achieve apparent gains in emotional functioning too, for example, Sarah.

Increasing psychological attention is being paid to the end point of the health career, when the patient has a terminal illness and friends and relatives are bereaved. A variety of approaches have been fruitful in this area and work with a dying child is described in Part 2.

Applications can be found in treating patients in almost every branch of clinical medicine. The cases in this section represent some of the common areas of work including medicine (cardiology), surgery, gynaecology, neurology, rehabilitation, general practice and primary health care. Cases in other sections touch on problems in paediatrics and the well-established fields of psychiatry and geriatrics.

Despite this dispersal, the models and methods used retain the distinctive features of clinical psychology. Of great significance are the themes that behaviour is changeable and that there is potential for learning and adaptation. These are repeatedly used in formulating a hypothesis of the aetiology of the presenting problem and in designing a treatment or management plan. Examples are presented where the medical formulation is of a fixed unchangeable condition — for example, basic neurological deficits as in the cases of Sarah and Mr Wood — or the notion of symptoms being maintained by stable personality characteristics, such as 'hysterical' personality, in the case of Catherine. These and other cases demonstrate the potential for change using a variety of learning approaches including skills training, graded practice, operant procedures and biofeedback.

A variety of cognitive approaches are in evidence too, from the assessment of cognitive functioning and the consideration of cognitive retraining with Mr Watkins, to anxiety reduction through information giving with Derek and cognitive representations of illness and sick-role interpretations with Neil. Developments in cognitive psychology and in cognitive/behavioural methods clearly have an important role to play in this as in other fields of clinical psychology.

More specific to this area are approaches to the conceptualization of pain where the addition of cognitive and emotional/motivational components have contributed to basic physiological formulations (illustrated in the cases of Neil, Mrs Ellis, Derek and stress management in the treatment of angina). Similarly, psychophysiological analysis has led to the understanding of problems previously attracting a non-explanatory 'psychosomatic' label. Examples are given of relaxing painful muscle contractions (Catherine and Janet) and of the control of angina by stress management procedures.

While most of the cases deal with direct one-to-one work with patients, there are illustrations of introducing psychological skills to other health professionals (training for health visitors) and of an evaluation project designed to ascertain the needs for psychological care of the victims of serious burn injuries (planning psychological care in a burns unit). It is important to develop these alternative methods of working if the full potential of psychological approaches is to be delivered throughout the health care system.

Finally, the clinical psychologist's use of guiding theories, hypothesis testing, attention to evidence and the collection of potentially discomfirming data using single case study or group comparison designs are vital assets in introducing psychological models in a field dominated by biomechanical models. The much disputed applied scientist role demonstrates its effectiveness in these cases.

28 Mr Watkins: investigation of a head injury

Problem and background

Mr Watkins was a 46-year-old man admitted to a regional neurological unit for investigation. Four years previously he had been the driver of a car involved in a multiple collision. The driver of one of the other cars in the accident had died as a result of his injuries. Mr Watkins was taken by ambulance to the local district general hospital, and on admission through casualty about an hour after the accident was noted to be unconscious and to have bone fractures. For the latter he spent some weeks in the care of the orthopaedic surgeons, but the bones healed well with no significant long-term sequelae. Shortly after the accident he lost his job as a security guard; the reasons for this were obscure. The fact that his marriage had subsequently broken up made it difficult to get an independent account of details of this kind.

His GP referred Mr Watkins to the regional unit because he continued to have complaints of loss of memory and concentration. The situation was considerably complicated by legal proceedings. The widow of the driver who had died in the accident was suing Mr Watkins for damages. He denied responsibility but, in his turn, was attempting to sue the driver of another vehicle involved in the accident. Although the question of future management might well arise, the initial evaluation of this tricky case was important because of its impact on the litigation. As expected, both the psychologist and the neurologist involved were asked to submit reports to solicitors and to attend court hearings.

Formulation

In considering a problem of this nature a number of issues arise. The first is the severity of the head injury since severity, as measured by the length of post-traumatic amnesia (PTA), does relate to many different aspects of outcome (Brooks, 1984; Miller, 1979). A second question is what, if any, psychological impairments have resulted from the injury. Another factor that has to be considered in cases like this, where the possibility of compensation arises, is whether the patient has some form of compensation neurosis or accident neurosis (Miller, 1979; Miller, 1961). The further complication in this instance is that the possibility of the court finding Mr Watkins responsible for the death might also be helping to maintain symptoms. Finally, initial contact with Mr Watkins revealed someone who was rather slow and ponderous in movement as well as slow to respond to questions. Emotional tone seemed flat and, if anything, a little low. This coupled with the fact that his complaints about his alleged mental failings were vague and difficult to pin down raised the possibility that the whole problem might be complicated by depression.

Detailed investigation

As it turned out the question of depression proved by far the easiest to resolve. Detailed questioning about such things as appetite, diurnal variation, suicidal ideas, etc. indicated that Mr Watkins came nowhere near meeting the DSM III criteria for depression (American Psychiatric Association, 1980). All that emerged was some apathy and a lack of interest in things — a finding equally compatible with the after-effects of head injury. Administration of the Wakefield Self-Assessment Inventory for Depression (Snaith et al., 1971) also gave a score well outside the range associated with depressed psychiatic patients.

Estimation of the severity of the head injury proved difficult. Detailed questioning of Mr Watkins failed to elicit any clear idea as to the length of retroactive amnesia (RA) or PTA. He could recall nothing about the accident itself nor could he indicate what had been his last memory prior to the accident. He was similarly vague about when his memory returned afterwards but when pressed hard suggested that it was days rather than hours or weeks afterwards. The other possible source of information was the notes from the hospital that had admitted him after the accident. As is all too common, these contained a lot of information about his orthopaedic problems but little on his mental state. He was said to be unconscious on admission, with another vague comment about five days later indicating that he might still have been a little confused. This is also complicated by the fact that he underwent a major operation about 24 hours after admission to deal with an orthopaedic injury. Putting it all together suggests a PTA of 24 hours at least and seven days at most. At the lower end of this range significant long-term effects on psychological functioning are possible but not inevitable. With a PTA of a week such consequences are highly likely.

To investigate possible psychological impairments a number of tests were administered. The WAIS IQ was around 100 (Wechsler, 1981). This is of little interest in itself since even after quite severe head injuries IQ returns to pre-injury levels following a temporary decline (Brooks, 1984; Miller, 1979). What it does show is that scores on other tests are not likely to be depressed because of a low general intellectual level. Memory was assessed using Warrington's (1984) Recognition Memory Tests. Retention of both words and faces was at about the tenth percentile for people of his age. Given the low correlation between IQ and memory performance this is low enough to hint at the possibility of a mild memory deficit but not enough to be unequivocally outside the range that might have been expected.

Attention and concentration were examined using the Paired Auditory Serial Addition Test of Gronwall and Sampson (1974). Again the score was a little on the low side but certainly not low enough to give a strong suspicion of an impairment. Judgement of spatial relationships is something that is often affected by severe head injury, but performance on the test devised by Benton et al. (1978) was well within the normal range. There were no signs of aphasia (language impairment due to brain damage).

Those who have suffered severe head injuries quite often show the kinds of personality change and other behavioural effects usually associated with frontal lobe lesions. Mr Watkins' general behaviour did not appear to be disinhibited nor did he show any of the other common 'frontal' signs. If anything he gave the reverse impression in seeming to be a little depressed and withdrawn. More formal testing, including the assessment of verbal fluency (Miller, 1984a) was entirely normal.

The final point that needed consideration was the possibility of an accident neurosis (Miller, 1961). H. Miller claimed that vague complaints of such things as lack of concentration and memory, dizziness etc. were commonest after mild head injury. He indicated that these were maintained by the possibility of substantial compensation. The status of such complaints in the absence of a demonstrable cause is much less clear than H. Miller would have it (Miller, 1979). Deliberate faking to get compensation is probably very much rarer than H. Miller suggested, although it would be surprising if there were not a few who would try to exaggerate or even fake handicaps for financial gain. Clinical experience suggests that this can happen but is by no means common. In this case the complaints were of loss of memory and concentration but there were no complaints relating to other features of accident neurosis such as headache or dizziness. As the results showed, Mr Watkins did not take the obvious opportunity to do really badly on the tests. There are thus no good grounds for thinking he deliberately tried to fake or overplay any impairments.

Discussion

This case is a little more difficult than usual, partly because the severity of injury is in doubt. The fact that things are unclear forces a much more careful consideration of the basic issues and may provide a better illustration of what is involved than if there had clearly been a very severe head injury with obvious serious psychological consequences. If it was possible to be confident that the PTA was of the order of seven days or longer, then long-term sequelae would definitely be expected. The rather equivocal results on memory testing might then best be attributed to a failure of the tests to indicate clearly enough an impairment that was probably there. With a PTA at the shorter end of the possible range, it is possible that Mr Watkins might have escaped relatively unscathed. The fact that other tests, especially those of spatial judgement and attention/concentration, also failed to give any convincing sign of impairment despite being commonly affected by severe head injury suggests that any long-term psychological consequences were not very large.

As indicated earlier, a failure to demonstrate impairment cannot be taken as sure evidence that no impairment exists. Tests measuring slightly different functions or tests with greater sensitivity might have revealed convincing evidence. It was the memory test that produced the lowest scores and further examination of memory might have been justified. Unfortunately there is a lack of good memory tests and, in any case, a clinical judgement has to be made as to when the likely return from further investigation ceases to justify the effort involved. As it happens, a research memory procedure was also administered and this offered no further light on the situation. From the point of view of writing the legal report the conclusion was the negative one of having failed to demonstrate appreciable long-term effects that might seriously affect Mr Watkins' life but that some lesser degree of impairment might be present which was not detectable by the tests available.

The question of a possible accident neurosis has to be taken much more seriously in cases like this than would be justified by the balance of more recent evidence on this alleged problem. Because lawyers are aware of this possibility, and so that the psychologist's evidence will be seen as maximally credible in some circumstances, it is necessary to have been seen to take it into careful consideration.

Although this case was considered to require assessment and was investigated with a view to the likelihood of having to prepare a report for solicitors, there are potential implications for long-term management and rehabilitation. If good evidence of deficits in functions such as memory cannot be obtained, then an approach to rehabilitation based on cognitive retraining would not be appropriate. If the evidence suggests that impairments are minimal or non-existent yet the individual complains of an inability to function adequately, then the situation can be conceptualized in a number of other ways. One is to consider it an inappropriate adoption of the sick role (or handicapped role) and to approach the problem by the way of cognitive therapy, in terms of what the patient appears to understand that he has suffered and the implications he sees this as having for his life. These cognitions, if erroneous or distorted, could then be tackled in much the same way as the cognitive therapist would deal with the distorted or erroneous cognitions of a depressed patient.

29   Mr Wood: the effect of practice on naming in aphasia

Background

Although there is room for debate on the matter, Miller (1984b) has argued that the evidence for the efficacy of treatments for aphasia (disturbance of language due to brain damage) is far from compelling. Those interested in aphasia therapy have usually based their interventions on rather broad general principles which are held to apply to more or less the whole range of aphasic disorders. In contrast Miller (1984b) has suggested a step-by-step approach based on dealing with specific aspects of aphasia and without any assumption that what might benefit one particular type of language problem will necessarily be of value for another. This more detailed approach is also ideally suited to single-case research because of the very wide variation that can be found between different aphasic subjects.

This report describes a simple, single-case study carried out on an aphasic subject who had, among other things, a severe difficulty in naming objects. One of the major schools of treatment for aphasia is derived from the ideas of Wepman (1951) and known as stimulation therapy. These ideas have strongly influenced many authorities on aphasia therapy such as Schuell et al. (1964) and Taylor (1964). The general tenets of this approach are vague but, at least according to some interpretations, naming should not be beneficially affected by practice alone, except under relatively unusual circumstances. In addition, anything causing an improvement in naming one set of objects should enhance naming in general, thus providing widespread generalization. This study explores both these assumptions by means of a single-case experiment.

The subject

Mr Wood was a 66-year-old man admitted to hospital after a left hemisphere stroke. His main handicap was in language and he had a moderately severe aphasia. This was investigated in some detail along the lines advocated by Benson (1979). Spontaneous speech was fluent with occasional loss of words and paraphasias (substitution of incorrect words or syllables). Naming as tested by the Graded Naming Test (McKenna and Warrington, 1983) was markedly impaired. Repetition of phrases was good but reading and writing were both affected with reading being more clearly disturbed. Performance on the Token Test (de Renzi and Vignolo, 1962) was very poor indicating a marked difficulty in comprehension. The picture corresponded most closely to that of a transcortical sensory aphasia (Benson,

1979). In addition this patient had all the features of the Gerstmann syndrome which is associated with left-sided parietal lesions (Hecaen and Albert, 1978). This alleged syndrome consists of right-left disorientation, disturbances of calculation (dyscalculia), an impairment in writing (agraphia) and an inability to discriminate individual fingers when these are touched and without being able to see them (finger agnosia).

Intervention

In essence the intervention was designed to see if simple practice would affect naming ability and to get some indication as to whether any positive effects of practice would generalize to an unrelated set of words. The experiment was conducted over a period of about a week during Mr Wood's admission to hospital. Two separate sets of pictures of objects served as the stimuli to be named. These were in fact the pictures forming McKenna and Warrington's (1983) Graded Naming Test and those of the Boston Naming Test (Kaplan *et al.*, 1983).

Mr Wood attempted to name both sets of stimuli on the first morning. He then had one presentation of the McKenna and Warrington set each morning and afternoon for five presentations. The Boston set was also administered on the fifth occasion. On each presentation the subject was required to name each picture and a correct response was indicated as such. An incorrect response or a failure to respond in 20 seconds resulted in the correct word being supplied by the tester.

In the second block of sessions the pattern was reversed, with the Boston set being administered each half-day. On the last testing the McKenna and Warrington set was administered once again.

Results

These are shown in Figure 29.1. They are fairly clear-cut and are comparable to those obtained from an earlier case subjected to a similar intervention but where a complete set of data could not be obtained.

It can be seen that performance on the McKenna and Warrington set increases quite markedly over the block of testing while, if anything, that on the Boston set declines slightly. The reverse occurs in the second block with the Boston set showing improvement and the McKenna and Warrington set remaining more or less static. The drops in performance for the untrained sets in each block are small and probably of no significance. This is especially true of the McKenna and Warrington set in the second block since performance on this test was very nearly perfect at the end of training and any random variation in performance would be most likely to produce a slight fall at the end of the second block.

Discussion

The results suggest that simple practice can have a marked impact on the naming of pictures of objects in at least this one subject. The fact that no improvement occurred in the untrained set over the first block suggests two things. One is that the improvement in practice cannot be attributed to spontaneous recovery since this would also be expected to influence the untrained set. Such a conclusion is not really justified for the second block because the then untrained set was constrained by a ceiling effect but it would be strange if spontaneous recovery were to act over the second block without influencing the first. The other conclusion is that there is no indication of training on one set generalizing to the other. This study therefore

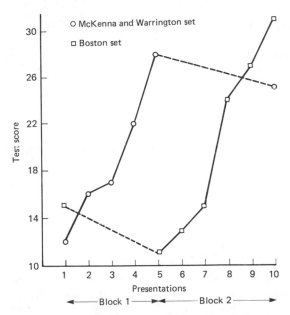

Figure 29.1 Performance on two naming tests as a function of practice

offers no support to the expectations derived from the stimulation therapy approach to treating aphasia.

Although practice does seem to have a beneficial effect in this experiment it is not clear how effective it would be with other subjects and other materials, especially words of some importance to the subject's life rather than those which were just convenient for the investigator to use. It is also unlikely that therapists working with aphasic patients would want to place much reliance on practice alone. Most probably they would want to do other things such as using different kinds of prompts to try to elicit the correct response (e.g. Howard *et al.,* 1985). However, because simple practice does appear to have an effect, studies of the efficacy of other procedures should use practice as a control condition in order to show that their effect is not just mediated by the fact that they also necessarily involve the subject in practising the production of words.

The fact that the present data give no sign of generalization reinforces Miller's (1984b) view that aphasia therapy needs to be directed at those language situations that are important for the patient's everyday life rather than using a range of materials handy for the therapist and assuming that generalization to the real-life situation will automatically follow. Nevertheless it would be wrong to use these results as strong evidence against any generalization. The two sets of words were very different from one another and it is not possible to rule out the possibility that generalization of practice effects might occur if the two sets were related to one another in some way (e.g. by belonging to similar semantic categories).

Finally, this study gives little indication of what might be the optimal frequency of practice. Practice twice daily seems to have a definite effect but a gap of two to three days is too long for the effect of one practice session to carry over to the next. Further elucidation of this question would require more extensive investigation. Nevertheless this simple experiment does indicate that worthwhile questions about the treatment of aphasic patients can potentially be resolved by single-case experimentation.

30 Sarah: remediation of apraxia following an anaesthetic accident

Introduction

Sarah was 20 years old in 1983 when she sustained extensive damage in an anaesthetic accident. Four months later she was admitted to a rehabilitation centre for adults with acquired, non-progressive brain damage. Although able to walk and talk Sarah was in other ways severely handicapped and was virtually unable to do anything for herself. On the Vineland Social Maturity Scale (Doll, 1953), for example, she was failing items below a 1-year level. Before the accident Sarah had been working as a secretary and was fluent in three languages. She had obtained three A level passes, so it can be assumed fairly safely that she had been of above-average intelligence. Sarah's first admission to the rehabilitation centre was for 14 months. During that time several assessments were undertaken and a clear picture of the nature of her problems emerged.

Assessments

Because of physical and cognitive problems Sarah was too disabled to be given many of the conventional neuropsychological tests. With the help of her occupational therapist, physiotherapist and nurse, the clinical psychologist was able to complete a Vineland Social Maturity Scale (Doll, 1953) shortly after her admission to the rehabilitation centre. Her overall social age at that time was estimated to be around the 1–1½-year level, with her first failures at the 0–1-level (she was unable to grasp or reach for objects) and her highest success at the 2–3-year level rested on the fact that she always asked to be taken to the toilet.

After four months the Vineland was re-administered and Sarah had improved in all areas. She still needed help with eating and drinking, which led to failures at the 2–3-year level, but enjoyed reading books, newspapers and magazines, thus gaining her highest success at the 11–12-year-old level. She could also spell, converse in French, name colours and indicate whether or not objects or shapes were the same. However, she could not always identify objects and she could not perform tasks involving movements. Thus she could not write, draw, carry out constructional tasks or even point with her finger. She could 'eye-point' and several tasks such as colour-matching were performed in this way.

Sarah's motor problems were not due to paralysis or weakness. She had good strength in her limbs and a full range of movements. It was concluded that her motor problems were due to apraxia, a term which refers to a variety of movement disorders which cannot be explained by paralysis, weakness, poor comprehension or refusal to cooperate. Apraxia, like several other neuropsychological syndromes, is defined by exclusion. With Sarah it was possible to exclude weakness because she could walk, raise her arms in the air and even grip the psychologist's finger tightly (although she could not always let go when she wanted). In comprehension, Sarah understood what was required in a task, she could repeat information and attempt to perform the task. Refusal to cooperate was ruled out by Sarah's efforts to complete tasks to the best of her ability, sometimes even to the extent of becoming embarrassed at failures. For example, when asked to demonstrate how to wave goodbye, she said, 'Don't ask me to do that, you know I can't do it and I feel stupid.'

Plan of first treatment

The most handicapping and distressing aspect for Sarah was her almost total inability to do anything for herself. Improving her self-help skills therefore became a priority for treatment. The Vineland was used to determine the lowest developmental failure in this area. Her earliest failure turned out to be inability to drink from a cup unaided. A treatment programme for this task was devised jointly by the occupational therapy and clinical psychology departments. The approach adopted involved breaking the task down into small steps, rather like a chaining procedure used typically in teaching self-help skills to children with mental handicap (for example, Carr and Wilson, 1980).

Designing the treatment programme

The first stage of treatment consisted of direct observation. Sarah's occupational therapist and clinical psychologist simply watched her trying to drink from a cup. Typical responses were: she was unable to direct her reach, so could not touch the cup; she held the very top of the cup so that it was unstable; when she found the handle she could not grip it; and when she held the cup she was unable to put it back on the table.

Following these observations, the task was broken down into nine steps. The observers selected the steps partly as a result of their observations and partly through intuition concerning Sarah's ability to accommodate certain steps. The nine steps were:

(1) Put your hand flat on the table.
(2) Keep your hand low.
(3) Put your thumb through the handle of the cup.
(4) Grasp the handle.
(5) Lift the cup to your mouth.
(6) Drink.
(7) Put the cup down on the table.
(8) Open your fingers.
(9) Release your fingers and take your thumb out of the handle.

After the seventh teaching session an additional step was added between 5 and 6. This required Sarah to 'Look for the red rim' (a red marker was placed on the rim of the cup nearest to her mouth). This step was needed because she often held the further rim of the cup to her mouth, thus causing most of the liquid to spill down her dress.

179

Scoring was as follows:

(1) Sarah completes step alone
(2) verbal prompt needed
(3) physical prompt needed (a light touch)
(4) physical guidance needed (i.e. the therapist held Sarah's hand and placed it in the correct position).

The treatment took place during Sarah's daily occupational therapy sessions between 9 a.m. and 10.30 a.m. It began four months after her admission to the unit, that is eight months after her accident. In the sessions she was seated with a half-filled cup of coffee or fruit juice placed on a table in front of her. First she was asked to drink her coffee. If she then put her hand flat on the table without help this step was scored as one. If she failed to carry out this step she was given the verbal prompt, 'Put your hand flat on the table.' If she succeeded in doing this she would score two. If not, the occupational therapist gently nudged her hand in the right direction and a score of three would be awarded if the step was then completed successfully. If neither of the prompts led to successful completion of the step her hand was guided to the correct place and a score of four awarded. The same procedure was followed for each successive step.

Table 30.1 Teaching Sarah to drink from a cup unaided

Date	Session	Steps								
		1	2	3	4	5	6	7	8	9
24/10	1	4	4	4	4	4	1	3	2	2
	2	2	2	2	2	1	1	2	2	2
	3	1	1	1	1	1	1	1	1	1
24/10	1	2	2	2	1	1	1	1	1	1
26/10	1	1	1	2	3	4	1	1	1	1
	2	1	2	2	4	4	1	1	1	1
	3	1	2	2	1	1*	1	1	2	1
27/10	1	1	2	1	3	4*	1	2	1	1
	2	1	2	1	2	2*	1	1	1	1
	3	2	2	2	2	1*	1	2	1	1
	4	2	2	3	2	1*	1	1	1	1
31/10	1	1	1	1	1	1	1	1	1	1
1/11	1	1	1	1	1	1	1	1	1	1
2/11	1	1	1	1	1	1	1	1	1	1
3/11	1	1	1	1	1	1	1	1	1	1

* = additional step inserted

Scoring: 1 = complete step
2 = verbal prompt
3 = physical prompt
4 = guidance

Outcome of the first treatment

It can be seen in Table 30.1 that Sarah learned rapidly to drink from the cup unaided. The first time the programme was followed she was able to complete only one of the steps alone and needed full guidance for five of the nine steps. However, by the third attempt (within the same session) she was completing all the steps unaided. In the following sessions in the first week Sarah's success was variable, but in all the sessions during week two she completed all the steps unaided.

Since that time Sarah has always been able to drink from a cup unaided. Although her movements remain rather jerky and she has to feel for the table initially, she is certainly independent of others in this activity.

Given the rapidity and somewhat dramatic nature of the successful completion of this task, the therapy team wanted to know whether the method employed would be equally effective for other tasks. A second task was selected for treatment and this time Sarah's physiotherapist helped to run the programme.

Plan of second treatment

The second area the team concentrated on was Sarah's inability to pull her chair to the table. Initially, she had been unable to seat herself upon a chair without help. Again it was established that this was due to apraxia and not to weakness or paralysis. Sarah stood near the chair, fully aware of what was required. She would move around the chair but would be unable to position herself correctly in front of it in order to seat herself upon it. Although she learned how to seat herself in the first four months at the unit, her inability to pull the chair she was sitting on towards and under a table persisted. She could not decide where to put her hands or how to move during this operation. Following the earlier pattern, the task was broken down into a number of steps:

(1) Stand up.
(2) Bend over.
(3) Put one hand at the side of the chair.
(4) Grasp the chair.
(5) Put your other hand at the side of the chair.
(6) Grasp the chair.
(7) Put your head up and look where you are going.
(8) Walk forward with little steps while holding the chair.
(9) Put your head up and look where you are going.
(10) When you touch the table sit down.

The scoring system remained the same as in the first treatment.

Outcome of second treatment

It can be seen from Table 30.2 that Sarah learned the second task even more quickly. This may have been because the second operation was simpler. As with drinking from a cup, Sarah has retained her ability to complete this second task for a period of two-and-a-half years since the programme was first introduced. Furthermore, the method has been employed to teach Sarah certain dressing skills.

Table 30.2 Teaching Sarah to pull her chair to the table

Date	Session	Steps									
		1	2	3	4	5	6	7	8	9	10
10/11	1	1	2	2	3	4	2	4	1	4	2
	2	1	1	2	1	2	2	2	1	2	2
	3	1	1	1	1	1	1	2	1	2	1
11/11	1	2	2	1	1	1	3	2	1	2	1
15/11	1	3	1	3	1	3	1	2	1	2	1
17/11	1	3	1	3	1	3	1	2	1	2	1
18/11	1	3	1	1	1	1	1	1	1	1	1
	2	3	1	1	1	1	1	1	1	1	1
21/11	1	2	1	1	1	1	1	1	1	1	1
22/11	1	2	1	1	1	1	1	1	1	1	1
	2	1	1	1	1	1	1	1	1	1	1
23/11	1	1	1	1	1	1	1	1	1	1	1

Scoring: 1 = completes step alone
2 = verbal prompt
3 = physical prompt
4 = guidance
(see text for discussion of steps)

Discussion

Natural recovery cannot account for the rapid and dramatic success of this treatment procedure as Sarah has never learned to complete a self-help task without a similar structured programme. Without a step-by-step programme it would seem that she cannot hold a plan of action in her mind in order to initiate and carry out an activity. Certain types of apraxia have indeed been considered as disorders of planning by some neuropsychologists. For example, one of the earliest writers on apraxia, Liepman (1920) believed that ideational apraxia resulted from an impairment of the idea or plan of movement. Luria (1966, 1973) claimed that frontal apraxia was due to a disruption of both the plan or intention for action and of the ability to compare one's performance with the plan to see if the goal has been achieved. Heilman (1979) has a somewhat different explanation for ideational apraxia. He believes it is due to a disorder in the verbally mediated motor sequence selector.

Both hypotheses may be near the mark in explaining Sarah's difficulties. If we accept that she is unable to plan her actions because of problems experienced in selecting the correct sequence, which in most people is verbally mediated, then we can suggest a possible explanation for her success in the programmes. They provided the verbal sequence so that Sarah was able to carry out the appropriate actions in the right order. She did not overtly verbalize the sequence nor did she read the instructions, but she was nevertheless able to learn the task once she had been taken through the sequence a few times. Thus the most likely explanation is that her verbalization was covert or unconscious.

Follow-up

When Sarah left the rehabilitation centre she went to a college for handicapped people. One year later (nearly 30 months after the initial brain injury) she was re-admitted for one month for a further period of rehabilitation. Cognitive assessment showed that she was more alert and oriented and able to point more accurately. However, her self-help skills had not improved. She was still able to drink from a cup alone and pull in her chair, but had not learned new skills. During her one-month stay she was taught successfully to pull her pants up and down, put on her coat and jacket, and make herself a cup of coffee provided help was given in pouring the boiling water. These tasks were taught in the same manner as the earlier ones. It would appear that Sarah is capable of learning numerous tasks provided these are broken down and taught in the manner described above.

31 Catherine: biofeedback treatment of recurrent shoulder dislocation

It used to be assumed that shoulder dislocation which occurred frequently and persisted in spite of surgery was an hysterical phenomenon and the patient would be expected to show psychological abnormalities (Rowe *et al.*, 1973). These authors reported 26 cases of whom two had the diagnosis of hysterical personality and six others had psychiatric labels ranging from acute schizophrenia to opiate dependence. Unfortunately, none of these was defined. They concluded that these patients' failure to improve after operations to stabilize their shoulders appeared to be an extension of their emotional symptoms and that psychogenic factors should be assessed.

Presenting problem

Catherine, a 24-year-old married woman was admitted to an orthopaedic rehabilitation unit with pain and jerking in her left shoulder whenever she tried to reach forward. This seriously affected her ability to work as she was a sales assistant needing to reach across a counter many times a day. Usually she experienced increasing tension at the top of the shoulder during the week, and by the weekend it was extremely painful.

She had first attended for an opinion about her shoulder some years before because she had lifted a heavy case of merchandise and immediately noticed pain. This cleared up quite quickly but whenever she tried to raise her arm from this time on it 'stuck'. She had an operation to prevent this problem, went back to work and had no further trouble for two years.

Then she reappeared with jerking in the shoulder. No evidence of damage was apparent but the joint dislocated several times a month and often needed to be put back in hospital. She had another operation which only partially improved the situation and a feeling of instability remained. Standard physiotherapy was also unhelpful because the precise nature of the problem had still to be elucidated. She was therefore readmitted for further assessment.

At this point there were three possible explanations of the problem: the shoulder had suffered some damage which could reasonably be expected to improve with surgery (there had never been any supporting evidence for this idea); a muscle pattern had been learned which maintained instability in spite of surgery; and if muscle learning had occurred the patient had some reason for keeping the problem and warranted the label 'hysterical'. Opinion was greatly in favour of the third of these when Catherine was referred.

Assessment

Catherine showed no evidence of any personal difficulties at clinical interview. A short MMPI (Kincannon, 1963) was administered to test the hypotheses that she would have high anxiety or symptom exaggeration or learned symptom complaining, since high scores on scales measuring symptom complaining are said to be diagnostic of conversion hysteria (Hanvik, 1951). However, these were not substantiated by the test results which were entirely normal.

Analysis of the electromyographic (EMG) activity in various shoulder muscles was carried out by the surgeon and showed an overactive pattern in pectoralis major (Figure 31.1).

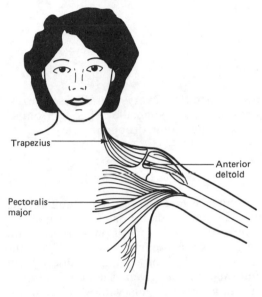

Figure 31.1 Left arm, anterior view

An EMG biofeedback machine, which uses adhesive electrodes attached to the skin over the required muscle, was employed to give simple information about this electrical activity during use of the arm. Biofeedback uses machines which convert electrical signals from body systems (heart, skin temperature, brainwaves or, as in this case, muscle activity) into auditory and visual signals (clicks and needle movements on a meter) so that information about these body systems, which would not otherwise be consciously monitored, can be made available to the individual. Psychologists have been familiar with the use of biofeedback in the context of galvanic skin response as a measure of anxiety. The person is trained to reduce the amount of electrical activity and thus reduce the tone of the signal coming from the machine as a means of learning anxiety control. In Catherine's case the same principle applies: by attaching electrodes to the skin over the pectoralis major muscle and using a machine to feed back information about activity in this muscle during use, Catherine can learn to modify abnormalities in the muscle pattern. Figure 31.2 shows the machine in use.

The machine confirmed that the muscle retained about 40 microvolts of activity at rest. Normal resting activity is about 5–10 microvolts. Under standard conditions of moving the arm forward (protraction) and back again (retraction) across a table

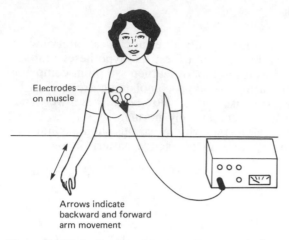

Electrodes
on muscle

Arrows indicate
backward and forward
arm movement

Figure 31.2 Biofeedback machine recording signals from pectoralis major

65 centimetres high, partial dislocations occurred on every trial. These corresponded to increases in activity in pectoralis major as the needle deflected from 40 to 80 on the meter at the moment the shoulder joint dropped.

Formulation

The available evidence suggested that Catherine had learned to tighten certain muscles in an attempt to stabilize the shoulder and minimize pain. Unfortunately, the muscle tension was itself causing joint instability. Standard physiotherapy for this problem has traditionally involved general strengthening which may have the effect of reinforcing the activity in those muscles which produce the dislocation. It was hypothesized that if appropriate information was given, she could learn to repattern muscle activity to produce functional movements without discomfort. EMG biofeedback seemed the treatment of choice to enable this learning to occur. Records had to be kept of relevant machine settings and the proportion of trials of movements in which relaxation of the muscle was achieved and dislocation was prevented. If no progress followed this regime, then further assessment decisions could be made following the generation of new hypotheses based on carefully collected data.

Treatment

Stage one

Relaxation of pectoralis major using reduction of click frequency and decreased needle deflection as feedback of success was demonstrated and Catherine practised on a graded programme of increasing sensitivity until normal resting states were possible. This pattern was then incorporated into activities which simulated the significant aspects of her job, beginning with a relatively low table, 55 cm high.

The programme consisted of repeated trials of reaching forward and relaxing to the criterion of 5 microvolts until 20 consecutive successes were achieved. Then the height of the table was increased by 10 cm to encourage more normal amounts of flexion and the trials were repeated. Records were kept of progress in each session.

Stage two

After four days of treatment, spasm at the top of the shoulder in the trapezius muscle (Figure 31.1) was a problem as it would have been at work. Initially a tape of deep muscular relaxation (Jacobson, 1938) was tried to see if inducing a state of general relaxation would reduce this specific muscle tension. Unfortunately, discomfort in the shoulder remained, and it was necessary to train Catherine to control it by giving biofeedback information about the activity in the trapezius muscle specifically, demonstrating the advantage of biofeedback.

After another four days, during which her activity built up to approximately normal levels to simulate work, no spasm occurred. Trapezius had been used to compensate for increasing pain from the shoulder, but this itself exacerbated the problem. If both pectoralis major and trapezius were relaxed, better and more normal function was possible. The patient, however, still complained of sudden jerks on retraction.

The biofeedback machine was then employed to test the relative activity of other muscles, demonstrating that anterior deltoid was also part of the abnormal pattern (Figure 31.1). This muscle showed a sudden increase in activity at the beginning of the reaching forward movement, and another during the moving back phase, when it should have relaxed smoothly.

Recent experiments with muscle biofeedback linked to a computer enabled the production of a plot of anterior deltoid activity in both arms under the same conditions of moving forwards and back again. These are shown in Figure 31.3. The excessive increase in initial activity and the failure to relax smoothly were presumed to be the pathological features which caused the dislocations.

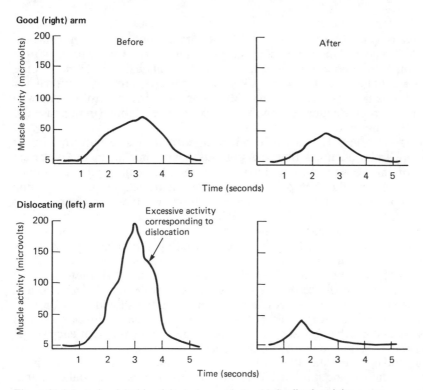

Figure 31.3 Anterior deltoid activity before and after biofeedback training

Stage three

The final part of the programme involved protraction/retraction as before, but this time concentrating on achieving a smooth increase and decrease in the use of anterior deltoid.

Initially the activity pattern was about 200 microvolts in the protraction phase and remained at about 100 during most of the retraction phase. On the right the pattern was about 75 and then reduced smoothly to 0. This pattern was achieved on the left after a further eight days of practice.

Catherine continued on the programme for another two days without feedback to ensure generalization and her records showed no dislocations.

Outcome

New readings were taken from the computerized system and are shown in Figure 31.3. Catherine was discharged home and returned immediately to work. Initially there was a small increase in the amount of discomfort felt by the end of the week, but no spasm, jerks or dislocations. She was very well at nine months follow-up, reporting no discomfort at all.

The majority of a sample of people with recurrent shoulder dislocation need no other treatment at a follow-up period of up to two years under this kind of regime (Fisher, in preparation).

Discussion

A major problem with EMG biofeedback is that data are not available for muscle recruitment during normal movements. One study (Inman *et al.*) as far back as 1944 recorded 'action current potentials' during motion, but only half the range of some movements was studied. It also seems likely that patterns are not identical for repetitions of the same movement. Using patients as their own controls is one way of investigating appropriate muscle activity if the contralateral joint (in this case the right shoulder) is normal.

It is not clear how people learn to produce abnormal muscle patterns, but it cannot any longer be assumed that the patients have some form of hysterical conversion. Not only does the notion of hysteria need to be challenged in the minds of the medical staff and the therapists, but also the theoretical model of learning has to be demonstrated to take its place. A stepwise objective approach to assessment and treatment goes some way to achieving these aims. It must be argued that hysteria cannot be a diagnosis made by default because other seemingly relevant treatments have failed. Even in the case where psychological abnormality can be identified, its contribution to the patient's particular complaint must be elucidated before it can be assumed to be a causative factor. Without any such evidence, as is the case with Catherine, simpler hypotheses can be generated and tested. Since she did not have any avoidance or gain from the shoulder discomfort, traditional kinds of psychotherapy did not fit the model, and a feedback theory of learning was applied which allowed clear changes to be demonstrated at each stage. As Fordyce *et al.* (1973) have pointed out, if such problems arise from personality difficulties, a good outcome should only be achieved by methods aimed at resolving the intrapsychic conflict, and it is hard to account for the success of a goal-directed, behaviourally oriented programme.

Although the use of the MMPI is controversial in this country and should not be considered a valid instrument for the identification of psychological disturbance without some other corroborative information, it is useful when asking questions about learned symptom complaining rather than about the more traditional issue of the organic/functional dichotomy (Fisher, 1984).

This problem may, however, be considered a psychological one for several reasons. The body of knowledge on operant learning should be consulted (e.g. Skinner, 1938) and in addition since biofeedback therapy is not simply a stimulus-response learning paradigm, as it is often mistakenly assumed to be, the involvement of a suitably experienced professional in the therapy design is important.

Clinical psychologists have long experience using feedback of autonomic systems to control various dysfunctional states and this experience needs to be extended to problems which initially appear to have a purely organic basis. Psychological expertise was able to contribute to Catherine's management in a number of valuable ways. First, it enabled data to be collected that allowed clarification of each stage of the problem and its solution. Second, it removed the unhelpful assumption that the problem was inherent in the patient's personality and therefore amenable only to lengthy psychotherapy. Third, it reduced helplessness in both the patient and the therapy staff by structuring the task in clearly defined ways, and fourth, it was instrumental in the development of EMG biofeedback treatment for other patients which was previously not available.

A word of caution is necessary about the use of biofeedback. A literature review undertaken by Alexander and Smith (1979) has suggested it has no better results than non-machine-based relaxation in the management of pain *per se*, and given the problems encountered in the generalization phase of treatment, it is probably best avoided. However, where actual muscle incoordination can be demonstrated to be the cause of a movement disorder resulting in lack of function or other discomfort, its contribution can be tried as long as other validating data such as fewer dislocations, or a greater range of movement are also collected.

A final point is the problem inherent in all treatment trials as to their effectiveness when tested against chance factors. In this study no attempt was made to manipulate false feedback. Catherine used her three months on the waiting list to monitor her own situation and was aware that spasm in the trapezius muscle occurred after a few days at work, and she noticed that the arm jerked on every attempt at retraction. On initial assessment this was noted to happen on 100% of trials. On discharge assessment it occurred on 0% of trials. No other treatment had been effective in the meantime and in particular surgical intervention and standard physiotherapy had failed to prevent the problem. Since it seemed to be self-perpetuating as the muscle patterns were not available to consciousness except by specific feedback, it appears likely that this and Catherine's motivation to modify them were the effective components.

32   Neil: learning to live with pain

Introduction

Chronic pain usually refers to persistent complaint of pain for over six months and psychologists view this pain as a multi-dimensional experience with physiological, cognitive and more easily observed behavioural aspects. These dimensions are not synchronous, and treatment attempts will generally focus more on one or another aspect.

It is gate control theory (Melzack and Wall, 1965) that provides the theoretical background to this multi-dimensional approach, as it delineates the complex interaction between the various dimensions of pain. This theory highlights the effects that brain processes can have on the experience of pain. For instance, general anxiety, beliefs about the pain or worries over the consequences of pain all seem to potentiate the pain experience (Holzman and Turk, 1986). Also, the sets of pain behaviour once elicited (guarding, grimacing, complaining, pill-taking), can be strengthened by the learning contingencies that psychologists are so familiar with (Fordyce, 1976).

The main psychological approaches to pain have been conceptually separated into those treatments that target pain experience, and those targeting pain behaviours (Broome, 1985). Recently research has focused more on the patient's own perceptions and experiences such as beliefs about pain (Dolce *et al.*, 1986), the coping styles adopted (Rosentiel and Keefe, 1983; Turner and Clancy, 1986), and the need to match treatment goals with personal characteristics and family involvement (Rowat and Knafl, 1985) in dealing both with pain experience and pain behaviour. The emphasis is towards more individually tailored treatment plans (Turk *et al.*, 1983), a sensitivity to the stages in the patient's career (Kotarba, 1983) and the development of self-efficacy (that is, the person's belief that they can effect change) (Saltzer, 1982).

The present case study demonstrates how much negotiation has to take place to render the patient accessible to coping techniques rather than 'cure'. With chronic pain a particular difficulty is the anger often seen at referral to the psychologist, apparently as a result of disappointment at the failure to cure the pain and the feeling of being dumped, or labelled a 'mental case' by the referral (Turk *et al.*, 1983; Broome, 1985; Kirby, 1985).

Background

Neil was 19 years old when he was referred for psychological management to help deal with the chronic mastoid pain he had been suffering for over four years. The neurosurgery for pain in his mastoid area (behind the ear) had given no alleviation of symptoms, and there was some evidence that perhaps there had been a slight additional change in reported sensations since this operation. It was therefore agreed that psychological methods should be tried during this plateau phase, before any further invasive methods were attempted, particularly in view of the risks of additional exploratory surgery and the possibility that scar pain might add to his already severe baseline pain.

In addition to feelings of helplessness and isolation, mobility was a problem. Neil did not walk more than three or four steps without crouching on the floor holding his head, and at these times he described himself as 'completely out of control', and unable to cope with any other events. For instance, he described one occasion when he crouched down in the gutter and was quite oblivious of traffic passing within a few inches of his head.

Neil lived within a close and supportive family network with his elderly father and married sisters who lived nearby. Although his father was chronically ill with heart disease, he performed most of the household duties and maintenance tasks. His father collected allowances from the post office, cooked, cleaned and generally maintained his son and the household.

During the initial interview his father became noticeably distressed and solicitous when Neil displayed pain behaviour. He was available at his son's beck and call in the house to play chess or snooker, and Neil was socially isolated from his own age group.

Overall, he seemed to have an isolated lifestyle with high dependency on his father and restricted social life.

Pain assessment

At the first interview Neil reported continuous and severe head pain rated 4/5 on a 0–5 scale of severity. He claimed he was unable to monitor his pain for a baseline saying that the monitoring made him focus more on the pain and hence increased his suffering.

Neil appeared to be socially unskilled, with a wide range of pain behaviours, the most noticeable being facial grimacing, and continuously fingering and applying pressure to the painful mastoid area.

Formulation

After the first interview a number of problem areas were identified:

(1) the maintenance of sick-role behaviour by Neil's family, particularly his father,
(2) the social isolation from his peer group,
(3) the lack of information on Neil's pain and its pattern,
(4) the lack of information on the range of coping mechanisms Neil had available, and which might be used to advantage during treatment.

However, none of these processes could be further investigated until Neil began to enter into a more equal relationship with the psychologist and to become an active problem-solver in dealing with his own problem.

In discussing this, Neil appeared to resist the idea that he could help himself. He became aggressive and upset at the idea that he had anything to contribute to the solutions, and that he could take an active approach to improve his situation. Neil wondered whether it was thought he was exaggerating or imagining his pain. More significantly, he felt controlled by the pain, rather than the reverse. He admitted to feeling helpless.

Intervention

Dealing with tension

Because he seemed so resistant to focusing any more attention on the pain, and also to the idea that he could problem-solve, it was not possible to investigate further his pattern of pain (the physiological component) or the cognitive elements that related to his pain. Although he did not agree to monitor the pain, he did, in negotiation, agree to learn to relax.

As there is often some relationship between tension and pain experience, this seemed a worthwhile place to start. Pain is often accompanied by tension, possibly as a result of guarding against more pain or because of the pain-tension-pain cycle that can be caused by lack of information, so fear about the cause of the pain can increase fear and tension (Broome, 1985). Neil was taught a form of autogenic relaxation using a visualized image that he found distracting and relaxing. He also learned to use a self-hypnotic technique during the next two sessions. This was seen as a technical educative venture and, as he became better at recognizing certain sensations as tension, he monitored with more enthusiasm and noticed some tendency to acute pain episodes if he was tense at the start of the day.

By negotiating with Neil and changing the focus from the pain to his level of relaxation and tension, the psychologist was building on the only area of agreement at the formulation stage. As Neil became more skilled in relaxation and more interested in its relationship to his pain, he and the psychologist graphed the information together, working out the clearest method to demonstrate the relationship between tension and pain. It appeared to both that the acute pain episodes occurred more often in combination with high baseline tension. Although there was still no clear information on the frequency of acute episodes, Neil felt that, by controlling the resting level, it might be possible to decrease the likelihood of acute pain episodes.

By this time Neil was becoming quite enthused by the idea of problem-solving. He suggested that he monitor his pain more carefully to try to unravel the connection between specific activities and his tension and pain. Once identified, he started looking at events that made him feel more tense and anxious. He began to recognize these more easily since undertaking the relaxation training, and began to separate out those activities which caused him pain problems.

Tackling changes in his social life

As Neil began to problem-solve he began to wonder about his employment. He signed up for a professional training course by correspondence and was helped out by a local self-help group which organized his finance, supervision of assignments etc.

It was now possible to discuss with him the rather unusual way he spent his time and his social isolation. Because of Neil's great fear of mobility, it was decided to tackle this first and then look at general social integration through the monitoring of his activity level. Neil resisted simply increasing his activity level. He appeared to be avoiding both the pain he feared (Slade *et al.,* 1983), and the social role which he had had limited opportunity to learn. An emotional session followed, centring symbolically on whether he should keep the wheelchair he used and, if he started to cope more successfully, what threat this might pose to his disabled status, both in financial and social terms.

Neil's habit had been to walk a maximum of four steps until he hurt so much that he felt a loss of control. He had previously coped with this activity problem by using a wheelchair, which his father pushed, so that he could simply take two or three steps from the wheelchair until he hurt so badly that his father would bring the wheelchair up behind him and he would sit down. In the clinic, walking practice and learning the extent of his limits were discussed. Walking was rehearsed with him so that he walked one to two steps, rested and relaxed, and then took two more steps. During the next three weeks Neil gradually increased his walking, taking a systematic approach. By resting and relaxing he found he could increase by two or three steps each day without a significant increase in pain. At the end of three weeks he was heard slowly walking the length of the corridor to the office door without stopping. He found that at home he could gradually reach the end of the street by walking slowly, but generally without stopping. Building up his walking in this way meant he now had a slightly wider range of social possibilities.

Local activity targets were agreed; Neil planned to get a little further afield and possibly to meet friends of his own age. He was now able to walk a little further, but was still unable to go anywhere without using a taxi or the wheelchair as a prop to get him nearby and then walking a few steps. Using these methods he was now able to get to the local pub, to the shops, cinema, and to his local chess club.

Family contingencies

Neil and his father were very close. His father managed the practical side of housekeeping and Neil managed household decisions, paperwork etc. However, at the stage in Neil's treatment when he was beginning to shift from a dependent equilibrium to increasing his activity and social contacts, his father's health forced Neil to take over many more housekeeping functions. His father became quite acutely ill, was taken into intensive care and had to have a pacemaker fitted. (Sadly, he had a series of heart problems and has since died.) However, at this point these changing events caused Neil to anticipate when he would be entirely on his own and would need a wider range of independence skills in order to cope on his own.

Outcome

Discharge was discussed when Neil was able to relax to keep his baseline level of tension down. He felt that his acute bouts of pain were reduced, he was getting further afield with his slightly increased mobility, and his social contacts and career prospects had improved.

With longer and longer follow-up periods from the clinic and his father's deteriorating health, Neil began to take more and more responsibility for his own independence. He began to take driving lessons, passed a driving test and got his own car. He continues to follow the correspondence course to gain a professional qualification, but still anticipates only working at home. His aspirations do not stretch to taking an office job. His pain is still rated 3/4 on a 0–5 point scale.

Discussion

When Neil first came to see the psychologist he was very resistant to psychological treatment approaches, although he was fearful of the alternative of further neurosurgery. However, by joining in a problem-solving exercise he began to make the best of the situation. He now appears to have reduced the acute painful periods that were so debilitating to him, and although he still rates his pain at the same general level, he does register fewer acute bouts when he self-monitors. His lifestyle has also changed considerably, partly because of therapy but also because of radically changed family circumstances. He looks forward to the future, is undertaking work training, and has limited social integration, having had to take over a number of household duties to function independently.

Although Neil's case has attempted to follow some of the clear guidelines for psychological treatment, the stages in treatment were highly dependent on matching Neil's changing motivation and the opportunities offered by the family context. The need to develop an active problem-solving approach through specific behavioural intervention led to a useful analysis of the relationship between resting tension levels and acute pain bouts.

At discharge Neil functioned in some ways as an independent adult, although his pain remained at very much the same level as when he was referred. On a two-year follow-up Neil's social activity, educational achievements and the extent of his mobility remained very much the same as on discharge from the psychology department.

33   Mrs Ellis: frequent attendance and anxiety in a primary care setting

Presenting problem

Mrs Ellis was referred by a trainee GP to the clinical psychologist working in the practice because of anxiety-related physical symptoms which led to a high frequency of attendance at the surgery. At the time of referral, the symptom was head pain, but at other times she had consulted with chest pain, vulval itching, joint pains and so on. Her mood was quite depressed, with considerable anxiety about her head pain and a general tendency to worry. The record of her surgery attendance (see Figure 33.1) indicates a considerable excess over the average consultation rate of two to three a year (Hicks, 1976). Typically her GP could find nothing wrong and it was clear from his report and the entries in her notes that her visits were a source of considerable frustration.

Background

Both Mrs Ellis and her second husband were 56 years old. Her first husband had died suddenly in an industrial accident 14 years previously. She had one daughter with whom she had quite a close relationship and who lived locally with her husband and two children. Mrs Ellis's husband had five grown-up children, four of whom lived with them and the youngest of whom, aged 19, was on probation. She worked part-time as a home help. She did not regard her husband as very supportive and clearly thought that her first marriage had been better.

Her medical history showed that in addition to the complaints mentioned, she had had a hysterectomy ten years previously and at an earlier stage had had breast cysts removed and surgery to the bladder.

Previous treatment

Two previous formulations had led to treatment with antidepressant medication and attempts at Balint-type psychotherapy (Balint, 1964). The latter involved interpretation of her presentation to the doctor, including transference interpretations, and was offered both by her own GP and by a psychiatrist specializing in psychodynamic therapy who did sessions in the health centre. Neither approach had helped.

First formulation and treatment approach

The initial hypothesis was that Mrs Ellis was experiencing a considerable amount of daily stress or hassle in dealing with this large household, that she was relatively unsupported by her husband, that her worries led to increased physical tension which she perceived as symptoms, and that the experience of her first husband's death led her to fear the worst. Early attempts by the psychologist to see the husband resulted in failure, to some extent confirming part of the hypothesis but also ensuring that there would be no opportunity to explore the possibility of changes in the marital relationship. Equally, it was impossible to get Mrs Ellis to keep even the simplest record of her worries or symptoms.

The treatment approach adopted focused on coping with anxiety (relaxation training, coping self-talk, systematic desensitization). These procedures were unsuccessful as Mrs Ellis did not keep appointments and tended to come to the surgery when she was very distressed and unable to learn the procedures.

Examination of the first six months of Figure 33.1 shows her frequency of visits to her GP over this period. The apparent reduction in attendance during April/May (marked *) is spurious as Mrs Ellis attended three district general hospitals during this period; she initiated these visits based on previous contact she had had with the clinics when no organic abnormalities had been found.

It was concluded that, while the formulation of the problem might still be correct, the attempted intervention had not been successful.

Second formulation

Patients consulting their GP frequently have high levels of anxiety (Banks *et al.*, 1975). It was hypothesized that the services offered may play an important role in maintaining illness behaviour in these patients. Similar models, with supportive data, have been presented by Fordyce *et al.* (1968) on pain behaviours, by Hallauer (1972) on symptom presentation and by others in the field of physical disability.

In this formulation, her illness behaviour, including her physical symptoms, her distress and her health centre attendance, were all viewed as operant behaviours maintained by her GP's contingent reassuring attention. The analysis was presented to Mrs Ellis by suggesting that perhaps some of the symptoms she experienced were started off by the bodily changes that went with worrying; at an early stage, she would decide that these symptoms were not bad enough to consult her GP, but her continuing worry led to the build-up of the bodily symptoms to a point where going to her GP could be justified and, when she got there, he reassured her. She found this plausible, perhaps because it was the first time that her reluctance to visit the GP had been acknowledged and both she and her GP were prepared to try an intervention based on these ideas.

Intervention

The aim of the intervention was to break the contingent relationship between the high level anxiety behaviour and the postulated reinforcer of reassurance and relief obtained by visiting her GP. The first target was to gain control over her health centre attendance, thereby interrupting the anxiety-symptoms-anxiety spiral and making her visits to the health centre less disruptive and perhaps more productive. Other targets were to teach her methods of dealing with the anxiety and to reduce the frequency of her health centre visits.

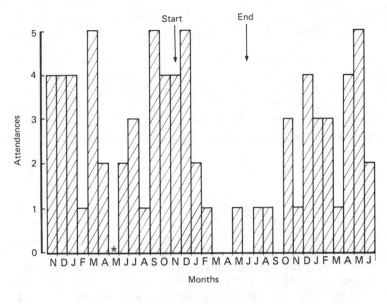

Start = start of programme   End = end of programme   * see text

Figure 33.1 Mrs Ellis's monthly visits to her GP before, during and after the programme

Mrs Ellis was reinforced by a planned appointment with the psychologist each week, contingent on no GP visits. These appointments lasted 5 to 15 minutes, allowed her to discuss any symptoms if she wished, rehearsed coping statements and rehearsed non-illness responses to common social greetings, such as 'How are you?'. Thus health centre visits were independent of symptom experience.

This programme was followed for six weeks, was suspended or reversed for three weeks (while the psychologist was on holiday), continued for six weeks and then spaced to two-week intervals and finally handed over to the GP. The design can be described as:

A-B-A(reversal)-B-B(thinning)-B(transfer)

During thinning Mrs Ellis was telephoned by the psychologist on the intervening week.

What happened

The programme proceeded remarkably smoothly after the first week when she visited her GP and therefore did not see the psychologist. The sessions were spent usefully and independent reports from the local community (health visitor, lady in the wool shop and others) suggested that Mrs Ellis spent far less time discussing symptoms.

Her understanding of her visits to her GP seemed to change. In the first phase she visited her doctor because she had been feeling bad, but she thought it was 'due to worry'. During the thinning period she visited her doctor and both he and she sought out the psychologist to explain that this was different and that these symptoms were real; it appears that she was learning to discriminate between symptoms based on worry and other symptoms.

On one occasion during the thinning period a one-week interval was used as she was not confident that she could cope for two weeks, but otherwise the programme ran as planned.

When the programme was handed over to the GP he immediately extended the period to three weeks as she appeared to be so well. She quickly started to break down and require more appointments. Control was again regained at one week and then at two weeks, but was interrupted when the GP himself became ill. The psychologist was no longer working at the health centre and the programme collapsed.

Outcome

Figure 33.2 shows the weekly record of her visits to the psychologist and her GP during the programme, reversal and thinning. Mrs Ellis visited her GP in the first week and therefore did not see the psychologist (marked **), but the following weeks show a pattern that suggests some control. During the period of reversal to previous conditions she visited her GP six times in less than three weeks, but control was quickly regained when the programme was reintroduced and maintained during thinning. Summary data are shown in Table 33.1.

It was not possible to monitor her anxiety systematically over the period of the programme as Mrs Ellis could not keep even very simple records. However, when she visited the psychologist or was contacted by telephone, her mood was assessed using the following rough and unvalidated categories:

Cheerful: showing no anxieties which she could not resolve.
Worried: worrying about her health, but without overt behavioural distress.
Distressed: overtly distressed, tearful and agitated.

Reports by the GP and by the health centre receptionists, together with comments in her medical notes and occasional observations by the psychologist, suggest that most attendances prior to the start of the programme would have fallen

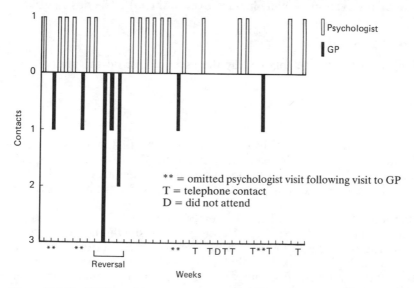

Figure 33.2 Mrs Ellis's weekly contacts with psychologist and GPs during the programme

Table 33.1 Contacts with psychologist and GP during the programme and reversal

Period	No. of weeks	Contacts		No. of contacts	Mood	
Programme	32	Psychologist {	attendances	18 } 26	Cheerful	19
			telephone	8	Worried	6
					Distressed	1
		GP	attendances	4		
Reversal	3	GP	attendances	6		

in the 'distressed' category. During the programme she was most often 'cheerful' (see Table 33.1). All attendances to her GP during the reversal period would have been categorized as 'distressed'.

The total health care time used was much less than would have been expected from the baseline. There were no attendances at the health centre in a state of high distress or without an appointment. Staff at the health centre, including receptionists, made spontaneous comments about how pleasant Mrs Ellis was now that they had seen her when she was not in a highly aroused state.

Discussion

Mrs Ellis was probably the patient who presented the health centre staff with most difficulty at the beginning of this intervention. For this reason it was decided to persist with a second approach to intervention after the first failed.

It is still possible that the initial formulation and the earlier formulations by the GP and by the psychiatrist were correct, but their application had achieved nothing for Mrs Ellis.

The intervention may appear to be harsh and unduly focused on the economic use of a doctor's time. In practice, it seemed much more sympathetic and less hurtful than the previous interventions. The structure provided by the programme allowed Mrs Ellis to be seen when her anxiety level was low enough for her to learn other, useful things.

It was not simply the better explanation that helped Mrs Ellis. When the programme reversed to the previous management, her behaviour and distress reverted to their previous level. But the explanation may have been useful in allowing Mrs Ellis to attend the health centre when she did not have symptoms.

There were clearly difficulties in handing the programme over to the GP. This method of care was very different from the normal demand-led consultation pattern and the primary care team had not been satisfactorily prepared to maintain the programme.

34 Stress management in the treatment of angina

Introduction

There are now numerous studies describing the contribution of psychological factors to the development of coronary heart disease. It has been shown that certain behaviour patterns constitute a significant risk factor. For example, Jenkins *et al.* (1978) found a significant association between Type A behaviour (a behavioural style including competitiveness, time urgency, impatience and hostility) and angina, a form of heart disease caused by narrowing of the coronary arteries. Hostility scores, a component of the Type A pattern, are predictive of the incidence of coronary heart disease and mortality (Barefoot *et al.*, 1983). These studies suggest that angina patients may benefit from a treatment approach which teaches how to recognize and control emotional arousal, anger and hostility (Smith *et al.*, 1984).

Stress management training (SMT) is now a well-established psychological treatment for patients who experience exacerbation of their symptoms by stress. A study by Ornish *et al.* (1983) shows that for angina patients SMT was associated with clinically significant improvements in exercise tolerance and a range of other indicators of heart functioning, while non-significant changes were shown in the control group. However, this study confounds the effects of dietary changes and SMT and there was no follow-up.

The current research study is a pilot investigation of SMT in comparison with routine cardiological care in the treatment of patients with chronic stable angina. The aim of the study was to establish whether SMT is an effective rehabilitation technique for angina on standard cardiological criteria (exercise testing and angina diary cards) and on criteria of psychological adjustment.

Design of the study

The cardiologist was able to identify up to 30 patients a year from his clinic who had stable angina of one month's duration and no heart attack within the previous three months. The psychologist administered standardized questionnaires to these patients to assess a range of psychological measures. The most important were measures of how anxious the person felt at the moment (state anxiety), as measured by the Hospital Anxiety Depression Inventory (Zigmond and Snaith, 1983) and of how angry the person felt at the moment (state anger), as measured by the Spielberger State-Trait Anger Inventory (Spielberger *et al.*, 1983).

Formal medical and exercise tolerance tests were completed by the cardiologist and a standard angina daily record card was administered on which patients recorded the incidence and duration of each angina attack. The exercise tolerance test is a well-established cardiological assessment procedure which aims to aid diagnosis in heart and/or lung disease; aid planning and evaluation of therapeutic intervention; monitor progress over time. The bicycle ergometer used was calibrated in 20-watt incremental steps from 0 watts to 500 watts. This was connected to a 12-channel electrocardiograph (ECG) recorder. Electrodes were placed on the patient's chest which then provided a continuous display of the ECG, and a recording was made every minute. Patients were instructed to pedal the bicycle at a constant speed, which could be seen on a visual counter in front of them. They were asked to continue until they were unable to go on because of chest pain or fatigue. The workload (that is, the amount of watts resistance at which patients were able to cycle) was increased by 20 watts every two minutes, up to the patients' tolerance level, that is, the point at which they expressed discomfort.

It was hypothesized that stress management training would reduce the amount of anxiety and anger experienced by those who received it, improve cardiological functioning (in lower blood pressure and heart rate) at the same workload on the exercise test and that patients would report fewer angina attacks on their daily diaries.

Procedure

Patients were randomly allocated to the SMT (experimental) or waiting list (control) groups. There were 16 in the SMT group and 14 in the waiting list control group. The SMT group were asked to participate in weekly group meetings lasting one-and-a-half hours for seven weeks. All patients in both groups were then fully assessed at the end of the treatment period and again at two months follow-up.

Stress management training

Stress management training can consist of a variety of techniques which are derived from one of the many models of stress. The model chosen in this case was that of Lazarus (1966) who defined stress as a product, not only of the environmental stimuli and the individual's response, but also of the individual's perception of the demands of stimuli as threatening or benign, and the appraisal of his or her capacity to meet those demands. The intervention therefore aimed to teach people how to identify stressors, the way in which appraisal could lead to effective or ineffective responding, and new skills and effective responses to stress. Since strong emotions such as anger are often reported by patients as provoking angina attacks, anger control was given special attention (Novaco, 1979).

Excessive sympathetic nervous system arousal, whether induced by exercise or stress, is associated with angina, so relaxation techniques were taught. These methods are a well-established technique for controlling anxiety states, and psychophysiological studies show that a reversal of the stress response is induced with parasympathetic responding and a pleasant mental calmness (Everly and Rosenfeld, 1981).

As angina patients often report being fearful of their symptoms and avoiding exercise associated with angina, it is possible that the anticipatory anxiety may in part trigger the angina attacks. Continued avoidance of exercise can lead to a steady decrement in physical capacity, which itself can lead to a lower tolerance for exercise before symptoms occur. A further function of relaxation is to control anticipatory anxiety and to reduce the oxygen demand on the heart during exercise so that a greater tolerance of exercise can be built up.

In order to create effective group treatment, some time was spent in building trust among the participants by self-disclosure and informal discussions. This was based around a simple factual presentation of a topic by the psychologist, backed up with the same information in written form. Group discussion was encouraged through individuals carrying out exercises within the session or as homework assignments which were then discussed at a subsequent session. For example, one exercise involved keeping a diary of stressful events and responses to those events, which provided a means of checking the adequacy of the individual's ability to respond appropriately and flexibly to different situations. This same exercise was repeated later in the classes so that participants and psychologist could see how much progress had been made.

An important ingredient was the active practice of techniques for coping, with the opportunity for the psychologist to provide feedback and guidance. Most of the active practice consisted of learning a range of relaxation techniques which were then practised at home with audio-taped instructions. A lesser amount of time was spent on role play or rehearsing thought control techniques in imagination, the simplest of which involved spotting unhelpful thoughts, such as 'This pain is awful, I am going to die if it gets worse, I can't cope' and substituting more rational and, hence, more calming responses.

What happened for Peter

Peter Brown, one member of the SMT group, was 45 years old, married, with two children. He had been given a medical discharge from his work as a manager in a chemical company when he developed angina two years previously. He had had a severe heart attack one year ago. Currently he worked for himself as an agent for a rival company.

Session one: introduction to stress and heart disease
Peter was quiet and when questioned said he was concerned about discussing aspects of his private life. He listened attentively and responded well to the relaxation exercise.

Session two: identifying stressors
Information was presented on the role of chronic stress and life events, on the relationship between stress and performance and between stress and health. Information was also presented on the importance of the person's interpretation of an event as stressful in determining whether the person experiences stress or a more positive response. Self-monitoring (diary-keeping) and problem-solving methods were discussed. Peter volunteered that he had not had time to practise relaxation, and when questioned about this at the end of the session he said he now realized that some of his work problems arose because he did not set priorities and tried to please whoever shouted loudest.

Session three: thoughts and emotions under stress
The importance of identifying how one's appraisal of the stressful situation and one's capacity to respond affect the response was illustrated using examples reported by the participants from their personal stress diaries and their use of problem-solving skills. Peter reported some success in setting priorities at work,

and in achieving this he was able to see that the situations to which he tended to respond immediately were those which produced panic and fear of personal criticism. Thus a rapid response in these circumstances was a way of reducing the fear but was not always the best option nor always productive.

Session four: styles of thinking under stress
The identification of rational and irrational thoughts provoked Peter to realize that he could question his thoughts and be his own 'wise counsel'. Using a questionnaire that identifies underlying styles of thought which may underpin the development of emotional problems such as depression (Beck, 1976), Peter recognized that his tendency to overreact to personal criticism reflected a high need for approval. For example, Peter had 'strongly agreed' with these items: 'A person should try to be best at everything he or she undertakes'; 'If I fail at my work then I am a failure as a person'; 'I should bc able to please everybody.' As a result of the group discussion he realized that these expectations were putting unrealistic demands upon him.

Session five: anger and angina
The causes of anger and its relationship to angina were discussed. Peter acknowledged that both fear and anger, particularly frustration engendered by being unable to get others to see his viewpoint or to do things his way, often resulted in angina.

Session six: anger control
Two methods of anger control, problem-solving and anger inoculation, were presented. Peter reported that he now used problem-solving techniques regularly. The self-preparation methods of anger inoculation were explained and he rehearsed using these methods for coping with predictable but unavoidable 'wind-up' confrontations with his colleagues.

Session seven: lifestyle and healthy habits
The importance of a healthy general lifestyle and a balance between work and leisure, activities and relaxation, avoidance of unhealthy habits such as overeating, drinking and particularly smoking were discussed. Peter's goal became to find a balance between work and leisure, and to incorporate light exercise into his routine as well as regular practice of relaxation exercises.

Some measure of the success of the intervention for Peter was provided by the continuing reduction in frequency and duration of angina attacks on his post-treatment assessment, despite the fact that his new business had collapsed. His angina attacks went down from an average of four to two per week and their mean duration decreased from three minutes to one. There was no change in the workload measurement (the length of time he was able to cycle on the exercise test); his blood pressure had decreased and his heart rate increased slightly after exercise.

Results

The results of the tests administered at the pre-treatment interview were analysed to ensure comparability between the experimental and control group members. T-tests were computed and showed no significant differences between the groups on the cardiological measures or on the measures of state anxiety and anger.

After the treatment the results showed significant differences between the groups on the measures of state anxiety (p <0.01) in favour of the experimental group. At two-month follow-up the anxiety scores of the experimental group were also lower than the control group. Analysis of variance revealed a significant group × time interaction (p<0.01); that is, the experimental group's anxiety scores continued to decrease over time (see Table 34.1). The significant difference between the groups

Table 34.1 Mean state anxiety scores*

	Time 1 Pre-treatment	Time 2 Post-treatment	Time 3 2 month follow-up
Experimental group	10.9	9.2	6.5
Control group	10.2	7.9	9.7

* Anxiety sub-scale of the Hospital Anxiety Depression Scale

in the amount of time patients were able to cycle on the exercise test (p<0.02) was accounted for by deterioration in the control group. There were no differences between groups in the workload and heart rate tests. According to the patients' daily diaries, there were significant differences in favour of the experimental group in the number of angina attacks per week and in their intensity but there was no difference in the duration of the attacks or the amount of medication taken.

The results show that patients who attended the SMT classes had better cardiological status on the exercise test after treatment than the control group. The control group were unable to work for as long as the experimental group before experiencing chest pain or stopping the test. That is, the control group had deteriorated in comparison with their earlier results and the experimental group had maintained their capacity for exercise. According to the patients' daily diaries the experimental group were reporting fewer attacks of angina and these were less severe than those experienced by the control group. Also, they were less anxious and angry at the post-treatment interview. Analysis of the follow-up data showed that beneficial reductions in post-treatment state anxiety were maintained. Further analyses of the cardiological variables are still required before it can confidently be stated that the physical improvements post-treatment were maintained at follow-up.

As yet it is unclear which components of the package are effective but clinical experience seems to show that as people get stressed by different events and have different methods of coping with stress, the salience of a component will differ according to the needs of the individual. Although some people report most benefit from the relaxation techniques, the sections on the cognitive components of stress have been more important for others. For the person described in the case example above, immediate symptomatic relief was obtained using the relaxation components but longer-term changes were probably based on his response to the cognitive components of the programme.

Discussion

One of the major practical problems of this study has been the significant number of drop-outs (three from the SMT group and three from the control group, a total of 20% overall) between the pre- and post-treatment assessments, although nobody dropped out between the end of the treatment phase and the follow-up. These have occurred for several reasons, the majority of which were due to an unexpected deterioration in the patient's physical condition. However, in three cases, patients expressed reservations about the exercise test or the psychological test or the supposed stigma of attending a psychological group. There are no obvious remedies for the deterioration in cardiological status, but greater attention will now be given to explaining to patients the rationale for each of the different types of assessment, and a more detailed discussion with the psychologist before referral to the group may help reduce some of these difficulties.

A second practical problem in running the stress management group has been the rather differing needs of the patients who are retired or who are medically retired at an early age due to their chronic angina, and those patients who are still in some form of active employment. The latter patients suffer the traditional work stress problems and problems of conflict between work and home, while the former group tend to suffer problems of underload.

The third question is perhaps more fundamental. While the studies referred to in the Introduction indicate that certain lifestyle and personality variables may predispose certain individuals to develop angina, little research has attempted to delineate whether patients with identified angina have distinctive and perhaps pathological psychological characteristics which distinguish them from other patients. Further research is needed to investigate whether these patients are simply showing the relatively high prevalence of psychological morbidity associated with a chronic disabling condition or whether they show specific behavioural characteristics, such as high rates of hostility, which have a direct influence on their current angina symptomatology. The early results of this pilot study appear to confirm the generally favourable effect of SMT on the workload and angina symptomatology of angina patients which was also shown by Ornish *et al.* (1983). However, as neither study has used an active treatment comparison group or a placebo control group it is not possible to determine whether the results were achieved by any specific aspect of SMT intervention as opposed to general non-specific placebo effects.

35 Derek: anxiety management in a general hospital surgical setting

The problem

Derek was a 41-year-old married electrician who had been referred by his general practitioner for a surgical opinion concerning abdominal pain. Subsequently he was diagnosed as suffering from inflammation of the gall bladder and admission to hospital for its surgical removal was then suggested. No major surgical complications were anticipated although the patient was noted to be obese and to be a heavy smoker. Derek stated, however, that he would not be able to tolerate admission to hospital in his current psychological state because of a long standing 'claustrophobia' problem which caused him to feel anxious and to avoid any situations in which he felt trapped. The hospital situation, in particular during the immediate post-operative state, would represent an extreme example of this problem. In this context a behavioural psychological opinion was requested in an attempt to help Derek accept and tolerate admission for surgery.

Assessment

Behavioural analysis of the 'claustrophobia' revealed a number of situational difficulties and anxieties. The problem had a history of approximately 15 years, apparently originating during an incident in which Derek was working under the floorboards in a house, became physically stuck, felt himself to be trapped with insufficient air to breathe and experienced a severe panic reaction before being able to release himself. Subsequently Derek avoided such situations. He also found that the problem had generalized in several ways. At the time of referral he had for some years experienced anxiety and dizziness if he lay flat even when trying to sleep. He consequently slept at night propped up with a number of pillows and, knowing that he would need to lie flat without pillows for at least part of his post-operative stay in the hospital, he experienced considerable anticipatory anxiety at this prospect. He also disliked being in any room without 'fresh air' circulating and was therefore anxious lest, while in the hospital ward, he would be unable either to get to an open window or to open one when he wished. This, he anticipated, would be particularly difficult when on a post-operative drip. He also feared the sensation of dizziness which he expected to experience when given a general anaesthetic.

His panic sensations could develop within seconds and were characterized by physical tension, dizziness, subjective difficulty in breathing and an urge, usually uncontrollable, to leave the situation. He did not report depersonalization, excessive sweating or palpitations. His panic states would often last for some minutes and on occasions for hours. Derek denied being anxious about injections or being anxious or embarrassed about social interaction with other patients while on the ward.

Psychological formulation and intervention procedures

The rationale for the behavioural intervention was derived largely from two sources. The first of these was the work by Janis (1958), and Lazarus (1966) and Lazarus and Folkman (1984) which has suggested that appropriate psychological preparation for surgery may reduce the level of post-operative pain and may facilitate coping. The second was the work of Ley and his co-workers (Ley, 1977; 1982) which has highlighted the role of adequate and comprehensible information as a powerful determinant of patient satisfaction and compliance with health advice. In the light of these findings a cognitive-behavioural intervention was suggested to Derek.

On the basis of Janis' and Lazarus' work, discussion was undertaken to ensure that Derek understood the likely patterns of anxiety in response to surgery. It was explained that the normal pattern was for anxiety to increase just prior to surgery and subsequently to take several days to settle down. A realistic explanation of the likely level and pattern of pain and discomfort for the few days following surgery was also given. Repetition with use of specific examples couched in simple comprehensible language was used to maximize understanding of the information provided.

Attempts were made to make the situation less novel and more predictable and to provide Derek with realistic and prepared coping strategies for self-management of the anxiety he would experience during hospitalization. This included the following:

(1) a visit to the relevant surgical ward to give Derek a clear perception of what to expect, to meet the sister and ward staff and to agree with the ward sister that he could have a bed near a usually open window. The old-fashioned circular structure of the ward with beds placed on the circumference and facing inwards to a central seating area was, interestingly, rated by Derek as less subjectively anxiety arousing than the common rectangular ward structure. It was unclear exactly why this was so but it appeared to be because Derek had a sense of more 'personal space';
(2) self-control strategies involving training in muscle relaxation, controlled breathing and distraction, coupled with positive self-statements of successful coping, aimed at reducing dizziness, anxiety, panic and post-operative pain;
(3) *in vivo* desensitization to lying flat on a stretcher trolley in a white-tiled treatment room, as a parallel to lying flat on a bed or theatre trolley. This was supported by home practice at sleeping with progressively fewer pillows in preparation for the immediate post-operative stage of hospitalization;
(4) reassurance that regular access to the psychologist would be possible throughout the period of hospitalization to discuss experiences and strategies to control anxiety.

A total of six out-patient sessions over a period of six weeks was used to carry out the above procedures in preparation for admission. The surgical team was asked to arrange admission for approximately four to six weeks from the original assessment in order to give Derek a structured expectation of admission. This was agreed and the admission date scheduled for approximately six weeks from initial assessment. Because of the inherently rather unpredictable times of bed availability, Derek received only three days notice of the exact date of admission. However, he was by that time ready to accept the admission offered.

What happened

Surgery was scheduled and carried out successfully on the day following admission. Derek was visited briefly on the ward by the psychologist on the evening of his admission and then briefly before his pre-operative medication on the morning of surgery. He was seen again after surgery on the evening of the same day and on the first, fourth and seventh post-operative days, for approximately 15 minutes on each occasion.

He was asked to complete the Hildreth Feeling Scales (Hildreth, 1946) as an index of his psychological state on each day of his admission except the first post-operative day during which it was considered that he might feel too physically unwell to complete the scale. The Hildreth is an early, not very sophisticated self-report measure of emotional state. For each of the items, the individual selects one of ten scaled alternatives as most appropriate. One item, for example, contained statements ranging from 'never felt better in my life' to 'couldn't feel any worse'. In a formal research study, more recent and sophisticated multi-dimensional measures of mood and response to surgery would be necessary. However, in the present case, the function of the assessment was to be part of the psychological intervention itself (that is, giving structured feedback to Derek about his emotional state) rather than part of the analysis of the problem or the evaluation of the treatment interventions.

The pattern of the data obtained was fed back to Derek to confirm with him that his psychological state was following the predicted pattern. Figure 35.1 displays the pattern of Hildreth scores over time and the pattern is similar to that reported by Janis (1958) as characterizing the response to major surgery among his sample. No attempt was made to provide Derek with a comparison between his scores and those of other patients from normative samples, although his highest scores were similar to those of newly admitted patients. However, the changes in his scores over time were emphasized.

During these in-patient contacts Derek was given reassurance that his experience and progress were appropriate for the particular stage of his hospitalization and was

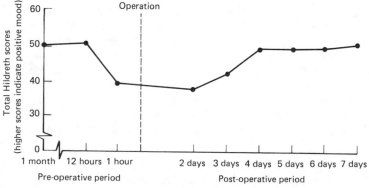

Figure 35.1 Pattern of pre- and post-operative Hildreth scale scores

reminded of and encouraged to use the self-control strategies. By his accounts and from informal nurse observation he did use the strategies. He accepted on only two occasions the minor tranquillizing medication offered by ward staff to post-operative patients. No specific advice had been given either to Derek or the ward staff about the suitability of such medication as an alternative or adjunct to the self-control strategies. On no occasion did Derek experience uncontrollable panic or its behavioural concomitants and the closest he came to this state was on the way to theatre when he had to sit up briefly on the theatre trolley. He did report considerable pain during the first few post-operative days but this gradually receded in the predicted fashion. He was discharged seven days after surgery to out-patient follow-up.

Outcome

Derek was seen on three further occasions as an out-patient for psychological follow-up at six, seven and 11 weeks after his discharge from in-patient surgical care. He had been offered the opportunity to initiate earlier contact if he wished to do so and had been asked definitely to contact the psychologist at the six-week follow-up stage if he had not done so previously. At this latter time, he stated that he had not experienced any panics in relation to his surgical progress since discharge. He had experienced some anxiety over whether the dark colour of his urine might indicate the passing of blood and therefore a complication in his progress, which had led him to consult his GP. After an out-patient urological investigation which revealed no complications he had felt reassured concerning his progress. He reported no subsequent anxiety concerning this.

The two subsequent appointments were largely concerned with Derek's attempts to stop smoking and lose weight. He had successfully not smoked at all since the day before his operation, having reduced his consumption from 30 to 20 per day in the pre-operative period on the advice of his surgeon. He reported little in the way of physiological craving and appeared to have been largely a habit smoker who would go for several hours without a cigarette without any distress. He had voluntarily lost approximately two stones in weight during the five months since he had first been advised that surgery was necessary and that stopping smoking and losing weight would be advisable. He had achieved these two changes in behaviour with little direct advice from the psychologist although several possible strategies had been briefly discussed.

Non-directive discussion of the relationship between Derek and his 19-year-old son, who had left home after a family row, was also undertaken at Derek's initiative. The likely benefits and difficulties of different courses of action were examined although no definite decisions were made by Derek during the sessions.

By the final follow-up appointment, Derek was successfully back at work full-time. He had experienced only one episode of his 'claustrophobia' problem. This had occurred while watching a magician on a television programme shutting a volunteer in a box! He had felt compelled to go to the door to breathe 'fresh air' and experienced a sense of anxiety for several minutes. He still avoided some enclosed situations at work, but felt himself better able to cope with his anxieties in these settings. He stated that without the behavioural intervention he did not believe he would have been prepared to go into hospital for the operation except as an absolute emergency. He attributed his ability to cope with the experience to the procedures he had been taught and had used, and to the opportunity to discuss and to obtain reassurance about his progress.

Discussion

A single case study of the type described here has the obvious major limitations of being uncontrolled; it cannot generate conclusions which have proven generality across a range of clinical conditions, patients, therapists or situations. Because of the relatively fixed trajectory and time periods of surgical admissions to hospital, it is very difficult to examine the effects of behavioural and communication interventions using A-B-A, multiple baseline or other single-case experimental designs. This means that group comparisons, currently the more frequently reported experimental strategy (Ley, 1982; Melamed, 1977), will probably remain the most common methodological technique for assessing experimentally the contribution of psychological techniques to the management of surgical anxiety.

Disentangling the relative value of the different interventions that can be used at the individual case level will remain an important and interesting problem. Whether the anxiety and pain management procedures, the graded practice and densensitization, the presentation of adequate information, or some combination of these, were major influences on the successful outcome of the present intervention cannot be established with certainty. It is also interesting that, after a single recommendation to stop smoking and to lose weight, this patient successfully, and with relatively little external advice, achieved at least short-term successes with both these behaviour changes. In view of the fact that many individuals fail in their attempts to change these habits, it is important to ask why and how this individual succeeded at this time. It may be simply that Derek had not previously considered it relevant to change these behaviours because he had no awareness of the reasons to do so, never having been adequately informed before. Alternatively, unexpressed fears of surgical complications or even of death may have been a major motivation. The health beliefs, attributions and personality of the individual may also have been relevant in view of the increasing evidence that the locus of control orientation of individuals may relate to the acquisition and successful use of health-related advice (Lefcourt, 1981; Strickland, 1977).

As well as these theoretical issues, this case study seems to have three direct clinical implications. First, potential patients and health care staff involved with surgical care may gain by being alerted to the possible role of cognitive/behavioural approaches in managing problems of this type. This can usefully include members of the primary health care team as well as hospital staff. Second, clinical psychologists will need to be prepared to become actively involved in the surgical care environment itself. Finally, close liaison between medical, nursing and clinical psychology staff will be essential if these approaches are to be effectively implemented at the individual patient level.

36 Janet: psychosexual problems following radical surgery for genital cancer

Introduction

Psychosexual problems frequently occur following radical surgery for cancer of the vulva which involves mutilation of the external genitals and distal portion of the vagina. Anecdotal reports of post-vulvectomy patients (Springer, 1982) as well as more systematic case reports (Anderson and Hacker, 1983) suggest that following vulvectomy there is a reduced level of sexual activity and sexual satisfaction and increased incidence of depression.

Cancer of the vulva affects 3–4% of all women over the age of 50. However, the incidence is increasing in women in their third decade (Hilliard *et al.*, 1979).

The most prevalent but apparently innocuous physical complication of this surgery is oedema (swelling) of the legs. While it does not directly affect sexual function, it is visible to observers and may influence how attractive the person feels. Also common are problems of pain while sitting, as fatty tissue is removed from the groin and the scar tissue can be very sensitive. Women may feel embarrassed by the difficulty they have in directing the flow of urine as the distal portion of the urethra is lost. Mutilation of the external genitals and distal portion of the vagina results in loss of sensitivity in portions of the body important to foreplay, and removal of or damage to the clitoris can result in loss of orgasmic potential.

Referral

Janet was referred to the clinical psychology service by her gynaecologist. He had performed a radical vulvectomy six months earlier for early carcinoma of the vulva. This involved removal of all external genitalia, although her vagina was intact, and there was no interference with bowel or bladder function. He had informed Janet that the cancer had been removed, but normal practice was for regular follow-up. He had referred her for psychosexual therapy as she had not resumed sexual intercourse and he had detected that Janet was reluctant to be internally examined and had developed vaginismus (an involuntary spastic closure of the vagina) when he had tried to examine her.

Background

Janet was 33 years old with two children aged 7 and 5 by her first marriage. After her divorce and 18 months earlier, she had married Paul. They had met three years previously. She had left education at the age of 16 and after working in clerical jobs

211

she married and did not work outside the home thereafter. Paul was aged 47. He had been married before and had three children, all now in their late teens and living with their mother. He worked from home as a life insurance salesman. At the time of the first interview, Paul's father had died one month earlier, following two other deaths of elderly relatives in his family.

Assessment

Janet and Paul were initially very reluctant to discuss their problem, perceiving the consultation as connoting mental abnormality. Paul refused to see the psychologist alone to give a sexual history, stating that he was 'quite normal'. Janet was somewhat reluctant but on her own began to be more forthcoming. Over the course of two interviews an assessment was made of her adjustment to her cancer, her previous sexual history and her current sexual functioning. This included using the Derogatis Sexual Functioning Inventory (DSFI) (Derogatis, 1978) which assesses previous sexual experience, current attitudes and information, sexual activity or drive and the range of sexual fantasies and sexual satisfaction. It also includes an assessment of sex role orientation which is scored on a dimension from exclusively feminine (or for males, masculine) orientation to a more combined masculine/feminine role. There is also a measure of psychological adjustment as states of anxiety, depression and poor body image and anger are known to detract from sexual functioning.

Adjustment to cancer

Janet had been taken by surprise by the whole episode. She had felt some irritation and a lump on her vulva for two months before seeing her doctor who referred her for a biopsy. Within one month she was admitted for radical surgery. She felt very angry at her misfortune as she found out this cancer is more typical among older women. She did not report feelings of guilt over the cancer itself but she felt guilty at the disruption of the marriage. She felt unattractive and unfeminine and was concerned that Paul must feel sexually frustrated. She believed she was cured of the cancer but also admitted to fears of recurrence of the disease. She did not believe her reluctance to resume sexual activity was related to the occurrence or recurrence of her cancer. Mood scales of the DSFI confirmed a picture of moderate depression.

Physical problems

Janet reported many of the complications of women who have undergone vulvectomy, including soreness around the vulva, which made sitting and driving in particular uncomfortable. She had difficulty in controlling the direction of urination. She reported oedema of her legs and distaste for her appearance and she could not insert tampons as she felt too tight and sore.

Psychosexual functioning

She reported an unremarkable psychosexual history. Her parents had a relatively permissive parental attitude to sexuality and she was given adequate sex education. Her first intercourse was at 18 years, just prior to her first marriage, which was sexually fulfilling, although she found her second husband, Paul, more adventurous. Pre-operatively, their range of sexual experiences were typical of a normal healthy couple, and were similar to the healthy population reported by Derogatis and Melisaratos (1979). She reported satisfaction with her physical attractiveness at that time.

However, her sexual functioning at the initial assessment showed she was considerably distressed, and uninterested in almost all forms of sexual contact. Her profile is given in Figure 36.1. Scores above 50 are considered to be strengths, below are considered deficits. Compared to the average scores of Anderson and Hacker's (1983) sample of 15 vulvectomy patients, she was having fewer sexual experiences and less satisfaction, and the total score was also lower. In particular, she reported kissing her partner on the mouth only two to three times a week and only occasional sexual fantasies, and she did not masturbate or have any form of foreplay or intercourse. Also, she had a poor body image. She still felt her weight, height and body hair were attractive, but she felt revolted by her genital area and periodically swollen legs. She dreaded being seen unclothed by her partner. She reported that Paul had looked at her pelvic area in hospital, and once at home in the bath, but she had avoided looking, even while washing herself. She and Paul had attempted intercourse once, five months after the surgery and one month before her first appointment. It had been initiated by Janet in response to encouragement by her gynaecologist, and she stated that she felt so guilty for 'depriving Paul of his sexual fulfilment'. There had been limited foreplay and she had reported no sexual arousal. Intercourse had not been possible as she experienced pain at the entrance to her vagina.

Formulation

The main problem was Janet's phobic response to her mutilated genitalia, and the problem of pain associated with attempted penetration. Second, she reported mild depression, her thoughts centred on the possible effects of her disability on the marriage and the recurrence of cancer. Third, she had physical discomfort from the operation.

Treatment for phobic avoidance was based on three assumptions. First, that Janet held misconceptions as to the extent of the disfigurement. Second, that she was ignorant of the possibility of sexual arousal through stimulation of areas other than the clitoris and vagina, coupled with the overriding fear that Paul would reject her changed appearance. Third, that the lack of sexual arousal and the fear at the time of first attempted intercourse resulted in poor lubrication and therefore pain, due to friction at the attempted insertion of the penis, resulting in the protective closure of the vagina (vaginismus).

Treatment

The treatment plan involved sexual re-eduction of Janet, and later Paul, to include more accurate knowledge of the degree of disability and awareness of other forms of sexual arousal. In addition, homework exercises were prescribed. Through these, Janet learned to gradually explore her genitals and to develop through masturbation non-clitoral means of sexual arousal. Specific exercises were geared to helping her to overcome the vaginismus response. As Janet was so concerned about the impact of her problem on the marriage, it was thought to be important to carry out a fuller exploration of both partners' expectations of each other in order to establish mutually satisfactory sexual relations and emotional fulfilment. Finally, Janet's depressive mood was clearly related to her concerns about the marriage and the possible recurrence of cancer. A cognitive behavioural approach was thought to be appropriate and was pursued in parallel with the sexual therapy.

Janet was seen over eight sessions, excluding two assessment sessions. Paul only attended the first, and Janet reported each time that he had intended to come but work had prevented his doing so. After assessment sessions, and when the treatment plan had been discussed, Janet was keen to pursue treatment and herself suggested that she seek information on her condition from books and by talking to a distant relative who had also had this operation.

Janet agreed to the self-exploration and vaginismus retraining procedure, but was sceptical about the need to incorporate masturbation and fantasy. Stages of self-exploration were discussed at the beginning, and she was taught basic relaxation techniques in order to control her level of apprehension concerning examining her genital area and thinking about her illness and disfigurement. After the first treatment session, she was set the homework task of achieving a level of exploration which was minimally discomforting; that is, examining her body in the mirror including her breasts but excluding her pelvic area. In order to encourage her to explore her physical responsiveness, she was asked to find out how different areas of her body responded to touch by her hands, rubbing with oil, stroking with soft cloth and so on. The second phase was to examine the pubic area including the operation scar, and to examine the sensations experienced by touching these areas. We had anticipated she would experience hypersensitivity at the scar area, and she was not concerned by the slight discomfort she experienced. At the third session, she was instructed to use specific exercises to gain control over the spastic reaction of the pelvic floor muscles (Kline-Graber and Graber, 1978). This involves learning to tense and relax the muscles of the outer third of the vagina. She was instructed to place a clean finger in an artificial lubricant and to gently insert the finger into the relaxed vagina. Over the course of the subsequent three weeks, she was able to contain one finger and, by the fifth session, she could contain two fingers. She was also encouraged to explore her sexual response by masturbation, but she refused to do this. However, while agreeing that intercourse was still impossible, she readily agreed to invite Paul to engage in mutual masturbation.

At the sixth session, she reported a setback. She and Paul had attempted intercourse, after some persuasion from Paul. Penetration had not been possible as she experienced pain, and the subsequent attempt at inserting her finger had been more difficult. After discussing the importance of refraining from intercourse until control of the vaginal response was satisfactory, and rehearsing some assertive ways of dealing with sexual pressure from Paul, she resolved to resume the treatment as planned. By the seventh session, vaginal control was sufficient to allow gentle penetration with Janet gently guiding Paul's lubricated penis from the female superior position. After this, she felt able to pursue intercourse, and declined further advice. Two follow-up appointments were made in order to monitor progress and some further advice was provided to Janet in relation to asserting herself more in her relationship with Paul, and in relation to her fears of the recurrence of cancer. By the eighth session, she reported feeling reassured by her most recent visit to the gynaecologist, and also by the experience of non-painful intercourse.

Outcome

At her final appointment, she completed the DSFI again and her scores are shown in Figure 36.1. Although assessment was carried out only one year after the operation, she was functioning just above the average of the total levels achieved

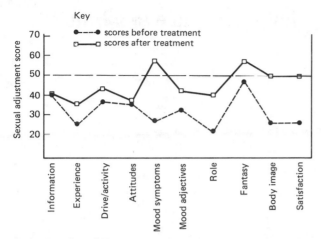

Figure 36.1 Sexual functioning before and after psychological intervention

by the Anderson and Hacker sample assessed on average five years after the operation. However, she was considerably disabled compared to her pre-operative functioning. The scores for sexual satisfaction, body image, sexual fantasy and mood (anxiety and depression) symptoms are similar to the mean for a normal population (Anderson and Hacker, 1983). There was improvement in the breadth of sexual experiences, and acceptance of a less exclusively feminine sex role. While the level of sexual drive was improved, it was still well below the level for both sexually dysfunctional women and normal women. Specifically, intercourse was achieved one to two times per week, masturbation and sexual fantasies were very limited but kissing and petting were more frequent than before the operation at a rate of two to three times per week. As the couple reported this to be satisfactory, although not ideal, treatment was terminated.

Discussion

Given that there are no published prospective studies of the psychological adjustment of women after vulvectomy, it is impossible to assess whether this patient's adjustment was facilitated by treatment or whether this would have been achieved spontaneously. Follow-up in later years will enable us to determine whether sexual functioning is maintained, or indeed whether it has returned to a more nearly normal level. As she was functioning post-surgery at about the level achieved by Anderson and Hacker's patients at approximately five years post-surgery, it seems probable that psychological intervention acted to prevent the development of the high levels of sexual avoidance and dissatisfaction noted in this sample. Given that Janet's problem of phobic avoidance stemmed partly from ignorance of the physical impact of the surgery, it seems probable that the provision of more detailed information by the gynaecologist at an earlier stage and possibly assessment of the couple's psychosexual functioning pre-operatively, would enable earlier intervention to be planned. For example, in this case, encouragement of gradual self-exploration and the use of artificial lubricants and mutual masturbation as an alternative to intercourse in the early stages, could have prevented the development of pain on intercourse and may also have facilitated enlisting the involvement of the husband in the treatment plan.

37　Planning psychological care in a burns unit

The problem

Burn injuries are dramatic, emotive and tragic. They produce a sudden and largely permanent alteration of the body surface and deeper structures. The injury itself is often shocking and painful and the treatment in a specialist burns unit over weeks and sometimes a lifetime is often a greater trauma than the injury itself. Above all, the injury usually occurs as an acute crisis to an intact person resulting in chronic disability, disfigurement and stigmatization (Bernstein, 1976). It is therefore unsurprising to find that adverse psychological sequelae to a major burn injury are prevalent and generally exceed those to be expected for an acute hospital admission (O'Connell, 1985). An additional irony is the often reported finding from epidemiological data that the population of people who are most at risk for burns are usually handicapped on indicators of social deprivation and familial conflict, and have higher than normal rates of pre-existing physical disability (particularly neurological disorders) and psychological disturbance both in the patient and in the family of the patient (Bowden et al., 1979; Klorman, 1983; Wiseley et al., 1983).

Since the Second World War, the medical treatment of burns injuries has seen dramatic advances in surgery and in the control of infections which has enabled previously unsavable patients to survive. Research into the quality of life of the survivors has largely been confined to anecdotal report or follow-up of patients who are by no means representative of a total burn population. Of 159 studies reviewed by Bowden et al. (1979) only 49 were empirical, and only 16 were concerned with outcome after discharge.

In the early years of the establishment of Fenmoor Regional Burns Unit, reports by the social worker showed apparently high levels of psychological disturbance in the burned children (Woodward, 1959). In the 1970s, a psychiatric study showed that while at least one-third of adults had evidence of pre-existing psychological problems, two-thirds had evidence of psychopathology using a standard psychiatric interview technique (White, 1982).

A recent survey of the sisters-in-charge of the 43 burns units in the UK (Wallace and Lees, in preparation) showed that the 28 respondents were unanimous in recognizing the shortcomings of burns units in providing psychological care for burns patients. Many recognized that their unit lacked input from specialist staff such as clinical psychologists and psychiatrists. Lay support is also scarce; one unit runs a patient-lead support group, two are co-run by patients and staff, and one is in the planning stage. An individual counselling service is run by the father of an ex-patient and another unit has a help line run by a parent of an ex-patient.

In the mid 1980s, the staff of the Fenmoor Unit recognized that the psychological trauma of the burn patient is exceptional, but were at a loss to determine how to detect those patients with significant pre-existing problems, how to minimize the psychological trauma of treatment, and how to promote long-term psychological adjustment. With the availability of time from a clinical psychologist for approximately seven to ten hours a week, the question was presented of how best the unit could provide psychological care.

Formulation

Clinical casework would necessarily be confined to a caseload of only two to three patients as there were 500 new patients a year admitted to the unit, and in addition patients were re-admitted for reconstructive surgery. As the patients' problems were often closely linked to their rapidly changing physical and emotional state, this work is necessarily intensive. Problems selected included anxiety, depression, aggression towards staff, difficulty in coping with pain and food intake requirements, and problems of disfigurement and disability.

In order to promote the psychological care of all patients, the remaining time was allocated to supervising research undertaken by graduate psychologists in order to provide an evaluation of the effectiveness of existing services and a baseline for introducing changes in care suggested by these projects. One project examined the effectiveness of the current anaesthetic regime, from which suggestions have been made to improve the matching of techniques to patients' pain and the psychological preparation of patients for pain (Lawrence, 1986). Future investigations will examine the use of forewarning, distraction and relaxation and possibly self-hypnosis.

The second study, described below, was initiated to determine the levels of psychological disturbance of patients and their perceived use of and need for professional and self-help support.

Design and procedure

As the study was conducted by a relatively inexperienced undergraduate, standard screening questionnaires were employed to measure mood state, adjustment to illness and self-esteem (see Table 37.1). The questionnaires selected were appropriate to the age range of patients from a few months to the very old. It must be recognized that these methods may only produce minimum estimates of disturbance since more skilled questioning is often needed to elicit problems such as alcoholism. An open-ended questionnaire was designed to elicit perceived need for support. Factors thought to predict which patients would develop psychological problems, such as the presence of facial disfigurement and size of burn injury, were also noted from the medical case notes.

A series of patients was interviewed in the week of discharge from the ward and six months later in the clinic or at home. A further sample of patients who had been discharged two years earlier were selected in order to determine whether psychological problems diminish once the major treatments are completed.

Every effort was made to obtain a complete sample of patients discharged from the unit within a six-week period. However, patients with little English or major communication problems such as senile dementia were excluded, although where possible information was obtained from relatives. Patients were seen in the clinic or

Table 37.1 Psychological adjustment of burns patients

Patients	Measure	Proportion showing abnormal adjustment					
		Discharge		6 months after discharge		2 years after discharge	
		N	%	N	%	N	%
Adults (over 16 years)	Hospital Anxiety Depression Scale (HADS):						
	Anxiety	5/16	31.25	3/16	18.7	4/15	26.6
	Depression	2/16	12.5	3/16	18.7	3/15	20.0
	Psychosocial Adjustment to Illness Scale (PAIS)	–	–	6/15	40.0	5/14	35.7
	Burn Specific Health Scale	–	–	8/17	47.1	5/15	33.0
Children and adolescents (3½–16 years)	Child Behaviour Checklist (CBCL):						
	Behaviour	0/3	0	1/8	12.5	2/12	16.7
	Social Competence	2/3	66.7	5/8	62.5	3/12	25.0
Children (2½–3½ years)	Behavioural Checklist (BCL)	2/2	100	0/1	0	9/12	75.0

at home appointments, but three refused to be interviewed, and six were untraceable, leaving 85 patients who were interviewed at least once. Forty-five patients comprised the discharge and six-months sample, and there were 40 in the two-year post-discharge sample.

Results

It was expected that the sample would reflect the high degree of psychosocial problems typical of major burns injury. Table 37.1 shows the levels of psychological disturbance of patients in comparison to the norms available for the measure. As the sample contained patients across the whole age range, inevitably there are relatively small numbers represented in some of the age groups. For the adult patients at discharge from hospital, 30% of the patients showed clinically significant levels of anxiety, and 12.5% showed clinically significant levels of depression. The rates of depression were similar to those of a mixed medical sample, but the rates of anxiety were twice as great (Zigmond and Snaith, 1983). There was evidence of a slight decrease in anxiety by six-month follow-up, but the sample at two years showed no overall reduction in symptomatology. It is also interesting to note that 47% of patients at six months were experiencing significant problems of psychosocial adjustment on the Burn Specific Health Scale (Blades et al., 1982). Also, in the two-year sample, 22% of patients were showing a level of disability greater than the mean of the normative sample. Using the Psychosocial Adjustment to Illness Scale (Derogatis and Lopez, 1983), the estimates of 'psychiatric caseness' (that is, the number of patients disturbed enough to warrant psychiatric treatment) were 40% at six months and 35.7% at two years.

The small samples of child and adolescent patients, over 3½ years and under 16 years, make interpretation difficult. There was no evidence on the Child Behaviour Checklist (Achenbach, 1984) that patients showed behavioural problems at discharge. But at six-month follow-up one out of eight and at two-year follow-up two out of 12 patients were showing behavioural problems typical of a clinic population. Approximately two-thirds of patients at discharge and six months, and a quarter of patients at two years were showing problems of social competence. Of the children under 1 year at the time of injury, when assessed two years later on a behavioural checklist (Richman and Graham, 1971), 75% were showing problems of significant behavioural disturbance.

T-test comparisons were made between scores at six months and at two years on all measures with sufficient data, and there were no significant differences. This may indicate pre-existing differences between the two samples or, alternatively, it may disprove the supposition of some surgeons that psychological problems diminish once the major medical treatment has been completed.

Burns patients' and parents' preferences for support

It is not surprising that medical staff are most often reported as communication contacts. However, it is perhaps more surprising to note that 32% of patients and parents at discharge did not report significant contact with the medical team, and that 53% did not report significant contact with the nursing staff at discharge. Overall, the pattern is for at least as much communication to be available from another patient as from professional staff; the majority of patients do not report significant contacts with the other regular members of the team such as the physiotherapist, and fewer with the consulting staff. There is more reliance on relatives than anyone else at six months, and fewer than 20% of the sample at two years reported a significant contact related to the burn in the week prior to interview.

The usefulness of contacts, where available, were generally fairly high at discharge, but much reduced at six months and two years.

The majority of patients or parents (62%) would welcome some form of regular meeting at discharge, with a slight diminution of responding by six months (45%). However, 23% still welcome some form of regular meeting at two years, and nearly 58% felt that some form of group should be available, but they were unsure whether they would themselves attend. However, all patients or parents wanted additional information or support. Other forms of contact such as a newsletter, self-help group, hospital talks and social meetings also received support from the majority of patients. Chi square analyses revealed that it was not the same patients who wanted all types of contact; this suggests they may fulfil different needs. As might be expected given the great distances travelled to the hospital by some families, and the additional social problems of many of these patients, rather fewer patients expressed an interest in organizing such contacts. However, there was interest in participating in many activities, particularly where some form of professional support would also be provided.

Analyses of the risk factors for adverse psychological sequelae, such as the presence of facial injury, the size of the burn and pre-existing psychological problems, showed that it was not possible to predict which patients would become poorly adjusted. However, there was a tendency among adults for those with concurrent psychological problems to be most in favour of some form of professional or self-help support.

Conclusions

The methods used are only likely to produce minimum estimates of psychological disturbance. The psychosocial adjustment results confirm that clinically significant levels of mood disturbance are manifest in between 20% and 40% of adults, and although the numbers of children available for testing at each point were relatively low, some children were showing levels of behavioural disturbance equivalent to those of clinic populations. None of the patients were receiving professional help for their problems. Although the samples at discharge and six months, and the sample at two years were different, there was no evidence that the majority of problems diminish by two years post-injury.

There is evidence of a continuing need for psychosocial care for extended periods after a major burn injury for at least 20–40% of patients, and probably all patients and families would benefit to some degree by further information and support. The survey indicates that there are no obvious ways of targeting the help to particular at-risk groups. Therefore, services will be opened up to all patients and parents.

Initially, in order to tackle the need for basic information, the unit plans to provide a series of booklets for patients and parents covering aspects of in-patient and post-discharge care. Second, as most people preferred a professionally lead rather than self-help group, it is planned to provide a discussion group for families of in-patients. As children under 2½ years were not tested for psychological disturbance, the levels of psychological problems are not documented by this project. However, those children who were under 1 year at admission, were tested at two-year follow-up, and 75% were behaviourally disturbed. The proposed discussion group for parents of in-patients may have a preventive function if it prepares parents for handling behavioural problems to be expected after discharge.

For all age groups, the reported contacts with staff were very low. Negotiations are underway with medical, nursing, paramedical and social work staff to ensure that these staff provide some input to the discussion groups. It is also planned to provide videotapes of interviews with parents, children and adult patients who have successfully coped with such experiences to make a focus for group discussion and to reduce the burden on staff. Finally, as about one-third of the sample at two years after discharge wanted a self-help group, it is planned to encourage members of the in-patient discussion group to form a self-help group with some professional back-up from the psychologist.

Within the limited time available from the clinical psychologist, this research project has shown how the service, with back-up from the psychologist, can learn how to target the scarce staff resources to improve the psychosocial care of all patients. However, it is likely that a proportion of patients with severe psychological problems will require specialist psychological services, and it is agreed by the staff that this will be provided by a full-time psychologist funded by the Fenmoor Regional Unit.

The evidence from the burns unit survey shows that the problems of this unit are by no means unique. If further research shows the interventions to be effective it is possible that these services will be more widely integrated into the total care of burns-injured people whose problems so often persist beyond the time when physical healing and reconstruction are over.

38 Training for health visitors

Introduction

In their contributions to primary health care, clinical psychologists have naturally tended to focus on patients and the general practitioners who referred them. GPs often speak in their referrals of their patient's anxiety or depression. This probably reflects their initial expectation concerning a clinical psychologist's interests. Frequently, however, their patients describe serious family, marital or sexual relationship problems. An additional reason for concern about patients' close personal relationships is the fact that other people in a patient's surroundings often seem to play an important role in creating or maintaining the patient's problems.

Some of the patients referred to the psychologist had young children or a member of the household who was ill. The health visitors and community nurses attached to the practice often knew about those patients' problematic relationships. They had become aware of them while visiting their homes. However, they felt uneasy about having recognized the problems because they had not been trained in how to handle them. As a result the clinical psychologists in the district developed the training course described in this case.

While clinical psychologists are not uniquely qualified to provide such training, there are several reasons for them to take the initiative. In the districts with which the author is familiar, clinical psychologists have provided the only NHS-based help for people with sexual and marital relationship problems. There is a body of clinical psychological research concerning sexual problems, relationships and their breakdown which has a long history and is based primarily on work by social psychologists. Finally, sexual and marital relationship problems, some of them related to illness or disablement, are so common among the population, and have such serious consequences for those affected, that psychologists should see the education of others in the NHS as a professional obligation.

The course is an attempt to transfer some of the psychologists' knowledge and skills to the health visitors and nurses so that they are more able to fulfil their patients' needs. It is not an attempt to pass on work that would otherwise be done by a clinical psychologist. It has not yet been written up in the form of behavioural objectives ('At the end of the course the student will be able to . . .') but the purpose is to help the participants use and extend the skills they first bring to the course.

Participants are selected for the course by their manager and have included not only health visitors but also district nurses, community psychiatric nurses and

221

family planning nurses. District nurses often have to care for patients who have sexual (and consequential marital) problems as a result of surgical procedures or physical illness but are unsure of the best way of helping their patients or coping with the situation.

Design of the course

The course was first provided in 1977 and, with some modifications each time, has been taught ten times to a total of over 100 health visitors and other community nursing staff.

The in-service training course for health visitors and community nurses on marital and sexual relationship problems requires 18 hours. It is offered an afternoon a week for six weeks, each session lasting approximately three hours with a 20 minute break. There are nine to 12 participants with one, or occasionally two tutors. The course has three main components. The first two sessions are primarily concerned with developing the participants' counselling skills and raising their confidence in the skills they already have. The third and fourth sessions are concerned with teaching a model of normal sexual response and using that to identify what can go wrong. The fifth and sixth sessions review the characteristics of two-person relationships, relate therapy to a model of relationship break-down and look at case-management issues. Family therapy is mentioned but in the time available it is not possible to do more than that. Questions of referral and consultative work are discussed at the end.

An important feature is homework, the inclusion of which is intended to provide a model for work with patients. The idea, familiar enough to psychologists but apparently less familiar to other health care professionals, is that the main benefit to the patient derives from the activities which are carried out at home between the sessions. Printed hand-outs are used liberally throughout so that participants have a resource to guide them in their everyday work.

Description of the course

Session one

The aims of the session are:

to identify participants' interests and needs;
to review the principles of counselling;
to practise listening skills with particular reference to the non-verbal aspects of the counselling process;
to identify sexual language appropriate to the locality for use in counselling sessions.

Homework
Experiment with non-directive interviewing to practise listening skills.

Counselling is practised in groups of three — a 'patient', a 'counsellor' and an observer. 'Patients' are asked to discuss some problem of genuine personal significance since this gives them a real feeling of what it is like. Participants often remark on the personal benefit they experience from even a brief role-play. This provides an easy lead-in to a brief discussion of confidentiality. The final activity reflects a recognition that a counsellor needs to be at ease with whatever language the patient may find easiest to use. It is a group activity which involves writing down on a large sheet of paper all the current words for sexual activities and parts of the body. Far from being embarrassing, this invariably ends the session on a high note!

Session two

The aims of the sessions are:

to review the management of difficult clients, such as silent, angry or frightened people;
to practise influencing and advising skills;
to practise talking to couples;
to help participants explore their attitudes to sexual relationships, behaviour and problems.

Homework
Practise advice-giving in a current case.
Interview a couple.

The session starts with a review of the homework during which participants report, often with genuine surprise, the successes they have had. Health visitors and district nurses spend a lot of time giving advice. An analysis of why people don't always take advice, based on the book by Mager and Pipe (1970), reinforces the importance of appreciating the patient's problem from the patient's point of view. The first counselling exercise is carried out one-to-one. A role play of an initial interview with a couple suffering from mutual disappointment and resentment and a consequential sexual problem provides practice in talking to a couple and raises questions for discussion about participants' attitudes to sex roles and permissible behaviour.

Session three

The aims of the session are:

to teach the stages of normal sexual response;
taking account of epidemiological evidence, to identify common problems and disorders;
to review the sexual needs of people with handicaps;
to provide a structure for assessing the problems of a couple with a sexual problem.

Homework
Carry out a structured interview with a couple in which one partner has hinted at a sexual problem.

The model of normal sexual response is Kaplan's triphasic model (1979, 1982). Sexual response is seen as having a 'desire phase', based on a neuropsychological appetite or drive; an 'excitement phase', based on reflex physiological vasodilation; and an 'orgasm phase', based on reflex muscular contractions. Having been explained, this model then provides the basis for a group activity where participants predict, from first principles, what disorders of sexual response are likely to occur. The tutor describes some research evidence about the frequency of sexual difficulties in the general population. District nurses have particular opportunities to help and advise people whose sexual life has been impaired by illness or injury. Issues arising have included the continuation of desire in the absence of physical capability or the presence of catheters; self-image problems resulting from mutilating operations or deformities; and fear of further injury as is found, for example, in those with heart disease. The information about sexual disorders is then re-presented in terms of the way people actually present their problem to professional services; in other words, potential causes are related back to common statements such as 'I don't seem to have any interest in sex' and 'I get aroused but I don't have a climax.'

Session four

The aims of the session are:

to analyse one or more homework cases;
to explain concepts of reciprocity in relationships;
to describe a communication training activity known as mutual pleasuring or sensate focus;
to describe some useful methods for therapy and to demonstrate how an individual programme of therapy can be designed;
to examine some of the books on sexual problems currently available in the locality.

Homework
Try the communication training activity with a partner at home.

The analysis of homework cases provides an opportunity to identify the differing roles of anger and anxiety in real-life sexual problems.

Individual programmes of therapy for each of the common sexual problems are designed as a group activity. The need for trust, cooperation and effective communication between the partners becomes self-evident. The methods are those described by Masters and Johnson (1970) and Kaplan (1979), attention being drawn to the difference between anxiety reducing and arousal increasing approaches. Although the participants may never attempt to undertake counselling for sexual problems in any systematic way, this session demystifies this area of work and permits them to reassure patients whom they may then refer on. The book by Brown and Faulder (1977) is reviewed as one which it is appropriate to recommend to patients. The homework provides another opportunity for some participants to find out what it is really like for themselves.

Session five

The aims of the session are:

to explain and analyse communication and control problems in relationships;
using those methods and ideas, to identify some strategies for therapy;
to practise work with couples on the above problems.

Homework
In preparation for the final meeting, identify a case and prepare an analysis based on a first interview and information in the case records about significant social and emotional life events.

The main theoretical bases for this session are Duck's (1984) model of the dissolution of relationships and the analysis of pathological communications provided by Watzlawick *et al.* (1967). On the basis of research, Duck has identified five stages in the dissolution of a relationship, at each of which different issues and therapeutic methods are most relevant. In brief, the process of breakdown often begins with one person's dissatisfaction with the quality of the relationship. This dissatisfaction may pass through a threshold represented by 'I can't stand this any more', to a second phase in which the partner becomes the focus of dissatisfaction. The third phase is dyadic. With thoughts in mind about whether it will be possible to continue the relationship, the dissatisfied person confronts their partner with the need to reformulate the relationship. If the situation does not improve, the breakdown of the relationship becomes public as each partner recruits support and assistance from friends and families. If the breakdown has passed a point of no return, there is a final phase which Duck calls 'grave dressing'. Each partner, now separated, has to lay the past to rest and rebuild their self esteem by marketing their own version of the break-up and its causes. A role-play, focusing specifically on relationship issues, helps participants to integrate what they have learnt about counselling individuals about their relationship problems, including those where there are sexual difficulties. This is the most difficult session to teach because of the complexity of the material and it is the only session about which dissatisfaction has been reported by participants in their evaluation forms.

Session six

The aims of the session are:

to demonstrate programme planning through a review of participants' cases;
to arrive at an understanding about when participants should handle their own
    cases, when they should consult and when they should refer;
to have participants complete a course evaluation form;
to arrange a follow-up meeting in three to four months' time.

This session often raises the important question of whether, having undertaken the course, the participants will provide a service in the district for people with sexual and marital relationship problems. The answer is no, and it is not the intention of the course that they should. The provision of a routine service would require resources which the participants do not usually have the authority to commit. The time and facilities that would be required to provide a service of satisfactory quality are such that the decision to commit the necessary resources would have to be taken by senior district managers. So far, neither of the districts in which the course has been provided would have seen such a service as being of higher priority than the work currently undertaken by these staff. Therefore the course is undoubtedly about extending skills and not about establishing a new service.

Evaluation

The course is evaluated on a simple form. It consists of a sheet for each session, headed by the aims set out above, the title of the homework, and a list of the hand-outs and visual aids used during the session. Participants are asked to comment in their own words on any aspect of the session or course materials which they found particularly helpful, difficult or hard to understand. After the course, the evaluation sheets for each session are collected together and the comments used in the preparation of the next course.

Evaluations have always expressed appreciation of the course because it covers information and skills not included in basic training but highly relevant to the participants' jobs. It has proved difficult to include enough information about the effects of disablement and illness on sexuality to satisfy the district nurses' needs, yet leave a minimum of time for the discussion of relationships in the later part of the course. Also, participants often have difficulty with some of the homework tasks because they do not have suitable cases at the time of the course, but this does not prevent them becoming sensitized to problems addressed by the homework.

A measure of the success of the course is the number of participants who attend the three-month follow-up meeting, and their experiences when trying to put what they have learnt into practice. Generally, about two-thirds of the participants of a course attend, the rest sending their apologies relating to the demands of their current work. Their experiences suggest that, as individuals, they are able to make some use of their new skills in their everyday work but that this makes little impact on the pattern of work of the service of which they are a part.

The content of the course is not static. The clear differentiation of three components to the course was a response to participants' comments in their evaluations. The five-stage model published by Duck (1984) was of great value in giving some unity to the last two sessions.

Part 5

Service development and working with organizations

Introduction

Bernard Kat

Many of the case studies in this book are concerned with the assessment and treatment of individual clients. A few are concerned with treatment of clients in groups of people with similar problems and a few more are concerned with training for staff who will be working with clients. This section is different. The focus of concern is a system or organization for providing care or treatment.

Do organizations raise new or different issues for psychologists? The answer is undoubtedly, yes. There is more to an organization than the individuals of which it is composed. Nadler (quoted in Turrill, 1986) describes organizations as consisting of four components. The organization exists for a purpose; it has a *task* to perform. Organizations have a *formal structure*, which defines the relationships among the roles of the individuals within the organization in terms of their responsibilities, accountability, budgetary authority and so on. But organizations work because of their *informal structure* which consists of the personal expectations, relationships and loyalties of the individuals fulfilling the various roles. And finally there are the *individuals* themselves, without whom the organization would not exist but who may come and go without much effect on the tasks and structure of the organization. When attempts are made to change the task of the organization, the other three elements tend to resist the change in characteristic ways (Turrill, 1986). Individuals may impede it out of fear, lack of skills or other reasons. The formal organization finds that authority is challenged and normally responds by trying to regain control. As the informal networks are damaged or destroyed; attempts to retain power are likely and, sometimes contrary to everyone's interests, the power to get things done despite the imperfections of the formal structure may be lost. Readers seeking introductions to the literature on organizations might consult Payne (1984) or Handy (1985).

However, many of the issues raised by organizational work are not new to psychologists and are central to the work of psychologists working in health care. For example, quantitative methodologies, scientific enquiry, objectivity and goal setting are key psychological skills which can be applied in organizational settings.

Clinical psychologists have been familiar with organizational issues since the early 1970s. The early attempts to apply behaviour modification methods to wards and hospitals led to a number of reports concerning the problems of such ventures and also the widely quoted paper by Georgiades and Phillimore (1975). The cases in this section are mainly concerned with service development: in other words developments or modifications in the tasks to be undertaken by certain services, and the support and training required as a consequence by the individuals involved.

The reader will find very few references to the formal structures of the services. Two reasons are apparent. For the sake of brevity, a knowledge of the structure of the health and social services is assumed. Second, for the most part the authors have taken on a role as consultant to the manager of the service in question. The manager or authority sets an agenda for change which the psychologist facilitates or carries through. Issues of authority and control are therefore outside the field of immediate concern.

There are also very few references to the informal power relationships that existed within the services, and this is more surprising. The authors hint at the need to anticipate resistance and the problems of ensuring that changes are maintained, but give little information about how they handled those issues. Yet they must have done so. It seems that they often encouraged the individuals affected by change to participate in the decisions about the nature and pace of the changes to be undertaken. The authors have been concerned to draw attention to the developments in services that were achieved, which is natural in clinicians, but the reader should not forget these other issues with which they were also concerned but have not reported in detail.

So these are stories with the salty tang of real life about them. In the first, 'Caring, professionalism and management: using what is already happening to help Norcroft Hospital change', the author was setting out to develop services where previously there had been none. But where to start? The answer was with two influential members of staff who were identifying the need for change and were willing to support it.

In the second, 'Goal-oriented planning with clients in Torbridge Social Services Department', the author was asked to look at the services of a new day centre to see whether it was providing what its users needed. A simple enough question on the face of it, but one which presumed that the users' needs were known. It rapidly became clear that they were not. Feedback of information from structured interviews concerning current referrals prepared the day centre for a new assessment format which would help the centre's staff to target their work more accurately on clients' needs.

The author of 'Developing a psychogeriatric day hospital' was chair of a joint health and social services planning team for services for the elderly mentally infirm. The work undertaken by the psychologist reflects the detail necessary to prepare an organization for its task. This included discussions with the architect about the design of the bathroom and toilets, as well as drawing up schedules for the staff to use in the assessment of patients, training in behaviour management techniques, looking at the referral patterns to the unit and the development of support groups for those caring for the old people.

'Systems change in a home for old people' continues the theme of responding to a request for help. The psychologist was part of a larger change effort which acknowledged that the pace of change cannot be imposed and that change costs money. Training the staff to undertake a PASS assessment of their own home helped them to own the results of their work and also to become committed to a normalization approach. The experience of undertaking the assessment helped to motivate them for the changes required as a result of their findings. The second stage of the intervention required working parties of staff and residents. The author hints at some resistance to change and problems of maintenance, but notes that 'the particular home on which this project is based was inadvertently damaging as many as 62 residents at any one time. The solution to such a scale of problem must lie in systems intervention which confronts the true size of the problem, no matter the complications that arise from working with so many people simultaneously.'

In 'Penchester Community Education Project on solvent abuse' the psychologist's aims are clearly delineated and would, as he says, have been grandiose and unrealistic without the help of a citywide multi-agency committee to validate, facilitate and support the work. Establishing groups of like-minded people to carry change through is an important factor in ensuring the success of change programmes (Georgiades and Phillimore, 1975).

'Fernside District: service developments in mental handicap' refers to another large-scale project. This author also documents the detailed work which needs to be undertaken by a psychologist attempting to facilitate organizational change and provides a useful account of the range of issues to be considered.

'Glenwood Community Alcohol Team' draws attention to a number of points of wider relevance. The psychologist was one of a number of people with a special interest in alcohol problems who started to meet to plan a community-based service. Their plans took a sudden leap forward when the psychiatrist responsible for the in-patient alcoholism treatment unit initiated the closure of the unit and the transfer of the staff to the new service. The resulting team followed the pattern of the leaderless planning group and, at the time of writing, intended to maintain a system of decision-making which does not rely on an appointed leader or director. The author notes that such innovations tend to rely on the existence of a cohesive group of individuals working closely together and reports that the staff who transferred when the in-patient unit closed, who had not been involved with the initial planning, did not easily accept the new community-oriented approach.

This case also discusses the evaluation of the development and reports some performance indicators. Evaluations can be divided into formative and summative evaluations. Formative evaluations are conducted to provide the managers of a service or project with information about how to improve it. Summative evaluations, on the other hand, are intended to assess the ultimate impact of the service or project on the target population — its effectiveness in achieving its objectives. Cook *et al.* (1977) provide a review of the scientific issues concerning summative evaluations. The case is more concerned with formative evaluation, the information being collected as an attempt to monitor adherence to the service aims and objectives. The case closes with a brief account of the turbulent environment within which the service finds itself and to which it will have to adapt if it is to survive. Those familiar with a systems approach to family therapy will immediately recognize the points being made.

39 Caring, professionalism and management: using what is already happening to help Norcroft Hospital change

Introduction

As other writers have noted, the literature on helping institutions change contains much advice, many generalizations and principles but little evidence and few reports of successful change (Milne, 1984). Stolz (1981) commented on the absence of a general theory. Wilcock (1984) used an opposite approach — simply presenting a diary of his efforts. An intermediate approach might be to deny the necessity or even possibility of a general theory of organizational change, and instead use the psychology we already have to influence appropriate individuals within the organization. This case describes attempts to follow this middle course. The main purpose is to draw attention to the opportunities for change presented by current developments in the National Health Service in Britain. The first of these is the current interest in caring and the quality of care. The second is changes in the role and standing of nurses. Third is general management. Some psychologists (for instance, Lewis, 1984) are anxious about the developing role of nurses, and as a profession we are apprehensive about the effects of general management. The argument here is not that either is without problems, but that each also brings benefits and opportunities for improving the care that we and other professions provide.

Background

Mental illness and mental handicap hospitals are generally contracting. Many professionals reacted with initial approval despite doubts about the reasons for the contraction. Increasingly approval has been tempered by concern about the adequacy of the community facilities which were supposed to help people resettled from hospital to lead better lives. A further reaction is concern about the implications for the people who will not move to community care. What will life be like for the people who remain in the smaller and more efficient hospitals of the future? This last question has been a major concern here because Norcroft Hospital, in which the work discussed has taken place, will still be home for 500 people in 1995.

The overall aim has been to improve the quality of care provided to hospital in-patients. The work began late in 1984 when the writer moved to a new post with clinical duties in Norcroft mental illness hospital which was not then receiving any psychology services. New psychology services were not just desirable but necessary.

Caring

What new services and working with whom? At an early stage, nurse tutors and a senior nurse manager expressed concern about the style and quality of nursing care provided in the hospital — task-orientated rather than individualized, and custodial rather than caring. It was an encouraging sign of the times to find clinical nurses echoing these worries and showing eagerness to work with psychologists to improve their care. These are widespread concerns. Sarason (1985) provides many examples of the distress caused when health professionals give too little consideration to their ordinary social interactions with clients. The Association of Community Health Councils adopted a Patients' Charter in 1986 which set out principles concerning the rights and responsibilities of patients and health care providers. The recent focus on quality in health care (Maxwell, 1984) raises related issues.

Two projects developed from these requests. The first was a joint project with nurse tutors to evaluate the effectiveness of workshops in teaching 'therapeutic conversation' (Goldberg et al., 1984). The workshops used videotapes, previously used successfully in teaching psychiatrists the conversational model of psychotherapy (Maguire et al., 1984). There is both local and national interest from nurses in this approach to developing therapeutic skills (Faugier and Reilly, 1986). The purpose of the project has been to investigate whether sustained changes can be produced in the behaviour of nurses in interviews with patients. The desired changes include explaining the purpose of interviews, adopting a negotiating rather than dogmatic style, picking up verbal cues from the patient, and focusing on solving present problems. At present a pilot study involving learner nurses is being written up. This showed a number of significant improvements which were maintained at three months' follow-up. Having demonstrated the effectiveness of brief teaching, the next stage is to offer the workshop to trained staff.

The second project involved working with nurse tutors towards improving their methods of selecting new learners. A literature search yielded little of practical use. The nurses concerned were candid enough to admit that they often differed widely in selection interviews. The problem was then seen as the more general one of first specifying desirable characteristics of staff in particular posts, and then finding ways of assessing these qualities in candidates. The longer-term purpose was to make selection criteria and processes more explicit and rational throughout the hospital.

Partly because the nurses involved were particularly interested, the method chosen was repertory grids which were used to investigate nurses' opinions of the qualities of good and bad nurses in various grades. There was strong interest in the project because of concern at many levels about staff selection. The next step is to present the results — the opinions of nurses in post — and then try to obtain agreement on desirable attributes. The third stage, selecting for these attributes, is the most daunting. However, even to agree on desirable characteristics and then continue with interviews would be progress.

Professionalism

The current concern with models of nursing (Aggleton and Chalmers, 1984) is a stage in the development of nursing as a profession with a distinct and independent caring role. The nursing process (Hargreaves, 1975) marked an earlier stage. Project 2000 (Davies, 1986) looks like the next stage. Project 2000 is a report of the UK Central Council for Nursing, Midwifery and Health Visiting (UKCC) proposing major changes in nurse education.

These changes have implications for the ways in which psychologists work with nurses. In the past, psychologists have offered themselves as teachers and supervisors to nurses, usually promoting behavioural approaches. It now seems less acceptable to nurses to concentrate on what they see as a single therapeutic approach, and still less so for them to work as nurse therapists assisting psychologists. A more congenial approach is for psychologists to ask nurses what services they need. Three initiatives have followed this pattern and a fourth is intended.

One project began with a brief survey of nurses' views of the problems, services received, and needs of the patients they knew well. From this a summary description based on individual needs was drawn up for each ward showing main problems, activities and treatments, contact with relatives and so on. Each ward's description was taken back to the staff concerned and discussion focused on the extent to which activities met needs. These discussions were all constructive. Typical outcomes were developing, with psychology assistance, a treatment group for people with depression; producing a procedure and minimum set of information for patients and visitors; and planning a support group for relatives. Nurses are fully supporting the evaluation of all these activities.

A related project used the Ward Atmosphere Scale (Milne, 1986b; Moos, 1974) to assess nurses' views of the activities that are and should be provided on their ward. The Ward Atmosphere Scale provides real and ideal ratings on ten dimensions including involvement, support, personal problem orientation, and programme clarity. The ratings of all nursing staff on a ward are collated into a single set of scores for that ward. Numerical estimates of the discrepancies between real and ideal scores on each dimension can then be presented. The first use of the scale has been to present these discrepancies to the staff on each ward as indications of the areas of their work they appear to want to change. This has been received constructively. Several wards showed large discrepancies on the dimensions of programme clarity and personal problem orientation, reinforcing some of the findings of the previous project. A later stage will be to evaluate change by repeating the assessments with the scale.

A third change, also welcomed by nurses, has been the decision to evaluate therapeutic activities wherever possible as a matter of policy. Nurses readily saw evaluation as a useful source of information on their work. They have welcomed the assistance of psychologists.

Services are unlikely to be responsive to needs unless the consumers themselves are asked what they want and how satisfied they are with what they receive. This is a delicate subject in traditional institutions where it is easy to dismiss patients' views. The professionals seem to know best because patients are mentally ill after all. However, there is growing interest in consumerism in the NHS (Ham, 1985). It was gratifying when nurses themselves, after discussing their views of the services needed, suggested that patients' opinions should be sought in a systematic way. This is a difficult area (Lebow, 1982) but one that will be pursued.

Management

General management has brought a number of worries: increased personal pressure, disappointments, short-term objectives, and an undue concern with financial savings and efficiency rather than improving services and effectiveness. However, the fact that general managers have been set specific goals of achieving changes in services makes it more likely that change of some kind will occur. There is also a new emphasis on training and improving the quality of care (Merry, 1986; Coad and Hyde, 1986). The ideas discussed in the management literature on successful organizations and organizational change (Goldsmith and Clutterbuck, 1984; Beckhard and Harris, 1977) are easily compatible with the behavioural approach adopted by many psychologists. General managers and psychologists share the language and ideas of formulating problems, setting goals, planning changes and evaluating interventions. Furthermore, the management literature confirms that there are no ready-made solutions to organizational change problems. Each problem must be analysed and a suitable plan devised. Psychologists are used to this way of working. It is obvious that psychologists need the support of general managers; the reverse may also be true.

One kind of help that has been requested concerns occupational stress — another area of wide concern (George, 1986). Workshops on this were provided for the department of one of the professions allied to medicine. After further discussion with personnel and training colleagues, similar events are shortly to take place for unit general managers. The purposes are to inform them about the various sources of stress at work, the different ways in which people respond, the importance of stress to the individual and the organization, and to encourage coping at three levels: the individual, the informal social group and the organization. The total time taken is one working day, split into two sessions a month apart. The second, shorter, session is for evaluation and reviewing progress on homework projects. Stress is painful to the individual sufferer and costly to the employing organization (Cooper, 1986). The aim of the workshops is to cover both aspects, to help participants deal with their own stress and to promote a less stressful (more open and caring) management style (Firth *et al.*, 1986).

Occupational stress is perhaps the most obvious problem with which psychologists can assist general managers. Requests have also recently been made for help with quality assurance, staff appraisal and individual performance review. Psychological skills in goal planning and evaluation are clearly of value to general managers.

Conclusions

The work described here attempts to make use of and contribute to recent changes. None of the individual projects has yet been properly evaluated, and the longer-term impact in changing practices throughout a large hospital is as yet unknown. Psychologists have of course tried and failed to change institutional practices before. But now there are two important differences. First, despite all the drawbacks and reservations, there are certainly new pressures to achieve and demonstrate change. Second, just as nurses have developed their role, so psychologists appear to be clarifying the best use of their skills. This involves working on a project basis developing and evaluating services, and doing so in close cooperation with direct care staff. This gives a new perspective, helping psychologists to take a wider and long-term view and so plan interventions which are part of a longer term strategy.

40 Goal-oriented planning with clients in Torbridge Social Services Department

Background

Four years ago a clinical psychologist was seconded full-time to work with Torbridge Social Services Department reaching the parts that other NHS psychologists cannot reach (*sine qua non* Heineken).

The Social Services Department (SSD) spreads across four health authority districts, and employs 2500 staff, offering home-based, office-based, day and residential services for a wide range of clients. More than 30 000 people apply for a social service each year, and approximately 13 000 people are receiving a service at any one time. Although some of the initial requests for services are simple enough to grant (e.g. 'Can I have a 'disabled' sticker for my car?'), many problems are extremely complicated and urgent, often with significant resource implications (e.g. 'You'll have to take my mum into a home.'). Once a decision has been made to allocate a service to a client, that decision is then subject to repeated reviews when decisions are made to alter or terminate services. With this volume of demand for services, professional decision-making at the start and during the course of the department's involvement with clients appears worthy of very close scrutiny. This case deals with the work of one clinical psychologist, aided in the early stages by a trainee clinical psychologist, attempting to enhance the quality of routine social work planning with clients.

Presenting problems

Upon taking up secondment to social services, the psychologist was asked to look at the services provided by a new multi-purpose day centre to see whether it was providing what was needed by its users. It soon became evident that there was no way of judging the appropriateness of the day services without first finding out what the service users actually needed. Discovering such information from the client files was difficult, since the social work assessment that was routinely made of all clients' circumstances at referral contained so many ambiguities. It was proposed therefore to carry out a detailed assessment of a cohort of referrals to the day centre over a three-month period.

Assessment

A proposal was made to the SSD managers in the area that their field and day centre social workers should cooperate in a study of the way day centre applications were dealt with. This would involve structured interviews with these SSD staff, with parallel interviews being conducted with the client and, if appropriate, with the person who had first referred the client requesting a place at the day centre (GPs, health visitors etc.). From the start it was agreed that such a study would conclude with recommendations to improve practice in the way requests for day centre attendance were handled by the SSD.

Formulation

With the authority of the local managers offering credibility to the study, the cooperation of all parties was extremely high. Referrers, clients, assessing social workers and day centre staff all appeared to welcome the opportunity to analyse their involvement in the referral process.

After interviewing all parties concerned with 22 referrals over a three-month period, the following conclusions were reached.

First, assessment following referral for day centre attendance usually focused on the limited question: 'Is this client going to be appropriately placed at this day centre?' It did not involve assessment of the clients' lifestyles in the evenings and at weekends; nor did it generate consideration of plans other than day centre attendance. By contrast, when specifically asked in structured interviews what opportunities they were lacking, 66% of the clients listed 'company in the evenings'; and the assessing social workers saw this as a significant lack in 62% of the clients referred. The initial decision to suggest a day centre plan had effectively foreclosed a full assessment of the total person and consideration of a broad range of service plans. Such stereotyping was particularly worrying when many of the initial referrers were heard to say they didn't really know what went on at the day centre.

Second, the assessment information that was included in standard reports was almost entirely geared to what might be described as the matching of clients to the day centre. Listing the problematic features of the clients' daytime circumstances on referral, the written assessments proposed day centre plans which would alleviate the clients' current distress. The problems were treated as full justification for day centre attendance. Moving directly from analysing the problems to devising the plan to alleviate them tended to focus any debate as to the appropriateness of the day centre plan on questioning the reality of the problems as listed. What was usually missing in the assessment reports, and as a result missing in any debate on the suitability of day care as a plan, was any clear notion of the positive outcome clients or others were seeking to achieve. Put in the language of a transport manager, 'If you don't know where you want to get to, I can hardly tell you how to get there.' Without agreement on the desired end goals, there is no basis on which to suggest the best direction of travel, nor the best vehicle, nor the likely journey time, nor the likely cost; nor, most significantly, can there be any hope of recognizing when the journey is over and the destination reached.

Stereotyped and problem-oriented assessments for day care were serving to frustrate legitimate dialogue about the use of the day centre resources, and stifling the real need for flexible services to be developed to help different clients achieve their unique aspirations.

237

Intervention

On the evidence of the structured interviews, all parties involved were capable of taking a much broader overview of client and family problems on referral. Equally, all parties, with sufficient encouragement, were willing to risk describing the future they were seeking to achieve. How could these reorientations be built into routine assessment practice?

The virtue of SSDs from a psychologist's perspective is that many social work tasks are governed by standard procedures which allow discretion in how the task is done, but require a standard format for the presentation of output. In this case it was accepted practice for all assessments for day care to be summarized in writing using a common set of headings. The report which was submitted following the study of the day centre referral process proposed a new set of headings, with a suggestion that a volunteer should be sought from each field social work team to pilot the new assessment format and help to revise it in the light of experience. The format which was piloted, developed and implemented in 1984 is essentially as follows:

(A) *The past:* chronological life history, listing the date of each event and the age of the client at the time;
(B) *The present:* current lifestyle, typical 24 hours in the week and/or at the weekend; specific problems in current lifestyle (who's doing what, too much, at the moment?);
(C) *The future:* specific goals for future lifestyle (who will beneficially be doing what, more, in the future?); desired future lifestyle, typical 24 hours in the week and/or at the weekend;
(D) *Planning:* what services would best assist a shift from the present (B) to the desired future (C)?
(E) *Ownership:* are there any disagreements about B, C and D? Signature and comments of client.

Several features of this format deserve note.

(1) The history of the client (A) is put in one chronological account, rather than allowing several parallel chronologies where the coincidence of different sorts of events (e.g. redundancy, divorce, onset of illness) are ignored because history is divided between different headings (e.g. occupational history, social history, medical history etc.).
(2) Specific problems (B) are set in the context of the client's overall lifestyle, thus avoiding the narrow selection of only those problems that can be met by the service which was originally requested.
(3) Goals for the future (C) are positively stated prior to consideration of service plans (D) which might enable their achievement. Thus, agreed goals for the future may remain undisputed while a legitimate debate is held as to the best means to achieve them.
(4) Client ownership of the assessment is ensured as a result of the signature and comments section (E). Thus the assessment process is changed into negotiation wherein clients are accorded responsibility for planning their own future.

Results

The revised format for day care assessments has been in use for one-and-a-half years with all referrals to day care in one particular area of the county (N=85).

Consumer satisfaction has not been formally assessed, but informal feedback suggests a strong commitment to goal-oriented planning from managers, field and day care social workers. Since this format was first used for day care referrals in one area of the SSD in 1984, there has been growing interest in extending the goal-oriented approach into service planning and allocation in other settings with other clients. For the last nine months, in two areas of the county, all children over 10 years old and their families have been asked to complete sections, A, B and C prior to their applications for services being heard at a resource allocation panel (N=90). All requests for services to old people in the county (N>4000 per annum) will shortly be heard on the basis of sections A, B and C, with B taking the form of a checklist of areas of functioning of the sort used in the Clifton Assessment Procedures for the Elderly (CAPE) (Pattie and Gilleard, 1979).

Discussion

What began as a small piece of action research pertaining to one establishment has spread into suggesting remedies for similar problems in other areas with other clients. After all, most requests for social services are presented as problems to be relieved and thus encourage the problem-oriented allocation of resources without proper consideration of what positive outcome they are to achieve. Procedures which ask staff and clients to define their goals before planning how to achieve them at least offer some protection to staff and clients (staff from pressure to commit resources prematurely and clients from the allocation to them of inappropriate and stereotyped services). What about the 30 000 new referrals to the department each year, and the 13 000 ongoing cases which require regular review? Is it possible to aim for goal-oriented assessment of all requests for departmental services? Theoretically, such wide applications are possible providing it is accepted, first, that the amount of detail will be less when the requested resource is cheap or likely to have relatively little impact on people's lives and, second, that lower levels of staff skill will require higher degrees of prescription (e.g. checklists) in the more sophisticated sections where specific problems and specific goals must be identified (B and C). It appears that the commitment to goal-oriented assessment which already exists in Torbridge Social Services Department can be maintained and enhanced. Certainly the many front-line staff who already have experience of using goal-oriented planning formats will find it easier to use new ones with clients for whom current formats are still problem-oriented at the moment, so generalization of this approach across client groups should get easier. In addition the very culture of social work is making developments such as this easier with increasing participation by clients in the allocation and design of services. What could be more appropriate than a procedure that insists that both staff and clients should agree on the outcomes they are seeking to obtain when they plan services?

Is the development of procedures for large-scale use really the job of a clinical psychologist? David Hawks clarified this issue well in his article in 1981 when he highlighted the nonsense of any equation which requires the personal application of a clinical psychologist to all cases where it might be useful. Systems work such as this requires a highly developed relationship between the clinical psychologist and the consumer organization (in this case a social services department) but allows a much greater spread of psychological intervention. If goal-oriented planning with clients becomes a part of the everyday culture in social services, then the primary professional commitment to clients will be satisfied.

41   Developing a psychogeriatric day hospital

Introduction

Several authors have pointed out how the contribution of clinical psychology to health care in general and older people in particular should rely on more than direct work with individual patients (Jeffrey and Saxby, 1984). One of the additional roles suggested is in the planning and development of services. At first sight the particular contribution of clinical psychology may not be clear. There may be only limited ways in which the psychologist's role is unique. However, the particular skills of applied behavioural science do offer a new perspective on the interaction between physical environment and human behaviour. As yet we have probably spent more time studying how to set out supermarkets than on the design of rehabilitative environments. Nonetheless there are examples of such work in the design of accommodation for older people (DHSS, 1976; Liebowitz *et al.*, 1979). More recently the relationship between such things as floor coverings and mobility have been the subject of behavioural analysis (Willmott, 1986).

Much of the very interesting work now emerging on the measurement of quality of life relies on both physical and psychological indices (Moos and Igra, 1980). There is good evidence that the layout of rooms and furniture affect social interaction (Davies and Snaith, 1980). Thus the psychologist may offer special knowledge as well as the common sense of any well-informed professional.

Background

The author's contact with this project arose ex officio from being the head of a specialist clinical psychology service for the care of the elderly and as the chairperson of the joint health and social services planning team concerned with services for the elderly mentally infirm.

In 1981 the Deanvale Health Authority and the Upland County Council Social Services Committee accepted a report prepared by the mental illness working group of their joint forward planning panel. This working group had identified as the first priority for development those services for elderly people suffering from mental illness, especially dementia. The results of their deliberations were contained in a report on psychogeriatric services which attempted to set down a strategy for the development of these services. One important deficiency among the many identified was in the provision of day care.

240

Perhaps because specialist health services for the elderly mentally infirm are generally provided within mental health services, such patients are often seen under the general category: mentally ill. In their pathology, the dementias are more appropriately seen as a part of neurology, although that specialty has never taken on their continuing care. In recent years the trend in psychiatry has been to reduce the emphasis on illness, in favour of social and psychological models. For the patient with senile dementia, however, it is often necessary to make the opposing point, namely that this is an illness, not just being awkward or growing old.

The view of the clinicians was that there were very different needs for those suffering from functional mental illness at whatever age, and those afflicted by a dementia. This suggested that in the long term, there would need to be two or more day facilities.

Determination of what level of resources is adequate is often a contentious issue. There has been considerable use made of norms, but in most cases these refer only to the average provision across the country. For a specialty which can be seen to have been under-funded in the past, the average may not be very high or very satisfactory. In the case of this day hospital, the DHSS norms suggested that for the population of the catchment area (which is 87 000 with 13 000 aged 65+) a unit with 39 day places would be desirable. There was no existing provision, so it was generally agreed that priority should be given to this project. Indeed the speed with which agreement was reached came as a pleasant surprise to those who were used to fighting to reach a compromise.

Plans for the hospital

A multi-disciplinary project team was convened consisting of representatives from the clinical departments (nursing, psychiatry, psychology), the district works department and the district planning department. A 15–20 place day hospital was planned which was to open five days a week. It was estimated that the day hospital would serve up to 50 individual patients. This may be compared with the estimated 1300 elderly people suffering from dementia in the catchment area.

The funding at present available was seen as sufficient for the setting up of a day hospital using easily converted existing accommodation. It was in fact a former nurses' home. It was intended that there should be a more permanent unit, purpose-built in due course. As a result, one of the points discussed was the suitability for the scheme being integrated into later development. It was made clear by the planning officer that the scheme which had been funded should be seen as one step towards developing the overall service for both psychiatric and psychogeriatric patients.

The layout of the building was greatly constrained by the design of the existing accommodation. The options available related to the layout within rooms rather than the arrangement of the rooms in relation to one another. There was some scope for modifying the use of rooms, but it would obviously be much easier to design a better environment from a 'green field' site. One thing that became apparent was that some of the design and works staff could benefit from briefing on the special problems of elderly mentally infirm people. Short descriptions of the behaviour and cognitive problems of dementia provided by the psychologist seemed to prove particularly helpful.

The need to balance physical and mental frailty with the promotion of independence was discussed a good deal. Decisions on this and other matters were reached by a consensus of those present.

241

With the limited space available, aids and adaptations tended to be geared to the needs of the most frail with some risk that the more able might not be as maximally independent as possible. The special problems of dementia such as disorientation (confusion about time, place and people's identity) and dyspraxia (difficulty in movement) often require supervision rather than mechanical aids, so space for extra people rather than equipment was often required. It is worthwhile noting that by comparison with some other types of help, psychological intervention is very sparing in its demands for specialist equipment.

One specific example of the dilemma of rights and risks could be seen in the discussions over the correct sort of radiators for the unit. These were seen as needing to be guarded lest a patient should suffer injury, even though as day patients many, especially those living alone, were certainly at more risk at home. Identifiable risks must be minimized, but those which cannot be seen are usually ignored.

As a result of the fire officer's comments on the architect's plans, it was established that there was only adequate day space for 16 patients. Thus the number of places available was determined ultimately by practical considerations rather than service need.

The consultant architect was able to discuss with clinicians such things as the best design for the bathroom and toilets. It was interesting to note how the use of simple reversible catches with the provision for doors opening both inward and outward could ensure that both patient privacy and safety were maximized. How important such details become when they are absent.

The day hospital finally opened in September 1984, just one month behind the schedule that had been set down 15 months previously.

Outcome

The day hospital has now been running for a little over 18 months. The part-time social worker, agreed by the social services department, has just been appointed, and the problem of office space is now in the fore. There is general agreement that there should be a separate consultant psychiatrist post for the elderly mentally ill in this sector of the service. This has just been placed at the top of the priority list for developments in consultant psychiatrist posts for the district.

The clinical psychologist involved with the day hospital has been involved with considerable amounts of staff training and in developing and evaluating the operation of the unit. This has included drawing up schedules for staff on the unit to use in the assessment of patients, training in behaviour management techniques, looking at the referral patterns to the unit and the development of carers' support groups.

Given that this unit is the only day care provision by both health and social services for this area, the question 'Should it exist at all?' is not of practical relevance at this time. It is seen as more appropriate to focus on the place for this limited amount of day care in the overall provision for this group of patients and their carers.

Consideration of this has led to moves towards developing domiciliary support to carers as has for some time been established for physically handicapped people.

Discussion

As clinical psychologists move out into broader areas of the development of patient care, traditional exclusive skills play less of a part and those of management predominate. Nonetheless, as already indicated, there are examples of how specialist knowledge can add to the efficiency and effectiveness of planning and development. In many ways it is particularly interesting to work closely with those whose expertise is in buildings and equipment. These professionals have knowledge and skills which they wish to apply to the benefit of patients. Unfortunately, the link between them and the consumers, both patients and staff, is often left to chance so that their efforts may be misdirected. It is all too easy to hear complaints in a new unit such as 'Why on earth did they build it like that?'. Clinical psychologists are well placed to assist in amalgamating the many disciplines involved and thus in the promotion of better services for patients.

The latest figures from the Upland County Planning Department indicate that from 1981 to 1991 the number of people aged over 65 in the hospital's catchment area will remain the same. However, the number of those aged over 85, among whom the incidence of dementia is highest, will increase by 37%. There is still plenty to be done.

42   Systems change in a home for old people

Background

In 1983, the Mountview Area Social Services Manager requested the help of the clinical psychologist in redesigning one of the homes for old people in the area.

It was Mountview area policy at the time to encourage the development of small-unit living within its larger residential homes as a way of improving quality of life for residents and minimizing the damaging effects of across-the-board institutional practices. The particular home for which psychology services were requested was acknowledged to have received less time and effort in this direction than other homes in the area, so psychological consultancy was commissioned as one part of a larger compensatory investment.

Presenting problem

Initial discussion suggested there was a mismatch of purposes between staff at the home and the surrounding social services department staff, with home staff worried about change and external staff seeking it.

Assessment

Assessment procedures had to be designed with this background in mind. The area social services manager involved was in the midst of a management process that was designed to remove the obstacles to change within the home. To this end he called a special meeting of all staff at the home and made plain his expectation that the service offered by the home would begin to change so as to come more into line with area thinking about services to old people. He made clear, however, that the exact nature and time-scale of any changes should be actively decided by staff and residents at the home rather than by external managers.

Having established that change from within was required, the area manager offered extra resources to allow the home's staff to do the job, permission to overspend on staffing costs, full cooperation from other social services staff within the area to help out if needed, an increased allocation of time from the residential and day care officer (who managed this home among others), and the use of a clinical psychologist from the NHS to act as consultant/adviser one day a week for a year.

The work of the clinical psychologist combined the role of external assessor with that of catalyst to an internal self-assessment. In January and February 1984 a more detailed assessment was carried out by the psychologist who worked four shifts as a care assistant, and spent four days talking to residents and staff to discover both the formal and the informal policies and practices of the home. Sure enough, there was much requiring change if residents were to be offered a service which enhanced rather than damaged their status. During March the work involved designing and setting up a rather more detailed assessment of the service, the latter to be carried out by staff at the home so that they themselves might begin to 'own' the critique of current services which was necessary before they could move on to designing an improved service. In this way the idea was to parallel the sort of self-assessment procedure which is often used as a way of helping individual clients decide that they need to change. In these circumstances, assessment is clearly part of the intervention where clients are involved from an early stage in formulating their own views of the problems they wish to tackle and the goals they wish to achieve.

After much discussion, six volunteer staff from the home along with their residential and day care officer, were briefly trained and then helped to carry out a detailed in-house inspection of their own services.

The staff from the home itself comprised the officer-in-charge, the third-in-charge, three care assistants and one domestic. The group of six, along with their residential and day care officer, were trained and helped by the psychologist and his immediate manager. They were trained over a two-day period off-site using a bungalow attached to another home for old people in the area, and then moved back on-site to collect data on the actual services offered in the home for a further three days. The training consisted of practice using the normalization rating scales developed by Wolfensberger and Glenn (1975) and set out in PASS 3 (Programme Assessment of Service Systems). These scales oblige participants to judge the degree to which a service damages or enhances the status of people who receive the service. The data was collected on-site in such a way as to ensure that all the participants would experience a consumer-oriented view of the home's services at the same time as gaining sufficient objective information to agree ratings on the 36 aspects of the home which were taken from PASS 3. Having spent two days training and three days experiencing data collecting, the study group met for a further two days off-site — the first agreeing consensus ratings of current services and the second devising a strategy to share the findings with other staff and residents and plan with them to achieve better services for the future.

Results of assessment

The conclusions were of necessity embarrassing for staff at the home, but on the whole staff and residents were prepared to acknowledge current failings because they were seen as only temporary since there was a clear mandate to move on to better things as soon as possible.

In brief, the main findings were as follows:

(1) The building was quite well sited in a residential area close to shops and pubs, with a reasonable bus route, close to the railway station. Nevertheless, immediate access to the building was appalling, with a congested car park, treacherous paths, high steps without ramps on most external entrances, and no pedestrian crossings on nearby busy roads. As a result, very few people were able to leave the building without exceptional effort, and many visitors, it was presumed, would be deterred from calling in.

(2) In-house staff were rostered to deliver across-the-board services to up to 62 old people. For example, all residents were served three meals a day together in a large dining hall at set times. Men were shaved one after another in the corridors outside their mixed lounge areas. Beds and baths were done in a set sequence that paid little heed to the individual needs of residents.

(3) Resident involvement in daily living was minimal with very little opportunity to give as well as receive services. Equally residents enjoyed no opportunities to share in the overall management of their home.

(4) The quality of the design, decor, fixtures and fittings was very poor, with many institutional features present and many normal household features missing.

(5) Space was extremely cramped, allowing very little choice as to where and how to spend one's time, and very little space to maintain one's own possessions.

(6) Staff interactions with residents often treated the old people like children, and much of the regime was dominated by a medical ethos, with the officer-in-charge called 'matron' and the staff called 'nurses' (indeed most wore uniforms like those worn by hospital nursing sisters) and the general office was located in a room with the sign 'Medical Room' on the door.

(7) Staff interactions with each other were often extremely fraught, with poorly defined senior staff responsibilities allowing a corridor-based staff culture where residents were often privy to gossip, rumour and internal staff dynamics.

The experience of participating in the study group inspection was a powerful one which certainly fuelled a complete rethink of the sorts of services which were offered. Low scores, reflecting a service which damaged resident status, were given on far too many scales to allow any sense of complacency in the group. On the 36 rating scales which were used, scores of one were agreed on ten of the scales and scores of two on 11 of them. In other words, on 21 of the 36 aspects examined it was concluded that the service was actually damaging to the welfare of the resident old people. Nine of the scales gained a rating of three, six of them got ratings of four and none got a positive rating of five or six.

Intervention

To find a way of improving this poor state of affairs, the final day of the study group was spent agreeing the following plan:

(1) All staff and residents would be encouraged to join working parties which would meet regularly to detail changes under the following titles:
  (a) making it easier to have access in and out of the home,
  (b) designing smaller living units,
  (c) encouraging a homely atmosphere,
  (d) recommending more homely clothing for staff,
  (e) informing, educating and publicizing.

(2) The conclusions and recommendations of each working party would be published along with the in-house assessment report.

(3) A systematic process of change would be agreed with local managers and timetabled to happen over a period of three years.

Results

The working party formula was moderately successful, involving on average three residents and seven staff in each. Although ownership of the deliberations was not as broadly shared as might have been hoped, the working parties did nevertheless succeed in devising far reaching recommendations for change, which were agreed by area management and have been largely implemented at the time of writing two years later.

The process of change has been a painful one for both staff and residents since both groups have undergone the sort of disruption which is an inevitable part of change. There has been resistance at some points en route, and misunderstandings have had to be dealt with in a new way, which has been difficult for staff who were hitherto unused to managing confrontation professionally. Nevertheless, two-thirds of the way into the three-year timetable, staff have reduced the number of residents, increased the amount of space available to them, established a small group pattern to daily living (with separate unit dining-rooms etc.), increased the individualization and personalization of the service to residents, and dramatically improved access to the building with a consequent increase in comings and goings by both residents and visitors. A recent interim review repeating the same normalization scaling exercise finds low scores of one on only one rating now (ten ratings got this score two years ago), a score of two on four ratings (11 in 1984), scores of three on 19 scales now (only nine previously), scores of four on 11 (only six in 1984), and for the first time there was a score of five (for 'innovativeness'). Overall then, a substantial shift in the quality of services to clients has been achieved, and there is still a year to go to meet the agreed timetable.

The most crucial outstanding task now is to intensify the supervision of staff so as to enhance their development of practices consonant with the flexible, consumer-oriented services which residents are coming to expect.

Discussion

What began as a one-year contract to act as consultant/adviser to a social-services-run residential home has been negotiated into a three-year project with substantial spin-offs in other areas of the psychologist's work. The PASS format has been found to be equally useful in other social services settings (for example training and helping physically handicapped people to inspect their own day centre services prior to submitting their own bid for improved services) and the social services department is extremely interested in extending their use of self-inspection formats so that services can be genuinely reorganized to improve the quality of life experienced by users of all types of service.

Is such project work as this really a legitimate example of clinical psychology? Certainly individual client benefit must provide the bench-mark against which the work can be judged, but this should not be taken to imply an exclusive focus on small-scale individual or family pathology. The particular home on which this project is based was inadvertently damaging as many as 62 residents at any one time. The solution to such a scale of problem must lie in systems intervention which confronts the true size of the problem, no matter the complications that arise from working with so many people simultaneously. Such systems work as this demands a highly developed relationship with the host organization, and clear and well-negotiated arrangements for steering the project en route. Providing such conditions are fulfilled, much can be gained by clients from the use of independent clinical psychologists in social services department settings.

43 Penchester Community Education Project on solvent abuse

Introduction

Solvent abuse is taken to mean the misuse by inhalation of volatile hydrocarbons. Reports to social workers in one major British city suggest that over 90% of this problem is young persons, under 16, misusing acetone- or toluene-based glues, although it is the hydrocarbons packaged as aerosols which cause most damage and problems.

Background

Penchester is a large metropolitan area with typical inner-city problems. At present, services for solvent abuses are not organized centrally in the city and there is, therefore, a wide disparity of approaches among agencies. Although health, social services, and education receive requests for help, the information in a recent directory shows that individuals rather than organizations offer specialist help (the five health districts, four social services districts and three educational divisions are not coterminous).

Voluntary services, such as Drugline, offer some help to abusers but, for the most part, young people are referred to a few specific individuals only when the problem seems to have become life-threatening or totally socially incapacitating. Two hospital departments (toxicology and psychiatry) also help, but attention is short term and not specific to solvent abuse problems.

The problem

Abusers and their families have always been exhorted to go and meet the experts or go and talk about their problems. However, it became obvious early in 1983 that no specific training had been given to those people who might be asked for advice most frequently, for example teachers, GPs, community nurses, social workers etc. The literature was concerned predominantly with the effects of solvents (Institute for the Study of Drug Dependency, 1980), rather than controlled studies for the best methods of decreasing such abuse. Many colleagues indicated that most of the information about the problem of solvent abuse was gleaned from newspaper articles rather than professionally produced documents. However, it appeared that many of those charged with giving help to such adolescents and their families were expected to rely on the problem-solving techniques used by their professions with other client populations.

The problem with such services to misusers was not only a disparity of approach, but also the lack of coordination between such services. During the year 1984/1985, there were four known deaths in the city which could be attributed to the effects of solvents — three where death was accidental, following the altered cognitions caused by the chemicals, and one by apparently intentional suicide. National deaths numbered 57 in 1983, 81 in 1984 (National Children's Bureau, 1986), and 116 in 1985 (Anderson *et al.*, 1986). It was deemed important by all concerned that, in spite of a desire to decrease public anxiety about such misuse, there should never be any glibness regarding the problem. Such a goal would only be achieved by an integrated community education programme aimed at misusers, their families and those professionals concerned.

Formulation

The aims of the psychologist's interventions were to reduce public anxiety about solvent abuse, and so decrease the number of direct referrals which needed minimal help (for example, those children who had perhaps been seen sniffing glue from a crisp bag in a park once, in the company of peers, since when their parents had successfully intervened). The second aim was to improve the quality of interventions provided by professional colleagues by additional teaching. The third aim was to provide information and guidelines for counselling for those professional colleagues whom the psychologist might not meet. Such aims would be grandiose and unrealistic without the help of a city-wide multi-agency committee.

The psychologist was in a convenient organizational position to help set up such an advisory group of professionals from those agencies in contact with the problems. Because the psychologist in this case was clinically trained, working as an educational psychologist and employed by the education department but nevertheless working with problems referred by the social services department, he was able to present the views of those working with adolescents in all three agencies and also to allow the information to go from and to other psychologists working in different fields.

In 1981 the Advisory Committee on Solvent Abuse was set up in Penchester representing the police, social services department, probation service, education, health, magistrates and voluntary agencies. The psychologist was a founder member and has remained as scientific adviser. The committee was set up in view of the anxiety about solvent abuse in the city, and the aims of the committee were: to ensure that assistance and advice can be offered to misusers and their families; to encourage training programmes; to participate in arranging seminars; to facilitate liaison between all agencies and voluntary organizations; to encourage research; to publish information; to assist in the promotion of health education, particularly in schools. The particular contributions of the psychologist to this project are outlined below.

Action

Information

It can be seen from the committee's objectives that the psychologist's role in the assessment and dissemination of information and advice in health education was seen as particularly valuable. Furthermore, in view of the contested results from what little research has been undertaken, and in view of the methodological problems of projected research, the psychologist was charged with attempting to collate and weigh the evidence of research and to disseminate it.

This role within the committee led to not only a review of appropriate references, but also the compilation of other documents which the committee would publish and disseminate. These included a notice to the media, advice to parents, a paper giving the behavioural approach to solvent abuse reduction, and a pamphlet, *Notes of Guidance*, which gave general points and tried to allay some of the misconceptions about solvent misuse, as well as giving some hints of what to do and how to reduce the problem.

Training

It was always assumed that the psychologist could be referred specific cases where intervention programmes might be of help, but it was also understood that the psychologist's role would cover staff training and an advisory role at city level. Direct client work ensured some credibility for the psychologist's methods in the eyes of colleagues and families as well as highlighting problems of service delivery. Often, direct client work leads to training staff to run behavioural programmes and, therefore, helps future misusers, and aids the general training of colleagues in that establishment.

Social services staff and parents
In addition to training in the formulation of programmes for individual clients, staff were also given general instructions on how to recognize and deal with emergencies and how to cope with clients who were in an altered state of awareness. This advice was sent to all children's homes in the city for discussion and display on office walls.

Because of the incidence of solvent abuse in children's community homes, specific teaching programmes were introduced by the psychologist and his colleagues from educational social work. Such courses began with giving information about methods and effects of glue-sniffing, the age range, its possible pay-offs, and the incidence of accidents, as well as the practical details of what to do and what not to do. Using role-play and video examples, discussion centred around what staff could do with young people who are found glue-sniffing and how to decrease further incidents.

Emphasis was laid on the fact that most deaths occur through accidents and that, therefore, intervention should be kept low-profile and individual, as the DHSS has recommended (Health Education Council, 1985). For this reason, it was suggested that no groups for glue-sniffing adolescents should be set up. It was also emphasized that children who had been misusing solvents should not be confined to small areas, and should not be allowed to go to sleep or rest before the solvents had been excreted. Procedures were laid down by each children's home for informing parents, GP and school, where this was agreed to be necessary.

Psychologists often found it difficult to divorce training about glue-sniffing problems from the wider issues of staff training, such as the application of learning theory in general. Problems also arose because of the fast change-over of staff and also because of the problems of oversight of the clients while training sessions were in progress.

Misusers and their families
A pamphlet, *Notes of Guidance*, was aimed at misusers, their families and the caring services, and an attempt was made to couch it in terms useful to any of those who might come into contact with the problem; 15 000 were circulated among the relevant agencies. These pamphlets contained general points about abuse, what to do in an emergency, and how to talk about the problem when the person was not intoxicated.

Professional colleagues from psychology, medicine, education and social services
Six seminars were given to such colleagues (over 60 attended on each occasion, divided into three workshops) using the document, 'A behavioural approach for decreasing solvent abuse' (Barlow, 1982b). This gave guidelines for analysing the antecedents and consequences of such misuses and suggested how more effective rewards could be made contingent upon incompatible behaviours, or how rewards could be given for no evidence of abuse. Recent research and a bibliography were presented, as were indicators for good practice in counselling (Barlow, 1986).

In spite of the low-key approach of most workers (Release, 1979 and 1980) all colleagues underlined the importance of adequate supervision for those who were intoxicated and the importance of looking at the individual circumstances and rewards of glue-sniffing, rather than attempting to describe the problem in general terms.

The police and magistrates
In addition to the above training initiatives, the police invited the psychologist to give training seminars to crime and beat officers and juvenile liaison officers, using the same information, documents and methods. This eventually led to direct information-giving and training in non-confrontation to officers directly involved in youth and community services. The documents disseminated have become a training package which can also be given to misusers and their families.

This format of allaying misconceptions, giving information and making suggestions for handling and disposal, (making assumptions, for example, that care or custodial sentences are usually inappropriate for constant misusers) has also been presented to magistrates of the juvenile bench (the chairperson of the juvenile bench sat on the advisory committee).

Other community approaches

A local community theatre, with a grant from the Arts Council, approached the psychologist about help with a script for a play on the subject of glue-sniffing, which was then to be produced in schools, community homes, youth clubs, and colleges of further education. The company presented workshops afterwards where half of those involved in the acting remained in role, so that some role-playing sessions were possible with the audience. Those who came out of role were able to comment and pass on realistic information provided by the psychologist. A teaching package was presented to groups who saw the production.

Although difficult to evaluate such projects, which may be preaching to the converted, this endeavour led to commendation and a direct increase in self-referrals.

Scientific advice

The Solvent Abuse Committee is now setting up a working group of professionals directly in contact with abusers, to allow them to support each other, facilitate cross-referrals and to advise the voluntary and statutory agencies at a managerial level on aspects of crisis reduction and prevention.

Following the placement of a non-offending youngster in a secure unit because 'his life was in danger' from glue-sniffing, and the subsequent representations by the psychologist, the social services department will in future challenge any such requests for placement. Similarly, no care orders can now be requested using solvent abuse as the only reason for the child being out of parental control.

The psychologist, quoting the work of Millham *et al.* (1975), Millham *et al.* (1978), Millham (1986) and Cornish and Clarke (1975), suggested care orders may be more damaging than the presenting social environment. If admission to care increases personal stress and contact with glue-dependent young people, glue-sniffing in child care establishments is likely to be frequent, and difficult to decrease.

The social services department, acting on the psychologist's advice, alerted children's home professional and domestic staff to the need for cupboards containing hydrocarbons to be locked. Aerosols can cause 'sudden sniffing death' (Bass, 1970; Anderson *et al.*, 1985; Anderson *et al.*, 1986). As has recently been noted, the number of people dying from the direct toxic effect of solvents exceeds those dying from accidents while under the influence of glue (Anderson *et al.*, 1986).

The same department has, through its senior management, asked for specific advice on teaching methods, policy, and prevention of solvent abuse. Two main points have arisen from this. First, staff should not be expected to counsel young people without adequate teaching. It seems unfortunate that, within the caring professions, there are so many definitions of counselling. In this instance, the psychologist takes counselling to be verbal methods of altering specific future behaviour. To increase the chances of success, a list of dos and don'ts was circulated which attempted to apply behavioural theory to this problem, but also added ethical and relationship considerations.

Second, managers responsible for young people's services need to identify separate funding and resources for solvent abusers. In 1986, much money was identified to alleviate all drug abuse. However, in the light of the deaths of young people and the anxiety of others about solvent abuse, there is a case for giving it separate consideration. The reasons are that, compared with other abuses, the age range of solvent abusers is different; the chemical pathway and induction and excretion of the solvent are different; and the availability and low cost of solvents makes them more easily accessible.

These factors all suggest that psychological intervention, whether in individual problem-solving or group management, must be separate from community services to other substance-abuse problems. The implication for prevention and health education is that the psychologist provides advisory work to non-psychologist managers and planners.

Conclusion

There are many complex problems involved in evaluating the outcomes of such large-scale social projects which operate in the context of numerous other environmental and social factors. However, it can be noted that in 1986 the number of referrals to psychologists in Penchester dropped to 62 from 190 in 1985. This might reflect public acceptance of the problem, as well as a general reduction in solvent abuse. Anecdotally, experimental abuse may well have decreased, but the number of chronic stress-reducing abusers may not have decreased, resulting in a higher mortality (Anderson *et al.*, 1986).

The objectives of the committee, which were formulated as actions to be taken rather than results to be achieved, have been met, and there is now pressure on the committee to become involved with problems of other substance abuse.

If psychologists are to be seen as intervening in social problems (McPherson and Sutton, 1981; Mitchie, 1981), they must apply their skills to health education topics. Solvent abuse is only one of a number of such topics.

44   Glenwood Community Alcohol Team

Introduction

In recent years, clinical psychologists have been at the forefront of the development of community services for a number of client groups. This is no accident. Training in psychology places emphasis upon the continuity between the normal and the apparently abnormal; it emphasizes the social context within which problems of living arise; and it puts a high premium upon 'giving psychology away' to other disciplines and agencies. Hence psychologists have tended to embrace the movement towards community mental health.

In general the community psychology approach (Cowen, 1980; Heller *et al.*, 1984; Koch, 1986) can be summarized by saying that it advocates a pro-active rather than reactive style in reaching out to locate and respond to problems in the community; it attempts to deliver services in settings that are as close as possible to and as similar in form to people's own homes; and it makes as much use as possible of natural community resources, in the form of people and facilities. Community psychologists will think in terms of delivering relatively brief treatments to relatively large numbers of people in need, as well as making available traditional forms of treatment which are more intensive and which reach smaller numbers. They will be engaged in collaborating with voluntary agencies and in training and supporting volunteers. High on the priority list is likely to be the indirect provision of services to clients, by means of a consultancy service (Brown, 1984) to a broad range of health, social service, and other statutory and non-statutory workers who themselves are in direct contact with those in need. Finally, the community psychologist will be seeking ways to prevent psychological problems arising, as well as to treat them once they exist.

The area of alcohol-related problems is one in which psychologists have contributed a great deal to the development of new ways of thinking. Although the terms 'alcoholism' and 'alcoholic', and the models of individual pathology which these terms imply, are still to be found, they have largely been replaced by new terminology and new models. New thinking on this subject has led in the general direction of social learning theories which underpin recent models adopted by clinical psychologists (e.g. British Psychological Society, 1984; Heather and Robertson, 1986; Orford, 1985; Royal College of General Practitioners, 1986).

Two reports were particularly influential in laying the groundwork for the development of community alcohol teams. The first, *Responding to Drinking Problems* (Shaw *et al.*, 1978), reported that, although many agencies dealt frequently with alcohol problems, their potential for helping was limited on account of attitudes they held. In particular, agents often lacked therapeutic commitment to working with alcohol-related problems. They were often pessimistic about the outcome of treatment, doubted their own ability to help, and even questioned the legitimacy of their involvement. In the same year there appeared a DHSS report, *The Pattern and Range of Services for Problem Drinkers* (DHSS, 1978). The report saw the continued need for alcohol specialists, but saw it as their main role to educate, support, and be available to be consulted by, the general or primary level agencies. The report thus opened the way for the future development of the community alcohol teams (CATs) which have become one of the principal models of service delivery in Britain in the 1980s.

Background

In Glenwood Health District a number of people with a special interest in alcohol problems started to meet together regularly during 1980. This group comprised professionals — social worker, psychologist, psychiatrist, community nursing officer and probation officer — and the Director of the Council on Alcoholism who, in keeping with the strong tradition of self-help and the role of voluntary organizations in this field, brought his own experience of having had a drinking problem himself plus several years experience of running a voluntary council on alcoholism, largely unaided. This group met weekly, elected its own chairperson, who changed from time to time, worked enthusiastically on proposals for the development of community services, and was remarkably free of restrictive rivalries. This experience was similar to that of Fairweather and his colleagues (1974) in the USA who found that the spread of an innovation in service delivery depended less upon whether the person who took the lead in an area was a doctor, an administrator, a nurse or a psychologist, than upon the existence of a cohesive, collaborating group of committed individuals who worked together.

At a fairly advanced stage in the planning of the community service, the psychiatrist responsible for the in-patient alcoholism treatment unit suggested closing this unit and transferring most of the staff to work from the community centre. There was little time to think through the full implications of this radical step, but it seemed at the time like an opportunity not to be missed and it was grasped eagerly.

The community alcohol team (CAT)

The CAT came fully into being in October 1981 with the opening of a centre in the town as recommended by the DHSS report (DHSS, 1978). This is a three-storey building, a quarter of a mile from the town centre. The first floor is leased from the district health authority (which made available and refurbished the house) by a voluntary organization, the local Council on Alcoholism.

The team, which consists of five full-timers (coordinator, two community psychiatric nurses, one social worker, one psychologist), 12 sessional or part-time workers (four of whom work for the voluntary Council on Alcoholism), and four volunteers, grew out of the leaderless, multi-disciplinary planning group. The team has continued its tradition of doing without an appointed leader or director. No one person or discipline is in charge or ultimately responsible. Although this state of affairs is uncomfortable to everyone from time to time, the absence of a more traditional hierarchical arrangement is something to be cherished, and the team has evolved a system of decision-making which it hopes is robust enough to stand any pressures that may be imposed from above towards adopting a more traditional form of leadership and direction. It is encouraging to learn from Katz and Kahn's (1978) valuable book, *The Social Psychology of Organisations*, that, among other things, members of a team who feel autonomous and who are most involved in decision-making get more satisfaction from their work: this has certainly been this team's experience.

The central component of this system is a weekly meeting of the whole team. In the first two years the team also had a management group which consisted of senior members of the disciplines involved in the team, most of whom were founder members. This has gradually become more democratic, first moving to being appointed by the full team and being accountable to it, and subsequently doing away with the name 'management' altogether. All members of the team can now attend the renamed Finances and Resources Group which reports to the full weekly meeting which alone can make final decisions.

A list of some of the team's activities during its first five years is given in Table 44.1. The psychologist members of the team have contributed to most of these activities: their role has largely been that of bringing a psychological perspective rather than engaging in clearly distinct areas of work.

Table 44.1 Activities of Glenwood Community Alcohol Team

Core activities

Providing an accessible counselling service for people with alcohol-related problems

Providing an accessible counselling service for those affected by the drinking problem of a family member or friend, whether or not the problem drinker is receiving help

Providing an education service for other professional groups and voluntary organizations

Providing a joint assessment or consultancy service for other workers who are in touch with people with alcohol-related problems

Providing a day centre and group work programme for those who require it

Providing therapeutic halfway house accommodation for those who require it

Providing a home detoxification service for those who require it

---

Research and development activities, including:

Running an alternative (i.e. non-alcoholic) pub for clients, staff, and members of the general public

Running a home management training course for clients of the CAT and other agencies

Running a course of alcohol education for probation service clients whose offences are alcohol-related

Screening new admissions to the district general hospital to assess rates of alcohol-related problems

---

Evaluation

All the usual problems of evaluating psychological intervention are greatly augmented when the case study consists not of a single psychologist's intervention with a single person, but rather the coming into being of a whole team with such a broad brief as the one which this team has taken on. The task is one of programme evaluation, of which a great deal has been written, especially in the USA. There are many different kinds of evaluation and this has led to much confusion. Rossi *et al.* (1979), for example, have drawn useful distinctions between 'programme planning' (assessing incidence, level of need etc.), 'programme monitoring' (testing whether the service is being delivered to the people and in the way envisaged), 'impact assessment' (testing whether outcomes are achieved), and the assessment of 'economic efficiency' (cost-benefit or cost-effectiveness analysis).

Table 44.2 CAT performance indicators (1 January to 30 June 1985)

Performance	Rating	No. of clients	Direction of change*
1. *To provide an accessible service*			
(a) Self referrals	43%	59	+
(b) Attending first appointment	93%	129	+
(c) Average delay between referral and first contact	3.3 days	129	+
(d) Clients outside the city seen at home	64%	29	o
(e) Average delay between first and second appointment	10.8 days	63	o
2. *To engage clients in therapy*			
(a) Losing contact after first appointment	14%	16	+
(b) Agreeing a drinking goal (and seen more than once)	81%	51	o
(c) Experiencing a change in counsellor	24%	15	+
3. *To involve friends and relatives*			
(a) Clients with spouse/partner who are seen together	42%	25	–
(b) Other important friends/relatives seen	30%	13	+
4. *To involve other agents and to communicate effectively with them*			
(a) Joint sessions with other agents (if another agent is closely involved)	33%	14	+
(b) Referring back to other agents at case closure	46%	38	o
(c) Writing to referral agent after first appointment	61%	36	+
5. *To achieve early intervention*			
(a) Receiving help for first time	45%	58	o
(b) Aged below 40	52%	67	o
(c) Married	41%	52	o
(d) Employed	34%	44	o
(e) Agreeing goal of controlled drinking	10%	13	–
6. *To achieve home detoxification*			
(a) Number arranged	3%	4	–
7. *To achieve successful case closures*			
(a) Drinking goal achieved	51%	54	+
(b) Closed in planned fashion	54%	57	+
(c) Offered follow-up appointment after case closure	11%	7	+

* Direction of change:

+ signifies that indicators move by 10% or more in the desired direction compared with previous six months
– signifies a change of 10% or more but in the undesired direction
o signifies a change of less than 10% in either direction

Another useful distinction is that between formative evaluation involving the collection of data which are useful in making changes to the service as it goes along, and summative evaluation which seeks summary conclusions about effectiveness. The former implies an element of action research, a model for researching organizations whereby a researcher assists members of an organization to formulate useful research questions, to collect relevant data, and to interpret the results in a way which helps the organization change in desired directions (Cope, 1981). This attractive model for doing research has obvious affinities with clinical case work where the clinician (like the researcher in action research) assists clients (like members of the organization) to assess themselves and their situations (like collecting data in an organization) in order to facilitate personal change (like organizational change). As Bromley (1986) writes in his stimulating book, *The Case-Study Method in Psychology and Related Disciplines*, case studies in psychology have often concerned individuals while case studies in the social sciences generally have as often concerned organizations, teams, neighbourhoods, or communities.

The style of evaluation which the team has adopted — and this has been one of the psychologists' few distinct roles in the team — has elements of programme monitoring, formative evaluation, and action research. Using a microcomputer system some information about each client and about the team's response to each client has been routinely recorded.

The accumulated information is fed back to the team at a regular review day held six-monthly. Most recently these data have been fed back in the form of performance indicators which enabled the team to see how well it had been doing in relation to a number of agreed aspects of good practice, such as responding quickly, involving families where possible, and seeing clients at an early stage of their problems. Examples of recent data of this kind are given in Table 44.2.

Discussion

The decision to close the hospital unit, which with hindsight can be seen to have been taken hastily and with insufficient thought, was probably the right one nevertheless. The principle of moving the base for the service from a hospital to a non-hospital site was right and it has led to a client service which is more accessible (the number of clients using the specialist services is far greater than it was, and the majority now refer themselves). It has also led to a service which is far more involved with other organizations and agencies, both in a training and a consultative capacity. It has also led to a number of special projects with a greater community orientation. Examples include the provision of a detoxification service for general practitioners' patients at home rather than in hospital, and the opening of a non-alcoholic 'pub' in the basement of the centre.

Without the transfer of staff which the closing of the in-patient unit made possible, many of the CAT's activities would not have taken place. On the other hand, a number of disadvantages followed, mostly to do with philosophy and aims. A number of the staff who transferred from the hospital were not involved in the initial planning and did not necessarily share enthusiasm for the new ideas about alcohol problems and community mental health generally. There was an uneasy settling in period of at least a year during which a number of the original staff left. Because the team took on responsibility for providing the district's client service, it has also meant that direct work with clients has been seen to be the most urgent task. Furthermore, because most team members have been trained in direct client work, it is this kind of work that they feel most confident about and find the most rewarding.

Hence, there has remained a very real danger that the team perpetuates, albeit in a different setting, some of the very practices which the new community movements have been at pains to redress. In particular the team may be accused of continuing to adopt what community psychologists such as Rappaport (1977) have called a 'waiting' mode of operation instead of a 'seeking out' mode. This is quite contrary to the view in community psychology that problems should be treated where possible in the localities and settings in which they arise (in the family, the workplace, or the local health centre or surgery) or to the philosophy that specialist agencies should, first and foremost, be educating and supporting non-specialist workers. The team's experience of doing educational and indirect or consultancy work has been that these have tended to take second place to direct client work. The same has been reported from general community mental health centres in the USA. Nevertheless, the amount of educational and consultancy work is now quite considerable. There is also a good case to be made for the view that direct and indirect client work are complementary rather than alternative activities, and indeed that the latter is best based upon a sound foundation in the former.

The ability of the team to control its own destiny is limited by the fact that, by and large, it has no budget of its own and crucial matters of staff appointments and promotion are not within its prerogative but are made within separate disciplines or organizations from which it is constituted (nursing, social work, Council on Alcoholism, etc.). It is to be seen as a small subsystem nested within larger systems (Bronfenbrenner, 1979). Hence, it cannot remain unaffected by wider policies. Indeed the main issue for the team in the last year has come from without, in the form of district health authority policy of establishing locality community mental health teams and the desire to place all services, as far as possible, in those localities. Paradoxically, since such a move is thoroughly consistent with the community movement of which the community alcohol team is a part, team members have found themselves resisting the move of nursing staff to localities because the advantages to clients of accessibility and quality of service are unproven and uncertain, and perhaps because the change appears to threaten the very existence of the team.

In a paper in *Personnel Review* (a journal not normally read by clinical psychologists), Pettigrew (1975) describes typical changes that occur in specialist organizations in their first few months or years. He observed how an initial pioneering phase, associated with feelings of optimism, was regularly followed by a period of self-doubt. Depending upon whether the response to this phase was adaptive or maladaptive, the result could be the unit's absorption or demise by default, planned demise or absorption, or consolidation and renewal.

Postscript

Since this case was written, the CAT has ceased to function, at least as a joint statutory/voluntary venture. Many of its functions will continue in the district it served and psychologists will continue to make an input, but the CAT, with its almost unique multi-agency structure and democratic system of management which lasted for six years, is no more.

45 Fernside District: service developments in mental handicap

Introduction

The work of clinical psychologists in mental handicap has moved from an emphasis on changing the lives of individuals and groups towards advising and training carers (both professional staff and so-called non-professionals such as parents and volunteers), and to participating in organizational changes. This shift has been the result of several factors including an increased recognition of the role of clinical psychology, the need to make more efficient and effective use of the relatively small number of the profession employed within the services, and an acknowledgement by services that major changes are required.

What contribution can a clinical psychologist make to planning? What follows is an attempt to answer the question, but it should be remembered that others can also act as change agents. For a further discussion of change in mental health organizations, see Fairweather *et al.* (1974) on whose work these points are based.

An understanding of psychological processes
Psychologists' professional expertise can be applied not only to a discussion of what can improve the quality of life for people with mental handicaps and their families, but also for staff within organizations. Organizational structures and processes are dynamic and rely on human behaviour for their implementation. Good management practice relies heavily on psychological principles.

Perseverance
Change creates confusion and stress. Awareness of these issues and prevention of their negative aspects can help people to tolerate uncertainty.

Independence
Unlike many professionals, psychologists have no vested interests in keeping outmoded services. This is largely due to the way in which psychology, as a relatively new profession, has been organized. The flexibility of working styles and settings allows psychologists to avoid the main feelings of resistance and fear of loss (of status, benefits and skills) that other professional groups experience. Also they are not usually in control of resources and their thinking is not bound up in financial ties. There is little evidence that change relies on the availability of resources alone.

External intervention
Psychologists are often useful as change agents because they are external to both staff and their managers. External change agents who do not build up excessive resistances to their proposals can operate at several levels of a system and produce change more effectively than those at the top of the hierarchy.

Action orientated intervention
Intervention strategies orientated primarily towards behavioural compliance and task accomplishment are more effective than strategies aimed at cognitive awareness and attitudinal acceptance. Psychologists know the difference between what people say they will do and their observable behaviour.

Overcoming resistance to change
Even if those concerned with change can accept the fact of change, there is still a need to help them accept the emotional aspects that accompany change. People who are being asked to change need to feel that there will be benefits for them in the change and the psychology profession should be able to help in this process.

Power
Clinical psychologists recognize that there are limitations to formal power. The most senior people in the hierarchy cannot create change unless the rest of the hierarchy cooperates. They do not, therefore, feel helpless and can recognize that change can occur at any level. Similarly others can be helped to see how they might be effective.

Participation
Most change is the result of group effort. To be effective a group must be helped to form, cohere, interact, complete tasks, recognize success, withstand failure and remain committed. As a member of a group a psychologist can assist in these processes.

Change and learning
Service changes usually require staff to change their behaviour. Without the opportunity to develop alternative behaviours through training programmes, there is increased staff uncertainty and resistance. The psychological strategies that have been found to be effective with individuals need to be part of the repertoire of staff behaviour. Psychologists therefore have much to offer to staff training exercises.

An experimental approach
Many staff and relatives have justifiable fears about whether any proposed changes in services will in fact produce a better quality of life for people with mental handicaps. It is imperative to ensure the proper evaluation of new services so that faults may be promptly corrected if and when they occur. Also, feedback to staff is a powerful motivator and should be built into the system in a positive way. Resistances may also be overcome by the acceptance of an experimental approach rather than the blind belief that change, any change, will automatically be beneficial. Knowledge of the theory does not itself guarantee that psychologists will be able to put theory into practice. Continuous evaluation is essential to improve effectiveness.

Background

There is now widespread acceptance in principle that services for people with mental handicaps should be more humane, flexible and locally based, with small numbers of people in domestic-style residential accommodation with use, wherever possible, of ordinary community facilities. There is also greater awareness of the needs of individuals for choices, leisure opportunities, meaningful occupations, spiritual and artistic expression and for non-stigmatizing specialist support if this is necessary.

In the past, mental handicap services have been poorly resourced and have often centred on large institutions built in the days when custodial care was the aim. The damaging effects of institutionalization on residents and staff are now well known. To put the new ideas into practice on even a small scale can be difficult, but to change a whole service and provide alternatives to large hospitals can be a slow and daunting business. This case study outlines the work carried out over a three-year period (November 1983 to November 1986) in Fernside District Health Authority and illustrates how organizational changes can take place and how clinical psychology is involved.

The issues

The health services provided to people with mental handicaps in Fernside Health District centred on three hospitals (one of approximately 240 beds and two of approximately 50 beds each). The social services for the same population were arranged in three divisions, each offering an adult training centre (ATC) and a hostel for adults. Each hostel supported a few satellite group homes and offered short-term care to a relatively small number of people who lived with their families. In addition, a further hostel offered short-term care to children living at home for all three divisions. Two community mental handicap teams (CMHTs), of the four that were planned, had recently been set up. The total district population was approximately 360 000 and there were approximately 1000 people on the mental handicap register. The district health authority was not coterminous with the local authority social services department, and there was a small area of overlap with another social services department.

Despite valiant efforts by many individuals and groups in the health and social services, there were serious problems within both services. The main hospital had been the subject of a public inquiry in the 1970s and was run down, under-resourced, poorly managed and not able to recruit skilled staff. Crisis management appeared to be the norm and little support could be given to the newly established CMHTs whose work soon uncovered major additional needs within the community.

Social services did not have sufficient day or residential places to offer people in the community, either for long- or short-term care. Despite good working relations among individual members of staff within the two agencies (health and social services), when a problem arose, each agency would resent the fact that the other could not usually help. There was increasing reliance in emergencies on voluntary and private services which often deflected funds from planned improvements. A downward spiral was in progress.

To make matters worse, highly critical reports were received from the National Development Team (an independent advisory body on mental handicap services) and from the English National Board (the body which monitored nurse training at that time). The senior officers in both agencies were roused to action.

The planning of change

In November 1983 a joint working party (JWP) was set up, consisting of officers, managers, and planners from health and social services. This group included the district clinical psychologist. The education department was invited to send representatives, but declined the invitation at this stage and joined the JWP later. Representatives of parent groups were not invited to begin with, as their presence, it was thought, would inhibit the free and frank discussion that would have to ensue if progress was to be made.

The task of the JWP, as with any planning group, was:

(1) to build up a picture of the present situation
(2) to identify problems and future needs
(3) to conceptualize the desired service of the future
(4) to compare the desired state with the present state
(5) to identify the required changes
(6) to decide on the action to be taken to bring about the changes
(7) to monitor and evaluate the changes.

The cycle then begins again using the results of the evaluation. During this process the present services need to be maintained and the planning group has to be kept cohesive and task-orientated.

Finally, the implications of the chosen plan have to be matched to available resources.

First steps towards implementation

The JWP began by sharing ideas about what services were being offered, together with problems and deficiencies. A mental handicap register had been established which identified the names, addresses and a crude ability rating on a five-point scale for each person with mental handicaps whose main residence was in the health authority catchment area. The points on the ability rating scale range from 'mostly independent, living alone' to 'in need of 24-hour support'. Other details were also compiled for the register, including an outline of all the services used by each individual provided by education, health, social services, voluntary and private agencies.

The register was used as an information base, and rough outlines of need were identified. A sub-group worked on defining principles on which the future services would be based and the resources needed to provide them. The financial advisers for the agencies worked together to translate the services required into resources, and all available monies over a decade were identified. It was agreed that all monies would be pooled and a priority list was drawn up to be continuously updated as changes in the existing services occurred or as new service needs emerged.

Throughout the autumn of 1985 a public relations campaign was carried out with a leaflet describing the proposed service changes being sent to every family on the register. A video explaining the changes was made and shown to groups of relatives, staff and managers at meetings which were attended by members of the JWP who were there to answer queries and hear comments. Notes taken at the meetings were discussed at the JWP. One consistent comment was that relatives should be represented on the JWP. This was agreed and two relatives were elected. A major criticism of the plan from relatives was that it involved closing the main hospital. Several meetings were held to try to resolve this difference and in the end it was agreed that relatives and JWP members would together visit examples of 'good' campus services. The debate on this issue continues, although the visits did allow relatives to see some of the same problems in these services. Also unresolved at present are the issues of how the service will be managed, although the notion of a single agency service has been rejected.

Local groups have been set up for each of the four towns within the catchment area. These groups consist of representatives from health, social services, education, parents and housing. Their remit is to check the priorities and timetable of changes and resource allocations for each local area and to obtain more detailed information against which to test the plan. They are also the groups who will oversee implementation of the strategy at local level by appointing staff, renting, buying or planning buildings in line with the principles, the resources and the timetable of priorities. The implementation of the plan started in April 1987.

In summary, the plan will involve £9 million capital expenditure over ten years with a revenue budget of over £7 million per annum. (At present, health and social services spend just under £5 million per annum.) The number of residential places in the community will rise from 194 to 524 and day places from 395 to 587. There will be additional staff for the three current CMHTs and a fourth team will be formed shortly. The increased number of therapeutic staff, including psychologists, will be linked to the CMHTs.

Activities of the clinical psychologist

The planning exercise briefly described has involved clinical psychology as part of both the general work and in specific aspects. The main contribution has been made in the following areas:

(1) the outline of the philosophy on which the new services would be based
(2) the identification of needs on which to base planning as an overview
(3) the public relations exercises
(4) the services to be provided for people with the most challenging or difficult behaviours
(5) the training of untrained staff and the retraining of trained staff
(6) the evaluation and monitoring of the strategy.

The first three areas represent work that has been completed, whereas the final three areas are still being discussed. One important issue in each area has been how much psychological advice would be acceptable to the wide range of interests represented on the JWP without serious dilution of the psychological principles involved. The following is a summary of the results achieved.

The outline of the new service philosophy

The new service principles were based on the assumption that the main needs for people with mental handicaps are care, education, training, work and leisure. Families should be given more support if their relative still lived with them, but by the age of 30, all the people on the register should have a choice of alternative accommodation. Any support or help given to an individual should be tailored to their needs with an emphasis on the use of ordinary services where possible. The principle of normalization which, among other things, states that any help should be given in a socially valued way, was adhered to as far as resources would allow.

263

Identification of needs for planning base

Taking into account the principles which have just been outlined, the resources needed by people in each of the five groups identified by the ability rating scale were looked at, for example accommodation, types of daytime occupation opportunities that should be available as options, and the support required from staff. It was estimated that people in each group would require a range of inputs from a psychologist, starting with regular assessments and advice on training and behaviour modification for those with the most needs, to counselling and psychotherapy for the most able. This assumption, made on the basis of previous experience and expected needs, allowed the JWP to conclude that four more psychologists were required. (At the start of the period covered by this case study there were 1.5 whole time equivalent (w.t.e.) psychologists working in the mental handicap service, and this included the district clinical psychologist. At the end of the period there was a total of 2.5 (w.t.e.) psychologists and 4 psychology technicians. The future total will therefore be 6.5 (w.t.e.) trained psychologists, once the posts for the new services have been funded.)

The public relations exercises

A leaflet and video were used to disseminate the ideas put together by the JWP on how the new services would affect individuals, their families, staff and managers. A series of meetings was held for both families and staff to express their views and ask questions. The approach adopted by JWP members at these meetings was to note all comments, correct misunderstandings, explain the reasoning behind the plan, clarify how changes could best be brought about, acknowledge the difficulties, emphasize the benefits and be understanding about the uncertainties.

Changes were made to the plan as a result of these discussions. A balance had to be found between pushing ahead despite initial resistance to the plan so that the objectives could be achieved, and recognizing how important it was to acknowledge and include, even in small ways, the views of the consumers.

Services for people with the most challenging behaviours

Debate still rages on this topic. The plan includes resources for four assessment and treatment centres which would each provide ten residential places for people who might benefit from behavioural intervention. It is assumed by the majority of JWP members that not all these establishments will be required and the psychologists are suggesting a peripatetic team to provide intervention in the client's usual environments. It is hoped a principal psychologist post will be obtained in the near future so that a pilot team can be set up to investigate the effectiveness of such a model, reduce anxieties on the issue and perhaps remove the need for any specialist units.

Staff training

A sub-group of the JWP, consisting of staff development officers from health and social services, trainers, management representatives and the district clinical psychologist, has been working for the last year with managers of the residential and day-care facilities in both agencies to propose how best to meet training needs. It has been agreed that the managers, helped by members of the sub-group, will train their own staff. A timetable of such events is being drawn up after the identifying of staff training needs was completed by questionnaires and meetings. A library of video training materials has been set up and the managers will use these for discussion and training. The sub-group will adopt a 'pyramid sales' approach, starting with managers, to nurture a learning climate. These managers will then train their juniors, who will in turn train their staff and so on. The main advantage of this method is that it models the approach that the service hopes to adopt with clients, namely that of a participative learning approach. The evaluation of this method is being planned and it is hoped to use feedback from the first year to modify the second year's operation.

Evaluation and monitoring of the strategy

The main aims of the evaluation are:

(1) to increase the existing data base of the register and update it regularly;
(2) to establish systems for the assessment and review of individual client progress;
(3) to collect consumer views from clients and families;
(4) to sample the effects (if any) of changes on individuals;
(5) to measure quality-of-care issues;
(6) to gather views from staff on the plan as it evolves;
(7) to see whether or not the service principles have been achieved;
(8) to provide regular feedback to the JWP on progress and problems so that the plan may be continuously revised in the light of experience.

Researchers will be employed to carry out the data collection.

Concluding comment

The clinical psychology contribution to the planning process is made more effective by demonstrating the practical application of psychological principles directly with clients and indirectly with staff and families. During the period of organizational change described, other clinical psychologists, not directly involved in the planning process, were working in the district mental handicap service. They worked in accordance with the philosophy and principles of the new service, thereby demonstrating its feasibility. By enabling relatives and staff to observe the new type of care in action, their work enhanced the more formal public relations exercise. Their practical experience of working within the hospital and the CMHTs provided valuable information to augment the suggestions being made to the JWP and facilitated the planning work of the district clinical psychologist.

References

ACHENBACH, T. M. (1984) *Current Status of the Child Behaviour Checklist and Related Materials.* Burlington, USA: University of Vermont

AGGLETON, P. and CHALMERS, H. (1984) Models and theories. *Nursing Times,* **80,** 24–28

ALEXANDER, A. B. and SMITH, D. D. (1979) Clinical application of EMG biofeedback. In *Clinical Applications of Biofeedback: Appraisal and Status,* edited by R. Gatchel and K. Price. New York: Pergamon Press

AMERICAN PSYCHIATRIC ASSOCIATION (1980) *Diagnostic and Statistical Manual of Mental Disorders,* 3rd edn. Washington DC

ANDERSON, B. L. and HACKER, N. F. (1983) Psychosexual adjustment after vulvar surgery. *Obstetrics and Gynaecology,* **62** (4), 457–463

ANDERSON, F. N. and DEAN, H. C. (1956) Some aspects of child guidance clinic intake policy and practices: a study of 500 cases at the Los Angeles Guidance Clinic. *Public Health Monograph,* **42,** 1–16

ANDERSON, H. R., MacNAIR, R. S. and RAMSEY, J. D. (1985) Deaths from abuse of volatile substances: a national epidemiological study. *British Medical Journal,* **290,** (6464), 304–307

ANDERSON, H. R., BLOOR, K., MacNAIR, R. S. and RAMSEY, J. D. (1986) Recent trends in mortality associated with abuse of volatile substances in the UK. *British Medical Journal,* **293,** (6559), 1472–1473

ANTHONY, W. A. and FARKAS, M. (1982) A client outcome planning model for assessing psychiatric rehabilitation interventions. *Schizophrenia Bulletin,* **8,** 13–38

ANTHONY, W. Z. (1978) Brief intervention in a case of childhood trichotillomania by self-monitoring. *Journal of Behavior Therapy and Experimental Psychiatry,* **9,** 173–175

AZRIN, N. H. and NUNN, R. G. (1978) *Habit Control in a Day.* New York: Simon & Schuster

AZRIN, N. H., NUNN, R. G. and FRANTZ, S. E. (1980) Treatment of hair pulling: a comparative study of habit reversal and negative practice training. *Journal of Behavior Therapy and Experimental Psychiatry,* **11,** 13–20

BAKER, R. D. and HALL, J. N. (1983) *REHAB: A Rehabilitation Evaluation Rating Scale.* Aberdeen: Vine Publishing

BALINT, M. (1964) *The Doctor, his Patient and the Illness.* London: Pitman Medical

BANDURA, A. (1971) *Psychological Modelling: Conflicting Theories.* Chicago: Aldine Atherton

BANKS, M. H., BERESFORD, S. A. and MORRELL, D. C. (1975) Factors influencing demand for primary medical care in women aged 20–44 years: a preliminary report. *International Journal of Epidemiology,* **4,** 189–195

BAREFOOT, J. C., DAHLSTROM, W. G. and WILLIAMS, R. B. (1983) Hostility, CHD incidence and total mortality: a 25-year follow-up study of 255 physicians. *Psychosomatic Medicine,* **45** (1), 59–63

BARKER, P. (1982) *Behaviour Therapy Nursing.* London: Croom Helm

BARLOW, N. T. (1982a) Implementing a challenge to care. *International Juvenile Behavioural Social Work and Abstracts,* **2** (1), 17–30

BARLOW, N. T. (1982b) (revised 1985) A behavioural approach for decreasing solvent abuse. Birmingham Education Department, Tennal Centre, Birmingham B32 2EH

BARLOW, N. T. (1986) Guidelines for non-psychologists using behavioural counselling with people who abuse solvents. *British Psychological Society Newsletter of Special Interest Group (Children & Young People)* No. 2, June

BARMANN, B. C. AND VITALI, D. L. (1982) Facial screening to eliminate trichotillomania in developmentally disabled persons. *Behavior Therapy,* **13**, 735–742

BASS, M. (1970) Sudden sniffing death. *Journal of the American Medical Association,* **212** (12), 2075–2079

BAUMEISTER, A. A. and FOREHAND, R. (1973) Stereotyped acts. In *International Review of Research in Mental Retardation* (Vol. 9), edited by N. R. Ellis. New York: Academic Press

BAYER, C. A. (1972) Self-monitoring and mild aversion treatment of trichotillomania. *Journal of Behavior Therapy and Experimental Psychiatry,* **3**, 139–141

BAYLEY, N. (1969) *Bayley Scales of Infant Development.* Windsor: NFER — Nelson

BECK, A. T. (1976) *Cognitive Therapy and the Emotional Disorders.* New York: International Universities Press

BECK, A. T., RUSH, A. J., SHAW, B. F. and EMERY, G. (1979) *Cognitive Therapy in Depression.* New York: International Universities Press

BECKHARD, R. and HARRIS, R. (1977) *Organizational Transitions: Managing Complex Change.* Reading, USA: Addison Wesley

BENDER, L. (1938) *A Visual Motor Gestalt Test and Its Clinical Use,* Research Monograph No. 3. New York: American Orthopsychiatric Association

BENDER, M. P. (1979) Community psychology: when? *Bulletin of the British Psychological Society,* **32**, 6–9

BENSON, D. F. (1979) *Aphasia, Alexia and Agraphia.* Edinburgh: Churchill Livingstone

BENTON, A. L., VARNEY, N. R. and HAMSHER, K. DE S. (1978) Visuospatial judgement: a clinical test. *Archives of Neurology,* **35**, 364–367

BERKSON, G. and MASON, W. (1963) Stereotyped movements of mental defectives: III: situation effects. *American Journal of Mental Deficiency,* **68**, 409–412

BERNSTEIN, N. R. (1976) *Emotional Care of the Facially Burned and Disfigured.* Boston, USA: Little Brown

BITGOOD, S. C., CROWE, M. J., SUAREZ, Y. and PETERS, R. D. (1980) Immobilization: effects and side-effects on stereotyped behaviour in children. *Behavior Modification,* **4**, 187–208

BLADES, B., MELLIS, N. and MUNSTER, A. M. (1982) A burn specific health scale. *Journal of Trauma,* **22** (10), 872–875

BORDIN, E. S. (1979) The generalizability of the psychoanalytic concept of the working alliance. *Psychotherapy: Theory, Research and Practice,* **16**, 252–260

BORNSTEIN, P. H. and RYCHTARIK, R. G. (1978) Multi-component behavioural treatment of trichotillomania: a case study. *Behaviour Research and Therapy,* **16**, 217–220

BOWDEN, M. L., JONES, C. A. and FELLER, I. (1979) *Psychosocial Aspects of a Severe Burn: A Review of the Literature.* Ann Arbor, MI, USA: National Institute for Burn Medicine

BRANDES, D. and PHILLIPS, H. (1977) *Gamesters' Handbook.* Newcastle-upon-Tyne: Tyneside Growth Centre

BRITISH PSYCHOLOGICAL SOCIETY (1984) *Psychology and Problem Drinking: Report of a Working Party.* Leicester: BPS

BROMLEY, D. B. (1986) *The Case-Study Method in Psychology and Related Disciplines.* Chichester: Wiley

BRONFENBRENNER, U. (1979) *The Ecology of Human Development: Experiments by Nature and Design.* Cambridge, USA: Harvard University Press

BROOKS, D. N. (1984) *Closed Head Injury: Psychological, Social and Family Consequences.* Oxford: Oxford University Press

BROOME, A. K. (1985) Psychological treatments for chronic pain. In *Current Issues in Clinical Psychology,* 2, edited by E. Karas, pp. 59–76. New York: Plenum Press

BROWN, A. (1984) *Consultation: An Aid to Successful Social Work.* London: Heinemann

BROWN, P. and FAULDER, C. (1977) *Treat Yourself to Sex.* London: Dent

BURNS, B. H. and HOWELL, J. B. L. (1969) Disproportionately severe breathlessness in chronic bronchitis. *Quarterly Journal of Medicine,* **38**, 277–294

BUTLER, R. J. and ROSENTHALL, G. (1985) *Behaviour and Rehabilitation,* 2nd edn. Bristol: John Wright

BYRNE, E. A. and CUNNINGHAM, C. C. (1985) The effects of mentally handicapped children on families: a conceptual review. *Journal of Child Psychology,* **26** (6), 847–864

CAINE, T. M. and SMAIL, D. J. (1968) Attitudes of psychiatric nurses to their role in treatment. *British Journal of Medical Psychology,* **41**, 193–197

CAMERON, R., SHACKLETON BAILEY, M. and WALLIS, J. (1984) Difficult and disruptive behaviour: 2. Adopting a problem-centred approach. *Mental Handicap*, **12**, 152–155

CARR, J. and WILSON, B. A. (1980) Self-help skills: washing, dressing and feeding. In *Behaviour Modification for the Mentally Handicapped*, edited by W. Yule and J. Carr. London: Croom Helm

CHAMBERLAIN, P. (1984) *Personal Relationships and People with Mental Handicaps*. London: King's Fund

CHAMBLESS, D. L. and GOLDSTEIN, A. J. (1982) Editors. *Agoraphobia: Multiple Perspectives on Theory and Treatment*. New York: Wiley

CHILDREN AND YOUNG PERSONS ACT 1969. London: HMSO

CHILDREN AND YOUNG PERSONS ACT 1980. London: HMSO

CLARK, D. M. (1987) Cognitive therapy for anxiety. *Behavioural Psychotherapy*, **14** (4), 283–295

CLARK, D. M., SALKOVSKIS, P. M. and CHALKLEY, A. J. (1985) Respiratory control as a treatment for panic attacks. *Journal of Behavioural Therapy and Experimental Psychology*, **16** (1), 23–30

CLEMENTS, J. C. and HAND, D. J. (1985) Permutation statistics in single case design. *Behavioural Psychotherapy*, **13**, 288–299

COAD, H. and HYDE, A. (1986) Hot on the quality assurance trail. *Health Service Journal*, **96**, 518–519

COOK, T. D., COOK, F. L. and MARK, M. M. (1977) Randomised and quasi-experimental designs in evaluation research: an introduction. In *Evaluation Research Methods: A Basic Guide*, edited by L. Rutman. London: Sage

COOKE, D. and WATTS, F. (1987) Psychological research in the post-Griffiths era. *Clinical Psychology Forum*, **9**, 4–6

COOPER, C. L. (1986) Job distress: recent research and the emerging role of the clinical occupational psychologist. *Bulletin of the British Psychological Society*, **39**, 325–331

COOPER, P. J. and FAIRBURN, C. G. (1983) Binge-eating and self-induced vomiting in the community: a preliminary study. *British Journal of Psychiatry*, **142**, 139–144

COPE, D. E. (1981) *Organisational Development and Action Research in Hospitals*. Aldershot: Gower

CORDLE, C. J. and LONG, C. G. (1980) The use of operant self-control procedures in the treatment of compulsive hair pulling. *Journal of Behavior Therapy and Experimental Psychiatry*, **11**, 127–130

CORNISH, D. and CLARKE, R. V. G. (1975) *Residential Treatment and its Effects on Delinquency*, Study No. 32. London: HMSO

COWEN, E. L. (1980) The community context. In *Psychological Problems: The Social Context*, edited by P. Feldman and J. Orford. Chichester: Wiley

CRAFT, A. (1982) *Health, Hygiene and Sex Education for Mentally Handicapped Children, Adolescents and Adults: A Review of Audio Visual Resources*. London: Health Education Council

CRAFT, A. and CRAFT, M. (1979) *Handicapped Married Couples*. London: Routledge & Kegan Paul

CRAFT, A. and CRAFT, M. (1983) Editors. *Sex Education and Counselling for Mentally Handicapped People*. Tunbridge Wells: Costello

CRAFT, A. and CRAFT, M. (1985) Sexuality and personal relationships. In *Mental Handicap: A Multi-Disciplinary Approach*, edited by M. Craft, J. Bicknell and S. Hollins. Eastbourne: Baillière Tindall

CRAFT, M. and CRAFT, A. (1982) *Sex and the Mentally Handicapped: A Guide for Parents and Carers*. London: Routledge & Kegan Paul

CRAWFORD, D. A. (1979) Modification of deviant sexual behaviour: the need for a comprehensive approach. *British Journal of Medical Psychology*, **2**, 151–156

CRONBACH, L. J. and GLESER, G. C. (1965) *Psychological Tests and Personnel Decisions*. Urbana, IL: University of Illinois Press

CROWN, S. and CRISP, A. H. (1966) A short clinical diagnostic self-rating scale for psychoneurotic patients: The Middlesex Hospital Questionnaire (MHQ). *British Journal of Psychiatry*, **112**, 917–923

DAVIES, A. D. M. and SNAITH, P. A. (1980) The social behaviour of geriatric patients at mealtimes: an observational and an intervention study. *Age and Ageing*, **9**, 93–99

DAVIES, C. (1986) Nurse odyssey 2000. *Health Service Journal*, **96**, 986–987

DEPARTMENT OF EDUCATION AND SCIENCE (1983) *Assessments and Statements of Special Educational Needs*, Circular 1/83. London: HMSO

DEPARTMENT OF HEALTH AND SOCIAL SECURITY (1976) *A Lifestyle for the Elderly*. London: HMSO

DEPARTMENT OF HEALTH AND SOCIAL SECURITY (1978) *The Pattern and Range of Services for Problem Drinkers*. Report of a working party chaired by Professor N. Kessel. London: DHSS

DEPARTMENT OF HEALTH AND SOCIAL SECURITY (1986) *Social Trends.* London: HMSO

DE RENZI, E. and VIGNOLO, L. A. (1962) The token test: a sensitive test to detect receptive disturbances in aphasics. *Brain,* **85,** 665–678

DEROGATIS, L. R. (1978) *Manual of the Derogatis Sexual Functioning Inventory.* Baltimore: Johns Hopkins University Press

DEROGATIS, L. R. and LOPEZ, M. C. (1983) *PAIS and PAIS-SR: Administration, Scoring and Procedures Manual — I.* Baltimore: Johns Hopkins University Press

DEROGATIS, L. R. and MELISARATOS, N. (1979) The DSFI: a multi-dimensional measure of sexual functioning. *Journal of Sexual and Marital Therapy,* **5,** 244

DOLCE, J. J., CROCKER, M. F., MOLETTEIRE, C. and DOLEYS, D. M. (1986) Exercise quotas, anticipatory concern and self-efficacy expectations in chronic pain: a preliminary report. *Pain,* **24,** 365–372

DOLL, E. A. (1953) *The Measurement of Social Competence.* Educational Test Bureau. Minnesota: Circle Pines

DUCK, S. (1984) A perspective on the repair of personal relationships: a repair of what? when? In *Personal Relationships 5: Repairing Personal Relationships,* edited by S. Duck. London: Academic Press

EDUCATION ACT 1981. London: HMSO

EIDELSON, R. J. and EPSTEIN, N. (1982) Cognition and relationship maladjustment: development of a measure of dysfunctional relationship beliefs. *Journal of Consulting and Clinical Psychology,* **50,** 715–720

EISENSON, J. (1954) *A Manual for the Examination of Aphasia and Related Disturbances.* New York: The Psychological Corporation

EISER, C. (1984) Communicating with sick and hospitalised children. *Journal of Child Psychology and Psychiatry,* **25** (2), 181–189

ELLIS, A. (1962) *Reason and Emotion in Psychotherapy.* New York: Lyle Stuart

ELLIS, M. J. (1973) *Why People Play.* Englewood Cliffs: Prentice Hall

ELLIS, N. (1963) Toilet training the severely defective patient: an S-R reinforcement analysis. *American Journal of Mental Deficiency,* **68,** 98–103

EPTING, F. R. (1984) *Personal Construct Counselling and Psychotherapy.* Chichester: Wiley

EVERLY, G. A. and ROSENFELD, R. (1981) *The Nature and Treatment of the Stress Response: A Practical Guide for Clinicians.* New York: Plenum

EYSENCK, H. J. and EYSENCK, S. B. G. (1975) *Manual of the Eysenck Personality Questionnaire (Junior and Adult).* London: Hodder & Stoughton

FAIRWEATHER, G. W., SANDERS, D. H. and TORNATSKY, L. G. (1974) *Creating Change in Mental Health Organizations.* New York: Pergamon Press

FAUGIER, J. and REILLY, S. (1986) Taking time to talk. *Nursing Times,* **82,** 52–54

FELCE, D., DE KOCK, U. and REPP, A. (1986) An eco-behavioural comparison of small community-based houses and traditional large hospitals for severely and profoundly mentally handicapped adults. *Applied Research in Mental Retardation,* **7,** 393–408

FELDMAN, L. B. (1976) Depression and marital interaction. *Family Process,* **18,** 69–78

FEUERSTEIN, M., LABBE, E. E. and KUCZMIERCZYK, A. R. (1986) *Health Psychology.* New York: Plenum

FIRTH, H., McINTEE, J., McKEOWEN, P. and BRITTON, P. (1986) Interpersonal support amongst nurses at work. *Journal of Advanced Nursing,* **11,** 273–282

FISHER, K. (1984) Can we differentiate 'functional' from 'organic' pain? In *Readings in Psychology and Pain* (Proceedings of the First International Conference of the Pain Interest Group), edited by A. Broome. Dudley, West Midlands: Dudley Psychology Service

FISHER, K. (in preparation) Biofeedback treatment for recurrent shoulder dislocation: development of methodology and results

FLAXMAN, J. (1978) Quitting smoking now or later: gradual, abrupt, immediate and delayed quitting. *Behavior Therapy,* **9,** 260–270

FLEMING, I. (1984) Habit reversal treatment for trichotillomania: a case study. *Behavioural Psychotherapy,* **12,** 73–80

FORDYCE, W. E. (1976) *Behavioural Methods for Chronic Pain and Illness.* St. Louis, USA: Mosby

FORDYCE, W., FOWLER, R., LEHMANN, J. and DELATEUR, B. (1968) Some implications of learning in problems of chronic pain. *Journal of Chronic Diseases,* **21,** 179–190

FORDYCE, W. E., FOWLER, R. S., LEHMANN, J. F., DELATEUR, B. J., SAND, P. L. and TRIESCHMANN, R. B. (1973)

Operant conditioning in the treatment of chronic pain. *Archives of Physical Medicine and Rehabilitation,* **54**, 399–408

FRANSELLA, F. and BANNISTER, D. (1977) *A Manual for Repertory Grid Technique.* London: Academic Press

FRIMAN, P. C., FINNEY, J. W. and CHRISTOPHERSON, E. R. (1984) Behavioural treatment of trichotillomania: an evaluative review. *Behavior Therapy,* **15**, 249–263

GARDNER, J. M. (1972) Teaching behaviour modification to non-professionals. *Journal of Applied Behaviour Analysis,* **5**, 517–521

GARFIELD, S. L. (1980) *Psychotherapy: An Eclectic Approach.* New York: Wiley

GARNER, D. M., OLMSTED, M. P. and POLIVY, J. (1983) Development and validation of a multi-dimensional eating disorder inventory for anorexia nervosa and bulimia. *International Journal of Eating Disorders,* **2**, 15–34

GARNER, D. M., ROCKERT, W., OLMSTED, M. P., JOHNSON, C. and COSCINA, D. V. (1985) Psychoeducational principles in the treatment of bulimia and anorexia nervosa. In *Handbook of Psychotherapy for Anorexia Nervosa and Bulimia,* edited by D. M. Garner and P. E. Garfinkel. New York: Guilford Press

GARSSEN, B., VAN VEENENDAL, W. and BLOEMINK, R. (1983) Agoraphobia and the hyperventilation syndrome. *Behaviour Research and Therapy,* **21**, 643–649

GEER, J. H. (1965) The development of a scale to measure fear. *Behaviour Research and Therapy,* **3**, 45–53

GEORGE, J. (1986) Needed: care for the carers. *Health and Social Service Journal,* **96**, 13

GEORGIADES, N. J. and PHILLIMORE, L. (1975) The myth of the hero-innovator and alternative strategies for organisational change. In *Behaviour Modification with the Severely Retarded,* edited by C. C. Kiernan and F. D. Woodford. Amsterdam: Associated Scientific Publishers

GIBSON, H. B. (1965) *Manual of the Gibson Spiral Maze.* London: University of London Press

GOLDBERG, D. P., HOBSON, R. F., MAGUIRE, G. P., MARGISON, F. R., O'DOWD, T., OSBORN, M. and MOSS, S. (1984) The clarification and assessment of a method of psychotherapy. *British Journal of Psychiatry,* **144**, 567–580

GOLDIAMOND, I. (1974) Towards a constructional approach to social problems: ethical and constitutional issues raised by applied behavior analysis. *Behaviorism,* **2**, 1–84

GOLDSMITH, W. and CLUTTERBUCK, D. (1984) *The Winning Streak.* London: Weidenfeld & Nicolson

GOMES-SCHWARTZ, B. (1979) The modification of schizophrenic behaviour. *Behaviour Modification,* **3**, 439–468

GRAY, J. J. (1979) Positive reinforcement and punishment in the treatment of childhood trichotillomania. *Journal of Behavior Therapy and Experimental Psychiatry,* **10**, 125–129

GRAZIANO, A. M., DE GIOVANNI, I. S. and GARCIA, K. A. (1979) Behavioral treatments of children's fears: a review. *Psychological Bulletin,* **86**, 804–830

GREEN, R. (1985) Atypical psychosexual development. In *Child and Adolescent Psychiatry: Modern Approaches,* 2nd edn, edited by M. Rutter and L. Hersov. Oxford: Blackwell

GREENBERG, H. R. (1969) Transactions of a hair pulling symbiosis. *Psychiatric Quarterly,* **43**, 662–674

GREENBERG, H. R. and SARNER, C. A. (1965) Trichotillomania. *Archives of General Psychiatry,* **12**, 482–489

GRONWALL, D. M. A. and SAMPSON, H. (1974) *The Psychological Effects of Concussion.* Auckland: Auckland University Press

HAFNER, R. J. (1982) The marital context of the agoraphobic syndrome. In *Agoraphobia: Multiple Perspectives on Theory and Treatment,* edited by D. L. Chambless and A. J. Goldstein. New York: Wiley

HALEY, J. (1976) *Problem Solving Therapy.* San Francisco: Jossey-Bass

HALLAM, R. S. (1978) Agoraphobia: a critical review of the concept. *British Journal of Psychiatry,* **133**, 314–319

HALLAUER, D. S. (1972) Illness behaviour — an experimental investigation. *Journal of Chronic Diseases,* **25**, 599–610

HALLOPEAU, X. (1889) Alopecia par grottage (trichomania ou trichotillomania). *Annals of Dermatology and Syphilogy,* **10**, 440

HALMI, R. A., FALK, J. R. and SCHWARTZ, E. (1981) Binge eating and vomiting: a survey of a college population. *Psychological Medicine,* **11**, 697–706

HAM, C. (1985) Consumerism in the NHS: state of the art. *Health and Social Service Journal,* **95**, Centre 8 Supplement

HANDY, C. B. (1985) *Understanding Organisations,* 3rd edn. Harmondsworth: Penguin

HANVIK, L. (1951) MMPI profiles in patients with low back pain. *Journal of Consulting Psychology,* **15,** 350–353

HARGREAVES, I. (1975) The nursing process: the key to individualised care. *Nursing Times,* **73,** 89–91

HAWKS, D. (1981) The dilemma of clinical practice: surviving as a clinical psychologist. In *Reconstructing Psychological Practice,* edited by I. McPherson and A. Sutton, pp. 11–20. London: Croom Helm

HEALTH EDUCATION COUNCIL (1985) *What to do about Glue-Sniffing,* Leaflet M50. London: HEC

HEATHER, N. and ROBERTSON, I. (1986) *Problem Drinking: The New Approach.* Harmondsworth: Penguin

HECAEN, H. and ALBERT, M. L. (1978) *Human Neuropsychology.* New York: Wiley

HEILMAN, K. M. (1979) Apraxia. In *Clinical Neuropsychology,* edited by K. M. Heilman and E. Valenstein. New York: Oxford University Press

HELLER, K., PRICE, R. H., REINHARZ, S., RIGER, S. and WANDERSHAM, A. (1984) *Psychology and Community Change: Challenges of the Future.* Homewood, IL: Dorsey Press

HERBERT, M. (1987) *Behavioural Treatment of Children with Problems: A Practice Manual,* 2nd edn. London: Academic Press

HERSEN, M. and BARLOW, D. H. (1976) *Single Case Experimental Designs.* Oxford: Pergamon Press

HIBBERT, G. (1984) Ideational components of anxiety: their origin and content. *British Journal of Psychiatry,* **144,** 618–624

HICKS, D. (1976) *Primary Health Care: A Review.* London: HMSO

HILDRETH, H. M. (1946) A battery of feeling and attitude scales for clinical use. *Journal of Clinical Psychology,* **2,** 214–221

HILLIARD, G. D., MASSEY, F. M. and O'TOOLE, R. V. (1979) Vulvar neoplasia in the young. *American Journal of Obstetrics and Gynaecology,* **135,** 185

HOLZMAN, D. and TURK, D. C. (1986) *Pain Management.* Oxford: Pergamon Press

HÖPER, C., KUTZLEB, U., STOBBE, A. and WEBER, B. (1975) *Awareness Games.* New York: St. Martin's Press

HORNE, D. J. (1977) Behaviour therapy for trichotillomania. *Behaviour Research and Therapy,* **15,** 192–196

HOUNSLOW SOCIAL SERVICES DEPARTMENT (1983) *Sexuality of Mentally Handicapped People: Guidelines for Care Staff*

HOWARD, D., PATTERSON, K., FRANKLIN, S., ORCHARD-LISLE, V. and MORTON, J. (1985) Treatment of word retrieval deficits in aphasia. *Brain,* **108,** 817–829

HUNT, W. A., BARNETT, L. W. and BRANCH, L. G. (1971) Relapse rates in addiction programs. *Journal of Clinical Psychology,* **27,** 455–456

INDEPENDENT DEVELOPMENT COUNCIL FOR PEOPLE WITH A MENTAL HANDICAP (1982) *Elements of a Comprehensive Local Service for People with a Mental Handicap.* London: King's Fund Centre

INGLIS, J. (1959) A paired-associate test for use with elderly psychiatric patients. *Journal of Mental Science,* **105,** 440–448

INMAN, V. T., SAUNDERS, M. and ABBOTT, L. C. (1944) Observations on the function of the shoulder joint. *Journal of Bone and Joint Surgery,* **26** (1), 1–29

INSTITUTE FOR THE STUDY OF DRUG DEPENDENCY (1980) *Teaching about a Volatile Situation.* London: ISDD

JACOBSON, E. (1938) *Progressive Relaxation.* Chicago: University of Chicago Press

JANIS, I. L. (1958) *Psychological Stress: Psychoanalytic and Behavioral Studies of Surgical Patients.* New York: Wiley

JEFFREY, D. and SAXBY, P. (1984) Effective psychological care for the elderly. In *Psychological Approaches to the Care of the Elderly,* edited by I. Hanley and J. Hodge. London: Croom Helm

JENKINS, C. D., ZYZANSKI, S. J. and ROSENMAN, R. H. (1978) Coronary prone behaviour: one pattern or several? *Psychosomatic Medicine,* **40** (1), 25–43

KAGAN, C. (1985) (Editor) *Interpersonal Skills in Nursing: Research and Applications.* London: Croom Helm

KANE, B. (1979) Children's concepts of death. *Journal of Genetic Psychology,* **134,** 141–153

KAPLAN, E., GOODGLASS, H. and WEINTRAUB, S. (1983) *Boston Naming Test.* Philadelphia: Lea & Febiger

KAPLAN, H. S. (1979) *Disorders of Sexual Desire.* New York: Brunner Mazel

KAPLAN, H. S. (1982) *The New Sex Therapy.* Harmondsworth: Penguin

KATZ, D. and KAHN, R. L. (1978) *The Social Psychology of Organizations,* 2nd edn. New York: Wiley

KELLY, G. (1955) *The Psychology of Personal Constructs.* New York: W. W. Norton

KEMPTON, W. (1978) *Sexuality and the Mentally Handicapped; Slides and Commentary,* 2nd edn. Available from The Health Education Council and Concorde Films

KEMPTON, W. (1983) Sexuality training for professionals who work with mentally handicapped persons. In *Sex Education and Counselling for Mentally Handicapped People,* edited by A. Craft and M. Craft. Tunbridge Wells: Costello

KEMPTON, W. and FOREMAN, R. (1976) *Guidelines for Training in Sexuality and the Mentally Handicapped.* Philadelphia: Planned Parenthood of Southeastern Pennsylvania

KENDALL, P. C. and NORTON-FORD, J. D. (1982) *Clinical Psychology: Scientific and Professional Dimensions.* New York: Wiley

KEYS, A., BROZEK, J., HENSCHEL, A., MICKELSON, D. and TAYLOR, H. (1950) *The Biology of Human Starvation.* Minneapolis: University of Minnesota Press

KINCANNON, J. (1963) Prediction of standard MMPI scale scores from 71 items. *Journal of Consulting and Clinical Psychology,* **32,** 319–325

KING'S FUND (1980) *An Ordinary Life: Comprehensive Locally Based Residential Services for Mentally Handicapped People,* Project Paper 47. London: King's Fund Centre

KIRBY, K. A. (1985) Cognitive-behavioural treatment of chronic pain. In *Current Issues in Clinical Psychology, 2,* edited by E. Karas, pp. 77–87. New York: Plenum Press

KIRUSEK, T. J. and SHERMAN, R. E. (1968) Goal attainment scaling: a general method for evaluating community mental health programs. *Community Mental Health Journal,* **4,** 443–453

KLINE-GRABER, G. and GRABER, B. (1978) Diagnosis and treatment of pubococcygeal deficiencies in women. In *Handbook of Sex Therapy,* edited by J. Lo Piccolo and J. Lo Picollo. New York: Plenum Press

KLORMAN, P. B. R. (1983) The incidence of psychopathology in burned adult patients: a critical review. *Journal of Burns Care and Rehabilitation,* **4** (6), 430–436

KOCH, H. (1986) (Editor) *Community Clinical Psychology.* London: Croom Helm

KOTARBA, J. A. (1983) *Chronic Pain: Its Social Dimensions.* Beverly Hills/London/New Delhi: Sage

LaGROW, S. J. and REPP, A. C. (1984) Stereotypic responding: a review of intervention research. *American Journal of Mental Deficiency,* **88,** 595–609

LANG, P. (1971) The application of psychophysiological methods to the study of psychotherapy and behavior modification. In *Handbook of Psychotherapy and Behavioral Change: An Empirical Analysis,* edited by A. E. Bergin and S. L. Garfield. New York: Wiley

LANSDOWN, R. and BENJAMIN, G. (1985) The development of the concept of death in children aged 5–9 years. *Child: Care, Health and Education,* **11,** 13–20

LARNER, S. L. and LEEMING, J. T. (1984) The work of a clinical psychologist in the care of the elderly. *Age and Ageing,* **13,** 29–33

LAVENDER, A. (1985) Quality of care and staff practices in long-stay settings. In *New Developments in Clinical Psychology,* edited by F. N. Watts. Chichester: Wiley

LAWRENCE, L. (1986) The problem and management of pain on a burns unit: a pilot study of hypnosis as an adjunctive treatment. *MSc Thesis.* Birmingham: Birmingham University

LAZARUS, A. A. (1976) *Multimodal Behavior Therapy.* New York: Springer

LAZARUS, R. S. (1966) *Psychological Stress and the Coping Process.* New York: McGraw-Hill

LAZARUS, R. S. and FOLKMAN, S. (1984) *Stress, Appraisal and Coping.* New York: Springer

LEBOW, J. (1982) Consumer satisfaction with mental health treatment. *Psychological Bulletin,* **91,** 244–259

LEDERER, W. J. and JACKSON, D. D. (1968) *The Mirages of Marriage.* New York: W. W. Norton

LEFCOURT, H. M. (1981) (Editor) *Research with the Locus of Control Construct: Vol. I: Assessment Methods.* New York: Academic Press

LEVINE, B. A. (1976) Treatment of trichotillomania by covert sensitization. *Journal of Behavior Therapy and Experimental Psychiatry,* **7,** 75–76

LEWIS, C. (1986) *Becoming a Father.* Milton Keynes/Philadelphia: Open University Press

LEWIS, P. (1984) The teaching of clinical psychology skills to non-psychologists. *British Psychological Society: Newsletter of the Division of Clinical Psychology,* **45,** 32–35

LEY, P. (1977) Psychological preparation for hospitalisation. In *Contributions to Medical Psychology. Vol. 1,* edited by S. Rachman. Oxford: Pergamon Press

LEY, P. (1982) Giving information to patients. In *Social Psychology and Behavioural Science,* edited by J. R. Eiser. Chichester: Wiley

LEY, R. (1985) Agoraphobia, the panic attack and the hyperventilation syndrome. *Behaviour Research and Therapy,* **23** (1), 79–81

LICHTENSTEIN, E. (1982) The smoking problem: a behavioural perspective. *Journal of Consulting and Clinical Psychology,* **50**, 804–819

LICHTENSTEIN, E., HARRIS, D. E., BIRCHLER, G. R., WAHL, J. M. and SCHMAHL, D. P. (1973) Comparisons of rapid smoking: warm, smoky air, and attention-placebo in the modification of smoking behavior. *Journal of Consulting and Clinical Psychology,* **40**, 92–98

LIDDELL, A. (1983) (Editor). *The Practice of Clinical Psychology in Great Britain.* Chichester: Wiley

LIEBOWITZ, B., LAWTON, M. P. and WALDMAN, A. (1979) Evaluation: designing for confused old people. *American Institute of Architects Journal,* February, 59–61

LIEPMAN, H. (1920) Reported in *Clinical Neuropsychology,* edited by K. M. Heilman and E. Valenstein. New York: Oxford University Press

LINDSAY, W. R. and HOOD, E. H. (1982) A cognitive anxiety questionnaire. Unpublished

LINN, M. W., CAFFEY, E., KLETT, J., HOGARTY, G. and LAMB, R. (1977) Day treatment and psychotropic drugs in the aftercare of schizophrenic patients. *Archives of General Psychiatry,* **42**, 544–551

LOVETT, S. (1985) Microelectronic and computer based technology. In *Mental Deficiency: The Changing Outlook,* 4th edn, edited by A. M. Clarke, A. D. B. Clarke and J. Berg. London: Methuen

LURIA, A. R. (1966) *Higher Cortical Functions in Man.* New York: Basic Books

LURIA, A. R. (1973) *The Working Brain.* New York: Basic Books

McKENNA, P. and WARRINGTON, E. K. (1983) *Graded Naming Test.* Windsor: NFER-Nelson

McLAUGHLIN, J. G. and NAY, W. R. (1975) Treatment of trichotillomania using positive coverants and response cost: a case report. *Behavior Therapy,* **6**, 87–91

MacNEIL, J. and THOMAS, M. R. (1976) The treatment of obsessive-compulsive hair pulling by behavioural and cognitive contingency manipulation. *Journal of Behavior Therapy and Experimental Psychiatry,* **7**, 391–392

McPHERSON, I. and SUTTON, A. (1981) (Editors) *Reconstructing Psychological Practice.* London: Croom Helm

MAGER, R. F. and PIPE, P. (1970) *Analyzing Performance Problems or 'You really oughta wanna'.* Belmont, CA: Lear Siegler/Fearon Publishers

MAGUIRE, G. P., GOLDBERG, D. P., HOBSON, R. F., MARGISON, F., MOSS, S. and O'DOWD, T. (1984) Evaluating the teaching of a method of psychotherapy. *British Journal of Psychiatry,* **144**, 575–580

MANNINO, F. V. and DELGADO, R. A. (1969) Trichotillomania in children: a review. *American Journal of Psychiatry,* **126**, 505–511

MARKS, I. M. (1981) *Cure and Care of Neuroses: Theory and Practice of Behavioral Psychotherapy.* New York: Wiley

MARKS, I. and MATTHEWS, A. (1979) A brief standard self-rating scale for patients. *Behaviour Research and Therapy,* **17**, 263–267

MARLATT, G. A. and GEORGE, W. H. (1984) Relapse prevention: introduction and overview of the model. *British Journal of Addiction,* **79**, 261–273

MARZILLIER, J. S. and HALL, J. (1987) *What is Clinical Psychology?* Oxford: Oxford University Press

MASTERS, W. H. and JOHNSON, V. (1970) *Human Sexual Inadequacy.* London: J. & A. Churchill

MATTHEWS, A. (1983) St George's Hospital Anxiety Questionnaire. Unpublished, St George's Hospital Medical School, University of London

MATTHEWS, A. (1984) Anxiety and its management. In *Current Themes in Psychiatry, Vol. 3,* edited by R. Gaind, pp. 285–305. London: Macmillan

MATTHEWS, A., GELDER, M. G. and JOHNSTON, D. W. (1981) *Agoraphobia: Nature and Treatment.* London: Tavistock

MAXWELL, R. J. (1984) Quality assessment in health. *British Medical Journal,* **288**, 1470–1472

MEHREGAN, A. H. (1970) Trichotillomania: a clinicopathologic study. *Archives of Dermatology,* **102**, 129–133

MEICHENBAUM, D. (1977) *Cognitive-Behavior Modification: An Integrative Approach.* New York: Plenum Press

MELAMED, B. (1977) Psychological Preparation for Hospitalisation. In *Contributions to Medical Psychology, Vol. 1,* edited by S. Rachman. Oxford: Pergamon Press

MELZACK, R. and WALL, P. D. (1965) Pain mechanisms: a new theory. *Science,* **150**, 971

MERRY, P. (1986) Climbing up the NHS ladder. *Health Service Journal,* **96**, 1014

METROPOLITAN LIFE INSURANCE COMPANY (1983) Height and weight tables. *Statistical Bulletin,* January-June, 3–9

MILLER, E. (1979) The long-term consequences of head injury: a discussion of the evidence with special reference to the preparation of legal reports. *British Journal of Social and Clinical Psychology,* **18**, 87–98

MILLER, E. (1984a) Verbal fluency as a function of a measure of verbal intelligence and in relation to different types of cerebral pathology. *British Journal of Clinical Psychology,* **23**, 53–57

MILLER, E. (1984b) *Recovery and Management of Neuropsychological Impairments.* Chichester: Wiley

MILLER, H. (1961) Accident neurosis. *British Medical Journal,* 5230, 1 April, 919–925

MILLER, L. C., BARRETT, C. L. and HAMPE, E. (1974) Phobias of childhood in a prescientific era. In *Child Personality and Psychotherapy: Current Topics, Vol. 1,* edited by A. Davids. New York: Wiley

MILLHAM, S. (1986) *Lost in Care.* Aldershot: Gower

MILLHAM, S., BULLOCK, R. and CHERRETT, P. (1975) *After Grace — Teeth.* London: Human Context Books, Chaucer Publishing Company

MILLHAM, S., BULLOCK, R. and MOSIE, K. (1978) *Locking up Children.* Farnborough: Saxon House

MILNE, D. (1984) Change or innovation in institutions? a constructive role for the 'realistic hero-innovator'. *British Psychological Society: Newsletter of the Division of Clinical Psychology,* **46**, 34–38

MILNE, D. (1986a) *Training Behaviour Therapists.* London: Croom Helm

MILNE, D. (1986b) Planning and evaluating innovations in nursing practice by measuring the ward atmosphere. *Journal of Advanced Nursing,* **11**, 203–210

MINUCHIN, S. (1974) *Families and Family Therapy.* London: Tavistock

MITCHIE, S. (1981) The clinical psychologist as agent of social change. *Bulletin of the British Psychological Society,* **34**, 355–356

MONROE, J. T. and ABSE, D. W. (1963) The psychopathology of trichotillomania and trichophagy. *Psychiatry,* **26**, 95–103

MOOS, R. H. (1974) *Evaluating Treatment Environments: A Social-Ecological Approach.* Chichester: Wiley

MOOS, R. and IGRA, A. (1980) Determinants of the social environments of sheltered care settings. *Journal of Health and Social Behaviour,* **21**, 88–98

MORRIS, R. J. and KRATOCHWILL, T. R. (1983) *Treating Children's Fears and Phobias: A Behavioral Approach.* New York: Pergamon Press

MULHALL, D. J. (1977) The representation of personal relationships: an automated system. *International Journal of Man-Machine Studies,* **9**, 315–335

MULLER, S. A. and WINKELMANN, R. K. (1972) Trichotillomania: A clinicopathologic study of 24 cases. *Archives of Dermatology,* **105**, 535–539

MURPHY, G. (1980) Decreasing undesirable behaviours. In *Behaviour Modification for the Mentally Handicapped,* edited by W. Yule and J. Carr. London: Croom Helm

MURPHY, P. (1985) Preparation to mitigate the stress involved in invasive renal x-rays in paediatric patients. *BSc thesis,* North East London Polytechnic, London

NATIONAL CHILDREN'S BUREAU (1986) *Highlight No. 72: Solvent Abuse.* London: NCB

NELSON, H. E. and McKENNA, P. (1975) The use of current reading ability in the assessment of dementia. *British Journal of Social and Clinical Psychology,* **14** (3), 259–267

NOVACO, R. W. (1979) Cognitive regulation of anger and stress. In *Cognitive-Behavioural Interventions: Theory, Research and Procedures,* edited by P. Kendall and A. Hollon. London: Academic Press

OAKLEY, A. (1982) *Subject Women.* London: Fontana

O'BRIEN, J. and TYNE, A. (1981) *The Principle of Normalisation.* London: The Campaign for Mental Handicap

O'CONNELL, K. G. (1985) Self-perceived levels of depression, anxiety and self-image in the severely burned adolescent. *PhD Thesis,* Graduate School of Arts and Sciences of Boston College, Boston, USA

OLLENDICK, T. H., MATSON, J. L. and HELSEL, W. J. (1985) Fears in children and adolescents: normative data. *Behaviour Research and Therapy,* **23**, 365–367

ORFORD, J. (1985) *Excessive Appetites: A Psychological View of Addictions.* Chichester: Wiley

ORNISH, D., SCHERWITZ, L. W., DOODY, R. S., KESTEN, D ., McLANAHAN, S. M., BROWN, S. E., DE PUEY, E. G., SONNERMAKER, R., HAYNES, C., LESTER, J., McALLISTER, G. K., HALL, R. J., BURDINE, J. A. and GOTTO, A. M. (1983) Effects of stress management training and dietary changes in treating ischaemic heart disease.

Journal of the American Medical Association, **249** (1), 54–59

ORTON, H. D. (1984) Learning on the ward — how important is the climate? In *Understanding Nurses,* edited by S. Skevington. Chichester: Wiley

OTTENS, A. J. (1981) Multi-faceted treatment of compulsive hair pulling. *Journal of Behavior Therapy and Experimental Psychiatry,* **12**, 77–80

PAGE, F. (1984) Gestalt therapy. In *Individual Therapy in Britain,* edited by W. Dryden. London: Harper & Row

PARKS, T. E. (1966) Signal-detectability theory of recognition and memory performance. *Psychological Review,* **73** (1), 44–58

PATTIE, A. H. and GILLEARD, C. J. (1979) *Manual of the Clifton Assessment Procedures for the Elderly (CAPE).* Sevenoaks: Hodder & Stoughton

PAUL, G. L. and LENTZ, R. J. (1977) *Psychosocial Treatment of Chronic Mental Patients.* Cambridge, USA: Harvard University Press

PAXTON, R. (1983) Prolonging the effects of deposit contracts with smokers. *Behaviour Research and Therapy,* **21**, 425–433

PAYNE, R. (1984) Organisational behaviour. In *Psychology for Managers,* edited by C. L. Cooper and P. Makin. Leicester: Macmillan and The British Psychological Society

PETTIGREW, A. M. (1975) Strategic aspects of the management of specialist activity. *Personnel Review,* **4**, 5–13

PRIESTLY, P., McGUIRE, J., FLEGG, D., HEMSLEY, V. and WELHAM, D. (1978) *Social Skills and Personal Problem Solving.* London: Tavistock

RAPPAPORT, J. (1977) *Community Psychology: Values, Research and Action.* New York: Holt, Rinehart and Winston

RELEASE (1979) *Glue Sniffing.* London: Release

RELEASE (1980) *Leave These Kids Alone.* London: Release

REYNELL, J. and ZINKIN, P. (1975) New procedures for the developmental assessment of young children with severe visual handicap. *Child: Care, Health and Development,* **1**, 61–69

RICHMAN, N. and GRAHAM, P. J. (1971) A behavioural screening questionnaire for use with 3-year-old children: preliminary findings. *Journal of Child Psychology and Psychiatry,* **12**, 5–33

RIDGEWAY, V. and MATTHEWS, A. (1982) Psychological preparation for surgery: a comparison of methods. *British Journal of Clinical Psychology,* **21**, 271–280

RODIN, J. (1983) *Will this Hurt? Preparing Children for Hospital and Medical Procedures.* London: Royal College of Nursing

ROGERS, J. (1973) *Adults Learning.* Harmondsworth: Penguin

ROMANCZYK, R. G., KISTNER, J. A. and PLIENIS, A. (1982) Self-stimulatory and self-injurious behaviour: etiology and treatment. In *Advances in Child Behaviour Therapy, Vol. 2,* edited by J. J. Steffen and A. Karoly. Lexington, MA, USA: D. C. Heath

ROSENBAUM, M. S. and AYLLON, T. (1981) The habit reversal technique in treating trichotillomania. *Behavior Therapy,* **12**, 473–481

ROSENBERG, T. (1965) *Society and Adolescent Self-Image.* Princeton: Princeton University Press

ROSENTIEL, A. K. and KEEFE, F. J. (1983) Use of coping strategies in chronic low back pain patients: relationship to patient characteristics and current adjustment. *Pain,* **17**, 33–44

ROSSI, P. H., FREEMAN, H. E. and WRIGHT, F. R. (1979) *Evaluation: A Systematic Approach.* Beverly Hills: Sage

ROWAT, K. M. and KNAFL, K. A. (1985) Living with chronic pain: The spouse's perspective. *Pain,* **23**, 259–271

ROWE, C., PIERCE, D. and CLARK, J. (1973) Voluntary dislocation of the shoulder. *Journal of Bone and Joint Surgery,* **55A**, 445–460

ROWE, D. (1983) *Depression: The Way Out of Your Prison.* London: Routledge & Kegan Paul

ROYAL COLLEGE OF GENERAL PRACTITIONERS (1986) *Alcohol: A Balanced View: Report of a Working Party.* London: RCGP

RUSSELL, G. F. M. (1979) Bulimia nervosa: an ominous variant of anorexia nervosa. *Psychological Medicine,* **9**, 429–443

RUTTER, M., TIZARD, J. and WHITMORE, K. (1970) (Editors) *Education, Health and Behaviour.* London: Longman

SALTZER, E. B. (1982) The relationship of personal efficacy beliefs to behaviour. *British Journal of Social Psychology,* **21**, 213–221

SANDERSON, K. V. and HALL-SMITH, P. (1970) Tonsure trichotillomania. *British Journal of Dermatology,* **82**, 343–350

SANTO, S. J. and YULE, W. (in preparation) An objective measure of the efficacy of treatment of trichotillomania.

SARASON, S. B. (1985) *Caring and Compassion in Clinical Practice.* San Francisco: Jossey-Bass

SCHACTER, M. (1961) Trichotillomania in children. *Praxia der kinderpsychologie und kinderpsychiatrie,* **10**, 120–124

SCHUELL, H. M., JENKINS, J. and JIMINEZ-PABON, E. (1964) *Aphasia in Adults.* New York: Harper & Row

SHARPE, S. (1976) *'Just like a Girl': How Girls Learn to be Women.* Harmondsworth: Penguin

SHAW, S., SPRATLEY, T., CARTWRIGHT, A. and HARWIN, J. (1978) *Responding to Drinking Problems.* London: Croom Helm

SHEPHERD, G. (1983) Planning the rehabilitation of the individual. In *Theory and Practice of Psychiatric Rehabilitation,* edited by F. N. Watts and D. Bennett. Chichester: Wiley

SHEPHERD, G. (1984) *Institutional Care and Rehabilitation.* London: Longman

SHIFFMAN, S. M. (1979) The tobacco withdrawal syndrome. In *Cigarette Smoking as a Dependence Process,* NIDA Research Monograph 23, edited by N. A. Krasnegor. Rockville, MD, USA: Department of Health, Education and Welfare

SHIFFMAN, S. M. and JARVIK, M. E. (1976) Smoking withdrawal symptoms in two weeks of abstinence. *Psychopharmacology,* **50**, 35–39

SKINNER, B. F. (1938) *The Behavior of Organisms.* New York: Appleton-Century Crofts

SLADE, P. D. and RUSSELL, G. F. M. (1973) Awareness of body dimensions in anorexia: cross-sectional and longitudinal studies. *Psychological Medicine,* **3**, 188–199

SLADE, P. D., TROUP, J. D. G., LETHEM, J. and BENTLEY, G. (1983) The fear avoidance model of exaggerated pain perception — II. *Behaviour Research and Therapy,* **21** (4), 409–416

SMITH, M. J. (1975) *When I Say "No" I feel Guilty.* New York: Bantam

SMITH, T. W., FOLLICK, N. J. and KORR, K. F. (1984) Anger neuroticism type A behaviour and the experience of angina. *British Journal of Medical Psychology,* **57**, 249–252

SNAITH, R. P., BRIDGE, G. W. K. and HAMILTON, M. (1976) The Leeds Scales for the self-assessment of anxiety and depression. *British Journal of Psychiatry,* **128**, 156–165

SNAITH, R. P., AHMED, S. N., MEHTA, S. and HAMILTON, M. (1971) Assessment of severity of primary depressive illness: the Wakefield self-assessment inventory. *Psychological Medicine,* **1**, 143–149

SPENCE, S. (1980) *Social Skills Training with Children and Adolescents.* Windsor: NFER

SPIELBERGER, C. D., GORSUCH, R. and LUSHENE, R. E. (1970) *State-Trait Anxiety Inventory Manual.* Palo Alto: Consulting Psychologists Press

SPIELBERGER, C. D., JACOBS, G., RUSSELL, S. and CRANE, R. S. (1983) Assessment of anger: the state-trait anger scale. In *Advances in Personality Assessment, Vol. 2,* edited by J. N. Butcher and C. D. Spielberger. Hillsdale, NJ, USA: Lawrence Erlbaum Associates

SPRINGER, M. (1982) Radical vulvectomy: Physical, psychological, social and sexual implications. *Oncology Nursing Forum,* **9**, 19–21

STABLER, B. and WARREN, A. A. (1974) Behavioural contracting in treating trichotillomania: case note. *Psychological Reports,* **34**, 401–402

STANGLER, R. S. and PRINTZ, A. M. (1980) DSM III: psychiatric diagnosis in a university population. *American Journal of Psychiatry,* **137**, 937–940

STOLZ, S. B. (1981) Adoption of innovations from applied behavioural research: 'does anybody care?'. *Journal of Applied Behaviour Analysis,* **14**, 491–505

STREET, E. (1985) From child focused problems to marital issues. In *Marital Therapy in Britain,* edited by W. Dryden. London: Harper & Row

STRICKLAND, B. R. (1977) Internal-external control of reinforcement. In *Personality Variables in Social Behaviour,* edited by T. Blass. Hillsdale, NJ, USA: Lawrence Erlbaum Associates

TAYLOR, J. G. (1963) A behavioural interpretation of obsessive-compulsive neurosis. *Behaviour Research and Therapy,* **1**, 237–244

TAYLOR, M. T. (1964) Language therapy. In *The Aphasic Adult: Evaluation and Rehabilitation,* edited by H. G. Burr. Charlottesville, VA, USA: Wayside Press

TENNANT, L., CULLEN, C. and HATTERSLEY, J. (1981) Applied behaviour analysis: intervention with retarded people. In *Applications of Conditioning Theory,* edited by G. Davey. London: Methuen

THARP, R. and WETZEL, R. (1969) *Behavior Modification in the Natural Environment.* New York: Academic Press

TREACHER, A. (1985) Working with marital partners: systems approaches. In *Marital Therapy in Britain, Vol. 1*, edited by W. Dryden. London: Harper & Row

TROWER, P. (1984) (Editor) *Radical Approaches to Social Skills Training*. London/Sydney: Croom Helm; New York: Methuen

TROWER, P., BRYANT, B. and ARGYLE, M. (1978) *Social Skills and Mental Health*. London: Methuen

TURK, D. C., MEICHENBAUM, D. and GENEST, M. (1983) *Pain and Behavioural Medicine*. New York/London: Guilford Press

TURNER, J. A. and CLANCY, S. (1986) Strategies for coping with chronic low back pain: relationship to pain and disability. *Pain*, **24**, 355–364

TURRILL, T. (1986) *Change and Innovation: A Challenge for the NHS*, Management Series 10. London: The Institute of Health Services Management

VAN STRIEN, T., FRIJTERS, J. E. R., BERGERS, G. A. A. and DEFARES, P. B. (1986) The Dutch Eating Behaviour Questionnaire: assessment of restrained emotional and external eating behaviour. *International Journal of Eating Disorders*, **5**, 295–315

VERNON, J. and FRUIN, D. (1986) *In Care: A Study of Social Work Decision-Making*. London: National Children's Bureau

WALLACE, L. M. and LEES, J. (in preparation) Psychological support for burn patients

WALSH, F. (1982) *Normal Family Processes*. New York: Guilford Press

WARDLE, J. and BEINART, H. (1981) Binge eating: a theoretical review. *British Journal of Clinical Psychology*, **20**, 97–109

WARRINGTON, E. K. (1984) *Manual of the Recognition Memory Tests*. Windsor: NFER-Nelson

WATTS, A. F. (1948) *The Holborn Reading Scale*. London: Harrap

WATZLAWICK, P., BEAVIN, J. and JACKSON, D. D. (1967) *The Pragmatics of Human Communication*. London: Faber and Faber

WATZLAWICK, P., WEAKLAND, J. and FISCH, R. (1974) *Change: Principles of Problem Formation and Problem Resolution*. New York: W. W. Norton

WECHSLER, D. (1955) *The Wechsler Adult Intelligence Scale*. New York: The Psychological Corporation

WECHSLER, D. (1974) *The Wechsler Intelligence Scale for Children, Revised*. New York: The Psychological Corporation

WECHSLER, D. (1981) *The Wechsler Adult Intelligence Scale*. Windsor: NFER-Nelson

WEHMAN, P. (1979) *Curriculum Design for the Severely and Profoundly Handicapped*. New York: Human Sciences Press

WEPMAN, J. M. (1951) *Recovery from Aphasia*. New York: Ronald Press

WHITE, A. C. (1982) Psychiatric study of patients with severe burn injuries. *British Medical Journal*, **284**, 465–467

WILCOCK, P. (1984) Creating and maintaining behavioural change in an institutional setting: the Ivanhoe Project. In *Facing the Challenge*, edited by S. Simpson, P. Higson, R. Holland, J. McBrien, J. Williams and L. Henneman. Rossendale: British Association for Behavioural Psychotherapy

WILCOCK, P. (1985) The role of the clinical psychologist. In *Mental Handicap: a Multi-Disciplinary Approach*, edited by M. Craft, J. Bicknell and S. Hollins. Eastbourne: Baillière Tindall

WILLMOTT, M. (1986) The effect of a vinyl floor surface and a carpeted floor surface upon walking in elderly hospital in-patients. *Age and Ageing*, **15**, 119–120

WINDHEUSER, H. J. (1977) Anxious mothers as models for coping with anxiety. *Behavioural Analysis and Modification*, **2**, 39–58

WING, J. K. (1978) Clinical concepts of schizophrenia. In *Schizophrenia: Towards A New Synthesis*, edited by J. K. Wing. London: Academic Press

WING, J. K. and BROWN, G. W. (1970) *Institutionalism and Schizophrenia*. Cambridge: Cambridge University Press

WING, L. (1981) Asperger's syndrome: a clinical account. *Psychological Medicine*, **11**, 115–129

WINNICOTT, D. W. (1965) *The Maturational Process and the Facilitating Environment*. New York: International Universities Press

WISELEY, D. W., MASUR, F. T. and MORGAN, S. B. (1983) Psychological aspects of severe burn injuries in children. *Health Psychology*, **2** (1), 45–72

WOLFENSBERGER, W. (1972) *The Principle of Normalisation in Human Services*. Toronto: National Institute on Mental Retardation

WOLFENSBERGER, W. and GLENN, L. (1975) *PASS 3*. Toronto: National Institute on Mental Retardation

WOODS, P. A. and CULLEN, C. (1983) Determinants of staff behaviour in long-term care. *Behavioural Psychotherapy,* **11,** 4–18

WOODWARD, J. M. (1959) Emotional disturbances of burned children. *British Medical Journal,* 5128, 18 April, 1009–1013

WORLD HEALTH ORGANIZATION (1951) *Committee on Mental Health: Report on the Second Session,* WHO Technical Report Series No. 31. Geneva: WHO

YULE, W., SACKS, B. and HERSOV, L. (1974) Successful flooding treatment of a noise phobia in an 11-year-old. *Journal of Behavioral Therapy and Experimental Psychiatry,* **5,** 209–211

ZIGMOND, A. S. and SNAITH, R. P. (1983) The hospital anxiety and depression scale. *Acta Psychiatrica Scandinavica,* **67,** 361–370

Glossary

The following is not a comprehensive glossary of psychological terms. The definitions are given solely to clarify some of the terms used in the text. Full explanations can be found in standard textbooks. Some of the definitions are based on entries in *The Penguin Dictionary of Psychology* by Arthur Reber (1985), by kind permission of Penguin Books Ltd.

ABA design A design which evaluates the effects of intervention by alternating the baseline condition (A) when no intervention is effected, with the intervention condition (B). The baseline condition (A) is then repeated.

agoraphobia Fear of open spaces. The most common phobic disorder commonly manifested as fear of being caught alone in some public place.

agraphia Loss of the power, or the inability, to communicate in writing due to cerebral dysfunction.

aphasia A general term for all disturbances of language due to brain lesions in the absence of faulty speech muscles, disorders of articulation or mental handicap.

apraxia A disorder of voluntary movement in which the individual is unable to carry out purposeful movements in the absence of paralysis of other motor or sensory impairment.

Asperger's syndrome A syndrome most frequently occurring in boys and men who from early childhood show social and emotional abnormalities, poverty of expression and gesture, extreme self-centredness, unusual and constricted intellectual interests and idiosyncratic attachments to objects.

attachment object An object such as a soft toy or blanket used by a young child to obtain comfort in the absence of parents or other sources of comfort.

autogenic relaxation Methods of relaxation which originate within oneself and depend on individual preference and skill, for instance in sensory imaging.

baseline assessment The assessment of the level of incidence of a behaviour prior to intervention.

behavioural analysis An analysis of an individual's behaviour with particular reference to the antecedents and consequences of the behaviour in question.

behaviour therapy That type of psychotherapy which seeks to change abnormal or maladaptive behaviour patterns by the processes of learning. The focus is on the behaviour itself rather than on some analysis of underlying conflicts or other causes.

biofeedback Feedback of data on the subject's bodily functions such as blood pressure, EMG (q.v.) or brain wave activity. Although not conscious as such, autonomic nervous system functions are subject to learning.

claustrophobia Fear of being locked or shut in and of enclosed places.

cognitive behavioural coping procedures Clients are taught to alter self-appraisals, reconstrue the way they interpret their own responsibility for events, and change their expectations.

cognitive behavioural therapy An approach to psychotherapy involving an extension of behaviour therapy to the modification and relearning of cognitive processes such as thoughts, beliefs, fantasies and so on.

cognitive therapy Cognitive therapy views disordered behaviour and mood as the result of faulty thought processes. Thinking and perceiving negatively are considered to be the cause of negative feelings and behaviour. Therapy involves working with clients to directly change their thought processes.

conjoint therapy Psychotherapy involving both partners in a relationship which focuses on the interaction between the partners as well as their individual needs and problems.

contingency contracting An explicit statement of reinforcement contingencies between individuals who wish for some behaviour change (e.g. parents, teachers) and those whose behaviour is to be changed (e.g. children, students). Individuals agree to make particular reinforcers available if and only if particular goals in behaviour change are attained.

contingent A contingent event is one which is dependent on the prior occurrence of one preceding it.

conversion hysteria A reaction whereby a psychological problem is expressed by means of a physical symptom.

coping self-talk A cognitive therapy technique whereby an individual is taught to cope in problem situations by giving him- or herself pre-rehearsed instructions.

covert sensitization A technique used to decrease maladaptive behaviours such as overeating, drug abuse or sexual deviance. Individuals imagine themselves engaging in the undesirable behaviours. When the behaviour is clearly imagined they are instructed to imagine highly aversive events (such as vomiting or being observed by a family member). The aversive events are designed to suppress the behaviours.

delusion An irrational belief that is maintained in spite of argument, information and refutation which should (reasonably) be sufficient to destroy it.

dementia A loss of intellectual capacity to the extent that normal social and occupational functions can no longer be carried out. Senile dementia refers to dementia associated with old age.

depersonalization A loss of contact with personal reality accompanied by feelings of strangeness and an unreality of experience.

direct client work Any therapeutic intervention where the focus is direct face-to-face contact between client and therapist.

disorientation Inability to orientate oneself with regard to spatial, temporal and contextual aspects of the environment.

DSM III Third revision of the *Diagnostic and Statistical Manual of Mental Disorders* (American Psychiatric Association, 1980).

dyscalculia Inability to perform arithmetic operations.

dyspraxia Difficulty in moving or painful movement.

eclectic An eclectic approach to therapy is one which draws on techniques from several different models, as appears most applicable in the case of the individual client.

EMG (electromyogram) A graphic record of the changes of electrical potential in a muscle.

exploration of environment A scale from the Reynell Zinkin Developmental Scales for young visually handicapped children concerned with the child's understanding of areas beyond his or her reach. It consists of items such as exploring surfaces and purposeful movement towards objects.

extinction A reduction in response frequency following the cessation of reinforcement (q.v.).

facial screening The client's face is briefly covered with a cloth bib contingent on an undesired behaviour. Basically this is a specific form of aversive conditioning.

finger agnosia Inability to tell which finger has been touched in the absence of visual cues.

flooding (implosion therapy) A technique used in phobic disorders where the client is presented with the phobic stimulus until it no longer evokes anxiety.

forced-choice ranking paradigm A method of ordering in which the subject is required to select one item or answer from a series of sets of two or more alternatives.

generalization The transfer of a response to a situation other than that in which training has taken place.

Gerstmann syndrome A group of symptoms consisting of finger agnosia (q.v.), right-left disorientation, dyscalculia (q.v.) and agraphia (q.v.). Parietal lobe pathology is often implied.

graded practice Working towards some behavioural goal in a series of stages which gradually approximate that goal.

habit reversal A complex package involving training subjects to be aware of stimuli that set off the undesired habit, practising an incompatible response, relaxation training and self-recording.

hallucination A perceptual experience that is perceived in clear consciousness, in the absence of physical stimulus. In schizophrenia (q.v.) auditory hallucinations are most common, but other modalities — that is, vision, taste, touch and smell — may also be involved.

indirect client work A therapeutic intervention where the focus is on an intermediary such as nursing or care staff or parent. The therapist works with the intermediary who then implements the intervention with the client.

locus of control A general term which refers to the *perceived* source of control over one's behaviour. Having an internal locus of control refers to viewing oneself as being in control of one's own environment. A person with external locus of control sees him- or herself as being controlled by external factors over which they have no influence.

multi-modal behavioural analysis An analysis of behaviour which takes into account the fact that clients' problems can be manifest on a number of modalities or levels of functioning, such as cognitive processes, attitudes, emotions, behaviours and relationships.

multiple baseline design A method which examines the effects of intervention by introducing the intervention to different baselines (for example behaviours or persons) at different points in time.

negative reinforcement An increase in the frequency of a response following the removal of a negative reinforcer.

negative reinforcer An aversive event or stimulus the removal of which after a response increases performance of that response. Conversely the presentation of a negative reinforcer serves as punishment (q.v.).

nondirective discussion One in which specific counselling, advice or direction on the part of the therapist is kept to a minimum.

normalization A principle which states that, when planning services for 'disadvantaged' people (such as those with a physical or mental handicap or mental illness), decisions should be judged against values that are held by members of society as a whole for their non-'disadvantaged' members. Services based on normalization principles will, therefore, provide opportunities for clients to experience the same lifestyles that are valued by people who are not 'disadvantaged' and will use socially acceptable means to help clients develop skills to make the best possible use of these opportunities.

operant behaviour Any behaviour that is emitted by an organism without specific eliciting conditions. It can be strengthened or weakened by manipulating antecedent and consequent events.

operant methods Methods in therapy which use the relationship between behaviour and various environmental events (antecedents and consequences) to influence behaviour.

overcorrection A procedure which involves an individual taking responsibility for her or his behaviour. Restitutional overcorrection requires the individual to first correct any disturbance and then improve the environment over its original condition. In positive practice overcorrection the appropriate behaviours must be practised repeatedly.

paraphasia Perverted speech, jargon; most commonly used to refer to a form of expressive aphasia in which the individual, although hearing and understanding words, is unable to speak correctly. Words may be wrongly substituted and sentences so jumbled as to become unintelligible.

parietal Pertaining to the parietal lobe of the cerebral cortex which lies at the top of the brain behind the central fissure.

parietal-occipital Pertaining to the area of the cerebral cortex between the parietal lobe and the occipital lobe (at the rear of the brain).

perceptual motor A skill or behaviour involving a motor response to a perceived stimulus (most commonly visual). For example, touching a moving object.

positive reinforcement An increase in the frequency of a response that is followed by a positive reinforcer.

positive reinforcer A positive reinforcer is defined by its effect on behaviour. If an event follows behaviour and the frequency of behaviour increases, the event is a positive reinforcer. Conversely, the removal of a positive reinforcer produces extinction (q.v.).

positive self-statements Statements (either covert or overt) made by an individual to her- or himself pointing out some positive characteristic or achievement.

post-traumatic amnesia Loss of memory for events that occurred following the event that is presumed to have caused a memory disturbance, for example head injury.

psychoanalytic Descriptive of Freud's theory of human behaviour and the therapy based upon this theory.

psychobiological An approach which takes account of both psychological and biological factors and the interaction between them.

psychodynamic A label used freely for all those psychological systems and theories that emphasize processes of change and development. Occasionally used as a synonym for psychoanalytic.

psychosomatic disorder A physical disorder such as high blood pressure or ulcers which originates in or is exacerbated by emotional difficulties.

punishment A decrease in the frequency of a response when it is followed by a contingent aversive stimulus or event. Two types of punishment are distinguished: punishment by removal, a decrease in the frequency of a response that occurs when a positive reinforcer is contingently removed, and punishment by application, a decrease in the frequency of a response which occurs when a negative reinforcer is contingently applied.

repertory grid A technique concerned with eliciting the pattern of relationships between sets of personal constructs (ways of interpreting events) for an individual. The individual is the prime focus and the construct pattern is not related to normative data.

retroactive amnesia Loss of memory for events that occurred prior to the event (head injury, toxin and so on) presumed to have caused a memory disturbance.

schizophrenia A general term for a number of severe mental disorders involving gross impairment in contact with reality. Some or all of the following signs may be present: hallucinations (q.v.), delusions (q.v.), thought disorder (q.v.), incoherent speech, social withdrawal and cognitive deterioration.

self-hypnosis A self-guided process in which the subject takes both the role of hypnotist and the 'patient' role.

self-monitoring Individuals are asked to monitor their own behaviour, feelings and reactions, either by keeping detailed diaries or completing questionnaires or other data counts regularly.

sensorimotor understanding A scale from the Reynell Zinkin Devlopmental Scales for young visually handicapped children, concerned with the understanding of concrete objects, their relationship with one another, and their properties such as texture, shape and movement.

single case design A methodology with the capacity to conduct experimental investigations with the single case, that is one subject.

social adaptation A scale from the Reynell Zinkin Developmental Scales for young visually handicapped children, concerned with social response to people and the development of self-help skills, such as feeding and dressing.

systematic desensitization A clinical technique used in behaviour therapy for phobias and other behaviour problems which have a strong anxiety component. The technique consists of getting the client to rank feared situations from least feared to most feared. The client is trained in relaxation and told that it is impossible to be relaxed and anxious at the same time. Stimulus situations are then presented in relaxed conditions beginning with the least feared. The presentation can be done in real life (*in vivo* desensitization) or by getting the client to imagine the scene (imaginal desensitization).

systems approach An approach which views the individual as one component of a more complex system such as a family. The system is seen as maintaining the individual's behaviour and therefore any intervention is addressed primarily to the system rather than to the individual.

thought disorder Disturbance of thought, speech and communication including delusions (q.v.), flight of ideas and inability to reason logically.

thought stopping Stopping a train of thought. A technique used in cognitive therapy (q.v.) whereby as soon as the individual detects an urge (often a thought) to engage in an undesired act, he or she says "no" to him- or herself. Preventing the initial step in an often complex chain of behaviour lessens the probability of the behaviour occurring.

time out from positive reinforcement A means of reducing target behaviours by the withdrawal of reinforcement. Following performance of the maladaptive act the individual is removed to a place devoid of reinforcement, that is a situation in which positive reinforcement is no longer available.

transference The tendency in therapy for the client to make the therapist the object of emotional responses.

Type A behaviour A pattern of behaviour, associated with coronary heart disease and characterized by intense competitiveness, easily elicited aggression and a sense of urgency in all activities.

Index

Hyperventilation in panic attacks, 30
Hysterectomy
  fear of, 31
  panic attack before, 28
Hysteria, conversion, 184, 280

Illness,
  fear of, 37, 38
  sexual problems and, 221
Inadequacy, 10, 11
  feelings of, 24
Incontinence, faecal, 56–61
Independence in adolescence, 80
Institutions, changes in, 232
Interactive patterns, 98
Interdisciplinary treatment programme, 178–183
Intermediate treatment centre, 111

Junior Eysenck Personality Inventory, 88

Kidney scans, preparing children for, 102

Language, disturbance of, 175
Language disability, 131, 134
Learning programmes, 178–183, 186, 187, 188
Locus of control, 210, 281
Loneliness, 63, 237

Managers, 66, 71, 233, 237, 244, 252, 262, 264
Marriage
  communication failures in, 9
  problems of, 24, 25
    training health visitors in, 221
Mastoid pain, 191
Medical genetics, 39, 43
Memory, loss of, 171
Mental handicap, 131
Mental health
  definition, 3
  problems, 3, 4
Mentally handicapped people, 131
  with challenging behaviour, 264
  hostels for, 261
  importance of family interaction, 154
  in hospital, 232
  living in community, 132
  meeting needs in ordinary house, 149–153
  microelectronic equipment, use of, 139–143
  needs of, 263
  normal living and, 132
  profound, 139
  register of, 262
  services for, 259–265
    changes in attitude, 260
    developments in, 231
    evaluation of, 265
    intervention strategies, 260
    issues involved, 261
    public relations, 264
    registers, 262
    role of clinical psychologist, 259, 263
  sex education for, 160–166
    staff training in, 161
  sexual counselling, 163, 164, 165
  sexual relationships, 132

Microelectronic technology, use with
    handicapped child, 139–143
Micturition, 57
Modelling, 83, 86, 89
Mood, changes of, 3
  after burns, 220
Mood diaries, 7, 25
Moodiness, 22
Mouth, bleeding from, 119
Multidisciplinary, 102, 121, 154, 241, 254
Multiple baseline design, 136, 210
Muscles, 185
  relaxation of, 170
Muscular dystrophy, 39

Negative reinforcer, 135, 281
Neuroblastoma, 94
Neuropsychology, 171–174, 175–177, 178–183
Neurosis, accident, 173
Night, walking during, 155, 156, 157
Normalization, 133, 150, 160, 245, 281
Nurses,
  district,
    training of, 221
  professionalism, 233
  selection of, 233
  services needed, 234
  training of, 76, 221, 233
    see also under Staff training
Nursing care, quality of, 233

Old people's homes, 240
  assessment of, 244
  presenting problems, 244
  result of intervention, 247
  staff of, 245
  staff-resident interaction, 246
  systems change in, 230, 244–247
Operant learning theory, 131, 135, 150, 189, 196
Organizations
  providing care and treatment, 229
  structure of, 229

Paediatric patients, 102–107
Pain
  abdominal, 206
  behaviour, 190, 191
  child's rating of, 106
  chronic, 190
    assessment of, 191
    family interaction, 193
    intervention, 192
    relaxation in, 192, 193
    results of treatment, 193
    social life and, 192
  conceptualization of, 170
  experience of, 190
  gate control theory, 190
  living with, 190–194
  postoperative, 209
  psychological approach to, 190
  relaxation in, 189, 192, 193
  theories of, 169